THE CONCEPT OF THE BELIEVERS' CHURCH

Addresses
from the
1967
Louisville
Conference

Edited by

James Leo Garrett, Jr.

HERALD PRESS
SCOTTDALE,
PENNSYLVANIA

To the memory of
KENNETH SCOTT LATOURETTE, PhD
1884-1968

Historian of the Orient
Professor of Missions and Missionary Statesman
Early Leader in the Ecumenical Movement
Historian of the Expansion of Christianity

this volume is respectfully dedicated.

Preface

What is the "Believers' Church"? The term has not been commonly used in the expanding ecclesiological vocabulary of twentieth-century Christians. The British speak of their Free Churches, and in the German-speaking nations the terms *Freikirchen* and *Freiwilligkeitskirchen* are often used. These European terms hardly apply in the United States, where every religious body, including the churches whose European counterparts are established churches, is "free" in respect to non-establishment by the Federal and state governments, and the same is true in vast areas of the other continents. Other terms such as "gathered church," "pilgrim church," "pure church," and "antipaedobaptist church" have to varying degrees been used. The use of the term "Believers' Church" is an effort to fashion an instrument of identification, however imperfect, for that segment of the Protestant Christian heritage which is distinct both from Classical Protestant and from Catholic—Roman, Eastern, Anglican, *et al*—understandings of the church by its insistence on the indispensability of voluntary churchmanship with its many implications. The advantages of such a term, and even more importantly the significance of the reality which it seeks to identify, may hopefully become more evident in the pages of this book. The term must, however, never be understood to imply any denial of true Christian believers in other confessional traditions or to signify the primacy of belief in its most creedal sense.

What are the meaning and the contemporary significance of the Believers' Church? For the answering of this question the Conference on the Concept of the Believers' Church was held on the campus of Southern Baptist Theological Seminary, Louisville, Kentucky, June 26-30, 1967. Here assembled were those from denominations which have been active in the councils and associations that transcend denominational lines and those from denominations which have not so participated. One church historian has called the conference itself a major event in modern church history.

The earliest proposal for a conference with characteristics similar to those of the Conference on the Concept of the Believers' Church originated in Europe. Under Mennonite sponsorship and the personal leadership of Professor J. A. van Oosterbaan a conference of "baptizer" theologians, chiefly from Europe, was planned for the summer of 1964 in Amsterdam, The Netherlands, but could not actually be held. Subsequently Dr. John Howard Yoder of Goshen-Elkhart, Indiana, urged the Southern Baptist Theological Seminary to take initiative in convoking a similar but more representative conference in the United States. Accepting Yoder's proposal, the latter institution, through its Dean of the School of Theology, Dr. C. Penrose St. Amant, invited various church historians and theologians who held membership in various "believers' church" denominations and who resided in the Kentucky-Indiana-Illinois-Ohio-Tennessee area to constitute an interdenominational planning committee for a North American conference relative to the "Believers' Church." The committee met twice, once in Louisville and once in Anderson, Indiana, and gave direction to the purpose, program design and personnel, and potential participants of the conference. Of valuable preparation for the Conference on the Concept of the Believers' Church was a conference of theological professors from the Mennonite, Brethren, and Friends traditions—the three historic peace churches—which was convoked by Earlham College, Richmond, Indiana, in June, 1964.

Certain characteristics of the Conference on the Concept of the Believers' Church should be noted. It was not a conference of elected or delegated representatives of various denominational bodies. It did not assemble to consider proposals for church or denominational mergers. Its participants chose voluntarily to accept their invitations to the conference, issued in the form of letters sent to hundreds of potential participants. In some ways it resembled a professional society of church historians and theologians, but the presence and participation of pastors, editors, denominational executives, and laymen made the conference something other than this. The conference was a cooperative attempt to explore the meaning and relevance of the Believers' Church as both faithfully and unfaithfully expressed within the various denominations represented. Moreover, the time in which this conference was held is itself significant, since the conference took serious account of the fact that the year 1967 marked not only the 450th anniversary of Martin Luther's posting of his Ninety-Five Theses but also the 500th anniversary of the distinct separation of the *Unitas Fratrum* in Bohemia.

The one hundred and fifty participants in the conference were identified with the following Christian bodies: American Baptist Association, American Baptist Convention, Assemblies of God, Austrian Baptist Union, Baptist Federation of Canada, Brethren Church, Brethren in Christ, Churches of Christ, Church of God (Anderson, Indiana), Church of the Brethren, Conservative Baptist Association of America, Christian Church (Disciples of Christ), Dutch Mennonite Church, Evangelical Mennonite Brethren Church, Evangelical Mennonite Church, Friends General Conference, Friends United Meeting, General Association of General Baptists, General Conference Mennonite Church, Mennonite Church, North American Baptist General Conference, North American Christian Convention, Presbyterian Church of Japan, Southern Baptist Convention, United Church of Christ, and United Methodist Church. Official observers from the National Council of the Churches of Christ in the U.S.A., the Roman Catholic Bishops' Commission for Ecumenical Affairs, and the New York office of the World Council of Churches were present, and observers from the National Association of Evangelicals had been invited. Participants and observers came from twenty-five states of the United States, the District of Columbia, four provinces of Canada, and five nations outside North America.

The thirteen conference addresses appear in this volume as they were delivered with the following exceptions. The addresses by Dr. Groff, Mr. MacDonald, and Dr. Malherbe have been to varying degrees rewritten, and those by Drs. Williams and Yoder are published in unabridged form, whereas time limitations compelled these speakers to omit portions when delivering the addresses to the conference. The editor has sought to protect the right of each of the writers to express himself in his own words and style. Only at two points has there been an effort to achieve uniformity. First, the term "Believers' Church" (capitalized) is used to convey the concept in its ideal form, while "believers' church" and "believers' churches" (uncapitalized) are used to indicate any or all of the denominations that may have expressed during their history some of the characteristics of the Believers' Church. Secondly, the term "believer's baptism" (singular) is used to emphasize primarily the significance of baptism for the person baptized, whereas "believers' church" (plural) is used to indicate the interpersonal and corporate dimension in the life of the church. Furthermore, the editor is responsible for the introductions to the various addresses.

So far as possible this volume seeks to be a faithful record of the Conference on the Concept of the Believers' Church. However, limitations of space prevent the inclusion of some important items. Morning worship services were conducted by Dr. John R. Claypool, minister, Crescent Hill Baptist Church, Louisville, Kentucky, and Dr. Hugh T.

McElrath, associate professor of church music, Southern Baptist Theological Seminary. Dr. Claypool's messages and the hymnody utilized by Dr. McElrath provided a representative example of one type of worship in the heritage of believers' churches and afforded an openness to God for all at the beginning of days packed full with conference sessions. Also omitted from these pages is any detailed account of the memorable and informal Friday evening session in which certain official observers—Mr. Ray Ryland, Father Bernard Quinn, and Dr. Robert C. Dodds—registered their impressions of the conference and its task and certain "elder statesmen"—Dr. Robert Friedmann, Dr. Cornelius Krahn, Mr. Lewis Benson, and Prof. Gan Sakakibara, author of studies of the Radical Reformation in Japanese—shared their convictions, criticisms, and evaluations.

The editor wishes to express his own and the conference's gratitude to the following who have contributed significantly either to the conference itself or to the preparation of this volume or both: Dr. Cornelius J. Dyck, director of the Institute of Mennonite Studies, Elkhart, Indiana, for the preparation of the bibliography in its final form; Dr. Ronald F. Deering, associate librarian, Southern Baptist Theological Seminary, for assistance in the verification of quotations and footnotes and for the transcription of tape-recorded materials from the conference; Dr. John Howard Yoder, for counsel at numerous points as well as his service as chairman of the findings committee; the eleven other members of the findings committee, especially its vice-chairman, Dr. William L. Lumpkin, minister, Freemason Street Baptist Church, Norfolk, Virginia, its secretary, Dr. John J. Kiwiet, then professor of historical theology, Northern Baptist Theological Seminary, Oak Brook, Illinois, and Dr. Donald F. Durnbaugh, associate professor of church history, Bethany Theological Seminary, Oak Brook, Illinois, who prepared the "Summary of Believers' Church Affirmations" and whose significant book, *The Believers' Church: The History and Character of Radical Protestantism,* is appearing as this volume is submitted to the publisher; the thirteen principal speakers, for their willingness for their addresses to be published and their cooperation in revisions and corrections; the eight respondents, whose responses have been incorporated into the introductions to the addresses; Dr. E. Glenn Hinson, associate professor of church history, Southern Baptist Theological Seminary, who served during 1965-66 as chairman of both the interdenominational planning committee and the Southern Baptist Theological Seminary committee; Dr. W. Morgan Patterson, associate professor of church history, Southern Baptist Theological Seminary, who served during 1966-67 as vice-chairman of the Southern Baptist Theological Seminary committee with responsibility for the responses and the panel discussions; President Duke K. McCall and Dean C. Penrose St. Amant of Southern Baptist Theological Seminary, who cleared the way for their institution to be host to and locale of the conference and encouraged the publication of its materials; Dean Gene W. Newberry and Dr. John W. V. Smith of the School of Theology, Anderson College, Anderson, Indiana, who served as hosts to the interdenominational planning committee in its meeting in Anderson; Mr. George W. Knight, then associate editor, *Western Recorder*, Middletown, Kentucky, who served as official news correspondent for the conference; Mr. W. M. Pattillo, Jr., executive assistant to the president, Southern Baptist Theological Seminary, for the preparation of the conference program; Mr. Maynard Shelly, editor, *The Mennonite*, Newton, Kansas, and Dr. Lawrence T. Slaght, editor, *The Watchman-Examiner*, Somerset, New Jersey, for the most comprehensive interpretations of the conference in periodicals; Dr. Wayne E. Ward, professor of Christian theology, Mr. Chester A. Molpus, then director of administrative services, and Dr. Paul M. Debusman, order librarian, Southern Baptist Theological Seminary, for supervision of conference registration, of conference housing, and of tape recordings of conference proceedings, respectively; Miss Mary Jean Aiken, whose efficient management of secretarial services at Southern Baptist Theological Seminary has been a *sine qua non* for both the conference and this volume; Captain (Chaplain) Vernon L. Fash, for valuable assistance; and the Mennonite Publishing House, Scottdale, Pennsylvania, for its willingness to publish these conference materials, and especially Mr. Ellrose D. Zook, its book editor, whose courteous and helpful guidance has been of inestimable value to the editor.

James Leo Garrett, Jr.

Regent's Park College, Oxford
October 31, 1968

Table of Contents

THE CONCEPT OF THE BELIEVERS' CHURCH

1

The Concept of the Believers' Church

Franklin H. Littell

Ever since the initial publication in 1952 of his Yale University dissertation which had been awarded the biennial award of the American Society of Church History, *The Anabaptist View of the Church*, Franklin Hamlin Littell has increasingly become an articulate, representative, and recognized spokesman for the Free Church type of Protestantism. His study of the Radical Reformers of the sixteenth century had been complemented by an extended period of residence in West Germany and careful study of the impact of Nazism upon the churches. Dr. Littell, a native of Iowa and the son of a college professor, had graduated from Cornell College and Union Theological Seminary, New York. An ordained Methodist minister and the author or editor of nine books, including three in German, and more than ninety articles, he especially has cultivated the fellowship of the leaders of the churches derived from Radical Protestantism, many of whom did not know one another. By lectures, travel, correspondence, and other means Dr. Littell has helped to evoke the new sense of awareness and destiny among the heirs of Radical Protestantism and to give an effective contemporary apology for the relevance and validity of Free Church emphases among Christians having other backgrounds. Formerly professor of church history at Emory University, Southern Methodist University, and Chicago Theological Seminary, he is now president of Iowa Wesleyan College, Mount Pleasant, Iowa, while retaining an adjunct professorship in Chicago Theological Seminary.

Dr. Littell had delivered the opening address for the Seminar on the Church in the World at Earlham College, Richmond, Indiana, in June, 1964, on "The Historic Free Church Tradition." This seminar brought together theologians from the three historic "peace churches"—Mennonites, Friends, and Brethren. The interdenominational planning committee for the Conference on the Concept of the Believers' Church understandably invited Dr. Littell to deliver the initial address at Louisville.

Dr. Littell's address, in addition to providing the contextual framework within which the conference speakers would tend to function, had at least two specific effects. First, his delineation of six "basic principles" or marks of the "Believers' Church" provided conference participants with a useful guide for identifying such marks and at the same time stimulated others to offer their own identifications.

Secondly, Dr. Littell's tendency to identify "Free Churches" and "Believers' Churches" was to be countered by an opposite viewpoint, held by Dr. John Howard Yoder and others, which distinguishes the two more sharply and regards "Believers' Churches" as a less comprehensive category than "Free Churches." Such variant understandings were destined to be faced by the continuation committee of the Conference on the Concept of the Believers' Church after June, 1967.

Members of the panel who responded to Dr. Littell's address were Dr. Maurice Blanchard, pastor, Austin-Second Baptist Church, Chicago, Illinois; Dr. J. P. Jacobszoon of The Netherlands, visiting instructor in church history, Eastern Mennonite College, Harrisonburg, Virginia; and Dr. James D. Mosteller, professor of church history, Northern Baptist Theological Seminary, Oak Brook, Illinois.

Dr. Blanchard posed the question as to possible differences between the statement of the ideals or goals of Anabaptism and the degree of realization of these ideals. He also asked whether those baptized as youthful believers in the present day actually turn out to be better Christians at age twenty-five than the ones baptized as babies. Dr. Jacobszoon insisted that the church according to Menno Simons involved both new persons and a new society or fellowship. There is, he continued, a need today for more attention to be given to a theology of children and their place in the church. Furthermore, we must offer answers to the problem issues of our day and not merely repeat the answers of four hundred years ago. Dr. Mosteller agreed with Dr. Littell's marks of the Believers' Church but asked how these can be applied to the problems of congregational integrity and discipline today, especially in view of the prevalence of freedom of conscience and in view of the fact that believer's baptism is not in itself a guarantee of church integrity.

Most of the American churches claim to stand in the Free Church line, but the case is curious. To be sure, nowhere in the world is there such universal respect for religion as today found in America. At no time in history have so many people been voluntarily associated with religious programs, supporting them with their prayers, their presence, and their gifts. Nowhere else has there ever emerged such mutual respect between communities of the most varied teaching and style, often leading to joint meetings and cooperative work. Not only are we reaping our share of the harvest of Catholic-Protestant amity planted by good Pope John, but to a degree never known in two thousand years of family quarreling Christians and Jews are living and working side by side as brethren. From every outward evidence this should be reckoned one of the golden ages of religion.

Yet there is a profound uneasiness in our churches and synagogues. Perhaps our Calvinist racial memory will not let us be joyous in the face of such manifest ecclesiastical prosperity. Or perhaps the suspicion grows that we have wandered far from the highroad on which our feet were once set. The "Young Turks" among theologians and religious philosophers warn us of impending judgment. Even authors in popular magazines write of "the crisis in American religion" and "the breakdown of Protestant clergy." Wherein lies the crisis, and to what shall we attribute the mood of prosperous melancholy? Is it perhaps true that belief and church are separating like cream from skim milk? We hear much of "religionless Christianity," especially among the students.

Are we coming to the end of an age, with no sure guidelines for the future? Are student demonstrations, for example, so often associated with religious groups and leadership, a kind of "dance of death" signalizing anew the end of a universal discourse? Are our religious movements, like so many which shared the decline of past civilizations, building their greatest institutions and buildings precisely at the moment when they have peaked and begun to decline in authority and worth? When the President of the United States proposed to build a monument to God in the national capitol, to stand in honor beside the stone tributes to other dead heroes, was he perhaps speaking more significantly than he knew?

The thesis of this writing runs to the contrary. With all due tribute to the watchman on our walls, it is the writer's belief that the foot-faulting so evident in church and synagogue reveal dislocation rather than disaster. Our religious movements, with their great numbers of uninformed and untrained volunteers, have a potential for good and a basic soundness which are hidden behind the outward unease and uncertainty of direction. They are like eager choruses which, compelled by rapidly changing circumstance to sing from new scores, have not yet found the pitch. They often appear confused and disoriented, and the tuning forks and pitch pipes and drums all too often give contrary notes. But once we have passed through this time of confusion, there is in the massed voices a fundamental trueness and soundness of performance which puts to shame the jarring conflicts of the directors and sometimes even now confounds the skeptical with the glory of their singing.

Between the Times

We are living "between the times." The basic assumptions which governed the nineteenth century culture-religion are no longer sound. The tidy continuum of Christianity and culture which dominated Victorian England, tsarist Russsia, imperial Austria-Hungary, and the *Wilhelminischen Zeitalter* has been shattered. The integration of political and religious purposes which marked the Anglican, Orthodox, Catholic, and Lutheran establishments of another age has finally been destroyed. Only the bare skeletons of the edifices of a former "Christian civiliza-

17

tion" still stand against the skyline of Europe, disconcerting the casual viewer and diverting the attention of the serious from the real action. The keenest observers, both Catholic and Protestant, speak of the present situation in Europe as a "post-Constantinian era" or even a "post-Christian age." After two terrible World Wars, two depressions, two monstrously anti-Christian ideologies and systems (communism and fascism), only politicians still speak in Europe the language of the Holy Alliance. Among the spiritually sensitive a new language fit for a world come of age is sought and, when found on occasion, proclaimed.

Only in America, the last great civilization still largely "Christian" and unshattered by recent history, can virginal minds still speak of "Christian politics," "Christian higher education," "Christian social values," in the tone of voice once used by all of Christendom. In the southeast of the United States can today be found the largest intact bloc of Protestant culture left in the world. (The whole heartland of the Reformation is now occupied by communist power, and Christian minorities find themselves in the diaspora.) In America's major cities and in the upper Middle West there are still solid blocs of Catholic culture where the Church enjoys an influence still claimed for it at law in Spain and Italy but not enjoyed there. But whereas the power of the church is still real among her children in the land of liberty, all of the pretenses of anachronisms like Franco and Pieck cannot hide the fact that "Catholic Europe" and "Protestant Europe" have gone over to the adversary. Both are missionary territory, in the most precise sense of the word — whether we speak of the collapse of Christian credibility in the West or the public triumph of anti-Christian ideology in the East.

Christianity is also facing a credibility crisis in the United States. But so far, in spite of inroads in our society and occasionally in our churches by the communist and fascist belief and style, the problems of American church life are the problems of new Christians rather than the problems of tired baptized who have gone over to another and later dispensation. For the self-understanding of American Protestants the view of history is of fatal importance. Is the present era "post-Christian" in America as well as in Europe? Or is it "post-Constantinian"? When does the church address internal membership, and when does it speak to society at large, and is it aware of the difference?

In all of this, the key question is how the first period of church history in America, the period of the colonial state-churches, is to be understood. For in that place and time the decisions fell which determined for subsequent generations whether state-churches or believers' churches should dominate the American scene. Was it the high tide of our religious life when American Christianity was a peninsula of British Christendom? Since the collapse of New England's Standing Order has all else been anticlimax? Whither are we tending in American religious life, now that the principle of pluralism gains increasing acceptance? Is religious belief alone a secure principle on which to base religious association? Are there social or political reasons for vigorous churches so compelling that their support and standing cannot well be left to "mere chance"?

Puritanism in America

Of Nathanael Emmons (1745-1840), New England Puritan divine, Professor Williston Walker wrote:

> In his incisive style he declared that a Congregational Church is "a pure democracy, which places every member of the church upon a level, and gives him perfect liberty with order." In a Congregational Church, in all matters of business, the pastor "is but a mere moderator...."[1]

Today, such radical egalitarian principles ring rather well. But how shocked the founders of Massachusetts would have been by Emmons' opinions! And as for Professor Walker's, they would have been virtually unintelligible to the men who to defend order and established authority drove Roger Williams into the winter wilderness and Sir Henry Vane the Younger back to the comparative freedom of the Protectorate.

Nevertheless, the kernel of the matter was there from the beginning, even though the consequences of the concept of a Believers' Church were not drawn until the generation when Lyman Beecher returned to praise the benefits of the passing of the state church in Connecticut, a passing which in 1818 and 1819 he had striven mightily to prevent. Religious liberty was not utterly strange to conservative Puritanism, and neither was the principle of church membership based on belief rather than accident of birth.

John Cotton (1584-1652), the friend of Anne Hutchinson who abandoned her in the midst of her controversy with the establishment, remained verbally committed to the concept of a voluntary covenant of believing persons. This principle, affirmed also in the Mayflower Compact, was finally to blow the New England Standing Order apart at the time of the split between Trinitarian and Unitarian Congregationalists. According to an early record,

19

Mr. Cotton, preaching out of the Book of Kings, 8, taught, that when magistrates are forced to provide for the maintenance of ministers, etc., then the churches are in a declining condition. There he showed, that the ministers' maintenance should be by voluntary contribution, not by lands, or revenues, or tithes, etc.; for these have always been accompanied with pride, contention, and sloth, etc.[2]

John Norton (1606-1663), writing for the Massachusetts clergy in response to the questions of an English clergyman, put the center of the matter at the source of liberty:

The Christian churches are neither a monarchy, an aristocracy, nor a democracy, but a theocracy or, if you will, a Christocracy.[3]

The Cambridge Platform of Church Discipline (1648) summed up the matter as the New England founding fathers understood it:

In respect of Christ, the head and King of the Church, and the sovereign power residing in him, and exercised by him, it is a monarchy; in respect of the body or brotherhood of the church, and power from Christ granted unto them, it resembles a democracy; in respect of the presbytery, and power committed unto them, it is an aristocracy.[4]

Most evidently it was then an aristocracy, "a vocal aristocracy in the face of a silent democracy." But just as evidently the kernel of the concept of the Believers' Church was there—whether stated in the language of voluntary commitment and support or put forward in affirmation of obedience to Christ, the one and only king in the church. For the essential matter of the Free Church is the affirmation of the *potestas Christi* in all things religious.

Religious liberty begins not with a political detente, as an exaggerated form of toleration; it begins with a high view of the church. And the Free Church begins not with the question of church-state relations, as though the political factor were to define a true church. The churches were separated from the state in the Nazi administration of the Warthegau (1941-43), but the Christians did not enjoy religious liberty. The churches are separated from the state under the decrees governing religion in the Deutsche Demokratische Republik (Communist East Germany) today, but there is no true religious liberty. The matter of religious liberty begins with the understanding of the church, and this is the missing side of the argument in that fine declaration, *Dignitatis Humanae*, from Vatican II,[5] a declaration which, like Pope John's encyclical *Pacem in Terris*, grounds liberty and integrity of conscience in natural law.

The understanding of the church accents the believer's authority in the Free Church. John Owen (1616-1683) put it this way:

> But as *this whole church-power* is committed unto the whole church by Christ, so all that are called unto the peculiar exercise of any part of it, by virtue of office-authority, do receive that authority from him by the only way of the communication of it—namely, by his word and Spirit, through the ministry of the church. . . .[6]

The believers' authority and the Believers' Church come from Christ. Any other construction misses the whole point, both historically and theologically. This sequence may seem to belabor the obvious. But in a day which is fond of discussing religious liberty without churches, churches without belief, religion without Christology, and freedom of conscience without church discipline, it seems worthwhile to point up where the believers' church begins and what its associations are.

The Question of Origins

Where does the believers' church take its start in history? Most of our churches of the Anabaptist, radical Puritan, Free Church line have traditionally asserted their point of origin to be the Church of the New Testament. In the last hundred years the development of source study and the comparative method in theological and historical science has muted this kind of talk. In an age when our brethren of the Catholic communion are studying and affirming the authority of Scripture and the normative character of the church of the apostolic age, when the latest studies of the sub-apostolic age are read avidly and discussed by scholars of the most varied backgrounds, entering into disputation over competing claims of prior occupancy seems hardly likely to edify.

Where then shall we begin in the modern period to sift out the believers' church? The introduction of the historical discussion with references to Congregational testimony from early New England (plus John Owen) was done with deliberation. For there has been entirely too much effort in times past to prove the case by locating the landmarks and exploiting the genetic fallacy. And then, where the traces were obscured or evidence of direct influence broke down (e.g., in the relationship between continental Anabaptism and the radical sectaries of the English Commonwealth), bold conclusions were drawn across on slender supports or the posited bridge was rejected altogether by the tough-minded. The case for the Believers' Church does not depend upon any proved or disproved succession of unbroken church order across the centuries.

John Robinson (1576?-1625) put the matter very simply, in lively dispute with an opponent:

> And for the gathering of a Church . . . I do tell you, that in what place soever, by what means soever, whether by preaching the gospell by a true Minister, by a false minister, by no minister, or by reading, conference, or any other meanes of publishing it, two or three faithfull people do arise, separating themselves fro[m] the world into the fellowship of the gospell, and covenant of Abraham, they are a Church truely gathered though never so weak, a house and temple of God rightly founded upon the doctrine of the Apostles and Prophets, Christ himsef [sic] being the corner stone, against which the gates of hell shall not prevayl, nor your disgracefull invectives neyther.[7]

A good place to begin the discussion this year is through calling attention to the 500th anniversary of the founding of the *Unitas Fratrum*. For the Unity of Brethren was the community within which a number of the testimonies most dear to modern Free Churches first took determined shape. Five hundred years ago a small company of "brethren," influenced by Peter Chelcicky's view of the *Lex Christi* (Mt. 22: 37-39; Gal. 6:2), and led by the nephew of the Utraquist archbishop of Prague, founded a community at Kunwald. Eventually they broke completely with the established church and their three leaders, chosen by lot, received ordination from a Waldensian priest. Later blending with the Lutheran cause, they were shattered and virtually destroyed by persecution following an abortive revolt against King Ferdinand I (1547). A few merged with the Utraquists, to prosper briefly until Protestantism was destroyed in Bohemia and Moravia following the Battle of the White Mountain (November 8, 1620). Others scattered into Russia and Poland. Most important for subsequent history was the part which about three hundred Brethren played in the founding and development of Herrnhut (1722 ff.) and in the emergence of one of the major movements of Pietism and modern missions: the *Brüdergemeine* or Moravians. To mention the names of Zinzendorf, Nitschmann, Jablonsky, Spangenberg, de Schweinitz, Reichel, and Renkewitz is to raise the curtain on the modern age of ecumenical and missionary concern.

The Bohemian Brethren, or later the Moravian Brethren, emphasized those understandings and institutions of the New Testament which have risen again and again among the believers' churches of the modern period: a style of life modeled on the Sermon on the Mount (opposition to wealth and conspicuous consumption, denial of the oath and warring, separation from violence and coercion), literal acceptance of the Great Commission, imitation of the Church at Jerusalem, restitutionist views of church history, shunning of worldly morals and customs, foot-washing and the apostolic style of church leadership, church discipline to replace government of the church by secular authorities, and a simple ordinance of the Lord's Supper (sometimes accompanied by restoration of the Agape).

Since the *Unitas Fratrum* appeared on the scene while Christendom was still somewhat intact, or at least the hope of restoring it through General Councils had not yet abated, absolute separation of church and state and believer's baptism, the sign of a strictly voluntary covenant, were then accomplished only in few places and seasons. The Moravians, three centuries after Chelcicky, still managed a mixed solution—functioning as a renewal movement among the churches of the Christian nations, but gathering separate congregations on the mission field. Two movements which were part of the same eighteenth-century revival of religion, the Society of Divine Inspiration and the Church of the Brethren, took another course. The Society, eventually settling in the Amana colonies in Iowa, built strict and self-sustaining Christian communist settlements in imitation of the Church at Jerusalem. The Church of the Brethren also emigrated to America, becoming one of the three great "peace churches" and like the others (Mennonites and Society of Friends) influencing American Christianity through its peace testimony and its charitable works (Brethren Service Commission) far out of proportion to its numbers.

But where does the discussion begin? If nonresistance is the key, the Mennonites and Quakers and Brethren, with occasional assists from Moravians, Methodists, Christadelphians, and Adventists, stand at the center. If the key is believer's baptism, then the Mennonites and Brethren are overshadowed by Baptists and Disciples, by churches which have in America far outstripped them in numbers and social status. If, with Rufus Jones, we stress the "spiritual" and repudiate "secularism," not Pilgram Marpeck but Caspar Schwenckfeld, not Alexander Mack but Hochmann von Hochenau, not the councils of churches but the Wider Quaker Fellowship, stand at center forward.[8] But Benson, Creasey, Tolles, Cooper and other Quaker scholars have now restated the obligation of Fox, Barclay, and Penn and their associates to biblical and Christian intellectual and structural norms, and opposing "spiritual" and "secular" is going out of date everywhere. If church-state relations are the key, does American Catholicism stand in the Free Church line and Spanish Catholicism belong to "the Fall"?

Robert Friedmann once suggested in a classic essay on the Anabaptists[9] that the selection of what idea is treated as central determines the way different sections of that movement may be grouped and bracketed.

This principle certainly applies when we draw a line which, after pre-liminary reference to Waldenses and Bohemian Brethren, moves from the sixteenth-century Anabaptists (Mennonites, Hutterites) through radical Puritanism (Baptists, Quakers, Congregationalists) and Pietism (Moravians, Church of the Brethren, Amana Colonies) and the Evangelical Awakening (Methodism, Welsh Presbyterians, Lady Huntington's Connexion), through the American churches (including the Church of the Latter-Day Saints, Jehovah's Witnesses and Christian Science, as well as the Disciples' Restoration Movement) of the nineteenth century of home missions, to the younger churches of the former foreign mission fields. But such a relativism of typology, like dependence upon genetic evidence, provides little help in developing working principles for understanding and defining the theological encounters of the day.

Churches Open to the Truth

The conclusion, it seems to me, is unavoidable: in the approach to the sources, the hermeneutical principle is controlling. For a long time it was possible for most scholars to dismiss without serious reflection, for example, the testimony of the Anabaptists, because the concerns which the *Täufer* held dear were of no great interest to Christendom. The defenders of the "magisterial Reformation"[10] condemned them as "enthusiasts" and "Donatists," and generations of theologians and church historians repeated the condemnation without ever checking the primary sources of the movement, because they were determined to maintain a stable continuum of political and religious values and authority. Today, when the presuppositions of the sacral society are no longer self-evident, the testimonies of those who separated the political from the religious covenant and pioneered religious liberty have become useful to all Christians. In earlier times, when leaders of the Catholic and Protestant state-churches were busy establishing fixed points of authority and doctrine, the openness of the radicals to a continuing revelation seemed volatile and irresponsible. Today, when so many "Christian Ziggurats" have been pulled down, when so many Christians in both East and West have been compelled by conscience to dwell in tents again, the teachings of earlier pilgrim churches become relevant and useful. We may not yet live in a "post-Christian era," as some assert; but that our thought and our style is "post-Christendom" seems to me beyond dispute.

Who then were those who first experienced some of the struggles of alienation and separation from the prevailing culture? Who were the proclaimers of the Word who first gathered the faithful on the basis of voluntary membership and support? If the Christians are necessarily future-oriented, if the dialogue with the past is carried on for the sake of the future of the Christian movement, then the usefulness of the teachings and experiences of those who refused to adopt fixed positions for all time to come and anathematize those who were open to change is especially great. No one can master the lessons of the past "objectively," if "objectivity" be defined as starting from a presuppositionless stance and moving to necessary and inexorable conclusions. The ocean of facts is infinite, and the swimmer who sets out to cross all waters and touch all shores will drown no wiser than when he launched forth. An "objective" reading of the past, in the right sense, is only possible under the rules of the dialogue, where real questions are asked and witnesses, even disliked witnesses, are carefully listened to. The word which was invented by a leader of the Left Wing of the Reformation, *unpartheyisch*, to govern the dialogue is precisely what is meant by the quality which governs non-ideological, open-faced discussion leading unto truth.

The radical Protestant approach to truth is also clear in its attitude to the Bible. Among the Anabaptists, the Bible was opened in the congregation and the Spirit gave guidance to interpret the meaning of the Word. They did not believe the Word meaningful apart from the work of the Spirit. The same attitude was taken to church law and structures: the Spirit and not the letter ruled. But the Spirit was the One who gives order, not atomism and anarchy. In a dramatic confrontation between Ulrich Zwingli and leaders of the Swiss Brethren, one of the latter objected to Zwingli's deference to the cantonal council in matters religious:

> Master Ulrich. You don't have the authority to put the decision in milords' hands. The decision is already fallen: the Spirit of God decides.[11]

The order which was purposed was not, however, a finished scheme. In the time of Archbishop Laud, both the episcopal party and conservative Puritans complained bitterly of the "principle of mutability" exercised by the radical Puritans. What the radicals claimed, however, was the right to change their minds, given further light. To them, this was an article of faith; to their opponents, it was proof that they could not be depended upon to stay put.

The truth was not, for the early Free Church men, a closed book. The Spirit broke the seven seals in the congregation, and the dialogue with the written word came alive. The Spirit governed and guided Christians in their common life and sent them forth in mission and service. The Spirit who today gathers men of the most diverse ethnic and institutional traditions into live encounters, imparting new wisdom the

25

while, is well known to those whose fathers repudiated "sectarian" (*partheyisch*) disputes and wanted fellowship with all who bore the Name and lived the covenant of a good conscience with God.

What are the contact points where lessons may be learned, where help for the present struggle of faith may be found? It is precisely the genius of the article by Michael Novak, "The Free Churches and the Roman Church,"[12] that the author approaches the sources with real questions and purpose to learn. As in many other fields of inquiry, useful answers can only be obtained by asking the right questions. Having learned from the Spirit governing the present inter-church dialogue, few of us who claim descent from Free Church fathers would assert that all answers to all questions are to be found in one or another moment enshrined in our heritage. We are prepared to learn from others. But we are convinced that, in many of the issues facing the Christian movement today and in the time ahead, the findings of the once despised "sectarians" can be strengthening to every community of faithful people.

What then are the issues which make the Free Church record relevant today? What are the key points of belief and practice which gave coherence and integrity to a chain of churches which earlier broke away from the established confessional and liturgical systems of Christendom? We must begin with their critical attitude to history before their own movement, for the view of the church and church history is basic to every major concern they expressed and position they adopted.

The notion of a Fall of the Church has played a large role in the thinking of reform, renewal, and restitution movements since the time of the Abbot Joachim of Fiore (*c.* 1132-1202). Joachim divided religious history into three periods: the Age of the Father, when the Law governed, as graven on stone; the Age of the Son, when the dogma of the church disciplined the mind of the faithful; the Age of the Spirit, when the divine would inform the free individual spirit directly and organized religion would wither away. Such periodization introduced discontinuity and revolution into church history. The Age of the Father ended with the destruction of the Judaic cultus; the Age of the Son ended with the setting aside of creeds, hierarchy, and the sacramental system. Followers of Joachim among the radical Franciscans came to view the pope and medieval church authority as "the Antichrist," because the one who sat on the throne of Peter refused to say the Magnificat and depart his rule in peace.

The signs of the different periods shifted among the Bohemian Brethren, the Anabaptists, the radical Puritans, and the Pietists, but

26

the sword of the Spirit which was drawn against the institutional church was never sheathed. The radical reformers came to divide church history into a Golden Age (the time of the Apostles), a Fall (the "dark ages" following the outward triumph of the Christian religion after Constantine, Theodosius and Justinian), and a Restitution dated with the rise of their own movement. Their program was the restitution of pure, primitive Christianity—which was at the same time the triumph of spiritual religion. "Spiritual religion" was the faith that wrought miracles, the faith before creeds and hierarchies controlled Christendom, the faith of those who had personally known the Christ. The hermeneutical principle is clear: the concepts of decay of the church as institution and the coming restitution of Christianity as pure faith provided a foundation for a new and explosive kind of religious movement. It was, moreover, a spiritual recovery suspicious of the arts and cunning of the human fall.

The fellowship of the restitution, within which believing men and women rediscovered the vitality of apostolic faith and life, was the setting within which the Truth became familiar and reliable for life and death.

The Basic Principles

1. The Believers' Church, although outwardly constituted by volunteers, is Christ's Church and not theirs. One of the grave misunderstandings of the established scholarship of a generation ago was to confuse the sociological and theological premises, to elide voluntaryism and voluntarism. This was especially true of the writings of Karl Holl, who considered the Free Churches of England and America heretical because they were "Freiwilligkeitskirchen."[13] The term is ambiguous and confusing. Many Free Church men, from the time of Pilgram Marpeck, have been hard-line Augustinians on the freedom or bondage of the will. The question of how the church is constituted in its visible form is quite independent of the concept of the relationship of divine initiative and human response. Most of the Anabaptists were Erasmians; most of the radical Puritans were Calvinists; but in both movements there was unanimity as to Who authors history and Who heads the church.

Because the Believers' Church is Christ's Church, it can never compromise with the principle of ethnicity in religion. In repudiating the whole idea and practice of Christendom, its adherents have—from Wilhelm Reublin and Wolfgang Brandhuber on—considered the whole world missionary territory. Such an issue as that raised again a few weeks ago by the Greek Orthodox establishment in requesting the Vatican to desist from "proselytizing," or such an issue as the similar denunciations of evangelical "proselytizing" in so-called Roman Catholic territory (Spain, Latin America, Italy) was already unintelligible to Free Church men four centuries ago. The church consists of those who are personally claimed by Christ, and without that relationship there is no church, however impressive the outward show. The point seems obvious today, until we recollect on what basis religious statistics are still compiled[14] and how delegates are to be chosen for the next Assembly of the World Council of Churches. The "hidden church" in Russia will probably, by the use of recklessly watered statistics, outnumber the delegates of several large churches of known volunteers. But if a "hidden church" is to be the argument, why not the "hidden church" of the Hutterite *Grosse Geschichtsbuch*, or of the Mennonite *Märtyrerspiegel*?

The true church is representative of *(stellvertretend für)* the claims of the Universal Church in one place. The congregational principle has been important to most Free Churches, but not all, in language such as this:

> . . . there is no greater church than a congregation, which may ordinarily meet in one place.[15]

But this congregation may not be counted faithful if it compromises with race, the present moment of truth for the churches; nor may it think of itself as a private club of restricted membership. "Believers' Church" does not mean that the church belongs to the members; it means that the members belong to Christ.

2. Membership in the believers' church is *voluntary* and witting. In the sixteenth century the proof text was the Great Commission; and since those verses imply adult baptism and no clear mandate for infant baptism can be found in the New Testament, believer's baptism became a sign for most believers' churches. Infant baptism may be, like circumcision, a sign of the covenant of fathers and sons. With subsequent use of confirmation (not to be confused with the medieval *Firmung*)—a rite which owes its development in good part to the encounter of Martin Butzer with the Anabaptists[16]—the importance of adult decision and deliberate choice was structured into the establishments as well. Adult baptism, which has a different significance in an area where children are automatically baptized or perhaps coercively baptized, from what it has in an area of religious liberty, is a point on which there is still substantial disagreement, as there was even among the early so-called "Anabaptists." But there is no disagreement on the point that church membership should be deliberate and voluntary.

This being the case, the Free Churches have tended to accent the dignity and voice of each member. When they sink back into their own style of culture-religion, as in some of the Russian Mennonite or American Hutterite communities, and lose the style of a missionary-minded and pilgrim people, new forms of authoritarian control may develop which are as deadening as the fathers felt rule by hierarchs or professional theologians to be. But as a movement the men of the Free Church line can claim with considerable justification that the "rediscovery of the laity" dates at least from the sixteenth-century restitution rather than from the twentieth-century church struggle alone.[17]

3. The principle of *separation* from "the world" is basic, although it has often been misinterpreted both by critics and by initiates. The critics, frequently basing their attack on Troeltsch's famous distinction between "church type" and "sect type" and forgetting his warning that the typology does not hold beyond the eighteenth century or in the Anglo-American complex, have attributed "Donatism" and "perfectionism" to the believers' church. The initiates, sometimes mistaking the tension between the eighteenth century and the twentieth century for the tension between the "church" and the "world," have sometimes settled into social fossils. The spirit of separation, however, lies between those who live the life of hope in the coming Kingdom and those captured by "the spirit of the times," between the Christians who are being formed for the world to come and the self-justifying and self-satisfied age of warring, dehumanization, violence, racism and murder which is passing away. When churches which have earlier escaped the bondage of state control and manipulation now settle into the pattern of social statics and social establishment which we call "culture-religion," it is a major mistake in reading Christian history and Christian vocation.

The first major struggle for Christian liberty and for "the Crown Rights of the King" began in an insistence that the political covenant and the religious covenant are two different sets of relationships. The Anabaptists, who knew only persecuting or tolerating governments (and few of the latter kind), had no chance to develop a political theory to match their concept of the church as a voluntary association. But from the time of the Commonwealth a new understanding has been emerging: the true church is to be free of unbaptized controls, the better to serve her Lord, and government is to be demythologized. The pretension of governments to serve ultimate ends, whether the old type of sacralism or the new type of ideological state is at the bar, is contrary to the presuppositions of religious liberty and destructive of the Believers' Church. But this separation, rather unfortunately called "separation of church and state"—as though the church were indifferent to social and political issues and the state free to function without a conscience—is but the beginning of the matter. The churches are freed to obedience, not to anarchy and indiscipline.

4. *Mission* and *witness* are key concepts for the Believers' Church, and all members are involved. The Anabaptist treatment of the "counsels of perfection" is illustrative. In the middle ages "the religious" were a small and select few among the baptized. The restitutionists made the counsels binding upon all believers, thereby numbering all members among the religious. It is sometimes said that certain of the more radical of the Free Churches have no clergy. A truer report would be this: several of them have eliminated the laity, at least in its usual passive condition.

The Hutterites mounted the most vigorous Protestant missions of the sixteenth century. The Quakers were the most energetic missionaries in the seventeenth, the Congregationalists and Baptists and Methodists and Moravians in the eighteenth. It is no accident that today three-fourths of Protestant missionary personnel and support come from churches of the Free Church line. If we include the work of Lutherans under Pietist influence and Anglicans affected by the Evangelical Awakening, the percentages would jump even higher. The truth is that an expansive world-view has always been a mark of the restitutionist church—long before the men of the "magisterial Reformation" admitted the Great Commission to be still operative, long before Hendrik Kraemer and Karl Barth and others began to question the triumph of ethnicity in "Christian" Europe. The "great century" of Christian missions, of which Professor Latourette has made us so keenly aware, was on the Protestant side the century of the believers' churches. Surveys of the mission fields and the younger churches from Parker (1938) to the *Weltkirchenlexikon* (1960) show several dozen countries of Central America and Africa where the staffs of the most radical wing of Protestantism (the so-called "Spirit-filled sects") outnumber all other missionaries, Catholic and Protestant, put together.

5. Internal integrity and *church discipline* are stressed. The religious primitivism of the left wing has often carried a technological or cultural primitivism with it. The Free Church fathers have been suspicious of human invention, craft, artifice and cunning, whether in complicated church government or in theological learning. "Let the simple Gospel suffice!" For this reason, as can be seen in the present conflict of the Amish with public school authorities in Kansas and Iowa, they have stressed the oral tradition more than the critical method. They

are not, as often charged, anti-intellectual; rather, they emphasize that dimension of learning which has to do with wisdom *(Logos)* rather than technical proficiency *(Techne)*, including proficiency in the science of theology.[18] For the oral tradition, memorization is important; and so is the dramatic reenactment of ultimate events: Lord's Supper, adult baptism foot-washing, personal religious testimony.

Church discipline of a critical kind is also practiced, based on Matthew 18:15-19. Without governmental decrees or licenses or officially sponsored theological faculties to give form and structure, the believers' church is dependent upon a pattern of apostolic church government modeled on that of the house-churches in the Acts. Of a good decision "talked up" in the congregations and made binding by consensus ("the sense of the meeting"), the faithful can report, "It seemed good to the Holy Spirit and to us" (Acts 15:28).[19] Without such an internal struc-ture—and here we must not forget the indebtedness of Calvinism to the Anabaptists[20]—no believers' church can maintain the life of the Spirit. It is unfortunately true that some Free Churches, having lost their practice of church discipline, are in worse condition than the es-tablishments, from which they once separated, that have at least main-tained their traditional confessions of faith and liturgical life.

6. Of great importance in contemporary dialogue is the *concept of the secular.* At the International Conference on the Theological Issues of Vatican II held at the University of Notre Dame, the importance of a theology of the created order came to the fore as unfinished business.[21] For if the church has been freed from the continuum of religious and political authority called "Christendom," the government and social welfare and the university and other "creatures" have been freed from the necessity of subservience to churchly imperialism. They have been granted an integrity and a dignity of their own and are not to be judged wanting if they fail to serve churchly interests.

Take "secular" government, for example, one of the greatest blessings of human liberty. The old style of Christian government and the new style of ideologically tainted government claim authority over the conscience. Secular government, however, knows its claims to be limited, knows itself to be a human invention to achieve specific purposes, recognizes the limits of the "creaturely." Such government complements the believers' church, and we do wrong to fall back into the old ideology of "Christian America," "America-Back-to-God," of Prayer Amendments, etc. The next major task for the believers' church where operating under reactionary sacralism (as in Spain) or reactionary Marxism (as in East Germany) is to declare and to dignify the integrity of the secular. In some important areas of American life the responsibility is the same, particularly in resisting the Ersatz-piety of the Radical Right.

°   °   °

In sum, the task before the believers' church today is to span the bow more tensely. Culture religion is neither "church" nor "world," but corrupting to both. For us who enjoy the blessings of religious liberty, the double task is to enrich the quality of the community of faithful people and in the secular order to learn to live with all men of good will without suspicion and without anxiety. The same Lord rules both church and created order, and in the end His purposes will obtain in both. In the day of the Kingdom there is promised the consummation of church history and also the consummation of the history of the world.

The Believers' Church is no Manichaean fortress, a tiny area of illumination in the midst of a creation given over to darkness. The Believers' Church knows, with the Psalmist of old and with the Anabaptists for whom it was a favorite text even in martyrdom, that "the earth is the Lord's and the fullness thereof" (Ps. 24:1). When we speak of restitution, we look to the fulfillment of God's purposes for the **Church and a final restitution of all things.**

A BELIEVING PEOPLE

William R. Estep, Jr.

2

Historical Background

William Roscoe Estep, Jr., has altered the pattern predominant among Baptist church historians of the second quarter of the twentieth century, especially W. T. Whitley and W. W. Barnes, of disassociating and differentiating as fully as possible the English Baptists of the seventeenth century from the continental Anabaptists of the sixteenth. Instead, Dr. Estep has participated in the renaissance of Anabaptist studies, has fostered the reopening of the question of English Baptist indebtedness to the Anabaptists, and has written a readable narrative on Anabaptism, *The Anabaptist Story* (1963). Now professor of church history at Southwestern Baptist Theological Seminary, Fort Worth, Texas, Dr. Estep is a graduate of Berea College in his native Kentucky, of the Southern Baptist Theological Seminary, and of Southwestern Baptist Theological Seminary. The pastor of various Baptist churches prior to his acceptance of his present chair in 1954, he has spent sabbatical years studying Anabaptism in Zürich, Switzerland, and Evangelical Christianity in Latin America in Cali, Colombia, and was managing editor of the *Southwestern Journal of Theology* from 1963 to 1967.

Dr. Estep's address was designed to inform conference participants of the origins of the various "believers' church" movements which have insisted upon the personal commitment of faith as essential to membership. With emphasis on indebtedness to preceding movements within the Believers' Church heritage his survey extends from the antecedent Lollards and *Unitas Fratrum* to twentieth-century Pentecostalism with Anabaptists, Mennonites, and Baptists receiving the more detailed treatment. Dr. Estep identifies seventeen characteristics of "Believers' Churches" and concludes that both the recovery of biblical faith and flexibility or accommodation are needed among such movements.

In response to the address by Dr. Estep, Dr. Cornelius Krahn, professor of church history and director of the Mennonite Library and Archives at Bethel College, North Newton, Kansas, cited additional evidence as to the rise and scope of the renaissance of studies concerning the Radical Reformation. Dr. Krahn pointed to the publication of source materials in Europe for at least a century prior to the work of C. A. Cornelius and to the significance of *Bibliotheca Reformatoria Neerlandica* and of the publications of the *Täuferakten Kommission* of Germany and Switzerland. He reported that more than one hundred and fifty PhD dissertations had been written on the Radical Reformation since World War II. Likewise, Dr. Krahn took note of the prevalence of the tendency to posit a pre-Reformation succession of "believers' churches" and attributed the scholarly support for this view mainly to Ludwig Keller, who influenced such Mennonite historians as C. H. Wedel and John Horsch. Dr. Krahn's principal criticism of Dr. Estep's paper was the lack of "concise formulations of what constitutes the concept of the Believers' Church or 'a believing people.'" Dr. Krahn recalled an observation made by Dietrich Bonhoeffer in lectures at the University of Berlin:

> Speaking of the Troeltsch-Weber church-sect theory, he observed that there was something wrong with it. He found it true that old magisterial churches are burdened with a lot of tradition and dead timber. He continued that it is Christ who can make even this church a true and faithful church. It is the same Christ who brings into being the younger free and believers' churches in protest against institutionalism. But like a teenager who revolts against the traditionalism of his parents, the younger churches also grow old and become burdened with traditions. It is Christ who keeps the church faithful and vital regardless of whether she is young or old.

o   o   o

The current definition of the church as "the people of God" emerged out of a change of directions in biblical scholarship which has taken place during the past quarter of a century. With the publication of C. H. Dodd's *The Present Task in New Testament Studies* in 1936, a call was sounded to reverse a century-old trend in biblical studies which had emphasized the diversity evident in the books of the Bible.[1] Within a few years a number of notable works in a similar vein were written by A. M. Hunter, G. Ernest Wright, F. C. Grant, H. H. Rowley, to name a few.[2] These works emphasized the basic unity of the books of the New Testament and the essential oneness of the biblical record. From this attempt to discover unitive threads that bind the biblical fabric together in a recognizable pattern, the term "the people of God" has been revived. Its popular reception was doubtless due quite as much to the term's ambiguity as to its biblical overtones. However, the inclusive nature of the term is the very characteristic which makes it unacceptable, unless qualified, as an adequate designation of those who comprise the object of study in this conference. The topic assigned me contains the first of four qualifying terms suggested by the program committee, "A Believing People: Historical Background."

In what sense are we justified in referring to the architects of the Believers' Church as "A Believing People"? The answer lies in the historical panorama. If the strength of one's faith is revealed by the price he is willing to pay for it, then history knows no people of greater faith than those who have committed themselves to the concept of the Believers' Church. Too, in spite of a fierce separatism that frequently led to the fragmentation of the very witness for which these earnest people gave their lives, they considered themselves members of the Church Universal by virtue of their relationship to Christ. Again, their identification with the church of the New Testament, as naive as it sometimes appears, saved them from an ahistorical stance and firmly rooted their faith in an historical event, the revelation of God in Christ. Since these dissenters readily disassociated themselves from Rome and the churches of the Magisterial Reform, they often attempted to supply the need for an historical identity by appropriating a miscellaneous collection of schismatics from the Montanists to the Waldenses. Even though a dubious procedure on historical grounds, the results did supply some deep psychological needs of the oppressed minorities.[3]

In each of the above ways the believing people transcended their rather narrow self-imposed lines of demarcation to establish a sense of oneness with God and His people. The concepts of First Peter 2:7-10 provide a most apt description of the self-image which many groups within the Believers' Church tradition have possessed. While establishing an implied continuity with Israel, this passage clearly indicates that with the advent of Christ a new people of God distinct from Israel has emerged. Peter writes, "Once you were no people but now you are God's people; once you had not received mercy but now you have received mercy."[4] Vatican Council II caught the spirit of this passage as well as that of the harbingers of the dawn in its *Declaration on the Relationship of the Church to Non-Christian Religions*. In the paragraph dealing with the Jews, the conciliar fathers told the world, "Although the Church is the new people of God, the Jews should not be presented as repudiated or cursed by God, as if such views followed from the holy Scriptures."[5] The sixteenth century Anabaptists would have agreed with this statement. While assuming a hermeneutic of radical discontinuity between the Old and New Testaments, they also manifested a lively interest in the conversion of the Jews, not by coercive measures but simply through a presentation of the gospel in love.[6]

Who were these new people of God that first conceived and implemented the concept of the Believers' Church? Were they products of the Renaissance, the Reformation, or the Middle Ages? While our answers to these questions may not be conclusive, we will at least make the attempt to base them upon documentary evidence insofar as it is available. For Lord John E. E. D. Acton's often quoted words, "History, to be above evasion or dispute, must stand on documents, not on opinion," are axiomatic. Yet history, and particularly church history, is much more than a compilation of facts. The statement of Jules Monnerot is particularly appropriate to our task when he writes: "History is something more than a process of ripping open dolls and turning them over to shake out the sawdust; it is also the midwife of values."[7] We now turn our attention to the historical development of those whom we have designated "A Believing People."

The Pre-Reformation Era

This year marks the fifth centennial of the *Unitas Fratrum*, better known as Moravians. The Moravians claim John Huss as their founder. Actually, it was Peter Chelcicky who salvaged the remnants of Huss's beleaguered followers and with some Waldenses formed the communion which can trace its history through five centuries of suffering and service. The Bohemian Brethren who emerged were far more evangelical in their theological complexion than was Huss. Huss, as Matthew Spinka has written, was "a child of his age, sharing many elements of the theology and the world-view of the late medieval era, although he differed from it by his greater emphasis on Scriptural authority and patristic teaching of the first five centuries."[8] Perhaps the Hussites would have passed into oblivion except for the intervention of a Lutheran Pietist, Count Nikolaus Ludwig von Zinzendorf. It was he who gave the few surviving Moravians refuge on his ancestral estate. But he did much more than that. He also injected his own fervent evangelical spirit into the little band. From 1722 on the revitalized movement electrified and stimulated Christians on both sides of the Atlantic for the better part of a century.

However, two other pre-Reformation evangelical movements antedate that of the Bohemian Brethren and were in various ways related to the Hussite reform effort. The more ancient of the two, the Waldenses, exist today in somewhat altered form.[9] The rise of the second, the Lollards, is associated with the work of John Wyclif, two and a half centuries after the time of Peter Waldo.

Wyclif became almost as influential in Bohemia as he was in England. For Wyclif, "Holy Scripture is the highest authority for every Christian and the standard of faith and of all human perfection."[10] Wyclif's teachings and his Bible supplied the materials out of which

38

Walter Brute molded the Lollards. Even though the Lollards disappear from the pages of English history by the middle of the sixteenth century, their ideas continued to find a sympathetic audience for some time. In fact, Lollardism persisted, according to A. G. Dickens, in the vicinity of the diocese of York until 1534 and even beyond.[11] In that year Henry VIII, who had been previously designated "Defender of the Faith" by the pope in gratitude for his writings against Luther, became a defector of the faith, and heresy almost became legitimate. By this time the teachings of Luther and of Zwingli were well known, and those of the Anabaptists to a lesser degree. As a result many Englishmen now were quite willing to accept Wyclif's view of Rome as a fallen and apostate church and his designation of the pope as Antichrist. The introduction of Tyndale's New Testament (1526) provided a most effective vehicle for conveying Reformation concepts from the Continent to the British Isles. [12]

Wyclif's reformatory efforts were apparently much more radical than those of either John Huss or Peter Waldo. The movements sparked by these Reformers became with the passing of the years increasingly evangelical. The role of the Scriptures in this development has not always been duly recognized. Yet the Lollards and the Bohemian Brethren consistently appealed to the authority of the Scriptures over that of the Church for the Christian life and faith.

It is also significant that no reform effort enjoyed a massive response until the Bible became readily available through the invention of a printing press using movable type. Five hundred and one years ago today, June 27, 1466, the first Bible printed upon the newly invented press was offered for sale. It was published by Johann Mentel in Strasbourg. Before Luther's September Bible appeared in 1522, no fewer than fourteen editions of the Bible in High German and four in Low German were published by various printers.[13] Yet few people possessed a thorough knowledge of the Scriptures. Luther claimed not to have read a Bible in his entire life prior to his student days at Erfurt. Even then he did not begin a serious study of its contents. In fact, he embarked on no such study until becoming a theological professor at the University of Wittenberg in 1512.[14] The publication of Erasmus' critical edition of the Greek New Testament in 1516 stirred an interest in the publication of the Bible in the vernacular unprecedented in the history of the Church. It appears that the Reformation of the sixteenth century waited for the Bible. It could hardly do otherwise, since it was dependent upon the apostolic witness to the revelation of God in Christ which the New Testament alone contained.

There is no understanding of Martin Luther if one ignores the role of the Bible in his experience. When Luther came to grips with the significance of Paul's discussion of the righteousness of Christ, he confessed:

> Then I began to comprehend the "righteousness of God" through which the righteous are saved by God's grace, namely, through faith; that the "righteousness of God" which is revealed through the Gospel was to be understood in a passive sense in which God through mercy justifies man by faith, as it is written, "The just shall live by faith." Now I felt exactly as though I had been born again, and I believed that I had entered Paradise through widely opened doors.[15]

Erich Hassinger asserts that Luther's fundamental insight which underlies the Reformation doctrines of *sola scriptura, sola fide,* and the priesthood of believers is his "rediscovery of the historical core of Christianity."[16] Bainton sympathetically reflects on this concept.

> . . . Luther's distinctiveness lay in his recovery of the historical element in Christianity. It is a religion of history. . . . It rests on a deed of God in a time when a decree went out from Caesar Augustus that all the world should be taxed. To Christ the centuries lead up, and from Christ the centuries lead out. In him God the inscrutable became God the discernible. In him God the all terrible became God the all merciful. God was in Christ, reconciling the world unto himself. Therefore Christianity is forever anchored in the past.[17]

Of course, the means of transmission through the centuries of the "deed of God" is the New Testament. This fact, as Luther discovered, gives the Bible a priority over Church and sacrament, for it alone confronts one with the apostolic witness.

Luther's insight regarding the nature of the biblical witness and the nature of the faith-response which that witness entails soon became the common possession of all elements within the Reformation. However, when the performance of the Magisterial Reform failed to match its promise, the disillusioned multiplied. Their disillusionment was the more bitter, for it was twice compounded, first with Rome and second with the Magisterial Reformers. The points at issue vary with the critics. However, the charges of ethical weakness and ecclesiological compromise recur repeatedly in the list of complaints.[18] The Reformers were not altogether oblivious to these weaknesses. There is evidence that they did attempt to rethink their ecclesiology in the light of fresh

Reformation insights. Each of them seems to have entertained radically new concepts of the church which were only partially realized. None appears to have been satisfied with the moral standards of his followers. They apparently were attempting to act responsibly in light of their own understanding, training, and political realism. But the built-in compromise of state-church structures took its toll, even in the thought processes of the Reformers.

Luther's loss of confidence in the common man and fear of the *Schwärmer* caused him to restructure his church along lines very similar to Rome. While holding that Rome was a fallen church, he refused to deny all churchly quality to the grand old medieval edifice. The evidence of continuity between his *Volkskirche* or *Landeskirche* and Rome was the sacraments. At this point Luther was persistently more Roman than Zwingli or even Calvin. For Luther, the prince took the place of the bishop, and all born within a Lutheran prince's territory were baptized in exactly the same manner as those born in Roman Catholic countries. The empirical church became, for Luther, the locus where "the Word is preached and the sacraments are properly observed." Thus he retained infant baptism and the concept of the real presence in the Eucharist, while denying other aspects of the doctrine of transubstantiation.[19]

Calvin, building upon the Zwinglian foundation and confronted by the vigorous Swiss Anabaptist movement, constructed a *Volkskirche* in his Genevan theocracy. He declared the church a spiritual reality where the Word is preached, the sacraments are properly observed, and discipline is practiced. Like Luther, even though more harsh in his denunciation of the fallen Church of Rome, he recognized its baptism and its ecclesial nature. More ethical and stern in the requirements of the Christian life than Luther, Calvin was even less tolerant of dissent. However, neither the Reformers nor the Catholics left any room for the dissenter. Freedom of religion was an impossible and dangerous concept for them. It remained for the Anabaptists to rethink more thoroughly and completely and advocate more courageously the implementation of a New Testament *ecclesiology* for the *empirical* church than any theologian of the Magisterial Reform. The concept of the Believers' Church found its clearest expression and most consistent implementation in the Anabaptist movement of the sixteenth century.

The Anabaptists

For more than four centuries a wanton confusion dictated the use of the term "Anabaptists" in popular parlance and scholarly works alike. Such usage still continues where ignorance or malice prohibits a more objective approach to the subject. However, neither reason nor justice can defend such a procedure. A move to reevaluate the Anabaptists upon the basis of available sources was initiated with the work of C. A. Cornelius more than a century ago. Gradually, but ever so slowly, the Anabaptists emerged from the limbo of discredited movements into which they had been cast by such partisans as Heinrich Bullinger, Christoph Fisher, Justus Menius, and Philip Melanchthon. In this country, John Horsch and his son-in-law, Harold Bender, became the pioneer evangelists in the revival of Anabaptist studies. A. J. F. Zieglschmid and Robert Friedmann made invaluable contributions in the discovery and editing of heretofore little known source materials. However, it was Franklin H. Littell's *The Anabaptist View of the Church* (1952) which called attention to the new era in Anabaptist studies perhaps more than any other single work. It was awarded the Brewer Prize by the American Society of Church History and rapidly became the most widely read book on the subject. Ten years later, after many new works and additional discoveries of source materials, Hans Hillerbrand compiled the most comprehensive bibliography of sixteenth-century Anabaptism yet published. Since Hillerbrand's manuscript was completed, at least a dozen notable books have appeared in English and German on the Anabaptists of the sixteenth century. It appears that the history of the Reformation must be rewritten in the light of fresh knowledge now available. For do we not have a situation comparable to that presented to New Testament scholars by the discovery of the Dead Sea Scrolls or to the historians of the early church created by the discovery of the Nag Hammadi Gnostic library?[20]

In any attempt to rewrite the history of the Reformation care must be taken to clarify the use of the term "Anabaptists." Those who in the past have been so designated should be divided into at least three major categories: *Spiritualisten* (Inspirationists), Anabaptists, and Rationalists. A general term used by Bainton to identify these is "the Left Wing of the Reformation." George Huntston Williams prefers the term "the Radical Reformation" and explains why.

> Though Anabaptists, Spiritualists, and Evangelical Rationalists differed among themselves as to what constituted the root of faith and order and the ultimate source of divine authority among them (the New Testament, the Spirit, reason), all three groupings within the Radical Reformation agreed in cutting back to that root and in freeing church and creed of what they regarded as the suffocating growth of ecclesiastical tradition and magisterial prerogative. Precisely this makes theirs a "Radical Reformation."[21]

There are other differences which make the suggested distinctions among elements of the Radical Reform necessary. The *Spiritualisten* chronologically arose within the context of the Lutheran movement a few years prior to the Anabaptists. The Swiss Brethren, the original Anabaptists, on the other hand, arose within the immediate context of the Reformation in Zürich. The Rationalists appeared half a century later in Poland under the influence of Faustus Socinus.

It is within the Anabaptist movement as it developed under the tutelage of and in tension with Zwingli and his reform that both the concept and the implementation of the Believers' Church enter into the stream of Christian history. The Anabaptist movement was not the fruit of Thomas Müntzer's labor nor that of the Zwickau Prophets, as Bullinger and many since his day have insisted. Rather it was, as Fritz Blanke has demonstrated, a Swiss movement that drew much of its inspiration and some of its insights from Zwingli's earlier teachings.[22] In this regard it is significant to note that Zwingli's preaching in the Grossmünster was from the very beginning an exposition of the books of the New Testament. He did not turn to the Old Testament until after the final break with his erstwhile disciples in January, 1525.[23]

The issue which marked the beginning of the break between Zwingli and the radicals was the latter's disappointment with Zwingli's unwillingness to abolish the mass and replace it with the Lord's Supper by Christmas Day, 1523, as he had promised. A measure of disagreement was evident during the second major disputation. On the first day of the disputation, October 26, the use of images was discussed and roundly denounced by all participants. On the second day the mass was repeatedly described as an abomination before God. At this juncture in the disputation Grebel, Stumpf, and possibly others had expected some explicit directions from Zwingli to the council on the abolition of the mass. Prior to the debate Zwingli and his young disciples apparently agreed to follow the Bible explicitly in their program of reform. Throughout the October disputation the common appeal of the speakers had been to the Word of God.[24] Undoubtedly Zwingli and his followers had dared to hope that the disputation would prepare the way for changing the mass into an observance of the Lord's Supper. But the close of the debate on the mass brought forth no instructions concerning its abolition. The burgomaster had already announced that the disputation would move on the next day from further consideration of the mass to a discussion of purgatory. Whereupon Grebel arose to request that the present subject not be forsaken until other abuses of the mass had been discussed and instructions given as to the means of its abolition. To this suggestion Zwingli replied, "My lords will decide whatever regulations are to be adopted in the future in regard to the Mass." This unexpected and rather curt statement from Zwingli provoked Simon Stumpf to exclaim, "Master Ulrich, you do not have the right to place the decision on this matter in the hands of my lords, for the decision has already been made, the Spirit of God decides."

Zwingli next delineated the difference between truth as determined from study of the Scriptures and the implementation of truth by the council. The closing remarks of Stumpf indicate that to him implementation of that which was so clearly enunciated in the New Testament was not the prerogative of the council. "If my lords adopt and decide on some other course that would be against the decision of God, I will ask Christ for His spirit, and I will preach and act against it."[25] Zwingli immediately responded to Stumpf's statement with a ringing affirmation. "*Das ist recht,*" he replied. "I will also preach and act against it if they decide otherwise. I am not putting the decision in their hand. They are not over the Word of God, and this goes not only for them but also for the whole world (*ja ouch alle welt nit*)."[26] Then once again Zwingli differentiated the diverse functions of the disputation and the implementation of its judgment by the council.

During the next fourteen months the incipient Anabaptist movement developed rapidly, and the resultant estrangement between Zwingli and the Grebel entourage increased. The final break came three days after the fateful disputation on January 18, 1525, when a small band of resolute men, determined to implement believer's baptism and thereby constitute a church after what they were convinced was the New Testament pattern, met to follow the Spirit's leading in defiance of Zwingli and the orders of the instituted authorities. The events of that unforgettable night are recorded in *Die älteste Chronik der Hutterischen Brüder.*

And it came to pass that they were together until anxiety (*angst*) came upon them, yes, they were so pressed with their hearts. Thereupon they began to bow their knees to the Most High (*hochstenn*) God in heaven and called upon him as the Informer of Hearts (*Hertzenkundiger*), and they prayed that he would give to them his divine (götlichen) will and that he would show his mercy unto them. For flesh and blood and human forwardness did not drive them, since they well knew what they would have to suffer on account of it.

After the prayer, George of the House of Jacob stood up and besought (*gebeeten*) Conrad Grebel for God's sake to baptize him

44

with the true (*recht*) Christian baptism upon his faith and knowledge (*erkanndtnus*). And when he knelt down with such a request and desire, Conrad baptized him, since at that time there was no ordained minister (*dienner*) to perform such work.[27]

After his baptism at the hands of Grebel, Blaurock proceeded to baptize all the others present. The newly baptized then covenanted together as faithful disciples of Christ to live lives separated from the world and to teach the gospel and hold fast the faith. On this fateful night the concept of a Believers' Church based upon a voluntary confession of faith confirmed by the act of public baptism found concrete realization in history. Thus, from a handful of radicals in Switzerland and South Germany who preferred to call themselves Brethren in Christ, the Free Church movement sprang. This fact alone gives the Anabaptists a place of unrivaled importance in the history of the church.

The Mennonites

From the very beginning the Anabaptists, although largely drawn from the peasant class, became a most literate people. Since the success of the movement was wholly dependent upon a personal response to their presentation of the biblical message, literacy became a necessary corollary to evangelism. Too, the relentless opposition of their enemies made an understanding of the faith with a corresponding commitment an imperative. Believer's baptism became the hallmark of this understanding and commitment.

The case of Claus Felbinger is a classic illustration of an Anabaptist confessing his faith under fire. Felbinger, a locksmith by trade, was arrested with another Hutterite, Hans Leutner, near Neumarkt in Bavaria. During the two months of his imprisonment hardly a day passed in which he escaped interrogation. Priests, monks, and theologians visited his cell. Upon one occasion Felbinger was questioned about recanting. He replied that he and his fellow prisoners would abide in the "simplicity of Christ." The chancellor was aroused to ask: "Are you simple? I do not believe it, . . . not one of a hundred could defend himself, and maintain his position as fairly as you have done."[28] In regard to his baptism Felbinger testified.

> Further I was asked with regard to *baptism*, how often I was baptized. I said, "Once, as God has commanded." They then asked if I had not also been baptized by the brothers. I answered, "The

devout brothers who baptized me in accordance with the command of Christ first taught me repentance and faith in the name of Jesus Christ. Then, at my request, they baptized me on confession of my faith; which faith, God, according to His promise, also sealed and strengthened with His Holy Spirit, who has until now kept me in the way of truth. And it is my hope in God that He take Him not from me until my end."[29]

The Anabaptists possessed no one theologian whose word became supreme among them. For one thing, no early theologian lived long enough. Balthasar Hubmaier, for an example, lived only four years after publishing his first reformatory work. All the initial leaders, with the exception of Wilhelm Reublin, were dead within five years. Zürich lost its three major Anabaptist leaders in short order. Grebel died of the plague in 1526.[30] Felix Manz became the first Protestant to die at the hands of Protestants in 1527,[31] and George Blaurock was burned at the stake in 1529.[32] The oppression of the Anabaptists in Switzerland led to their almost complete extermination. However, in the Canton of Berne, in spite of severe persecution, Anabaptists have maintained a vigorous witness through the centuries down to the present. Today, they are known as Mennonites, even though Menno Simons had nothing to do with their origin. Two other contemporary denominations which trace their history back to the Swiss Brethren are the Hutterites, who set up their first Brüderhof in 1528, and the Amish, who became a distinct party of the Swiss Mennonites in the seventeenth century.

A seemingly endless variety of religious opinion gave rise to new conventicles in almost every part of Europe. Where Anabaptist life merged with that of the *Spiritualisten*, such fanatical millenarians as the Münsterites arose, basing their movement quite as much on the Old Testament as the New, and with special revelations of the Spirit as the occasion suggested or as the opportunism of a John of Leiden demanded. On the other hand, where the stream of Renaissance rationalism converged with Calvinism and Anabaptism in Poland, the Polish Brethren became Socinians. The Reformation counterpart of medieval mysticism found exponents in Caspar Schwenckfeld, Sebastian Franck, and their followers. Even Catholicism could not escape the leavening influence of the Radicals through such intrepid spirits as Alfonso and Juan de Valdes.[33]

However, it was Menno Simons who became the most influential and certainly the best known theologian of the Anabaptists. Eventually the remnants which survived the blood bath of the sixteenth century became known by his name. Menno may not have been the most astute and accomplished theologian sixteenth-century Anabaptism produced, but he was by all odds the most important. It was he who gave the movement a leadership that enabled it to extricate itself from the odium of Münster and the vagaries of the Davidians and Batenbergers alike, as well as from the rationalism of the Pastorites. More than any other Dutch theologian he recaptured in life and thought the vision of the Swiss Brethren in spite of some Hofmannite overtones.[34]

The Mennonites occupy a position of unusual importance for our study: first, as preservers of the basic insights of sixteenth-century Anabaptism, and second, as transmitters of these concepts via influence and direct stimulus upon English Separatism.

The Baptists

With the Act of Supremacy in 1534 the Church of England was separated from Rome. This occasion signaled the beginning of the reform from within, carrying with it more promise of toleration than materialized. Anabaptists, hoping to find some respite from the reign of terror on the Continent, fled to England's shores in ever increasing numbers until the Marian years temporarily reversed the trend. Anabaptism thus became the third level of four strata supplying the ideological background from which English reform movements freely borrowed. The Lollard and Lutheran movements preceded the Anabaptist, and Calvinism followed.

The presence of foreign Anabaptists in England was soon marked by martyrdom. Irvin B. Horst indicates that the number of Anabaptists burned by Henry VIII was larger than the number of Lollards burned in the previous century.[35] The number of Anabaptists executed during Mary's reign, estimated as two-thirds the total number put to death in the five-year period, was considerably fewer than those executed on the Continent during the same period. However, they were numerous enough to remind Englishmen of their presence and to rebuke them for their inhumanity.

The Anabaptist witness in England was not without effect. The Brownists and Barrowists were apparently indebted to the Anglicans for their recruits, to the Puritans for the substance of their theology, and to Anabaptists for some aspects of their ecclesiology. *A most important fact often overlooked is that the very concept of the gathered church, which is the heart of Separatism, was Anabaptist in origin and not a conscious product of the Magisterial Reform.* None of the Reformers developed an ecclesiology of churches composed of committed disciples only.

The first English Baptist church emerged out of English Separatism only after direct contact with the Waterlander Mennonites in Holland. Early in 1609 or late in 1608 John Smyth and his congregation unchurched themselves and reconstituted their church on the basis of believer's baptism in the place of a church covenant. John Robinson, pastor of the Scrooby division of the original Gainsborough congregation, wrote in 1617 of Smyth's action:

> Mr. Smith, Mr. Helw: & the rest haveing vtterly dissolved, & disclaymed their former Ch: state, & ministery, came together to erect a new Ch: by baptism: vnto which they also ascribed so great virtue, as that they would not so much as pray together, before they had it. And after some streyning of courtesy, who should begin. . . . Mr. Smith baptized first himself, & next Mr. Helwis, & so the rest, making their particular confessions.[36]

What influenced Smyth and his small congregation to take such a drastic step? It could bring nothing but sorrow upon sorrow and forever alienate them from their fellow Separatists. Was this the logical outworking of Separatism? If so, why did not all Separatists adopt such a procedure and reconstitute their churches after the pattern of the continental Anabaptists?

The two possible stimuli that drove Smyth and his church to a fresh examination of their ecclesiology and believer's baptism were the prior conversion of some English Separatists to Anabaptism and a confrontation with the Mennonites themselves. Regardless of the reason, Smyth was apparently forced for his own satisfaction to search the Scriptures again for new light on the issues which confronted his church in an alien land. Once convinced of the rightness of the new position, he wasted no time instructing his congregation. The church was then reconstituted on the personal confession of faith and baptism of each one who determined to follow the leadership of the pastor. Smyth based his action squarely on the New Testament and the example of Christ and the apostles. Previously he had discovered the precedent in the Old Testament for constituting a church on a covenant. His former practice gave way to his new understanding. This is a most significant switch.

Possibly the English Anabaptists, formerly of Francis Johnson's church, provided the stimulus to examine New Testament teaching on baptism, for Smyth's act of self-baptism had been anticipated by them. Even if this were true, some Mennonite influence seems undeniable at this point. Smyth apparently did not seek baptism from one of the neighboring Mennonite churches, because he had not yet felt any necessity for such action. Nor was he prepared at this time to accept the Hofmannite Christology of his Mennonite friends.

Smyth was not one to keep his views to himself. He now began to engage his former Separatist brethren in a paper debate over the new practice. The ensuing controversy with Richard Clyfton forced Smyth to rethink his self-baptism. The result was a renunciation of his former action and a petition to the Waterlander Mennonites for admission into their fellowship. Before this step was taken, Smyth had led his church from Calvinism to the acceptance of the general atonement and other Arminian views. While at first rejecting the Hofmannite Christology, he finally capitulated on this point also. He was now prepared to accept with only slight alteration the whole of Mennonite theology. Since Smyth had come to recognize the Waterlander church as a true church, only one step remained. He declared his own baptism invalid and for the sake of order sought baptism at the hands of the Mennonites. The majority of the church followed his lead, but the Mennonites declined to accept the group without careful study. The break between Smyth and Helwys, which had begun with Smyth's adoption of Hofmannite Christology, was now complete. Smyth's progress toward a full-fledged Mennonite position can be followed in detail in the correspondence of Smyth and Helwys with the Waterlander Mennonite Church and the confessions which were exchanged. [37]

The degree to which continental Anabaptism directly influenced and modified the original Separatist position of the Gainsborough church of 1606 from which the Helwys church at Spitalfield sprang becomes a point of special importance in this discussion. Did Thomas Helwys completely reject all distinctive Mennonite concepts which by 1612 clearly marked the Smyth remnant, as has been claimed? Let us answer this question by turning to the sources.

Helwys listed in four points the major differences between himself and Smyth:

I. that Christ took his flesh of Marie, having a true earthlie, naturall bodie.
II. that a Sabbath or day of rest is to be kept holy everie first day of the weeke.
III. that ther is no succession or privilege to persons in the holie thinges.
IV. that magistracie, being an holy ordinance of God, debarreth not any from being of the Church of Christ. [38]

Helwys kept insisting that Smyth was seeking in Romanist fashion to maintain a succession in "holie thinges." This accusation Smyth rejected, declaring that succession was of no importance to him but that

49

correct order was. Helwys and Smyth seemed to have talked past each other.[39]

Helwys' writings and the Confession of 1611, which are readily available, reveal much concerning Anabaptist influence. It would appear that the association with and thinking of John Smyth as well as Mennonite thought had left an undeniable and indelible imprint. The available evidence seems to indicate that Helwys, Murton, and their followers comprised something new under the English sun. *They had emerged from the most difficult struggle of their tumultuous religious pilgrimage to project into English life that which was neither the Separatism they carried into Holland nor the Anabaptism they found there.* The salient features of the new position are given below.

1. The authority by which they arrived at such assurance of the rightness of their position was the New Testament Christologically interpreted. While they did not reject the Old as canonical, it certainly was not the ultimate source of authority for the Church or the Christian life. In article 9 of the 1611 Confession, the Helwys Church declared,

> That IESVS CHRIST is Mediator off the New Testament betweene GOD and Man, I Tim. 2.4, haveing all power in Heaven and in Earth given vnto him. Mat. 28.18. Being the onely KING, Luke 1.33, PREIST [*sic*] , Heb. 7.24, and PROPHET, Act. 3.22. Off his church, he also being the onely Law-giver, hath in his Testament set downe an absolute, and perfect rule off direction, for all persons, at all times, to bee observed; Which no Prince, nor anie whosoever, may add to, or diminish from as they will avoid the fearefull judgements denounced against them that shal so do. Revel. 22.18, 19.[40]

2. The ecclesiology was also essentially Anabaptist. For Helwys the church is not formed by a covenant after the pattern of the "Old Testament saints" as the Gainsborough Separatists first imagined but through a personal profession of faith and believer's baptism as Smyth discovered. Article 10 reads:

> That the church off CHRIST is a compainy off faithful people I Cor. 1.2. Eph. 1.1. seperated [*sic*] fro the world by the word & Spirit off GOD. 2 Cor. 6, 17. being kint [*sic*] vnto the LORD, & one vnto another, by Baptisme. I Cor. 12.13. Vpon their owne confessio of the faith. Act. 8.37. and sinnes. Mat. 3.6.[41]

Article 13 also makes this point clear:

That everie Church is to receive in all their members by Baptisme vpon the Confession off their faith and sinnes wrought by the preaching off the Gospel, according to the primitive Institucion. Mat. 28.19. And practice, Act. 2.41. And therefore Churches constituted after anie other manner, or off anie other persons are not according to CHRISTS Testament.[42]

The one thing that Helwys insisted upon is that such a church possesses the presence and authority of Christ.

And therefore may, and ought, when they are come together, to Pray, Prophecie, breake bread, and administer in all the holy ordinances, although as yet they have no Officers, or that their Officers should bee in Prison, sick, or by anie other meanes hindered from the Church. I:Pet. 4.10 & 2.5.[43]

3. In regard to the ordinances, like his mentor, Smyth, Helwys and his group rejected infant baptism and all sacramentalism. These concepts are evident in articles 14 and 15.

That Baptisme or washing with Water, is the outward manifestacion off dieing vnto sinn, and walkeing in newnes off life. Roman. 6.2,3,4. And therefore in no wise apperteyneth to infants.[44]

That the LORDS Supper is the outward manifestacion off the Spiritual communion betwene CHRIST and the faithful mutuallie. I. Cor. 10.16, 17. to declare his death vntil he come. I Cor. 11.26.[45]

4. While the soteriology is essentially Arminian, there is strong emphasis on original sin but not Adamic guilt. The Confession of 1611 places more emphasis on the sinful character of human nature than Helwys' previous statements on the subject.

5. On religious liberty and the limitations of the magistrate's office, the position of Helwys and Smyth and that of the Mennonites is identical. Even though Helwys' major concern was to clarify his position on the magistracy in the Confession of 1611 in articles 23 and 24, the concept of separation of church and state is implied.[46] The principles of religious liberty and separation of church and state are more clearly enunciated by Helwys in his *Mistery of Iniquity*, published in 1612. Perhaps Helwys' most eloquent passage is found in the inscription which he wrote on the flyleaf of the copy sent to James I.

Heare, o king, and dispise not ye counsell of ye poore, and let their complaints come before thee. The king is a mortall man, and not God therefore hath no power over ye immortall soules of his subiects, to make lawes and ordinances for them, and to set spirituall Lords over them. If the king have authority to make spirituall Lords and lawes, then he is an immortall God, and not a mortall man.

O king, be not seduced by deceivers to sin so against God whome thou oughtest to obey, nor against thy poore subiects who ought and will obey thee in all thinges with body life and goods, or els let their lives be taken from ye earth.

God save ye king.

Spittlefeild
neare London.

Tho: Helwys[47]

Within the book the themes of religious liberty and the temporal role of imperial authority are asserted repeatedly.

What Great Power and authority: what honor, names & titles God hath given to the King.

That God hath give vnto the K. an earthly kingdome with all earthly power against the which, none may resist but must in all thinges obey, willingly, either, to do, or suffer.

That Christ alone is K. of Israell, & sitts vpon Davids Throne, & that the K. ought to be a subject of his Kingdome.

That none ought to be punished either with death or bonds for transgressing against the spirituall ordinances of the new Testament, and that such Offences ought to be punished onely with spiritual sword and censures.[48]

Is not Helwys' stance at this point identical with Smyth's position as revealed in article 84 of *Propositions and Conclusions concerning True Christian Religion, containing a Confession of Faith of certain English people, living at Amsterdam?*

That the magistrate is not by virtue of his office to meddle with religion, or matters of conscience, to force and compel men to this or that form of religion, or doctrine: but to leave Christian religion free, to every man's conscience, and to handle only civil transgressions (Rom. xiii), injuries and wrongs of man against man,

52

in murder, adultery, theft, etc., for Christ only is the king, and lawgiver of the church and conscience. (James iv. 12).[49]

Helwys did not reproduce the Waterlander faith and practice in every detail. There were significant differences. But the determinative features of his theology, if we are not completely misled, are Anabaptist, remolded in the midst of controversy and in the light of his own understanding of the Bible. This is not to deny the role of the Scriptures in the formulation of Helwys' Baptist faith, but it is to acknowledge the catalyst that enabled him to recognize in the New Testament the essential features of that faith we readily recognize as Baptist. Helwys died in Newgate prison sometime prior to 1616.[50]

The first English Baptists became known as General Baptists since they, like the Mennonites, were Arminian in soteriology. The Particular Baptists who arose out of the Jacob-Lathrop-Jessey Independent Church in 1641/42 were Calvinistic in their theological complexion. Their origin reflects a merging of Independent Puritanism and Separatism under Anabaptist influence. This influence may have been mediated more by books and tracts than by personal contact. The careful student cannot rule out the possible influence of the General Baptists in precipitating this development. It is significant that here for the first time Calvinism enters into the stream of Free Church life without losing its basic theological orientation. These new Baptists, in addition to rejecting infant baptism, adopted believer's baptism by immersion only as valid baptism. The concept of the Church Universal which occurs in the Smyth Confession of 1612 and in the Helwys Confession of 1611 finds expression here also. However, the four scriptural officers of the local church reflect the Puritan heritage. Later this position is amended to support only two officers, pastor and deacons, as was the practice among the General Baptists. The authority to baptize, discipline, and celebrate the Lord's Supper, according to the London Confession of 1644, belongs to the whole church and not to the ministers only. This definitely reflects a pattern of General Baptist life rather than that of the Separatists. This was one of the burning issues that Helwys fought through in controversy with Johnson's Ancient Church.

The church established by Roger Williams at Providence was also Calvinistic in theology but within a short time became Arminian. Calvinism entered Baptist life again when, under the influence of the Great Awakening, many Congregational churches became Separatist, emphasizing the necessity of a regenerate church. They soon felt the heavy hand of the establishment. Imprisonment followed for those who would not conform.[31] The oppressed turned to the Baptists, whose principles of religious liberty were well known. A fresh study of the Scriptures under the sympathetic encouragement of their friends in adversity resulted in practically all of the New England Separatists becoming Baptists. George Whitefield complained upon returning to America after an absence of some time that all of his chickens had become ducks. The Separate Baptists (as they were known) soon became the most fruitful Baptists in the Colonies.[32]

The Quakers

George Fox at twenty-two years of age discovered the indwelling Christ after a religious pilgrimage of some four years. From this very personal and very moving experience the Society of Friends marks its beginning. Fox gathered his first converts from among the General Baptists of Nottinghamshire and nearby Mansfield. It is not surprising then that the Children of Light, as the Friends first called themselves, resembled so closely the General Baptists in their doctrines and polity.[33] William Tallack, in a work written a hundred years ago, discovered most of George Fox's teachings to have been prominent in the teaching and practice of the General Baptists, who maintained a close fraternal relationship with the Mennonites for so many years.[34] Many Baptist churches became Quaker conventicles in the early stages of the movement. However, Fox's teachings did constitute a departure from those of the General Baptists or there would have been no new movement.

Fox so emphasized the Inner Light as the common endowment of all men that the anthropology of the General Baptists appeared Calvinistic by contrast. Even though Fox's mysticism was nourished on the Scriptures, it appears from many of his writings that the Spirit, who provided him with certain revelations which he called "openings," became his ultimate source of religious authority. Fox rejected all external ceremonies, spiritualizing baptism and the Lord's Supper much in the manner of the Lollards before him. One of his more striking innovations was the silent worship characteristic of the first Friends. From the very beginning of the movement there was present within Fox that potent mixture of mysticism and social justice for which the Quakers have become so well known. An excerpt from Fox's *Journal* is typical:

And at a certain time, when I was at Mansfield, there was a sitting of the justices about hiring of servants; and it was upon me from the Lord to go and speak to the justices that they should not oppress the servants in their wages. So I walked towards the inn where they sat but finding a company of fiddlers there, I did not go in but thought to come in the morning, when I might have a more serious opportunity to discourse with them, not thinking that a seasonable time. But when I came again in the morning, they were gone, and I was struck even blind that I could not see. And I inquired of the innkeeper where the justices were to sit that day and he told me at a town eight miles off. My sight began to come to me again, and I went and ran thitherward as fast as I could. And when I was come to the house where they were, and many servants with them, I exhorted the justices not to oppress the servants in their wages, but to do that which was right and just to them; and I exhorted the servants to do their duties, and serve honestly, etc. And they all received my exhortation kindly, for I was moved of the Lord therein.[55]

The forces which molded George Fox's religious thought were varied, as varied as the religious menu mid-seventeenth-century England could offer. For four years Fox deliberately sampled it from the Anglican "steeple houses" to the General Baptist "house churches" with a generous side-dressing of Puritan ethics and Familist mysticism. But the Quaker movement was far more than the sum total of these ingredients. There is no explaining it apart from the faith and personality of Fox himself. Of course, he was not the entire movement. But his contribution, along with that of other early Friends such as Robert Barclay, William Penn, Margaret Fell, and Margaret Brewster, shaped to a considerable extent the character of the Quaker life and set its future direction.[56]

Pietism

Around the head of a German Lutheran, Philipp Jacob Spener, broke a storm and a revival. The mysticism characteristic of the movement which he initiated earned for him the Quaker label and for its enthusiasm the familiar term of reproach, *Schwärmer*. However, the appellation that stuck was "pietist." The theological faculty of the University of Wittenberg charged that the Pietists were guilty of at least 284 heresies.[57] The aim of the movement, as Spener envisioned it, may be gleaned from the complete title of his most important work, *Pia Desideria (or Heartfelt Desire for a God-pleasing Reform of the true Evangelical Church, Together with Several Simple Christian Proposals Looking Toward this End)*.[58]

Spener was greatly dissatisfied with the established churches of his native Germany and their blatant intolerance and endless bickering.

Their theological irrelevance, superficial externalities, and moral impotency drove him to launch a reform. In his *Pia Desideria* Spener set forth six concrete proposals based upon his understanding of the promises of God and the example of the early church. Tappert summarizes them.

> Here Spener calls for a more extensive private and public use of the Scriptures, a larger participation and activity on the part of the laity, a realization that in Christianity doing is important as well as believing, an education of ministers that couples piety with learning, and an introduction of preaching that has edification and the inner life as its goal.[59]

Neither Spener nor August Hermann Francke, his successor, was a Separatist. But they attempted to inject into German Christianity concepts associated with the Believers' Church, while disturbing neither the state-church structures nor the traditional doctrinal formulations of Lutheranism. The strategy of penetration which the Pietists followed was only partially successful. However, Pietism did become one of the most productive movements in Lutheran life, reaching far beyond Germany and the seventeenth century and bringing into life numerous new enterprises—missionary, benevolent, and denominational.

It is hardly possible to discuss at length all of the denominations which owe their origin to some extent to Pietism. Three are symbolic of many others which represent the same broad theological spectrum. The first of these is the Church of the Brethren, which dates its origin with the year 1708. In that year Alexander Mack led in the baptism of eight adults at night by trine immersion in the Eder River. In this fashion the small band of courageous believers attempted to constitute a church after the apostolic order as interpreted by the German historian, Gottfried Arnold.[60] The love feast and foot washing were also observed by these churches. Six years later Eberhard L. Gruber and John Frederick Rock founded the Quaker-like denomination called the Society of True Inspiration. They, like the English Quakers, rejected all baptism and emphasized the mystical aspects of the Christian life. However, the Inspirationists continued to observe the Lord's Supper, to which they added foot washing and the love feast. They followed the Church of the Brethren to the Colonies, where they established a communal society in the state of New York which was later moved to Amana, Iowa. The Methodist denomination through Moravian influence upon Charles and John Wesley became the most famous outgrowth of eighteenth-century Pietism. Subsequently, from the Brethren and from the Methodist denominations have come many other offshoots deeply tinged with Pietism. Among these one may list the ill-fated Ephrata experiment and the vigorous Pentecostal movement.[61]

The Campbell Movement

A nineteenth-century religious development which does not fit neatly into any previous category was that which was embodied in the Disciples movement under the leadership of Alexander Campbell and **Barton W. Stone.** Many different tributaries flowed into this river that soon covered Kentucky and Tennessee like a flood. The empiricism of John Locke combined with other forces, including Presbyterian and Baptist, to furnish the material out of which Alexander Campbell formed a new denomination which bore a close resemblance to the Baptists, but which was more akin in spirit to Socinianism.[62] In his own mind Campbell was simply restoring primitive Christianity. The changes which his thinking underwent from 1808 to 1843 may be followed by the interested student through the pages of *The Christian Baptist* and its successor, *The Millennial Harbinger,* or in his major debates.[63] Although Campbell's movement drew heavily from the Baptists, who lost entire churches to the "New Reformation," it represented basic changes in the commonly understood Baptist position of the day. Yet Alexander Campbell still remained, regardless of the estimate of his contemporaries, solidly within the Free Church movement.

Common Characteristics and Conclusions

Before attempting to draw any conclusions or suggest possible theses upon the basis of a historical study of the Believers' Church, we venture to suggest some characteristics which are common to almost all, if not all, major parties within the scope of our study. To some degree they seem to possess in common the following characteristics with differing interpretations:

1. An appeal to the New Testament as the ultimate authority in the church;
2. Primitivism, or the principle of restoration of the apostolic pattern in faith and practice of the church;
3. **The concept of the Believers' Church, which means that the** empirical church is primarily a fellowship, a fellowship of the regenerate;
4. A belief in the universal invisible Church as the body of Christ to which all believers belong;
5. Believer's baptism, with some rare exceptions;

6. The kerygmatic nature of the ordinances in contrast to the sacramental (*ex opere operato*) concept;
7. A rejection of Calvinism which varies from the modified form of most Baptists to total rejection by the Quakers;
8. An acceptance of the theology of the ancient symbols with a corresponding rejection of all creeds;
9. An emphasis upon the apostolate of the laity with the practical rejection of a professional clergy;
10. An affirmation of religious liberty with the rejection of an established church (*corpus christianum*);
11. Salvation through faith in Christ;
12. Christianity as primarily discipleship;
13. Discipleship as implying evangelism, ethics, and social action;
14. *Agape* (love) as the only adequate motivation of the Christian life;
15. Biblical pacifism (the widest divergence is probably evident at this point);
16. A sense of unity in Christ in spite of separate denominational structures;
17. An openness to truth under the Spirit's direction.

With some hesitancy I wish to venture the following conclusions which this study suggests.

1. It appears that no Free Church stands outside the stream of Christian history. The dependence of Free Churches upon prior antecedents, recognized or not, is an ever-recurring fact.

2. Indebtedness to the biblical witness is the one common denominator always present.

3. Apparently theological and spiritual renewal waits not for new structures so much as for the personal discovery and appropriation of a biblical faith.

4. Given the absence of coercion, Christianity is capable of forging new forms to meet the ever-changing conditions of a new age.

5. A certain degree of accommodation on the part of any Christian movement appears necessary if it is to speak effectively to its world. An inflexible unbending stance condemns Christianity to a fossilized existence and a rejected witness. On the other hand, with compromise at the point of its basic integrity or fundamental principles, Christianity easily becomes captive to its culture and thereby loses its soul to a new paganism that feigns itself Christian.

3

A BELIEVING PEOPLE:

Theological Interpretation

Warren F. Groff is dean of and professor of theology in Bethany Theological Seminary, Oak Brook, Illinois, the graduate theological school of the Church of the Brethren. A graduate of Juniata College and of Yale Divinity School and a PhD graduate of Yale University, Dr. Groff has a keen appreciation for the thought of the late Professor H. Richard Niebuhr and a vigorous interest in the issues of modern and contemporary theology—especially Christology and the relation of faith and conduct. A native of Pennsylvania, he formerly taught religion at Bridgewater College in Virginia and more recently spent a sabbatical year in postdoctoral studies at Harvard University. With Donald E. Miller, Dr. Groff has coauthored *The Shaping of Modern Christian Thought* (1968).

Perhaps more than any other, Dr. Groff's address to the Conference on the Concept of the Believers' Church marked the introduction of a new language not common among most of the denominations of the Believers' Church heritage. Dr. Groff evidences a greater awareness of the need for restating the relation of the church and the world than many who stand in this heritage and likewise is concerned to make ample place for a doctrine of original sin detached from any inherent connection with infant baptism. His concept of discipleship seems to be indebted to Dietrich Bonhoeffer as well as to the Anabaptists. Dean Groff's address served indirectly to remind conference participants that the language of Menno, Helwys, Fox, Mack, Wesley, Campbell, and others must have seemed to many of their hearers to be strangely and even dangerously innovative. On closer examination the new language was seen to point to the crucified and risen Man for others.

The response to Dr. Groff's address was made by Dr. J. K. Zeman, general secretary of the Home Mission Board of the Baptist Convention of Ontario and Quebec, Toronto, Canada. Dr. Zeman, whose "initial religious experience and training took place in the context of a United Lutheran-Reformed Church in Czechoslovakia" and whose theological training was "in Presbyterian seminaries in Europe and in Canada," referred to his own "radical experience of spiritual rebirth" subsequent to sacramental confirmation and its having "initiated a long period of search for a different type of church which would correspond more faithfully to the church of which I read in the New Testament." Out of this background Dr. Zeman asked whether "*the difference* between congregations which claim to be believers' churches and those which admit ·mixed membership' " was only "quantitative" (i.e., "a higher proportion of people with a genuine commitment to Christ") or both quantitative and "qualitative" (i.e., "a different type of spiritual experience"). Recognizing that faith could be understood sacramentally, intellectually, emotionally, or volitionally—all of which definitions tend to understand faith as "a human act," the Canadian leader insisted also upon faith as "an act of God," not in the Calvinistic sense that God supplies the faith to man, but in the Johannine sense that only men reborn have "the capacity to believe." Faith is "nothing less than the *ontological* invasion of the New Age into the being of a believer and of the believing community." Here Dr. Zeman was seconding Dr. Groff's assertion that "*the capacity to believe and obey is profoundly a gift before it is a task.*" Dr. Zeman's penetrating peroration was a quickening word to conference participants:

> If this is so [i.e., faith as "the work of the Holy Spirit"], then a believers' church is humanly helpless and totally dependent upon the work of God. A denomination which is constituted on the principle of "mixed membership" and on infant baptism can predict its numerical growth on the basis of national vital statistics. By way of contrast, a believers' church is only one generation away from extinction. Unless God the Spirit continues His gracious ministry of regeneration, such a church is doomed to death.

○　　○　　○

This conference provides occasion for treating the designated topic in the setting of conversation and sharing among diverse traditions. Although most of us are from the Free Church wing of Protestantism, we undertake our assignment with full appreciation for those not represented in our deliberations. There is certainly no merit in exaggerating the differences or in ignoring the similarities that may exist between the historic Free Churches and other major Christian groupings. We are also chastened by the isolation and even division among ourselves.

Where does the church gear into the broad experience of man and culture? What place does its life and work have in the overall design of God? Whatever else is meant by understanding the church as a "believing people," it basically has something to do with the determinative relationship to God and his purposes for human society.

Later we shall deal with related themes that cluster around our topic, such as baptism, voluntaryism, sin and grace, ministry, and the meaning of discipleship. But first we suggest the broad directions of an overall approach to matters of faith.[1]

I

We begin with an analysis of where the religious question and answer mesh with general culture. This in no way underestimates the defining particularities of Christianity, or the decisive normativeness of Jesus Christ as the living center of the church. We move in this way so that our specialized language about man's relation to God makes close contact with everyday considerations. To see how faith and life intersect is especially urgent when the church and its language seem aloof and unnecessarily alien to society at large.

To be a man is to be defined and limited (1) by other persons, (2) by goals and courses of action that direct our energies, and (3) by the future. This observation may seem so self-evident as to be theologically uninteresting. Quite the contrary! Its very commonness contributes to the importance of this primary insight into the nature of our humanity. It has far-reaching implications for understanding the particular function of the church's language.

Think of the way others contribute to our own personhood. As developing organisms—from the earliest years—we gain a sense of identity through relationship with influential persons.[2] From them we receive language, social values, notions of right and wrong, direction and purpose. To be sure, the larger cultural context also communicates its inhibitions, hatreds, fears, indifference, and crippling neuroses. Nevertheless, our capacities for growth and maturity are fundamentally conditioned by social relationships. Throughout the whole fabric of interpersonal connections we know what it is to be free and yet bounded. We become individuals precisely because we experience the boundary limits of other persons around us. We know who we are because we are known in these living encounters.

Similarly, we find life ordered and held together in relation to interiorized goals that claim our attention and energies. We are integrated as responsible agents by the projects to which we give ourselves. To illustrate, mark how some compelling objective—i.e., completion of a graduate degree in theology or a manuscript for publication—serves to marshal one's total resources in its pursuit. To attain such a projected end, certain intrinsic disciplines must be adopted: concentration of effort—literally willing one thing, restriction of leisure, sacrifice of time for the enjoyment of family and friends, and giving up a broad range of interests that do not directly contribute to the sought-after value. Life is filled with the pursuit of projects, some quite enduring and elusive, others more transient and easily achieved or displaced. We experience both success and failure in this process. In more than accidental ways we are constituted as persons by what we strive for in life. We are motivated and yet bounded by the many goals and courses of action that occupy us from time to time.

Man is likewise defined and limited by the future. It is the capacity to anticipate one's tomorrows that essentially distinguishes man and human society from other creatures and their groupings on this earth. We not only live out of a personal history, with its fund of individual-social relations, remembering what has been in the *past*; we not only strive for desired objectives in the *present* moment; we also look ahead to what may be in the *future*. Indeed, our anticipations become an ingredient in our present pursuits, even as they have informed all our relationships and actions in the past.

Man is a future-oriented animal, and in ways that are scarcely paralleled by the more instinctive reactions we observe even in lower forms of life. In our relations with other persons, and in our pursuit of projects, we know what it is to be open and yet bounded. But it is the future that marks the most decisive boundary limit. We know that our tomorrows will be shaped by the potentialities and the restrictive factors that have accrued to our past and present. Even more profoundly, we sense that our expected tomorrows may in fact not be. In the midst of life—at the very center of our strength and achievement—we face the poignant and inescapable prospect of death!

This is where the religious question and the possibility of the religious answer mesh with our general experience of being a man. We can phrase the religious question this way: who am I in my self-initiative and boundedness, as one who is defined and limited by other persons and sought-after goals, as one who is unqualifiedly bordered by a future which can be anticipated but is not mine to bestow? This question does not inevitably loom in the forefront of human consciousness. We live in a culture which is often able to function without explicit attention to this kind of primary awareness and introspectiveness. Although, even a society made up of "men come of age" deals at least implicitly with the uniquely human tendency to anticipate what lies ahead—with its enticement and element of mystery. Witness the exaggerated preoccupation with death and funerals that pervades American culture. In one way or another man in every era must deal with himself in his personal relationships, his volitional strivings, and his orientation toward the future which may be bulging with promise but which can finally only be received as a gift from beyond one's own powers.

In his personal encounters, his sought-after projects, and his anticipated tomorrows, man deals with that which "limits" and yet is highly influential in his life. Here then the religious answer arises as a recurrent possibility. The notion of God is a high-level generalization. It gathers up the lesser intimations of otherness and boundedness—whether in persons, goals, or the expected future. Such instances are not exhaustive of those everyday occasions where we deal with what bears on our lives from beyond, or that which transcends and yet impinges upon us. But they are pivotal in providing the experiential base for thought and speech about God. We can now phrase the religious answer in this fashion: *God is the name for that Limit than which no greater can be conceived*! It is he who defines and constitutes man in the keenest sense of all. It is he who is the deepest and most inescapable boundary of man's life and death. Thus, the call and promise of the future, as the distinguishing ingredient in man's past relationships and present strivings, takes on the personalized meanings that have become attached to the understanding of God, at least in those places that have been influenced by the Judeo-Christian heritage. We speak of God as the One whose purposeful presence and power is enduring and comprehensive enough to span future, no less than past and present.

But we must be clear that this kind of general analysis of what it means to be human does not in itself rule out the alternative that I am finally limited only by emptiness and silence, by Void, by the Abyss, by Nothingness. The future that I anticipate but cannot totally manipulate may be dark and inscrutable to the core. It perhaps has only that meaning which man projects upon it. Unaided reason cannot finally negate the conclusion that apart from other persons and the objects of my environment I am ultimately alone in the universe. Direct examination of experience does bring to consciousness an awareness of otherness and boundedness—especially in relation to persons, in pursuit of goals, and in our hoped-for tomorrows. But faith in God, as the ultimate Boundary Limit that conditions all of life, requires still other foundations.

II

What supports the religious/Christian option? How is the more general awareness of otherness and boundedness filled out so that one actually becomes a believer? What leads one to acknowledge God as that ultimate Boundary Limit of life and death?

Undoubtedly many subtle factors contribute to the process whereby the daily experiences of limitation, of boundedness in the midst of openness, are generalized into a full-orbed understanding of God. Most directly, though, the response of faith in God as purposive Being is precipitated and nurtured by the *persuasive power* of the biblical histories. The illuminating and shaping events of Israel's history, and uniquely the event of Christ, add vividness and detail to those hunches we may already have about larger boundary limits. Those who are captivated by these paradigmatic events are given a sense of identity, motivational guidance and energy, as well as a larger perspective on the purpose and direction of life. They receive the growing assurance that their actions are surrounded by an overarching providence, whose power is at the same time marked by care and good will. This is to say, they are given faith.

Think of the history of Israel. The life-story of this covenant people continues to mediate a response of faith in God, where he is understood as loving, acting, and purposefully directing the affairs of men and nations. Hereby the general and sometimes merely implicit intuitions of otherness and boundedness are universalized and personalized. Human existence, indeed all of creation, is grounded and ultimately delimited by the God of Abraham, Isaac, and Jacob.

Consider also the impact of Jesus, the man who lived, ministered, and was put to death on a cross. This formative history supports the insight that God may be characterized as suffering love, gaining victory for his intentions even through death. So responsive is the overarching providence to the condition of man that the One who impinges upon all of life allows himself to share the poignancy of finite limitation. Henceforth the ultimate Boundary Limit is known quite particularly as the God and Father of the Lord Jesus Christ.

Specifically the resurrection power that was released in the life and death of Jesus is the historical foundation of the Christian faith. The man who died on the cross—with his humble loving of God and neighbor, his obedience and faithfulness to God's will, his trust and hope in God's gift of the future even beyond the grave—is the enactment of God's present and coming kingdom. The style of existence which was realized in Jesus is the norm and goal of Christian life and community. The creative impact of the man from Nazareth, as caught up in a larger providential cunning, is the basis of Christian confidence and openness to that future which is made secure by God's mercy and care.[4]

Actually, what we have in mind here is a view of revelation as an historical *a priori*. The event of the man who lived and was subjected to death on a cross steadily impinges upon present experience. As a concrete item in the temporal process it has its own *a posteriori* character. But it lurks in communal and individual memory as an open-ended form, capable of gathering to itself the dispositions and aspirations of succeeding generations. It has the marks of universality and necessity in its status and functioning; it lives as a past datum that continues to shape personal-social existence in the direction of its own claims on the future. More than anything else, the revelatory dynamic of the Christ event as an historical *a priori* supports the religious/Christian option throughout changing times.

III

How does the church relate to the acknowledgment of God as the ultimate Boundary Limit of our life and death? In what way is it already presupposed in such a faith response?

Man's capacity to anticipate and shape his tomorrows, at the same time knowing that he is challenged and yet strictly bounded by a future he does not fully control, has profound social ramifications. This distinctively human openness to the future stimulates the imagination and takes different forms. What distinguishes the various human and cultural styles is the concrete point of reference which anchors and guides thought and life. The future beckons in freedom. It is not accessible to man without a residuum of mystery. What one expects and desires is based on persuasive clues along the way: perpetuation of the American way of life, continued success and economic security, enhanced popularity and prestige, fuller gratification of the sensual drives, progressive betterment of the human environment through technological advance, and/or the kingdom style of life actualized in the man on the cross. In these ways the shape of the future is anticipated and striven for on the grounds of pointers from the past and present.

All this is potentially community-creating. Where a secular society develops, the implied assumption is that man is simply "thrown" into existence, with only emptiness and silence as the ultimate boundary limit of his life and death. Such a culture is perhaps marked by the kind of productive activism which pervades our technopolitan, urban civilization. In this type of setting man often acts responsibly, and even with heroic discipline, in fashioning his future and that of his social order. The secular individual may reach great heights of imagination, courage, and regard for others. He may also succeed in bracketing the larger questions of purpose and ultimate destiny, contenting himself usually with provisional answers and highly restricted objectives. But quiet despair can still lurk underneath the surface calm. And man may occasionally fall to great depths of degradation through unchecked attachments to nation, wealth, power, or whatever seems—at least for the moment—to fill the throbbing void that is felt in the center of man's powers and attainments.[5]

We refer to church when a specifically religious answer emerges in an organized fashion around a defining focus: whether prophet, moment of illumination, authoritative teachings, or revealed documents. Where the persuasive and normative clues are from the biblical histories, and specifically from the man who lived for others and was put to death on a cross, we speak appropriately of the Christian church.[6] In these terms the church is a culture within cultures, a community within communities. It is marked by the conviction that man is not finally alone in the universe. Rather, it is the God of purposive intent and activity *who stands in the very midst of life* as the ultimate Boundary Limit of man and society. Consequently all that we are and do is prompted and judged in relation to the overarching providence of God.

The church has its life and reason for being as the provisional realization and agency of God's kingdom purpose. It is constituted by its mission, i.e., to help shape the future under the sovereignty and grace of God, whose intention has been declared and given firm historical rootage in Jesus Christ. As understood within the biblical histories, God's election of Israel, and the church as the new Israel, is not on the basis of inherent worth. Nor is it a conferral of arbitrary privilege or exceptional powers. God's election is for task, for mission, for extending the ministry of the man who met his death on a cross. Therefore the church witnessess to, celebrates, interprets, and disciplines itself in faithful pursuit of God's present and coming kingdom, or the style of life which is actualized in the shaping event of Christ.

In summary form, the church is defined essentially (1) by what it recalls, (2) by what it strives to do, and (3) by what it anticipates.

(1) The church is that part of the world whose remembered past, whose deepest self-awareness, is informed by the life histories of Israel and Jesus. The give and take of Israel's career, and especially the ministry and impact of the man who died on the cross, stimulate and sustain a consciousness of God's living *presence*. That which delimits man and society most profoundly is this identity-producing relationship. Where the church is truly the church—as the institutionalized memory and consciousness of God—pride and self-love are giving way

to a humble loving of God and neighbor.

(2) The church is that part of the world whose strivings toward individual and social fulfillment take the form of the kingdom of God and its inherent disciplines—humility and love, obedience and faith, trust and hope. The covenant ideal of Israel, and particularly the radical willing of God's will by the man on the cross, communicate and nurture a consciousness of God's life-shaping *power*. That which truly deserves to marshal and direct human energies is the kingdom of God. Every effort to build a society on earth, in the form of the "secular city" or whatever, is hereby pointed beyond itself toward that "city whose builder and maker is God." Where the church is truly the church—in its consciousness and provisional enactment of God's kingdom—rebellion and self-will are being replaced by obedience and faithfulness to the way of righteousness and peace, of justice and love.

(3) The church is that part of the world whose anticipations of the future are unleashed and productively shaped by the stability of God's promises. The victory of trust and hope in Israel, as realized most fully in the man on the cross, keeps alive a consciousness of God's *purposive* presence and directing power. That which is fully consistent with man's intended creativity, or his creation in the "image of God," is a posture of courageous openness to the gift of the future. Where the church is truly the church — as the consciousness and eschatological foreshadowing of what God has purposed for his world— the anticipation of what the tomorrows may bring does not issue in crippling dread and irrational withdrawals, but in the trust and confidence that God's providential care will prevail.

We obviously have been speaking about the church in normative rather than strictly descriptive terms. Congregations and larger ecclesiastical structures often fall far short of standing faithfully in Christ's own ministry of reconciliation, in obedience to the way of suffering love. The church in temporal development is itself human, all-too-human, and shares in the world's pride and self-love, disobedience and unbelief, distrust and hopelessness. And yet we are not minimizing the church's visibility or the importance of its concrete institutional character. In patterns that are open to sociological and political analysis the church lives in history in quite visible ways. It is identifiable through its preaching, sacramental life, instructional forms, inner disciplines, neighbor-concerns and social responsibility. But we are underscoring the point that the church as religious and cultic institution is itself subordinate to and judged by its own God-given mission. In short, the church is truly the church insofar as the purpose of God which was established in Jesus Christ is reenacted in its life and work. The church has its basic visibility as that group of believers who, through the grace of Christ and his continuing Spirit, are beginning to mirror the kingdom marks of humility and love, obedience and faith, trust and hope.

IV

The Free Church traditions have often featured the church-world distinction. But this is relative to a prior differentiation: i.e., between God and world! It is God—not the church—who fundamentally establishes and thus delimits the world. It may be a case of ecclesiastical pride if this prior distinction is forgotten when we talk about the "world" as though it were strictly over against the "church."

The church lives in and for the sake of the world: the same world which God made, into which God sent his Son to live and die, and which remains his good creation no matter how fully in the grip of those rebellious powers which are hostile to the kingdom purpose enacted in Jesus Christ. In short, the church is that part of God's world which is given the grace to recall God's mercy, to obey God's will, and to anticipate God's intended future.

The motif of the church as a pilgrim people has been implied in what we have been saying. This people has its continuity with the past, its true identity, to the extent power is given to obey the marching orders of the crucified and presently active Christ. The church is the *extension of Christ's own ministry of reconciliation*, through whom the world is being released from its alienation, its bondage, and its crippling dread. As a pilgrim people the church celebrates and witnesses to the faith that in Christ death itself has been conquered, as the last enemy to be destroyed. The church serves and disciplines itself for the coming of a world that may face an open but bounded future with the assurance "that neither death, nor life, nor angels, nor principalities, nor things present, nor things to come, nor powers, nor height, nor depth, nor anything else in all creation, will be able to separate us from the love of God in Christ Jesus."[7] "For he was made known to us in all wisdom and insight the mystery of his will, according to his purpose which he set forth in Christ as a plan for the fulness of time, to unite all things in him, things in heaven and things on earth."[8]

V

While it cannot be the only clue to its nature, an emphasis upon the church as *believing* people is appropriate in terms of our whole

68

analysis. Of course, if we make belief a basic mark of the church, it has to be understood in a total way. It includes fundamental attitudes, feelings, perspective, and life commitment no less than intellectual assent. The church is that part of God's world which is beginning to believe that God alone is sovereign and that he has established his Lordship in the kingdom style which was actualized in Jesus Christ.

To belong to the church as a believing people is not simply to join one more voluntary association. It is profoundly a free act, stimulated by the confession of others who covenant their allegiance to the "way of Christ." But the voluntaryism we are talking about presupposes the identity-producing, energy-releasing, life-orienting impact of the event of Christ. This event from its remembered past continues to intrude itself upon the present with new resolves and possibilities for facing one's tomorrows. Thus our free commitment is established in God's revealing act. We are here thinking of revelation quite historically, as an event that illuminates and shapes subsequent events. This was described earlier in more technical language as the status and functioning of an historical *a priori*. The event of Christ precedes every faith decision. It links believer to believer, and one historical period to another, through its generative power. As a peculiarly seminal moment in the life story of civilization and through what faith discerns as the providence of God, the man from Nazareth continues to shape personal-social existence in the direction of his own claim on the future. In this sense *the capacity to believe and obey is profoundly a gift before it is a task.* The act of believing is God's offer of himself in the man on the cross before it is a work of the disciple. It is a voluntary response that stems from the prior grace that roots in the one who lived and died for others.

VI

It is fitting that baptism symbolize the conscious commitment of the believer to the kingdom style enacted in Christ. This is not to overlook the degree to which conscious and unconscious elements intermingle in the life of the Christian in the community of faith. Nor is it to neglect the way degrees of commitment are always present in the ups and downs of a developing faith. Some traditions prefer to practice infant baptism as a way of acknowledging our dependence upon God's prevenient work in Jesus Christ. Substantial arguments support this position. But the tradition of the Believers' Church has found an even stronger case—both on the grounds of Scripture and theological reasoning—for linking the act of baptism with conscious levels of dedication. Baptism celebrates the reality of grace which has been realized in the man on the cross. It is also an occasion for the community to deepen its gathered life and effective witness through the responsible appropriation of discipleship on the part of the informed believer.

The justification for linking baptism with voluntary commitment is not only strong biblical precedent but the view of the church as a pilgrim people called into mission. As we have seen, the church is that portion of the world which recalls what God intends for man as declared in Jesus Christ. It not only celebrates and interprets the meaning of God's purpose for his creation but gives itself to the intrinsic disciplines of the kingdom: humility and love, obedience and faith, trust and hope. The church is covenanted to be an advance colony on earth of that life style which is at the heart of Christ's continuing ministry of reconciliation.

Hence, baptism is basically an ordination to service, to ministry, to the "priesthood of all believers." This too argues for the correlation of baptism with conscious appropriation of the tasks that belong to those who align themselves with the life-shaping power of the Christ event. It is difficult to specify the exact chronological age, or level of conscious choice, when baptism is most appropriate. But one criterion is sufficient maturity on the part of the participant that the service can carry the clear note of commitment to mission.

To link baptism with uncoerced decision is not to overlook the extent to which the level of mature faith is preceded and nurtured all along the way by the participation of the infant and growing child in the fellowship of believers. Nor is it to forget the presence and seriousness of sin. In fact, contrary to what is sometimes assumed, an emphasis upon the Believers' Church and adult baptism need not preclude a robust doctrine of original sin.

In speaking of original sin we refer to those deep-seated perversions that oppose the kingdom purpose which was declared in Jesus Christ. Instead of responding to one's anticipated tomorrows as the gift of a gracious providence that infuses man's life-style with love, faith, and hope, the movement of sin is to turn in upon itself in thwarting and self-defeating closedness. Sin is not simply a matter of isolated acts or surface imitation. It is a state of pride, of disobedience, of fundamental betrayal of man's true potential under God. It befouls the deepest springs of human creativity. It invades human institutions as well as the lives of individual persons. An assassin pulls the trigger and sends a bullet into the brain of a political leader. That particular man is responsible for his own blasphemous deed. But that man is the product of a deeper illness in the historical-social organism itself. His hatred is nurtured by those institutionalized patterns of human existence which breed inequality and discrimination, suspicion and distrust, frustration and violence. And so the kingdom of sin and the kingdom of God oppose each other in deadly conflict. Nevertheless, this conflict stands under the sign of the cross and the promise of the resurrection.[9]

But if we accept a view of the massiveness and universality of sin, then why not baptize infants? Are they not also—at least at a fairly early age—caught up in the cumulative and continually appropriated violations of true humanity? Even if we grant that sin snares us all in its grip, the central issue is this: how is grace mediated? Forgiveness and reconciliation are channeled fundamentally through the community of the faithful, with its own sacramental character—its role in making possible a response of faith. Baptism is basically a rite of ordination to the ministry of the whole people in mission. The need for healing and the dependency of children upon the believing community is acknowledged in ways other than the baptism of infants. For instance, services of child dedication are occasions when the blood family and the covenantal family join in renewed dedication to the tasks of witness and nurture, so that the developing person may experience the redemptive grace of God; so that he may consciously and responsibly espouse the kingdom style of life, with his faith identity and life posture clearly established in the event of the man on the cross.

VII

To understand the church as a believing people carries with it a strong emphasis upon Christian discipleship. We have seen how faith roots in, and is constantly nurtured by, the formative influence of the Christ event. The corporate context of personal commitment has also become evident. Such items are part of the larger frame within which we see the place of the individual follower of Christ.

In line with the distinguishing marks of the church we mention three important characteristics of the disciple: (1) He is one whose life is centered in the illuminating and shaping histories of Israel and Jesus. These events out of the remembered past, and most particularly the life and ministry of the man from Nazareth, contribute a keen sense of who one really is. The follower of Christ knows that he is a member of a blood family, a community, a profession or guild, a nation. He is individualized by the clan to which he belongs, the work he does, the place he lives, and the country that claims his loyalty. But even more he knows himself through his incorporation into the biblical story.

His affirmation—"I am a Christian"—is at least potentially the deepest identity he carries and discloses in his relationship with others.

(2) He is one who has begun to give priority to the disciplines of the kingdom. The disciple has caught glimpses of a pattern of life where man lives with his neighbor in peace and covenantal wholeness; where society is marked not only by love but by fundamental respect for the rights and dignity of others; where "justice rolls down like waters, and righteousness like an ever-flowing stream" (Amos 5:24). This vision becomes an inescapable imperative for the Christian, leading him often into places of tension in the world. In the interest of furthering the cause of the kingdom, he may be found in street demonstrations on behalf of a minority group, in a protest march against the war in Vietnam, or wherever a larger measure of brotherliness and fair play is needed and being promoted.

(3) He is one who shares actively in a community of believers. What especially distinguishes this community is the quality of hope and anticipation that pervades all its relationships and strivings. Instead of expecting only defeat for the way of righteousness and peace, this community says that the sign of the cross and the resurrection is writ large on the human story. In spite of the distortions and rigidities of sin, the life-orienting confidence of the disciple and his brothers in the faith is that the way of love will prevail. Even suffering and death cannot ultimately negate the victory of divine grace, whose first installments have already been given in the life and work of Christ and in those who have begun to follow the One who is indeed "the way, the truth, and the life."

4

A BELIEVING PEOPLE:

Contemporary Relevance

Confessing to be a "Neo-Quaker," T. Canby Jones, professor of religion and philosophy and chairman of the department, Wilmington College, Wilmington, Ohio, articulated in his address both his Quaker convictions and a general "vision" of the nature and function of a renewed Believers' Church. The son of a former president of Earlham College and a graduate of Haverford College, Yale Divinity School, and Yale University, Dr. Jones served in Civilian Public Service as a conscientious objector during World War II, was subsequently pastor to Friends churches in New York state, and was resident fellow, Woodbrooke College, Birmingham, England, during 1953-54. More recently he has been visiting professor at Earlham School of Religion, Richmond, Indiana, has led numerous spiritual retreats, and now serves as editor of *Quaker Religious Thought*.

Dr. Jones drew from previous experience of dialogue with Mennonites and Brethren and from his study of George Fox, about whose doctrine of redemption he wrote his PhD dissertation, and the seventeenth-century Quaker movement. He confronted his fellow conference participants directly and unmistakably with the challenge of personal concern about and responsibility for a renewed Believers' Church today. Finding original Quakerism to be only partially the product of Puritanism and indeed quite compatible with "the Anabaptist vision," Dr. Jones identifies the "Believers' Church" as a hearing, obeying, and witnessing community. His call to suffering is reminiscent of Anabaptism, his call to prayer of Pietism, and his call to nonresistance of the Quakers as well as of Anabaptists and Brethren. Yet here was no mere historical concern, for Vietnam, the "secular city," and ossified ecclesiastical structures called for answers. Dr. Jones anticipated the later stress of Dr. Burkholder on the wedding of evangelism and social action.

Panel members who responded to Dr. Jones's address were Dr. Cornelius J. Dyck, professor of historical theology, Associated Mennonite Biblical Seminaries, Elkhart, Indiana; Dr. Roger E. Sappington, professor of history, Bridgewater College, Bridgewater, Virginia; Dr. Robert R. Soileau, associate professor of theology, New Orleans Baptist Theological Seminary, New Orleans, Louisiana; and Dr. Earl Waldrup, supervisor of the associational unit, Sunday School Department, Sunday School Board of the Southern Baptist Convention, Nashville, Tennessee. Moderator of the panel was Dr. W. Morgan Patterson, associate professor of church history, Southern Baptist Theological Seminary.

Dr. Dyck commended Dr. Jones's address and called for further elaboration of the mission of the Believers' Church. He noted that Anabaptism had been the only Protestant missionary thrust of the sixteenth century and insisted that the Anabaptist witness was not merely individualistic in the later Pietistic sense. He pointed to the present need to "shore up the erosion along the border of the believing community" and asked what is unique in the "hearing" of the Believers' Church. Dr. Sappington raised the question as to the role of Scripture in understanding the voice of the living Lord. He confessed that it bothered him to hear a Quaker speak of obeying Christ "in all things" and to have exception made of baptism and the Lord's Supper. Dr. Sappington questioned Dr. Jones's emphasis on the possibility of human perfection and expressed the hope that present-day believers' churches would unitedly offer a peace witness. On the other hand, Dr. Soileau, while sharing a concern as to the horrors of warfare, expressed the view that it is sometimes a Christian duty "to restrain a tyrant." He spoke of the contemporary church as "a secular institution" and of its failure in communicating the Word of God. Dr. Waldrup proposed to add a fourth dimension to the Believers' Church as delineated by Dr. Jones: "A believing church makes a believable confession of its faith." Commending Dr. Jones for his stress on covenant, obedience, and discipline, he reported regretfully that some Southern Baptist churches are presently baptizing some children between the ages of five and eight.

o   o   o

Since this is the only "Quaker position paper" to be delivered in this conference, I feel that it must serve two purposes. First, it must present an interpretation of the Quaker background for a dialogue on the nature of the Believers' Church and, in the second place, attempt to speak on behalf of all of us gathered here at Louisville on the contemporary relevance of a believing people to the world today. I feel my limitations for this latter task very keenly, since I have only experienced careful conversation on these matters with Mennonites and Brethren in the past. About the rest of you and your convictions I feel extremely tenuous. Would that I were a panelist and could speak out of the context of mutual discussions!

First, I need to describe my own standpoint as one of those rare "birds" who might be called a Neo-Quaker. As such I believe that the early Quaker vision should be normative for all Friends today. Further, I think that the early Quaker vision has much to contribute to the recovery of a universal vision of a believing people of God, which I take to be the main purpose of this conference.

The Setting of Early Quakerism

I agree with Geoffrey Nuttall and Hugh Barbour that early Quakerism was to a significant degree a fruit of the Radical Reformation as it expressed itself in Puritan dress in seventeenth-century England. In many and various ways Friends were like Puritans. They shared the high Calvinist view of God's unlimited power and sovereignty, the conviction of man's depravity, and the characteristic Calvinist theocratic ideal that all human society should be transformed into a verisimilitude of the kingdom of God. Unlike their conservative Calvinist brethren, early Friends professed to live in the same Spirit and power in which the prophets and apostles lived. They were Holy Spirit radicals. Nevertheless, they avoided the extremes of Ranterism by insisting on observance of the ethics of Sinai. They were not violent Fifth Monarchy men because they eschewed violence on the basis of the Sermon on the Mount.

But I disagree with Nuttall and Barbour that Quakerism was solely a Puritan phenomenon. Such an uncanny similarity exists between the main points of the Quaker vision and the Anabaptist vision of the sixteenth century and the Anabaptist-Spener-Pietist vision of the eighteenth century that there must be some interconnection, although this is yet to be demonstrated. Harold S. Bender supported this contention when he said, "So much in the Quaker principles is similar to the principles of the early Anabaptists . . . that it seems impossible that there could have been no influence from Anabaptism upon the origin and ideas of the movement."[1] At the risk of repeating what others may say here at Louisville I would like to list the main characteristics of the Anabaptist vision as I understand them so that we may have them in mind as I go on to outline the faith of George Fox and the relevance of the Quaker vision to the vision of a believing church. In the Anabaptist vision are the following: (1) "Christ's church consists of the chosen of God . . . who hear and believe His word . . . and in patience and meekness follow in His footsteps." This meant "voluntary church membership based on conversion and a commitment to holy living." (2) The nonconformity of Christians and the church to the world, (3) The practice of true love and mutual aid among members of the church, (4) The principles of peace, suffering love, and nonresistance applied to all human relationships, resulting in the complete abandonment of war, violence, or taking human life as legitimate for the Christian under any circumstance, (5) The separation of church and state, and (6) Freedom of conscience.[2]

The Church of the Brethren shares this Anabaptist vision of the essence of Christianity as discipleship and obedience to Jesus, his way and commands. In it the Brethren see the realization of the restitution of primitive Christianity. But from Spener-Pietism the Church of the Brethren adds some distinctive demands, as Allen C. Deeter expresses them:

> (1) The primacy of devotional study of, and reliance upon, the Scriptures in public worship and in small intense groups . . . ; (2) frequent self-examination and recommitment to Christ . . . ; (3) mutual helpfulness . . . ; (4) mission, sharing their faith . . . wherever possible and transforming the church and society; (5) a sense of equal responsibility for the ministries of the church among all . . . ; (6) life, rather than doctrine or . . . institutional forms . . . the central concern.[3]

But the early Friends differed from both Puritans and Anabaptists. Lewis Benson summarizes the differences from Puritanism:

> Quakerism differed radically from Puritanism in its view of the Scriptures, its conception of the nature of the church, its doctrine of Christian worship and ministry, its view of the sacraments, its belief in the moral perfectability of both the individual and the church by the power of Christ, its view of the relation of the Christian to the state, and its understanding of the meaning of the cross. Quakerism was militantly engaged in an attack on Puritanism at all these points.[1]

Those are rather important points on which to differ and still be a species of Puritanism, do you not think? Perhaps Lewis Benson, Rufus Jones, and others are right that Quakerism represents a distinctive third force on the religious scene in seventeeth-century Britain. Quakers were leaders of spiritual reformation. But in calling them "spiritual reformers" we need to distinguish them sharply from the *Spiritualisten* of the Continental Reformation. The latter part of this address will show how closely the Quaker vision conforms to the Anabaptist vision and in so doing differs at the same points as the latter from men like Hans Denck, Sebastian Franck, Sebastian Castellio, and Caspar Schwenckfeld. Early Friends were not optimistic about natural man as these men were. Insisting that Christ had come to restore a visible Gospel order among disciplined people, Friends were not religious individualists as the *Spiritualisten* tended to be.

Neither were the early Friends mystics in the classical sense of that term. They were cast in the mold of the prophets of the Old

Testament and the apostles of the New. There is a species of Hebraic-apostolic-Augustinian mysticism in which God is experienced in transforming power acting through history, in groups and within the individual without destroying individuality or separate selfhood. The early Friends were this kind of mystic. They do not belong to the classical, monistic, total-absorption-into-impersonal-deity school of mysticism.

Quakerism differed from Anabaptism primarily in terms of spiritual emphasis. It stressed the spiritual presence of Christ, the spiritual authority of Scripture, the spiritual nature of obedience, and the primary role of the Spirit in motivation to witness. Otherwise conformity to the basic Anabaptist vision outlined above seems to me very close. Perhaps in this spiritual application of the vision may lie a key to relevance to twentieth-century man.

The Faith of George Fox

Important to an understanding of the Quaker vision is a brief discussion of the seven main points of the faith of George Fox. A careful reading of his writings brings one to the conviction that central to the faith of Fox was his belief in the *sovereign power of God in Christ*. Fox expressed faith in the "great and holy Eternal God, who made the world and all things therein, . . . Lord of Heaven and Earth and great King over all . . . ; he giveth to all Breath, Life and all Things, that they might serve and worship him." This God has made himself known through Christ his preexistent word and wisdom and express image of his substance. Christ is exalted ruler of creation to whom all authority has been given, just judge to cast fire on the disobedient, the Lamb who shall get victory over sin and hell, and the great restorer to restore all things to the Father so that God shall be all in all. Secondly, Fox experienced and postulated *a great ethical gulf* which exists between God and Satan, good and evil, light and darkness. Fox, in the third place, was convinced of *man's basic sinfulness*. Rebellious men are all dead in the first Adam. Adam's disobedience has destroyed God's image in man. Therefore "all men are plunged into Adam's death, and imperfection and darkness." All the evils of mankind are traceable to the sinful nature which has infected man since the disobedience of his first ancestor. A fourth and distinctive tenent of Fox's faith was his belief that *the light of Christ*, a measure of God's grace, is to be found in all men no matter how depraved. The seed of Christ which indwells fallen man is a sign and promise of his regeneration. The light of Christ is one, universal, and saving—provided men respond to it in faith. If men nurture this seed and live by the measure of grace within, they begin the life of hearing and obeying the Lord which will increase as they continue to obey.

Though pessimistic about sinful man, Fox, in the fifth place, had tremendous *confidence in regenerate man.* Those who have heard and obeyed the voice of the Prophet who teaches from within discover an inner power which enables them to live free from sin in this life. This is the experience of Christian perfection, power over Satan and his works. The Lord, maintained Fox, does not command his followers to actions without endowing them with grace and power to carry them out.` Or in the words of Isaac Penington, another early Friend, "As the soul in the faith gives itself up to obey, so the power appears and works the obedience. . . . The power never fails the faith."[9] The collective result, in the sixth place, of this power over sin in the life of the individual is *the restoration of God's true covenant people.* In this fellowship Christ has come to gather and teach his people himself and to restore them to the relationship with God known in the garden before the fall. The churches of the world have fallen into apostasy. But now Christ has returned in Spirit to restore his church to its primitive apostolic purity. A discussion of this gathered people who hear and obey the voice of the Lord in all things and witness to him in all places and conditions is the main burden of this paper. Finally, Fox proclaimed the call and mission of God's people to *enlist in the Lamb's war* and share in the victory of God. Christ as sovereign Lord of history has called out his restored and regenerate church to engage in a cosmic struggle against evil on every level of existence in this present world until the end of history. The sword of the Spirit is the weapon of this conflict. Those who instead rely on material weapons, throw away the spiritual. The Lamb shall have the victory and of his kingdom and of peace there shall be no end.

A Vision of Spiritual Reformation: Recovery of a Believing People

It is my conviction that a recovery of the early Quaker vision combined with a recovery of the Anabaptist vision will bring about the restoration of God's believing people in this generation. I will attempt to make this combination in what follows. I further believe that the recovery of this vision of a believing people represents the most relevant, needed, and important thing that we as a conference can say to modern, affluent, depersonalized man. The nature of the vision can be expressed in one sentence. What follows below is explication of the three main points of the sentence. Here is the sentence:

A believing people hears the voice of its living Lord, obeys him in all things, and witnesses unapologetically to his power in every phase of the life of the world.

1. A Believing People Hears

The first characteristic of the believing people of the spiritual reformation is its hunger and willingness to listen. It hears the voice of the One who speaks to it from Sinai, from Calvary, from the upper room, and from his martyr church throughout history. This is not a hunger to hear the printed word, the traditional word, the abstract word, but the new and living Word of its living Lord. The Word accomplishes that which it promises and sets out to do. This Word is no mere concept, sentence, or saying. It is a cosmic divine person who was made flesh and dwelt among us and has now come again to us in Spirit to draw all men to himself. Hearing this Word and feeding on him by faith in the heart is truly the only sacrament. He is the bread who came down from heaven to give life to the world. His living presence in the midst of his people has already begun that renewal of life for all.

The living Voice to which we listen is scriptural, normative, consistent with and faithful to biblical revelation. The Bible is not that voice but a record of that Voice and an indispensable witness to him and to the living words spoken by him to our spiritual forebears. If we should hear a word that contradicts scriptural revelation, we know that it is false. But the Word of God is a living person, the giver-forth of Scripture, not limited to Scripture but doing all things consistent with the precepts of Scripture.

The eternal Word is above all alive! He is the indwelling Spirit of Sinai, Carmel, Golgotha, and the Damascus road. He is personal, interiorized, and existential. He comes to us in our need and turns spiritual death and darkness into life and light.

The voice which we hear from on high is spoken to us through Jesus Christ, God's eternal prophet. Called by his voice, we

> stand before Mount Zion and the city of the living God, heavenly Jerusalem, before myriads of angels, the full concourse and assembly of the first-born citizens of heaven, and God the judge of all, and the spirits of good men made perfect, and Jesus the mediator of a new covenant, whose sprinkled blood has better things to tell than the blood of Abel. See that you do not refuse to hear the voice that speaks. Those who refused to hear the oracle speaking on earth found no escape; still less shall we escape if we

79

refuse to hear the One who speaks from heaven (Heb. 12:22-26, NEB).

Christ speaks to us as Prophet within, judging down sin and filling us with the terror and power of the light. From him no secrets are hid. To him all motives are known. His judgment burns out our fears, and we tremble lest we disobey. This Prophet has himself come to redeem, gather, and teach his people without human mediator and in the fullness of his power.

This voice we hear is the voice of God in Christ, Christ the king and sovereign Lord who rules in history. Just as God delivered Israel from Egypt in history and has rescued his people from bondage and oppression in every age, so he does in our own, and his concern is for all men. To Christ as king all authority has been given. Authority lies not in a book or in the will of man but in the good news that Christ has come to reign. In Lewis Benson's words, faith means "putting one's whole existence under the authority of Christ."[10] He is the first speaker and the last speaker. We hear his word and live. We refuse to hear and die.

The voice we hear is the voice of the good shepherd and the humble servant of all mankind. His sheep hear his voice and do not respond to the voice of a stranger. He is both the shepherd and the door of the sheepfold through which enter all who hear his voice. He is the humble servant who rose from supper, girded himself with a towel, and washed his disciples' feet. Christ, the way, the truth, and the life to all who believe, humbled himself and took on the form of a servant washing his disciples' feet and commanding us to do the same for all men. Both his servanthood and our obedience are beautifully expressed in First Peter 2:21-24, NEB:

> To that you were called, because Christ suffered on your behalf, and thereby left you an example; it is for you to follow in his steps. He committed no sin, he was convicted of no falsehood; when he was abused he did not retort with abuse, when he suffered he uttered no threats, but committed his cause to the One who judges justly. In his own person he carried our sins to the gallows, so that we might cease to live for sin and begin to live for righteousness. By his wounds you have been healed.

This marvelous description of the fulfillment in the life of our Lord of the suffering servant of Isaiah is the same servanthood to which we are called.

Finally, the voice which we hear, as we aspire to be a believing people, is the voice of the conquering Lamb who was, who is, and who is to come. At once sovereign Lord of all, he is the Lamb who conquers solely by persuasion, suffering love, the sword of the Spirit, and inner constraint. By these weapons he and his followers will bring all nations under his dominion and bring history to a climax of fulfillment and meaning.

2. A Believing People Obeys

God in Christ calls his believing people not only to hear his voice but to obey him in all things. We are first called to obey his call to covenant. In recent years I have been struggling to grasp the full meaning of the glorious concept of covenant found in Scripture. I am now convinced that in essence it is a personal relationship of love and mutual commitment between God and his people. Love is the ground of the covenant. Nowhere is this more beautifully expressed than in Deuteronomy 7:6-10, RSV:

> For you are a people holy to the Lord your God; the Lord your God has chosen you to be a people for his own possession, out of all the peoples that are on the face of the earth. It was not because you were more in number than any other people that the Lord set his love upon you and chose you, you were the fewest of all peoples; but it is because the Lord loves you, and is keeping the oath which he swore to your fathers, that the Lord has brought you out with a mighty hand and redeemed you from the house of bondage, from the hand of Pharaoh king of Egypt. Know therefore that the Lord your God is God, the faithful God who keeps covenant and steadfast love with those who love him and keep his commandments, to a thousand generations, and requites to their face those who hate him, by destroying them. . . .

The covenant of Sinai is not the Ten Commandments; these are the bylaws or rules of the covenant. The blood on the altar and then on the people represents only the sealing of the covenant. The covenant is a personal relationship of love and mutual commitment. Leviticus states it for us: "And I will make my abode among you and·my soul shall not abhor you. And I will walk among you, and will be your God, and you shall be my people. . . . I have broken the bars of your yoke and made you walk erect" (26:11-13, RSV). The only conceivable response to such love is obedience, total obedience, holy obedience, grateful obedience. Out of gratitude arises the will to obey and keep his statutes, commandments, and ordinances. Yahweh remains faithful even when we are faithless and disobedient. The only choice open to us is willful disobedience or glad obedience, for he will not let us go.

81

In the New Testament, covenant is essentially the same except that it focuses in a person who is God with us, Immanuel, Jesus the Messiah. Covenant in the New Testament also differs in that it has taken on fully and definitively the inward dimension promised by Jeremiah. His law has become a living thing written on our hearts. We are a people circumcised in heart and ears who hear and obey God's faintest whisper. We are called to observe the ethic of the Sermon on the Mount not through any self-help measures but through the grace of Another who has taken control of our wills. We live by faith in the Son of God who loved us and gave himself for us.

The good news to the believing church is that God's Son has come in the fullness of his power to restore his voluntary, gathered, regenerate people. He gathers through baptism by the Spirit into one body and one faith. Buried with him in his death, we are raised with him into newness of life. No water is necessary to this great act of mutual self-giving and covenanting. Water may even be a distraction. True baptism is into and by his Spirit. No physical element nor mode of its administration should be confused with the decisive spiritual act. Likewise, communion, the eucharist, is eternal, inward, and spiritual. We feed on him in our hearts by faith. The *magna charta* of communion is the sixth chapter of the Gospel of John. Jesus Christ is the bread coming down from heaven giving life to the world. Except we eat his flesh and drink his blood in an ever renewed act of the Spirit we have no life in us. There is really only one sacrament: this great act of God's self-giving love to redeem and save mankind and the world. Whenever and by whatever means we partake of this cosmic sacrament, he becomes Immanuel, God with us and in us. No bread or wine is necessary. The life-giving Word, the bread of eternal life, is in our midst, and that is sufficient. In a recent Faith and Order conference on the subject of baptism I polled the delegates present to find out whether I, a Quaker, could be admitted to membership in their churches without having to submit to water baptism. Only one would insist on water. All the rest would admit me on confession of faith and witness to baptism by his Spirit. I did not know whether to be shocked by this apparent lack of discipline or to be glad that spiritual baptism seemed to have such wide acceptance. I will choose the latter alternative and be glad.

Obvious to all who aspire to the voluntary gathered church is the fact that the only force that can be used to gather men into the fellowship is soul-force, the persuasive, constraining power of his Spirit. We must eschew all coercion as an unhappy reminder of the days of Constantinian Christianity. Our educational methods must be consistent with the suffering love of our Master and Lord. The sacrifice which God in Christ seeks above all is free and uncoerced obedience. No fellowship on earth can match in sheer joy and caring the fellowship of those freely gathered to him.

Obedience to the Prophet who speaks to us from heaven means also the recovery of discipline and what George Fox called "gospel family order." Though this be a spiritual reformation to which he calls his believing people, he does not call us to an invisible church. The Lord's presence in our midst is invisible, but the voluntary group discipline and order to which he calls us must be visible, tangible, particular, historical. The body of Christ, which is his people, is an extension of the Incarnation and is necessarily particular and historical just as he was when clothed in flesh. The doctrine of the invisible church, while a comfort to the persecuted, has often been used to avoid facing the sin of our divisions and, more important, as an excuse for disobedience.

This visible order of the gospel fellowship is, in the words of Lewis Benson, "not determined by the ordinances of the 'founder' during his lifetime but it is determined by what Christ does *now*. . . . He is at the center of this community and it is what he does that causes the community to appear and determines its form."[11] Institutionally minded churchmen must have a hierarchical priesthood, visible sacraments, and properly ordained deacons, ministers, and elders. The only structure or order the spiritually present Head of his people requires is a personal relationship of hearing, obeying, and witnessing. This master-disciple relationship results in a gathered community which nurtures the spiritual gifts of each member and causes them to live in unity and love to one another and in righteousness and obedience to the Christ within. Such gospel order is opposed to institutional Christianity.

As descendants of Radical Reformation groups we have had much previous experience with too rigid discipline. Sometimes we have been bound by too rigid adherence to the letter of Scripture or more commonly to the letter of Scripture as interpreted by the rigid human demands of culturally ossified Quakerism, Brethrenism, Mennonism, *et cetera*. The word of man and his authoritarian structures bound us to the letter of Scripture and the letter of our books of discipline, while quenching the life, the spirit, and the freedom of both. Some of the groups represented here, certainly the Quakers and to some degree the Church of the Brethren, the Disciples, and the

Church of God, have swung in reaction to the other extreme with resulting individualism and moral relativism. To what discipline, then, does the Lord, who would restore his church, call us?

He calls us to Christian liberty. For such liberty obedience is the source of freedom. When we voluntarily obey the voice of our inward Teacher, we are released and freed from conflict and guilt feelings within and from the desire to dominate and control others. This liberty in obedience results not in rigid individualism but in a profound experience of unity of faith through the one Lord who gathers us all as in a net. Liberty means hearing and obeying the voice of the Lord.[12]

Corporate obedience results. But there is no place in this gospel order for the ban or shunning the erring brother. Brotherly admonition is necessary, but supporting one another in love must be the criterion of such admonition. If real conflicts and disunity arise among those whom Christ has brought hither, the group in brokenness of spirit must seek the mind of Christ for a loving means of correction. If the group has not the mind of Christ, it cannot correct anything. But every member of the fellowship must hunger for group obedience, group witness, and the willingness to suffer as a group until the Spirit restores unity. The same standards apply to ordinary business meetings of the fellowship. We meet together to seek the mind of Christ for the fellowship in business matters in the same sort of spirit that we enter into worship. Taking votes which produces disgruntled minorities is highly inappropriate. In oneness of spirit we find the will of the Lord for the whole group, or we do not act until we do. Such corporate obedience results in corporate testimonies, as we shall see below.

Another form of obedience to which the sovereign Lord of his church calls us is holiness and power over sin in this life. Lesslie Newbigin has lumped all of us gathered here into the "Pentecostal third force" in Christianity today. So we might as well learn to enjoy this classification and claim its inheritance. If Christ has returned in the fullness of his power to restore his covenant community and commands that we live in a hearing and obeying relationship to him, he will enable us to live atop of sin in this life and overcome the kingdom of evil through his power at work within us. This experience makes individuals feel as George Fox, who felt he had "come up in spirit through the flaming sword into the paradise of God."[13] Sanctification means one work of grace in which we are justified, reborn, and enabled to walk in purity of life. As modern men we may shrink from claiming Christian perfection for at least two reasons.

84

First, the arrogance of claiming the absolute perfection found only in God repels us. Second, absolute laws have disappeared from man's understanding of science and the natural order. So who are we, therefore, to claim an absolute amid the constant emergencies of Christian moral decisions? Present-day pleaders for the power of sin accuse us of self-righteousness, if we say sin can be conquered in this life. This danger to which they legitimately point can only be avoided by crucifixion of self-will and sole dependence on grace. But is this not a lesser danger than saying that sin has won by default, because Christ has power only to save men from sin beyond the grave? But God's believing people know experientially that obedience to the voice of the divine Shepherd is possible! He makes it so. Just as he has won the decisive victory over death, sin, and Satan on the cross, so also he enables his faithful ones to walk in dynamic obedience as he walked in all humility and God-blindedness. The illusion of the unattainability of Christian perfection has become a massive excuse in this day for disobedience to the heavenly Voice. The possibility or impossibility of perfection in this life is really beside the point. The ethic of a believing people is an ethic of obligation. It is up to us to obey his voice. As we obey we come to the marvelous realization that as long as we continue faithfully to obey he gives grace to live free from sin. When a group of believers experiences such obedience, the aberrations and weaknesses of individual members are compensated for and the word of the Lord at the Red Sea becomes a realized fact, "Speak unto the children of Israel, that they go forward" (Ex. 14:15b, KJV)!

In the next place, obedience means walking not where but *as* Jesus walked. He challenged men to believe and enter the kingdom of God. He taught righteousness. He healed the sick. He judged down wickedness. He associated with and ministered especially to outcasts. Are we doing these things? What has happened, for example, to the healing ministry of our believing church? I was spiritually healed. The Lord saved my life; my physical life, I mean. Literally fulfilled ·for me were the words of Psalm 116:8, 9, 2b, KJV: "For thou hast delivered my soul from death, mine eyes from tears, and my feet from falling. I will walk before the Lord in the land of the living. . . . Therefore will I call upon him as long as I live." If we claim to live in the life and power in which the prophets and apostles lived, must we not recover this lost ministry as well as others?

But walking as Jesus walked means, above all, becoming a servant church. His disciples never understood his mission as Messiah, not even on the day when he was taken up from them into heaven. They still expected him to show a mailed fist and restore the kingdom to

Israel by force. But he was the Isaianic servant come to heal, love, persuade, and save men by his vicarious suffering. It remains an astonishing fact that it is the exalted Messiah of the Gospel of John who humbles himself and washes the disciples' feet. He commands us to do likewise. I think it very significant that at least three of the traditions represented among us here today still practice foot washing as an ordinance. What a sign for the servant church! But our Lord's command that we wash one another's feet did not mean that we should go into the universal foot-bathing business, complete with automatic coin-operated machines, but that we should serve man in all his needs—physical, economic, and spiritual—with both grace and joy. This generation no longer has patience with an authoritarian church that hands out edicts but responds warmly to Christians who empty themselves and take on the form of servants responding to personal needs as their Lord.

Finally, Christ calls us to a new intensity of obedience in a prayer life worthy of Thomas R. Kelly or true Spener-Pietism. How much do we really practice and depend on prayer? In this conference we are sharing various theories and stratagems for restoring the believing church. Do we really confess our helplessness to God and agonize for the rebirth of this people? I get a great "charge" out of men like the prophets of the Old Testament, Conrad Grebel, Balthasar Hubmaier, Alexander Mack, John Bunyan, and all the martyrs of our tradition. I thirst to be like them! To have their courage, their "guts," their devotion, their vision of mankind reborn into a gospel family order—I long for this fervently. Do you share this hunger? Do we all have it? I weep for the restoration of a Believers' Church, do you?

Most of us are harassed and busy men. We must cultivate in our prayer lives what I will choose to call "holy double-mindedness." As Tom Kelly instructs us, we must learn to live our lives on two levels at once. On the surface we are "snowed" by all the demands of industrialized or executive existence. But deep within, down below the time-torn surface, there can be a song of praise, an inner serenity, a consciousness that the Lord is with us, Immanuel. Such simultaneity of application to outward duty and inward listening really is possible even to men like you and me, men who are reeling from one harassed situation to the next. Our frenetic frenzy can be calmed and made radiant by disciplined wordless prayers and acts of inner adoration which soon become habitual. Paradoxically, holy double-mindedness leads to singleness of eye, and our whole bodies are filled with light.

We need to learn humility, too, but not the humility of a doormat. Enjoyment at being trampled upon is really a form of inverted spiritual pride. We must be humble like the prophets who were blinded by God and the demands of his righteousness so that they could see nothing else. To be humble is to live out Luther's dictum, to fear God and nothing else. Humility is bold because we fear nothing for ourselves. Thick-skinned, the bitter attacks of men do not disturb us, because we are secure in God's love.

In all our longing to restore God's believing people we must be ever conscious that in addition to humility each of us is called to walk in holy, joyous, radiant obedience to our living Lord all the days of our lives. Have you ever noticed the gorgeous little phrase the Revised Standard Version sneaked into the fifth verse of the thirty-fourth Psalm? It explodes: "Look to him, and be radiant." That's the whole bit! That is what this paper is all about. You may forget all the rest, if you will just remember to "Look to him, and be radiant."

But our prayers for the restoration of a believing people will be ineffective unless we believe it is already happening. God has already begun this spiritual reformation of which we dream. In Wilmer A. Cooper's excellent published lecture, *A New People To Be Gathered in the Power of the Lord*, the best sentence in the whole wonderful lecture is the affirmation: ". . . the fact is that new life *is* taking place among us and a new leadership *is* being raised up for the purpose of a new ingathering of people for our day."[11] Do you believe it? I do. This conference just could be the "constitutional convention" of such a new people.

3. A Believing People Witnesses

A believing people hears the voice of its living Lord, obeys him in all things, and witnesses unapologetically to his power in every phase of the life of the world. Witnessing serves as the primary means of demonstrating the contemporary relevance of a believing people.

Our first responsibility is *evangelism* by all means and all media and especially to mass, depersonalized, urbanized man. We witness to him that the voice of Him who is, who was, and is to come can be heard and known and that through obedience to him life can be transformed into a colony of heaven on earth. We must, as Lewis Benson puts it, lead men "directly to Christ who *is* the new covenant. As men turn to Christ, the light, they will be formed into a community—the children of light. Therefore, leading people to Christ is the strategy of renewal that belongs to the new covenant."[15]

This sharing of good news seeks to reach man who is at once self-sufficient, self-satisfied, the creator of a new technopolis—"man come of age"—and at the same time a prisoner of all the patterns of production, merchandising, and pleasure-fulfillment-gimmicks that he has created. Alienation, aloneness, noninvolvement describe his condition. What has the believing church to say to him? Precisely that "hearing and obeying the voice of the creator is the fundamental law of man's being."[16] Also that the living Christ brings assurance that power to obey is available and that life can be repersonalized through the new covenant of love for other men that results from the master-disciple relationship to Jesus Christ. We must witness to righteousness and power over sin into which Christ has brought us. The assurance that power to obey is available and the experience that obedience really occurs build an experience of cumulative moral energy that attacks evils both within and without.[17] The so-called unattainability of perfection and the temptation to moral relativism both become irrelevant, and man is released to "shake the country for ten miles around."

If Christ is God's eternal prophet and king who speaks and rules from heaven, his believing people must also develop a new concept of grace and mission. First, as Brunner, Newbigin, Elton Trueblood, Wilmer Cooper, and many others have reminded us, "the church does not just *have* a mission . . . the church *is* mission in the world."[18] A church or believing people that is not missionary is no church at all. It is an idol, the relic of a dead past. Quaker quietism felt that proselytizing was wrong and thereby wrote its own epitaph. This may have happened to some of the rest of you. Young people today, on the other hand, always want to go where the action is. Where the church is alive to its essence as mission, its dynamic witness will attract the young.

But the grace of Christ, the prophet who speaks within, is one, universal and saving and is extended to all men. Though men in any culture, religion, or anti-religion know him not by name, he is present within them, urging and prodding them to live up to and apply the best that they know. Does this suggest syncretism into one universal religion of the Spirit? Not at all. First, it is the Spirit of the God of Abraham, Isaac, and Jacob who has made himself known through a particular saving history and who was incarnated in his only Son. It is not the spirit of Amida Buddha or an impersonal absolute. Second, although individual men in many and various faiths and religions may very well be saved by obedience to the light of Christ within without knowing him by name, the vast majority of men *disobey* these inner promptings of the Spirit of our Lord and thus are concluded under sin. To disobedient men, the good news and the saving history through Christ must be preached. Thus, saving grace is extended to all, but Christian mission is preserved to win all men to Christ who is the head. Our missionary task is to bring men to hear and obey the living Lord who speaks from Sinai, from Calvary, from the upper room, and from his martyr church through the ages. One of the tragedies of contemporary Quakerism has been the separation of mission and service into opposing camps served by separate agencies and motivated by different philosophies. Quakers are known over the world for service and humanitarian concern in action. This is a wonderful thing. The Brethren Service Commission, patterned after the American Friends Service Committee, enjoys the unique distinction of having brought into being that service agency which represents most of us, Church World Service. But the balance between selfless service to war victims, refugees, and the needy and evangelism and mission to bring men to Christ has been preserved by the Mennonite Central Committee. We are called to become a servant church after the pattern of our Lord. But service must be motivated out of gratitude to him and the love he has shown to us. It is his voice that calls us to serve, and in obedience we minister to men in their need by work camps, by self-help projects, by diplomats' seminars, by teach-ins in the love with which he loved us. Pray with me that this Quaker schizophrenia, which some of you may also suffer to some degree, may be healed in the name of our servant Lord.

Harvey Cox and others call us to become "secular" in order to serve the needs of the world. To this challenge the believing church must say an emphatic "yes," if it means that we must get off our duffs and out of our four walls and our middle-class ecclesiastical ghettos and reach depersonalized, industrialized man in all his new social and power structures. The believing people represents religionless Christianity. It attacks the Constantinian institutionalized church. We do not just believe in the priesthood of all believers. We advocate the preacherhood of all. We seek not to abolish the ministry but to abolish the laity. There is no place for a *clergyman* in the believing fellowship, no place at all! We should penetrate and participate in the Ecumenical Movement but not in an uncritical fashion. Our Lord calls us to common life in him which is larger than the idolatrous denominational forms with which we are now saddled. We should pray, work, cooperate, and search together for his will for us all. But in so doing we must hold out for the restoration of noninstitutional believers' fellowship based solely on Christ and the master-disciple relationship of hearing and obeying. This means we will oppose structures which point toward monolithic organic reunion movements that end up in Constantinian compromises like episcopacy and apostolic succession. In such conversations we stand for the restoration of the living Jesus family with his spiritual presence the only normative structure. If we really sought the Lord in this spiritual sense, solutions to our differences on baptism, eucharist, apostolic succession, and other issues which divide would be found.

We need to say "yes" also to Cox's call to secular Christianity by getting involved as Christians in the life and structures of the nation-state, its political life, and its bureaucracy. It is hard for people in our tradition to admit, but I think that Christ died for the sake of just societies and states just as he did for individuals of all races, creeds, and political persuasions. God's believing people can no longer afford to say that the state and its structures must be condemned or shunned. They must be penetrated and either redeemed or condemned, whichever obedience to Christ demands.

On the other hand, an emphatic "no" must be said to Cox and his secularizers, if they mean that the church must become the world, compromising with it, thereby breaking the voluntary covenant of Sinai, Calvary, and Pentecost. The kingdom of heaven is like leaven. But if the leaven has lost its power to raise, the kingdom is lost.

One inescapable obligation our Lord Jesus lays upon his believing people in this and all generations is the demand for a consistent, unified Christian peace testimony. One of the blasphemies of Constantinian Christianity is its constant compromise with war, violence, and capital punishment. Jesus taught us to love our enemies that we might become sons of our Father in heaven. If instead we shoot, murder, bomb, and napalm them, we not only **disobey his explicit command but no longer remain sons of our Father** in heaven. A believing people exists by hearing and obeying. We must obey our sovereign Lord in this. Part of the American ethic seems to be, "If you have to kill to enforce the right, kill." To the Christian this concept is both blasphemous disobedience and treason. The only right a Christian has is to suffer wrong at the hands of another. Jesus was mocked, spat upon, and unjustly killed. Not only is persecution to be expected by his martyr church; it is a sign of God's blessing, his highest gift of trust, that we have been counted worthy to witness to the death if necessary. We are called to a new

90

kind of warfare, a warfare of the Spirit dedicated to saving men's lives, not to destroying them. Jesus' disciples sought hospitality in a Samaritan village. When refused, they wanted to play Elijah and bring down fire from heaven and burn up the place. Jesus rebuked them, saying, "You do not know what manner of spirit you are of; for the Son of man came not to destroy men's lives but to save them." (Compare Lk. 9:51-56.) This imperative of our Lord applies to his disciples today just as fully as it did then.

Justifying the participation of Christians in the armed forces of any nation fighting today's tribal wars, based on tribal ethics, is treason to Christ the king, sovereign Lord of history and of all men. We are citizens of his kingdom first. Our ultimate loyalty belongs to him. We are citizens of the kingdoms of this world and its nation-states only in a derivative, secondary, and subordinate sense. To disobey his command from Sinai not to kill and from the Mount to love enemies and rejoice when persecuted is treason to the high King of heaven, making shipwreck of our faith. This demand of Christian peace witness is not a luxury ethic reserved for the historic peace churches. It is a demand on all Christians, especially on all those who have the vision of the restoration of a believing church! Tertullian insisted that when Jesus disarmed Peter in the garden of Gethsemane, "he thereby ungirt every Christian."[19] Robert Barclay, Quaker theologian, expressed it: "To those whom Christ hath brought hither, it is unlawful for them to bear arms."[20] George Fox expressed it: "All such as pretend Christ Jesus, and confess him, and yet run into the use of carnal weapons, wrestling with flesh and blood, throw away the spiritual weapons."[21] Are we ready to readopt as a believing people this testimony of Christians for the first three hundred years? Readopt or perish! Just think of the shift in moral stance of the church in the eyes of modern men, if this should really happen!

The unifying concept of mission and witness which embraced the whole spectrum of the early Quaker vision was what was called "*the Lamb's war.*" As a believing people we are called to enlist in and fight in a new kind of army, the army of the Lamb. We are to struggle against evil in the name of Christ on every level of existence until the end of history, confident that the Lamb who has already conquered death and sin by his atonement and resurrection will bring all things under his feet. We turn to the Book of Revelation for a description of the Leader of this war and the nature of the conflict. We find two majestic descriptions of Jesus as sovereign Lord with eyes of fire, a voice like many waters, ready to rule all nations with a rod of iron and to smite them with the sword which proceeds from his mouth. In addition, we see the figure of the Lamb who was slain standing before the throne of God, judged alone worthy to open the sealed book of destiny. The word for lamb in Revelation is *arnion*, which means an active full-sized lamb. In this context this lamb is on the march. The Moravian Church seized on this lamb marching with a flag over his shoulder as the symbol of its fellowship. Around the seal is written the motto, "*Vicit agnus noster eum sequamur.*"—"Our Lamb has conquered, let us follow him." Let us borrow this emblem and slogan from the Moravians. This should be the emblem and motto of the believing church! In Revelation 17:14, RSV, we read of the conflict. Kings of the earth "will make war on the Lamb, and the Lamb will conquer them, for he is Lord of lords and King of kings, and those with him are called and chosen and faithful." And in 12:10-12a, RSV, after Satan and his angels have been thrown down, we read,

> And I heard a loud voice in heaven, saying, "Now the salvation and the power and the kingdom of our God and the authority of his Christ have come, for the accuser of our brethren has been thrown down. . . . And they have conquered him by the blood of the Lamb and by the word of their testimony, for they loved not their lives even unto death. Rejoice then, O heaven and you that dwell therein! . . ."

This is not a description of an obscure eschatological conflict tucked away at the end of history. It begins here and now as the struggle of the people of the Prophet who speaks from heaven to hear and obey in the conflicts of this present world. The key to understanding the whole conflict lies in the nature of its weapons. They are weapons of the Spirit. The sword proceeding from the mouth of the Lord is the sword of the Spirit which smites men, not with physical death but with spiritual judgment and with love in order to save them. The rod of iron is a symbol of total spiritual authority and does not mean a bar of ferrous metal. These are the same weapons more fully described in Ephesians 6:14-17, RSV: "the breastplate of righteousness," "the shield of faith," "the helmet of salvation, and the sword of the Spirit, which is the word of God." In this conflict we are to have our feet "shod . . . with the equipment of the gospel of peace." We are called to engage in this war of the Lamb who takes away the sin of the world. In this cosmic struggle the only weapons legitimate to the Christian for any purpose, the only conceivable weapons, are the weapons of the Spirit.

In Hugh Barbour's exciting book, *The Quakers in Puritan England*, he describes the way in which the early Friends conceived of the Lamb's war:

> Early Friends spoke of "the Lamb's war," the struggle to conquer evil within and without, led by the Spirit of Christ, who is the Lamb exalted to rule God's kingdom on earth. The Quakers called all men to join this struggle and to surrender their own wills to the constant judgment and guidance of the "inward Light" of God or Christ. . . . Fox and his friends felt there was a stark contrast between the world's ways and the way of Christ, but they called men to share in a world struggle and not to withdraw.
> . . . the Lamb's victory was an event expected within English history . . . , for them it was to be a real event. the actual climax of sacred history. . . . Friends expected to suffer as they shared in the Lamb's War; they also expected to win.[22]

The scope of the Lamb's war of the believing church is almost limitless. The ax is laid to the root of institutional Christianity and the relics of Constantinianism. Social and economic injustices among men are witnessed against and corrected. Relief is brought to the suffering, the needy are served, prisoners visited, the naked clothed. All structures of men's pride of class or race are hewn down. Civil rights, world peace, and the abolition of capital punishment are brought about. But most important, the citadel of man's pride, his hardness of heart is besieged with persuasion, suffering love, the gospel of peace, until all men are won to allegiance to Christ and through his grace to one another. He is the Prophet who speaks from heaven and from within and he will bring all men into a community who will hear, obey, and witness to him until the end of history.

As we recapture this vision of a believing people who hears the voice of its living Lord, obeys him in all things, witnesses unapologetically to his power, and uses his spiritual weapons to wage the Lamb's war until the end of history, our hearts are filled with hope, our eyes become bright with the vision of the triumph of God's purpose for mankind, and we sing with praise the new song: "Blessing and glory and wisdom and thanksgiving and honor and power and might be to our God [and to the Lamb] for ever and ever! Amen" (Rev. 7:12, RSV). And we hear his word behind us, "Behold, I am doing a new thing; now it springs forth, do you not perceive it" (Is. 43:19, RSV)?

A PEOPLE IN COMMUNITY

5

A PEOLE IN COMMUNITY:

Historical Background

The name of George Huntston Williams has come to be synonymous with careful and comprehensive scholarship pertaining to the radical wing of the sixteenth-century Reformation, though his professional labors have not been confined to this subject and his interests include a wide range of contemporary concerns. Dr. Williams is Hollis Professor of Divinity at Harvard Divinity School, the ninth Hollis Professor since the chair was established in 1721 by Thomas Hollis of London. A native of Ohio, he attended the University of Munich and then was graduated from St. Lawrence University and from Meadville Theological Seminary. After a traveling fellowship at the Institut Catholique in Paris and at the University of Strasbourg, Dr. Williams received his ThD degree from Union Theological Seminary, New York. After serving as assistant minister in the Church of the Christian Union, Rockford, Illinois, and on the faculties of the Starr King School for the Ministry and of the Pacific School of Religion, Berkeley, California, he became lecturer in church history at Harvard in 1947. He served as acting dean of Harvard Divinity School from 1953 to 1955 and edited *The Harvard Divinity School: Its Place in Harvard University and in American Culture*.

A member of numerous professional societies, Dr. Williams is past president of the American Society of Church History and of the American Society for Reformation Research and presently serves as chairman of the North American Committee for the Documentation of Free Church Origins. A Fulbright Lecturer at the University of Strasbourg in 1960-1961 and an alternate observer at all four sessions of the Vatican Council II, he has been chairman of the Massachusetts Commission for the Study of Birth Control and of the Massachusetts Council of Churches' Commission on Church and State.

All who today study the Reformation's radical wing are indebted to Professor Williams, especially for his coeditorship of *Spiritual and Anabaptist Writers*, an important collection of sources in English translation, and for his comprehensive volume entitled *The Radical Reformation*. Out of his comprehensive understanding of and sympathetic concern for the Believers' Church heritage, Dr. Williams presented to the Conference on the Concept of the Believers' Church a study of the usage by a selected number of believers' church and similar movements of the basic metaphors applied to the Christian church as a gathered community. The study was set in the context of a call to the recognition (a) of the debt that believers' or gathered churches have to the "given" churches out of which they came, (b) of the succumbing of believers' churches to the processes of institutionalization and acculturation, and (c) of the existence of an ecclesiological counterpart to the biological principle of the alternation of generations.

The response to Dr. Williams' address was given by Dr. Richard M. Pope, professor of church history, Lexington Theological Seminary, Lexington, Kentucky, an institution of the Christian Church (Disciples of Christ). Dr. Pope commended Dr. Williams for "a very solid, carefully researched, imaginative, even creative approach" to his subject and for his knowledge "of the total sweep of Christian history" and his "socio-psychological understanding of the nature of human community" as well as for "a detailed understanding of the history of the Believers' Church in its classical, formative years."

Dr. Pope emphasized the acculturation of the believers' churches. Therefore said he,

we must recognize that every form of the church, including the Believers' Church, is profoundly affected by the caste and class structures and all the other social and economic forces that play upon it in the cultures through which it moves in history. One is always surprised to find a Negro Mennonite, a share-cropper Unitarian, or a Disciple of Slavic background.

While acknowledging that the believers' churches had contributed to the breakdown of barriers of class, race, region, and nation, Dr. Pope insisted that in the history of the believers' churches this had been "only relatively true."

The one area of the world where their influence has been greatest, where, in fact, Baptists and Methodists constitute almost an "establishment" and where the Churches of Christ and Disciples are also numerous—the Southern region of the United States —a powerful caste and class society is upheld and mirrored in the churches themselves. . . . [Indeed,] the history of these churches in America would seem to indicate that in their preoccupation with individual conversion and purity of moral life, they have generally failed to reckon realistically with the ways in which such worldly vanities as love of preeminence, pride of race, sectional loyalty, party spirit, and desire for a power or financial success may subtly infiltrate the congregations of Zion. That is to say, separation from "the world" surely involves something more than an experience of regeneration and sanctification which abstains from tobacco, alcohol, gambling, and dancing, though these present problems are real enough.

But Dr. Pope also saw this acculturation of churches in the South spilling over into other areas.

Moreover, when a Southern Baptist from Appalachia, or a Church of Christ member from Tennessee, or a Disciple from Kentucky moves north to, say, Akron, Indianapolis, or Detroit, he may seek a congregation of his own faith in a spirit of genuine loyalty and sincerity. But his faith may unconsciously include not only a pure love of New Testament Christianity but also a very human and natural love of his own kind, a love, so to speak, of hot biscuits, grits, country ham, and red-eye gravy, that is, a love of people whose ways are familiar and with whom he shares a common memory of, and affection for, the old ways he knew back home.

Dr. Pope agreed with Dr. Williams as to the fact that today "the distinction between the [historically oriented] gathered church and the [historically oriented] given church is frequently not very sharp."

A Methodist church in Georgia may, for example, in its wealth and prestige and in the attitudes it engenders display some of the marks of the old established churches in Europe, while a Greek Orthodox church in this area may resemble in some of its attitudes and feelings the gathered churches of the Reformation.

Dr. Pope raised two basic questions concerning the address by Dr. Williams.

First, would it not have been more representative to have paid greater attention to the American experience in the history of the believers' church, since it is in this country that they have had what might be called their most conspicuous opportunity on the stage of world history, have achieved their most notable success, and, also, perhaps have suffered their most painful failures?

Second, does Dr. Williams give sufficient place to the power of ideas and doctrines in the formation of human communities? He asks, at one point, if the "Believers' Church" terminology is somewhat misleading, since articles of belief or creeds have not in fact played as large a role in their history as in that of the given churches. While this is true if one equates "belief" with formal or systematic theological construction, it is not true, I would hold, if belief is used to indicate deep and passionately held convictions of a theological nature such as the necessity for a regenerate church, a church free from state control, congregational autonomy, and so on. Wherever one looks in their history one finds, I should say, less willingness to compromise matters of belief for the sake of comprehension or unity than one finds in some forms of the given churches. Perhaps this is one reason why so many of the believers' churches have found it difficult to participate in the Ecumenical Movement in our time.

In conclusion Dr. Pope agreed with Dr. Williams that

it may well be that one of the contributions that the gathered churches can make to other Christians is their understanding of the Church as a covenant community of genuine faith, even as they in turn learn something about the corporate nature of the Church and the manifold richness of Christ revealed in the totality of its ongoing life.

o   o   o

It has been urged in the course of our conference that we should be at work on a theology of children. In accord with that proposal, I suggest that we begin with biology. The closest kinship between the **Believers' Church as we idealize it and as we glimpse it** particularly at the inception of this or that free-church denomination is the religious order or congregation within the Roman Catholic Church. And there, because of the vow of celibacy, recruitment, say of Franciscans, is wholly by call and conversion. But take, for example, Quakerism. Here there is accesssion to the group both by recruitment and reproduction. There are both the so-called "convinced Friends," and there are "birthright Quakers" who in due course usually follow their parents into the life of the Society. The first socio-biological fact to have clearly in mind in becoming historical about the believers' church as a people in community is that, unlike the monastery or convent, it is (with the exception of a very few "Protestant" communities like the Shakers), as it were, a conjugal form of coenobism with a very high, covenantal conception of marriage. Because in every believers' congregation there are both birthright continuators of the tradition and converts, the believers' church has some of the characteristics of an *ecclesiola in ecclesia*, like the Franciscans or the Benedictines in the Catholic Church, and also some of the characteristics of a complete but communitarian or ethnic church, like, for example, the Armenian Church with varying degrees or circles of solidarity and participation.

Now when I suggested that we begin our ecclesiology with a glance at biology, I had more in mind than the recognition that the Puritan congregation of disciplined saints had numerous offspring, while the Passionist Fathers, say, of Louisville, are celibate! I have in mind the biological and particularly the botanical principle of the "alternation of generations." In the plant kingdom the haploid and the diploid generations are, at the lower level of evolution up through the mosses and ferns, distinct and distinguishable variants of the species, visibly growths of different size, leafage, and function. In the flowering plants, this extraordinary alternation of two successive types of the same species in the life cycle is obscured to view by internalization, though the same alternation of generations is visible in the microscope of the observer of what goes on at the level of pistils and stamens.

In the life cycle of the spirit there is just such an alternation of generations, interiorized, obscured, and, to be sure, modified by the basic fact that we are creatures with wills, hearts, minds, memories, and hopes. The immediate relevance of the botanical analogy is that it suggests the appropriateness not only of the effort to work out a theology of progeny in the believers' churches but also (in our ecumenical climate, with psychological and sociological sophistication and historical insight) a theology, as it were, of the *corpus christianum*, out of which, as though in a slowly alternating cycle of generations, there is continually born or reborn the believers' church or a new order or a new sisterhood or a new storefront fellowship. There could not have been a congregation of a thousand Pentecostals in Colombia or two denominations of Pentecostals totaling a million in Chile, mentioned earlier in our conference, if there had not been a *corpus christianum Romano-Iberico-Incanum* out of which these Pentecostal assemblies, under the impulsion of the Holy Spirit, drew substance. In the sixteenth century the Anabaptist conventicles, unfolding in their astoundingly mobile and martyr-minded vitality within the interstices of a medieval Christendom in a period of both decay and renewal, represent a spiritual growth inexplicable apart from the previous generation with its disciplines and despairs.

A complete ecclesiology or theology of the Believers' Church must take seriously not only the matrix out of which it originally emerged, but also the cultural "*corpus christianum*" that it subsequently forms about itself in the process of biological growth, cultural accomplishment, and social accommodation. The believers' church inevitably acquires a stewardship of influence extending beyond the original believers' church fellowship in a way analogous to that of those often much larger communions that are not constituted formally on the basis of the believers' covenant. Believers' churches no less than monastic congregations grow out of soil enriched by the humus of departed saints and Christian sinners, out of the *corpus christianum* of intermingled sanctity and secularity, not out of rocky soil that has suffered irreparable erosion. The Moravian Brethren did not form among the Eskimos of bleak and rocky Greenland. They grew from seeds scattered in Germany by the Thirty Years' War; and growing strong on the estate of the protective Pietist count at Herrnhut, they assembled the spiritual power that sent them forth as missionaries to Greenland and around the world.

There are spiritual alternations of generations in the Great Church, in the monastic communities therein, in the free churches grown old and then again renewed. Let our ecclesiology include the Old Israel out of which came the New Israel. Let us find a place for the multitude who rejoiced with Jesus along the Palm Sunday road to

101

Jerusalem as well as for the seventy disciples and the eleven apostles who remained loyal to the end.

Luther and the Believers' Church

Martin Luther has been honored by our conference by a date on our program; but, as far as I recall, he has not been really mentioned in our conference thus far. In his *Preface* to his *German Mass*, as we all remember, he distinguished not only his new mass in the vernacular for the multitude of the *Volkskirche* and his *evangelical* Latin Mass for students and professors in the universal language of the church but also a third form for the devout. Luther in this paragraph presented an evangelical conventicle, meeting devoutly in a house, studying Scripture, baptizing in faith, sharing in the Lord's Supper, and singing psalms—a kind of *ecclesiola*. Lambert of Avignon sought to incorporate this devout congregationalism in his Homberg Church Order for Hesse. Much later the Missouri Lutherans found in this paragraph and other congregationalist *obiter dicta* of Luther a sanction for their polity. But the wonderful thing about Luther was that he could imagine within a few short paragraphs an international Latin liturgy and church, a vernacular church of the masses, and a highly disciplined conventicle that might in other circumstances have met all the specifications of the Anabaptists he so haughtily opposed. **But during the 450th anniversary of his posting the Theses, in the tradition of the free churches we can, in retrospect, honor Luther among so many other reasons for also having foreseen the place in the larger whole of the disciplined community of the devout, the Believers' Church.**

The Church Given or Gathered

A possible equivalent term for the Believers' Church is the *gathered church*. Its counterpart, neutrally or even ecumenically **or irenically labeled, would be the *given church*, understood as embed**ded in some kind of *corpus christianum*. This environing *corpus christianum* could turn out to be not only the surviving nationalized vestiges of medieval Christendom as in Sweden or Spain but also any associated national, ethnic, class, and regional subculture. We have already noted that the gathered church over the generations develops its own *corpus christianum* suffused with its ethos.

A believers' church, for example, of Southern Baptists could be gathered in the rapidly growing town of College, Alaska. Most of the recruits would turn out to be officers and students in the new land-grant university and a few townspeople who happened to have a Southern background and, by chance, Southern Baptist antecedents, although on principle, Eskimos and newcomers from other regions of the United States could be included among the charter members and would be warmly welcomed. A gathered church in other words has also a certain givenness. Similarly, a given church can also have a gathered character. For example in Oshkosh, Wisconsin, where there is another land-grant university, it is possible that there might, for commercial or other reasons, be just enough persons of Armenian background to form an Armenian Orthodox church, temporarily renting a hall, perhaps, in the Methodist church. A born Presbyterian in the history department in the state university, who had made a specialty of Middle Eastern history and who knew some Armenian, would surely be enthusiastically welcomed as an attendant at the divine liturgy in that rented room; he might conceivably even become a communicant member in the new church edifice projected. But he would be an isolated exception. The givenness of an Armenian parish or community consists not only in the pre-Chalcedonian Christology and the distinctive sacramental-liturgical life and language but also in eighteen hundred years of ethnic or national heritage and vivid memories of genocidal massacres and big-power divisions of the ancestral lands. A human being without further definition could more readily become a Southern Baptist in College, Alaska, than an Armenian Orthodox in Oshkosh, Wisconsin. But the point of adducing these extreme examples is to recognize that there is something of religio-cultural givenness in even the most exemplary believers' church and that there is surely something of gatheredness and even explicit belief in a church that historically we would characterize as a given church, but which in a variety of circumstances or in different sectors, due to transplantation, persecution, or inward redefinition of purpose, might acquire or recover many of the traits of the Believers' Church. A given church is one with its sense intact of its being *there* with all its historically accumulated polity, sacraments, and ordered wisdom. When we speak of the given church, we usually have in mind both the Catholic churches and the Protestant churches of the European state-church tradition, whether or not they still enjoy the privilege and responsibilities of state-establishment. But we are fully aware, of course, that the Orthodox community, say in Soviet Odessa, while it might indeed perpetuate even with assiduity the outer marks of a given church, would be inwardly or psychologically very much a gathered church of explicit believers, even though it would also try to perpetuate infant baptism. Similarly a Roman Catholic parish gathered in Tibati out of a polygamous society in Cameroun, though it be under the pope no less than the archdiocese of Toledo in Spain, would

103

surely qualify as a believers' church. Moreover, just as the Church in Rome in the first century was very much a church gathered out of the Jewish and Gentile groupings there, so increasingly the Roman Catholic Church of our day is refurbishing some of its ancient character as a believers' church and even in such ancient parts of old Christendom as Paris and Prague. By the same token, we all acknowledge that while the First Baptist Church of Dallas—to keep things at some distance!—might well observe with considerable refinement the practice of believer's baptism, yet it might well have about it several of the marks of what elsewhere in time and space we would call given or established Christianity. All this, of course, we know. Indeed we are here met to clarify the essential meaning of the Believers' or Gathered Church in the light of just such observations.

Cohesion Involves Exclusion

Called out of the world, the church nevertheless has a universal mandate in and for the world. The antinomy of universalism and particularism is indeed a problem for every world religion, for Christianity in particular, and for the Believers' Church in a special degree. For ecclesial cohesion involves also exclusion. The requirement of explicit faith disparages persons of insufficient temperamental, cultural, or intellectual endowment or aptitude. The group discipline of the Believers' Church tends to exclude in fact some of the very types and conditions of men and women and children who seem to have been most conspicuous among the first disciples of Jesus and the crowds on the margins who heard him preach and who were often individually or collectively the astonished beneficiaries of his charismatic bounty.

But the problem of cohesion and exclusion takes us beyond Christian beginnings, beyond even human religiosity and groupiness, to the very nature of social being. The full historical background of the Believers' Church as a people gathered in community would have to include some reference to the universal social phenomenon of how any community is formed partly through mutual solidarity within the group and partly through "creative" or formative antagonism over against other groups.

This groupiness of the human kind is indeed a phenomenon that extends throughout the whole realm of creation. For example, one troop of baboons is defined not only by mutual aid, exclusive loyalties, and hierarchical self-discipline but also by group antagonism over against various kinds of enemy species and rivals including other troops of baboons. When anthropological baboon-watchers separate twin baboonlets, leaving one with its mother in the troop of his birth and attaching the other to a bereft mother in another troop, it is observed that genetically identical or similar baboonlets absorb, to use the language of the anthropologists, the "social traditions" of the disparate troops, one baboonlet becoming, for example, a properly morose member of his morose troop, and the other twin a nervous member of an excitable troop. And each twin brother grows up to share also in the enmities that differentiate the two troops competing for feeding grounds and protective coverage. Nesting birds provide another example. Their territorialism, which is maintained largely by persistent song, is perhaps even more refined than the unsung comity arrangements between competing denominations in foreign or sub-urban mission territory!

Surely any survey of the Believers' Church as a people in com-munity must take seriously, even if not in elaborate detail, the sub-limated exclusivism which denominations, like other human groupings, share with the whole created order from birds to baboons. And this group-creative hostility or rivalry, separatism or schism—with its social, charismatic, temperamental, ethnic, and national components—is all the more complex and difficult to assess precisely in a Christian grouping for the reason that the Christian people, however sub-divided, in every subdivision perseveres in the claim to be true to, and concerned for, the universality of the reconciliatory love of the redemptive work of Jesus Christ, the foundation of all grace. Thus one task of the historian or interpreter of the Believers' Church as a people gathered in community is, at the first or at the last, to identify those components in every community, including therefore a com-munity of faith, which, while commonly or perhaps even necessarily present, are not the distinctive components of the community which we call the Believers' Church. Accordingly, while it will be these distinctively religious and more specifically Christian components in the bond among co-believers in historic formations of the believers' church which we shall have in mind throughout our inquiry, we have chosen to name and briefly characterize at the outset the other com-ponents of the bond of community.

Part I: Ten Metaphors of Ecclesial Community

1. Six General Motifs or Metaphors in Christian Togetherness or Community

Even before we reach the level of the more comprehensive com-munity we should probably mention also those bonds which bind only two or at most a very few persons in the relations, for example, of *spouses, friends,* and *companions,* because ecclesiological terminology often draws its imagery and self-understanding by analogy from this level of intimacy.

The most intimate and abiding of these three relationships is that of husband and wife. Spouses may be also companions and discharge other roles mutually, but that which is distinctive in their relationship is that it is conjugal, involving union and complementation of persons as man and woman. If their marriage is Christian, it is sustained in a lifelong covenantal or sacramental completion each of the other. In this relationship progeny and family institutions and concerns are the usual consequence, but inwardly wedlock is experienced as a major, though often hazardous, process of mutual self-risking fulfillment. The gathered church and the given church alike have in them something of both the risk and the richness of the conjugal relationship; and it is no coincidence that ecclesiology in quite divergent traditions readily resorts to nuptial and conjugal metaphors in order to set forth the mystery of the Church.

In contrast to the wedlock of Christian spouses the bonds of friends permit a plural ramification. But even friendship is not gregarious. It is, in fact, probably a rarer phenomenon in our mobile American society than in any other place and time in the history of civilization. There are not, one may note in passing, many modern equivalents of the classical and Renaissance essays *de amicitia.*

We know today perhaps a good deal more about another relationship much like friendship, namely, companionship. The distinctiveness of companionship is that it is more casual than friendship and that it need not involve equals. A man and his dog may be companions. In fact, it is often the case that the symbiotic relationship of companions derives its strength and satisfaction precisely from differences, marked complementarity, and comparable voids or aspirations but often in different areas of life. It is likewise more commonly sensed than articulated.

A specialized form of companionship is discipleship. The relationship between the teacher and his pupils and among the pupils themselves constituting a school is a fundamental pattern at the inception of most of the world religions and of most orders and denominations in Christendom. Co-discipleship has an exclusive as well as cohesive element, generating both loyalties, partisanship, and animosity.

Companionship, including discipleship, and friendship scarcely less than marriage involve an intimacy and mutual involvement that necessarily restricts the relationship. Christians have occasionally thought of themselves as friends of God, as disciples of Christ, and as companions of the Way.

Broadening down from the level of marriage, friendship, and companionship, which are quite individualized, are the relationships of *kinsmen, comrades,* and neighbors or *fellows.* These relationships embrace a larger cluster of persons than the foregoing. But here, too, all are known to each other not only by name but also by role and character.

The consanguineous relationship of siblings, cousins, cogenitors, and grandchildren is such a strong bond that it is almost regularly doubled without any emotional differentiation by way of in-law-ship; and, on the primary level of the nuclear family, it is fully achieved also outside consanguinity by legal adoption because the familial relationship and kinship beyond it constitute a system of intimate and trusting roles rather than merely of biological interconnections. The church has made ample use of the image of the family, especially in the metaphors of spiritual adoption and brotherhood by regeneration. In the primitive church and in all communities of faith, from their sectarian inception well into their maturation as denominations, participants have thought and spoken of themselves as brethren and sisters, while in the monastic orders, convents, and other ascetic congregations these terms and also "father" and "mother" have become formalized titles of address and monastic nomenclature. But siblings like nursing cubs or kittens are not necessarily loving; and the spiritual process of regeneration does not wholly eliminate the tussle and scrappiness of the reborn.

More consistently bound together than kinsmen by birth, adoption, and in-law-ship are comrades. In selecting the designation "comrades," I have eliminated a number of possible alternatives (such as "teammates" and "partisans"). However, in employing this particular word for our specialized purposes, one must supply a definition that will probably remain unique to this presentation, whereas most of the other terms we are using, like "spouse," "friend," and "companion," represent normal usage with at most just a little accenting for our purposes. The distinctiveness of the relationship of comrades first came to me in conversation with a former Catholic seminarian who, while remaining true to his religion, decided that he had not the priestly vocation and who thereupon entered a university history department for an academic career. In rehearsing the main features of his life, he, I noticed, referred to his fellow seminarians in Paris, whom he once went back to visit, as "comrades." As he completed his account, I went back to his term, asking him why he had not used "friends" or "companions" for the young men in training for the priesthood with whom his life had been so long linked. His answer was prompt and reasoned. He had chosen the term "comrade" precisely because of its analogy to the member of a Communist party. He said that he had revisited the seminary, thinking of the men there as indeed friends or companions of whom he was still fond, but that, after exchanging a few jokes, reminiscences, and indifferent inquiries, he realized that what had once bound him so closely with his fellows in seminary was the common discipline and self-sacrifice and above all the common purpose; "ideology," he said, not friendship. And from this I myself have generalized, holding that it is indeed true that within any church, party, team, corporation, labor union, military outfit, or college there is the powerful bond of a common cause and a common ideology, however defined, which makes of the recruits, the participants, the veterans, or *emeriti* a very strong comradery, indeed one of the strongest under the heading "community," but such a fellowship is based almost wholly upon the common "ideology" or objective. Relationships in this context are, accordingly, not primarily personal but purposeful, not permanent but interchangeable. In one sense comradeship is akin to companionship, which, as we have remarked, does not require equality, as does friendship; but unlike companionship this comradery endures only so long as an overriding purpose informs and unifies the company in time and space. Although the word itself is not so used, a good deal of sectarianism, denominationalism, and churchmanship is a matter of comradery. The crusaders—legates, idealistic knights, the military and eleemosynary orders, the outfitters, crewmen, tradesmen, camp followers, preachers, and almoners—might be taken as the representatives of the comrade component in the complex history of the Christian community; and, of course, with respect to this particular component the crusaders could not have differed much in comradery from the Saracens whom they collectively assailed.

On this level of multiple but still strong person-to-person relationship there is besides the kinsman and comrade, the neighbor. The neighbor, etymologically, is the adjoining farmer who has much the same interest as oneself in the conditions and events affecting the common enterprise, whether these be, as once, the common variables and afflictions of storm, vermin, flood, and fire or as today, for so many of us, traffic regulations, vandalism, or housebreaks on our street. But our experience of the neighborhood or of neighborliness has undergone considerable change, partly because of our social mobility and partly for a religious reason going back directly to Jesus. For Jesus in his parable of the Good Samaritan recast the meaning of neighbor to include also whoever passes by or into our life, regardless of his race or religion. Our neighbor in this extended sense might be the person with a problem right next to us on a transatlantic flight or, for the well-fed American, the famished Indian in drought-stricken India of whom he may indeed know more through television and popular magazine than he does about the occupant of the apartment on the floor below. Because Christianity and derivatively Western humanitarianism have extended the meaning of neighbor, it is true that the word itself has played no metaphorical role in the conceptionalization of the church as a community. Moreover with today's mobility, a network of working relationships based upon a kind of proximity other than property abutment is more nearly the modern American equivalent of the agrarian neighborhood; and this network, constituting the extended neighborhood of professional-social peers, does have such authentic features of neighborliness as compassion and mutual aid. The neighborly element, whether extended or literally proximate, is a real component in churchmanship; and we must find a convenient term that designates this reality even if we feel that "neighborliness" is unavailable for the purpose. When the Greek Orthodox or the Mennonites speak each of their community in such and such a place, they mean not merely the faithful at the divine liturgy or service on a Sunday morning but the whole complex of institutions and way of life, including perhaps a distinctive language carried over from the Old World which binds these people together whether in an urban complex or a rural settlement. Such a religious community is literally a transplanted neighborhood, as it were, of religious fellow **countrymen. But such terms as** "compatriotism of fellow landsmen in religion" and "ethnic-religious neighbors" also do not lend themselves to the extended usage which would serve our purpose in designating generically that component in every religious community, sometimes more, sometimes less, which far more than with faith or creed is connected with national origin; common class origins, vicissitudes, and aspirations; social behavior; and quasi-religious customs observed seasonally even outside the sanctuary. The Pilgrims and Puritan Congregationalists of Plymouth and Boston were only the first of such transplanted and extended neighborhoods which have become part of the growing structure of American society and religious life. The church has, indeed, in all times been able to think of itself as a spiritual neighborhood of sojourners or as a peoplehood of strangers, a remnant apart from the world, a new or true Israel, a peculiar people, a third race. We must accordingly have some generic name for this component in the formation of Christian communities. One could propose "classmateship" to suggest this very important non-theological factor in the rise and persistence of a church **as a people in community, this bond of class, race, and social** experience. There are recognizable signals and signs by which classmates know each other, interchangeably, as it were, for no other reason than their having undergone together roughly the same outward events at the same stage of maturation, for example, in college or in the armed services of a nation. By extension therefore one could speak of the bond which binds persons as mates in the same class and condition in society as classmateship. But one cannot force the language. And we are therefore left with only one really usable word even though it is not sufficiently specific: fellowship. Fellowship, containing in it the sense also of extended neighborliness, of transplanted compatriotism, and of sociological classmateship, is a very important component in the assembly, the settlement, and the cohesion of many sects and denominations, either in the process of upward or downward mobility in their own society or on colonization and adaptation to a new society with a new language and novel institutions.

We now have enough terms to designate both the more intimate and the more inclusive relationships by **which the Believers' Church** as a people in community has been held together and by which in some cases participants therein have actually described their solidarity metaphorically: wedlock, friendship, companionship (including codiscipleship), kinship (fraternity, sonship, etc.), (ideological) comradery, and (sociologically grounded) fellowship. These components in various proportions not only together help produce in part what we call Christian communities but they also in some instances supply the metaphors by which the Christian community, gathered or given, explains itself. But in addition to these components by which Christian communities are variously shaped and sustained, there are, of course, several distinctively or even wholly Christian bonds or covenants. It is by these **relationships that the Believers' Church and indeed every** church differs from communities without the Christian foundation, mandate, and expectation.

110

2. Four Distinctively Judaeo-Christian-Metaphors of the Christian Community

There seem to be four distinctively Christian components in the formation and self-consciousness of the church in general as a community in and under Christ.

The first is that of *membership.* Today one speaks readily of membership in a club as easily as membership in the church. Membership, however, is a metaphor that implies a body. And before there was the body politic and before there were corporations of various commercial and institutional types there was the body ecclesiastical; and that was the mystical Body of Christ. It is true that Stoic antiquity knew also of a cosmic body of which all rational men were members, a cosmic wholeness in which they knew themselves to live and move and have their being, as even St. Paul testified (Acts 17:28). But except for increment from antiquity the metaphor of the church as Body comes primarily from the church's own reflections on the meaning of the eucharistic sharing, beginning with St. Paul's own reference to membership one of another in the One Body of Christ (Rom. 12:4; 1 Cor. 10:17, etc.). In the tradition of this usage, in due course one spoke of the church as the *mystical* body, formed and sustained by the mysteries or sacraments of baptismal rebirth and eucharistic communion. The church in this tradition of the given church is preeminently the sacramental Body of which individuals are (reborn) members through diverse but conjoint functions for the good of the whole. In due course this mystical body, completely socialized as the medieval *corpus christianum*, developed a visible Head in the hermeneutical and institutional extension of the vicarial offices of the Bishop of Rome. And one form of reformed, national Catholicism or Protestant nationalism, namely, Henrician Anglicanism, found it congenial to think of a liturgically anointed King as the Head of the English Body politic and ecclesiastical.

In the distinctively English conflation of the conception of a church as Body and Realm it was Separatist Protestantism that first learned to disengage the transcendent *Kingdom idea* from any historic realm however Christianized. This second motif, creative of both folk and separatist churches, was in any case the original Christian basis for the new messianic community, which was the church. The Jewish kingdom idea was then in turn extended by the Constantinian imperial vision. Even today from the sacred liturgy of Greeks on Cyprus, through the Social Gospel of Protestantism and through the

Romanitas of the surviving triumphalists or integralists in the Catholic Church, to the millennialist preachment in the nearest Kingdom Hall of the Jehovah's Witnesses there persists the same basic commingling of two conceptions of the Kingdom, the Kingdom that breaks into time and the kingdom or commonwealth to be progressively Christianized. The metaphor of the Kingdom suggests subjects of a higher law and impending justice, as the metaphor of the Body suggests conjoint and mutually articulated members. The church either as the Kingdom yet to be established (also as a community of sojourners whose citizenship is in a heavenly city, Phil. 3:20; Eph. 2:19; and as the militia of Christ, the heavenly *imperator* or *capitanus*) or as the mystical Body of Christ is usually a hierarchically ordered society of Christians who as elect subjects or heavenly citizens, by virtue of these political, martial, or corporate metaphors, think of themselves as primarily related to each other through their suffering and risen Messiah, their heavenly Head, or eschatological Judge, rather than as primarily a fellowship of believers. Subjects are bound by a common allegiance but need not be personally known to each other.

A third distinctively Judaeo-Christian component of the church as a people in community is that of the believers as an *elect or chosen people of the covenant.* Election began in the history of Israel with a national covenant, but it was ever manifest also in individual circumcisions and other personal acts and asseverations. The covenant principle has in its transmutations through Christian history been several times re-nationalized, perhaps most spectacularly in the Solemn League and Covenant subscribed on the eve of Civil War in the kingdoms of Scotland, England, and Ireland. But the covenantal concept has also been constitutive of some of the smallest sects and must be counted, among the distinctively Christian components of the Christian sense of community, as the most significant in the formation of the Believers' Church as a people in community.

The fourth and the most exclusively Christian component of the church as a community is *communion.* Christians are communicants not only in their partaking of the same eucharistic elements by which they become one Body but also in the larger sense of their being drawn to each other through time and space in the ministry of the Holy Spirit. In communion they share the gifts and goods of the Spirit in all their transactions as the people of the Latter Days who are ever renewed, illuminated, and impelled to prophetic speech, groaning inwardly for adoption as the sons of God. At times in its history or in certain groupings of the *Ecclesia spiritualis* one can speak of Pneumatocracy, now with Montanists, now with the con-

112

fessor-monks, now with the Spiritual Franciscans, now with the revolutionary Spiritualists, now with the Quakers, now with the Revivalists.

For each of the four distinctively Christian component *relationships* deriving from the metaphors of faith we have yet to suggest appropriate terms. Accordingly, to the six not distinctively Christian component metaphors of community from wedlock to fellowship characterized earlier we can now add the following: for that relationship which is grounded in the metaphor of the mystical Body, we speak of *comembership*. For that relationship which is grounded in the metaphor of the impending Kingdom of the repudiated, risen, and returning Messiah: the *royal and mutual priesthood* of all believers. For that relationship which is grounded in the metaphor of the ever renewable covenant of the invisible Sovereign with a people drawn apart for a special purpose: coinheritance in election (or simply *coelection*) or *elective confederacy* in the new Testament or Covenant (*foedus*) through Jesus Christ. And finally, for the fourth relationship which is grounded in the sacrament or ordinance of sharing with all believers in all time and places not only in the covenantal Supper but also in all the gifts and goods of the Holy Spirit, which may include also quite temporal goods and mutual services: *communion* through the ministry of the Holy Spirit. Membership in the Body, the royal and mutual priesthood of all believers, elective confederacy and communion in the Holy Spirit—these are four distinctively Christian relationships, componently shaping every church as a people in community with their sense of the formative past and the future fulfilled.

3. Grace from Below and Grace from Above

Near the outset of this presentation it was remarked that every community, including also the community of faith and therefore the Believers' Church, too, takes shape partly by cohesion and partly by exclusion. Sometimes the cohesive force can lead to bigotry. Sometimes the exclusive impulse can lead to overt, tragic, and even monstrous animosity. A mob which becomes by rage psychologically structured (in contrast, for example, to a panicky crowd in a burning theater, each set upon his own life) will do things that none of the constituent individuals in the riotous group would do on his own or perhaps even realize that he had in himself. Similarly a nation, for example, Nazified Germany, could perpetrate an enormity in the history of inhumanity that no sane German would have even

113

thought of in 1933. There is a power for evil generated and channeled in a mob or a nation that is comparable to that of destructive floodwaters derived from drops of rain and rivulets of melting snow. This inducted and diabolic power of a group which seems far to exceed the mere totality of the energies and purposes of the individual constituents might be designated grace from below, in contrast to what Christians experience and know as a grace from above. Common to these two forms of grace is power, generated in, and conducted through, individuals who in their coalescence attain that critical mass which constitutes something more than their totality. There is a mystery here of human togetherness for good or ill. And a historian of Christianity will not overlook instances when, alas, even the Christian community has partaken of the nature of a coercive mass, inciting to war, sanctioning class or race privilege, carrying out inquisitions, hallowing an oppressive established order. In fact, the major concern of the historian of the given and the gathered churches as communities is to ascertain the extent to which the non-theological components thereof become licitly or illicitly Christianized and how also the distinctively Christian components of the community of faith can in their turn be secularized, socialized, nationalized, or otherwise distorted or misconstrued.

The two quite scriptural metaphors of Kingdom and Body have tended to be especially congenial to whatever Christian community has expanded socially and politically to include at least by intention the whole of the explicit and the implicit believers of a nation or society. For this condition the sociologists of religion have in fact devised the term culture religion. In many periods of history not only have the Body and Kingdom metaphors lent themselves to quite nationalistic, ethnic, or imperialistic conceptions of what constitutes the Christian community, but they can also, even in quite secularized or perverted forms, live on among *Deutsche Christen* of a Third Reich or among the radical rightists of a "Christian nation" with a manifest world destiny.

Discrimination is not all there is to the complexity of tracing and assessing the communal aspect of Christianity and especially of the Believers' Church. Besides the possibility of a change in voltage and an explosive alternation of spiritual current—grace from above, grace from below—there is the continuous historic shift in the relative strengths in society of those bodies which were once thought of as belonging respectively either to the temporal or to the spiritual order.

Generally there have been from the theological point of view just two groupings: those bodies belonging to the order of creation, like the tribe, the nation, the state, the family, the guild, etc., and those belonging to the order of redemption, namely, the church and her various subdivisions and instrumentalities. In between these two orders there has developed since the Reformation and especially from the eighteenth century on a wide range of voluntary associations many of them in fact modeled on, or inspired by, the Free or the Believers' Church. Many of these voluntary associations (to several of which most of us here also belong besides to our church), being humanitarian, eleemosynary, socially and internationally reconciliatory, and even in a sense redemptive in their purpose, would seem to belong in fact to an in-between order beyond the natural orders of creation and partaking of the nature and function of the church. Members of the given church no less than of the believers' church have rallied together in these societies, organizations, and *ad hoc* causes. The nun marching with a placard is one of the images of our age. And because of the proliferation of voluntary groupings of this kind, often akin to the Believers' Church but with a humanitarian or civic purpose, the Believers' Church may have some difficulty in defining itself in their midst.

This difficulty is compounded for many alert members of believers' churches by the world-wide propagation of whole new denominations of churches antagonistic toward the very denominations whose free-church principles they separatistically reembody and also by the emergence below the level of established parishes and congregations (mostly in the tradition of the given churches) of underground masses, house churches, sensitivity groups and fellowships.

At the same time because the substructure of nationalism is weakened among Westerners both by Marxist ideology and by modern technological capitalist compulsions and because also among the Asians and Africans nationalism is a phase of social development yet to be realized, religion in today's world, for either reactionary or progressive reasons, is tempted to offer itself as the social cement or sanction for the imperiled or the desired nationalism, or even for a rival conception of the nation. This is true of a revived Buddhism in Vietnam, of Hinduism in India, of Islam in Indonesia and in the anti-Israeli war. Certain proponents of Christianity also make the same offers with various motivations in Spain, Quebec, Communist Poland, and even in quite secularized America, where sectarian Christianity even in the tradition of the Believers' Church has occasionally added its voice to a strident Christianity in several sectors of the radical right.

If members of traditional believers' churches find self-identification difficult amid demands for black empowerment, amid fissiparous sectarianism, whether pentecostal or puritan, amid the neo-congregational-ism of group dynamics, amid quasi-religious voluntary associations of all kinds, they are also feeling the tug of ecumenicity in the sense of the desirability of some new form of global visibility and coherence among Christians in an increasingly hostile environment. This openness to ecumenicity among free-church congregationalists is to be explained in part by the recognition that globally Christianity has lost its establishmentarian character and is everywhere beginning to understand the church in terms of the saving Remnant.

If it is now agreed that Christianity in the tradition of the believers' church can, just as catholic Christianity, confuse the community of faith and something not properly identical with it, we shall find it helpful to examine some representative groupings of the past with a view to assessing the various components which at any given place or time were tributary in the make-up of what we would today regard as the idea of a Believers' Church.

Part II: The Ten Metaphors in the Believers' Church: An Historic Composite of Traits

As I begin a more detailed characterization of representative historic kinds of believers in community, let me express the conviction that a major ecumenical contribution of the experience and tradition of the believers' churches is (1) in helping to reduce or purify for all Christians those largely adventitious components on which all kinds of churchmanship, whether sectarian or stately, have in fact heavily depended and (2) in recovering also for all Christians the sense of covenantal belonging. The historic testimony and example of voluntary communicant solidarity may encourage the Christian people everywhere, but primarily in the major tradition of membership in the hierarchical Mystical Body, to rehabilitate their strategy for recruitment and service. In our complex and largely secularized society catholic Christians of whatever communion can no longer function as though the *corpus christianum* had not been irreparably disrupted; but, equally, the more sectarian Christians of explicit belief and congregational autonomy can no longer effectually witness to Christ in uncoordinated conventicles as though the Great Church and the classical Protestant imitators thereof *ipso facto* represented illicit concessions to the world or worse. For in today's global civilization Christians in the fellowship of the believers' church and Christians in the membership of the more comprehensive and corporate forms of Christian

116

life are alike fellow-sufferers in a world that has structurally out-grown all our familiar forms. We are, in fact, together, fellow-servants and kindred warners of a world which may drift toward universal destruction. A royal and mutual priesthood of all believers, co-members of an elective confederacy, Christians today of all types and traditions are converging in a new sense of communion with an emergent sense of what it means to be believers in the community of Christian faith amidst a world of both apocalyptic hazards and almost paradisaic potential.

In our glance backward, we shall make an effort (1) to ascertain, at representative moments in history, the relative strength of the ten or so communal component relationships we have distinguished and characterized; (2) to define the meanings of the constitutive *belief* (or faith) of believers in a believers' or gathered church; and finally (3) to characterize the constitutive acts whereby the believer thus defined has historically broken away from some other grouping on his formal entrance into the community of explicit faith.

Our representative moments have been chosen with a view to getting coverage of types and for that reason and for other reasons not all of the denominations represented at this conference are in-cluded. We shall be drawing on the formation of the Unity of the Bohemian Brethren just 500 years ago, the rise of the German Anabaptists *c.* 1525, the amalgamation of the Hutterite community in Moravia *c.* 1529, the schism of the immersionist Polish Brethren from the Helvetian Church in Poland *c.* 1563, the emergence of the Congregationalist puritans of England *c.* 1620, the rally of the Quakers *c.* 1675, the perpetuation of the Covenanters in Scotland *c.* 1687, the renewal of the Moravian Brethren under Count Nicholas L. von Zinzendorf *c.* 1722, the appearance of the Wesleyan Con-nection in England *c.* 1738, the separation of the New Light con-gregationalist Baptists of New England *c.* 1741. There are many other groupings that could have been selected; but I thought my presentation would be more compact if I selected no more than one specimen of believers' churchmanship from our own American back-ground. This happens to be the New Light Separate Baptists, of whom Isaac Backus was the chief spokesman. Except for this inter-esting group, we shall not draw upon Baptist history, although Bap-tists might be considered the very model of the Believers' Church. The present-day Baptists draw upon a number of historic impulses toward the pure church of true believers, even if one does not include the Continental Anabaptists among their antecedents. The fact that New Light or Strict Congregational Separates withdrew from the

117

Standing Order in eighteenth-century New England in the course of the Great Awakening and that several of these Separate congregations went on to disavow pedobaptism is an especially instructive analogue to what happened during the reformation of the Reformation in seventeenth-century England with the rise of General and Particular Baptists in the context of radical Puritanism.

I was, I should add, tempted to include a late medieval reformed or observant Franciscan convent for good measure, because it could be argued that the vow of the friar or monk to follow the counsels as well as the precepts of Christ and to live in self-sacrificial poverty and mutual obedience and self-discipline was often the medieval analogue or anticipation of covenantal baptism into the believers' church in the Reformation Era and of the Calvinist Baptist conventicle in the Era of the reformation of the Reformation in seventeenth-century England.[1]

Instead of dealing with the ten or so selected exemplars of the Believers' Church *seriatim*, I propose to allow the preceding analysis of different principles and metaphors of grouping to be determinative in the following presentation, although obviously all these terms are used somewhat loosely and mixed metaphors are the rule and consistency of sustained metaphor is the exception. What we want, I take it, far more than a rehearsal of the communal aspects of selected believers' churches, is a provisional composite of the Believers' Church as made up of traits common throughout the whole range of this kind of churchmanship. Accordingly, we shall first look at the metaphor of wedlock as transmuted for ecclesial purposes. And under this heading, as under each of the following nine metaphors of community, we shall also take note of what constitutes union and separation.

1. The Believers' Church and the Metaphor of Wedlock

In understanding itself as a community analogous in intimacy and involvement to marriage, the church in general and with it therefore the gathered church has not only assimilated and transposed the experience of conjugal life (as it was itself gradually Christianized over the generations) but has also sought to use the paradigm of the first mates in Paradise and then go on to meditate on the scriptural, patristic, and mystical understanding of the church as the Bride of the Second Adam. The fact that even old Israel could be boldly called by the prophets the Bride of Jehovah and that the New Testament made of the church the Bride adorned for her heavenly Bridegroom,

Christ, meant that from the very beginning of Christian history the nuptial and conjugal imagery was already a part of the vocabulary of revelation and not merely of the order of creation. Certain School-men eventually speculated that, although Christ established six of the seven **sacraments, one of them (to which he himself referred), was** primordial, being established in Paradise before the fall (Mk. 10:6 f.).

The Unity of the Bohemian Brethren were aware that some of the most radical of their Hussite-Taborite predecessors had been so eager to restore the innocence of Paradise before the fall that nakedness on certain occasions in their communal service on an island (to which they had withdrawn from the Taborite theocracy) was consid-ered an essential act of demonstrating the complete subsidence of the flesh in paradisaic harmony. Let this single instance suffice for a series of similarly motivated episodes reaching into Quaker history and beyond. The mystical elaboration of the nuptial imagery of Scripture and tradition facilitated the process by which the ordinary experience of marriage was directly reinforced by the individualization of nuptial ecclesiology, with each soul taking the place of the whole church as the recipient of the love of the heavenly Bridegroom.

By Melchior Hofmann, the charismatic preacher behind both **Münsterite and Mennonite Anabaptism, believers' baptism was** viv-idly likened to the bridal bliss of Israel (Jer. 2:2) in the wilderness of Sinai after having been brought out of bondage to Egypt. The ring of betrothal and the marriage banquet had with Hofmann their ec-clesial analogies. The communitarianism of the Hutterites was partly grounded in the language of paradise provisionally restored and partly in the nuptial language of mystical union and communion. Con-gregationalist puritans thought of pure congregations within the Established Church parish and particularly their new churches gathered in New England as the Beloved in the desert awaiting the embrace of that abiding Wisdom which is Christ (Song of Songs 8:5) or as the Woman in the wilderness which for its part will become the Garden (paradise) of the Lord (Rev. 12:6). The Familists, following Henry Niclaes, thought of the community of the spiritually reborn as preeminently a family and hence a house of love. The Familists con-stitute one of the tributaries of the Quaker movement. Count von Zinzendorf, founder of the Moravian Brethren, following a medieval, Lutheran, and pietistic tradition, made much of his church as formed from the wound in the side of the Second Adam, as Eve was formed by the removal of a rib from the side of the first Adam.

The bridal and marital language abounds in the history of Chris-tianity. The kiss of peace in certain contexts has been an extension

119

of the bridal metaphor. The covenantal conception of marriage, which among many groups of the tradition of the believers' church took the place of sacramental marriage, often involved the participants in divorce from an unbeliever and remarriage with a believer. Plural marriage established itself among the Münsterite Anabaptists on scriptural and pseudo-scriptural (Clementine) grounds fully as much as for reasons of martial and economic necessity. And a close supervision of courtship and marriage characterized almost all groups in the traditions we are considering. The German Anabaptists took religiously Jesus' injunction to let kith and kindred go; and, just as they considered sacramental pedobaptism a false baptism, so they considered an uncovenanted marriage no true marriage and separated themselves from spouses unwilling to incur the hazards of gathered, clandestine, and usually very mobile churchmanship, and they then remarried within the believers' covenant. When they excommunicated a wayward member, they often banned him or her bed and board. I have even come across an instance of a Separate Baptist woman being censured for insisting on walking to the meetinghouse with her dutiful but unrebaptized husband rather than with some full communicant neighbor!

2. The Believers' Church and the Metaphor of Friendship

Jesus, calling his followers not servants but friends (Jn. 15:15 f.), and James, characterizing the faith of Abraham as the sole basis of his being styled a friend of God (2:23), sanctioned for a minor tradition in Christianity a usage that has encouraged certain groups of Christians, especially in the traditions of the believers' church, to think of themselves as friends of God and friends of Christ and friends therefore of one another, absorbing into this friendship both classical and scriptural conceptions and recasting them ecclesiologically. The classical ideal of friends holding all things in common established itself in Christian tradition not only directly through the communism of the saints in the primitive Church in Jerusalem (Acts 2:44) but also pseudepigraphically in the so-called Fourth Letter of Clement of Rome to James in Jerusalem. This letter, derived from the Jewish-Christian Clementine literature with its conception of friendship in the context of golden-age communism, had already been long a part of canon law (Pseudo-Isidorean decretals) and monastic theory, when the letter, detached from canon law, circulated separately in the sixteenth century as a supposedly authentic document from the apostolic age. Certain Rhenish mystics called themselves Friends of God. Hans Hut, the former Müntzerite, readily spoke of the elect Friends of God, as did Caspar Schwenckfeld and the Hutterites. Both they and the Münsterites were acquainted with Fourth Clement and quoted it as an apostolic sanction for the sharing of goods and services among friends both in Münster and in the Hutterite communes or *Brüderhofs* in Moravia. The Racovian commonwealth of the pacifistic Polish Brethren was in part similarly motivated. The Quakers, aware of the long tradition of the word going back to Abraham, gave to their whole society the name of Friends. George Fox, when he so commonly referred to "friendly people" as those among the hearers of his message who seemed lovingly in rapport and sympathetic with his testimony, seemed also to be aware of the etymological meaning of "befriend," namely, to "love" and to "free" in the sense of "woo." In the eleven choirs into which the community of Herrnhut was divided the basis of grouping was similarity of age, marital status, etc., and hence of natural friendship. The same was true of the Methodist band of five or six and the classes of from twelve to fifty, although the language used by Zinzendorf and Wesley was less likely to be friendship than neighborliness and work in common.

Although "befriend" seems never to have emerged in any circle to mean adhesion to the Friends of God and of Christ in any of the circles considered, the opposite of friend was not unknown, outsiders being in the context of ecclesial friendship "slaves of the world," "friends of the world," or "enemies of Christ."

3. The Believers' Church and the Metaphor of Companionship

As we observed earlier, companionship differs from friendship in not being between equals and in not being necessarily permanent. There are companions in the sense of being fellow workers (Phil. 2:25); companions as followers of the same Way of suffering (Acts 19:29; Rev. 1:9); fellow pilgrims or *viatores*; and the very special companionship of co-discipleship under the same master. Companions in the Lord's work cooperate in common tasks and share their tools. Companions of the road give mutual aid and together withstand the hazards of the way. Co-disciples, revering a common master, perpetuate his precepts and rules in the School of Christ.

The term "School of Christ" is not scriptural; but the concept is readily grounded there in the rabbinical or magistral authority of Christ over his disciples. Many of the conventicles which were the original hearths of whole denominations in the tradition of the believers' church were initially convened for Bible study. The communions conducted by the Hussites in both elements on mountainsides under the open sky were modeled on the teaching assemblies of Jesus with his miraculous sharing in the loaves of bread on the hills of Galilee. Sustained by the great excitement of sharing not only in the wine limited hitherto to priests but also in the Word of God in the vernacular, the Unity of the Brethren were assiduous in the instruction of young and old in their assemblies. Those who became the first Anabaptists of Zürich originally knew each other as students of the Bible, meeting in homes and with the benefit of some in their number who also knew well the Hebrew and Greek texts. But formal learning was not the only criterion for the right to scriptural judgment. Both women and men, the unordained and even the unschooled as well as the few sometime clerics among them, were free to enter into the committed or covenanted deliberations as to the sense of Scripture. First Corinthians 14:23 ff. became a major sanction for the widespread conviction among the Anabaptists that all sitting about, studying Scripture, as co-disciples of Christ, the heavenly Pedagogue, and inspired by the Holy Spirit promised by Joel (2:28) and by Jesus, as destined to be poured out on old men and young in the latter days, had the right (*Sitzerrecht, lex sedentium*) to interpret Holy Writ.

The Racovian community of the Polish Brethren with its printing house and with its imprints in many languages, with its stress upon the work of teachers in preparing the catechumens for believer's immersion, and with its special understanding of Christ as himself not only Priest and King but also as Prophet-Teacher was a kind of School of Christ, which in the fully Socinian phase (after 1605) seemed, in fact, to have been an evangelical school more than a church.

The Thursday meetings for prophesying among the English Puritans had something of this instructional motivation. In the first place, they enabled the Puritan ministers themselves to get free from authorized sermons, but these gatherings for prophesying also partook of mutual instruction. The Congregationalists, following John Calvin, had a place in each congregation for both a pastor and a teacher, whose office was linked with the prophetic or doctoral office of Christ. In New England the congregational teacher was also literally the town schoolmaster, and even so advanced a school as Harvard College was regarded as a seminary or seedbed for ministers and magistrates in Zion.

Zinzendorf's Herrnhut thought of itself as a school of Christ for instruction of the offspring of the community, concerned also with the education of missionized natives, from Greenland to Latin America. Eskimos, Negroes, and Indians under Moravian tutelage became beloved disciples in the school of Christ. Although the actual word so characteristic of Wesleyan polity, the class, was originally a neighborhood rather than an academic term, the class meeting under the class leader soon became, in fact, the major means of teaching and disciplining the subdivisions of the various urban and countryside societies of Methodists. The intimate neighborhood bands and not much larger classes of early Methodism were the constitutive cells of that rapidly growing organism. In the bands and classes there was Bible study, mutual oversight, and, if necessary, rebuke. All bands of a given society came together for a quarterly love feast modeled on the New Testament *agape*. Since during Wesley's lifetime there was in England no separation of the Methodist people either from the Church of England or from the Nonconformists, all members of the societies were urged to attend upon the regular Sunday services of the parish or chapel and partake of its holy communion. In this context the love feast had a very special binding power and was not unlike the strictly kosher meal observed in the teaching fellowship or *chaburah* of Jesus' own day and of which his Last Supper was the most notable instance. So strictly was the Methodist love feast observed that one was admitted to the quarterly meeting only by showing to the doorkeeper a love-feast ticket that had been previously issued in one's name with date, on the occasion of a ministerial visitation for the purpose. The withholding of such a ticket was the equivalent of censure or dismissal. There is an instance of Wesley's exchanging band-meeting tickets for tickets that merely admitted the holders to the somewhat less exacting class meeting.

Among the Baptist Separates, Isaac Backus in a well-known autobiographical reference spoke of himself as having long been "a dull scholar in Christ's school" for having taken so long to see that faith must precede baptism. The only believers' church that has suggested the metaphor of the school in its official name is of course the Disciples of Christ, although the primary imagery here was more apostolic than academic.

If we pass from companions in the school of Christ to companions of the Way, we find that the metaphor never completely lost its power to create collateral terms consonant with it. The medieval world bequeathed to the Reformation Era the image of the simple *fidelis* as a *viator*, wayfarer. The Anabaptist was a pilgrim on the road to the Jerusalem that is above and that would in the latter days also descend, a *viator* prepared, in martyrdom, to go directly to that "city which has foundations, whose builder and maker is God" (Heb. 11:10 b). Short of that goal he was a missionary, testifying on the way. His was the message of Christ to those on the road to Emmaus and to Paul on the road to Damascus. The mobility of the Anabaptists on the roads and waterways of Central Europe was characteristic. They recognized each other by signs and gestures like medieval pilgrims to Jerusalem wayfaring through hostile lands. As late as the New England congregationalist Separate Baptists one finds the medieval term *viator* in the form of "walker," the contrasting phrases being the "disorderly walker" and "backslider," from whom the sturdy Baptist Separate should dissociate himself not only in walking to the meetinghouse but in walking about on his daily rounds in business or agriculture.

4. The Believers' Church and the Metaphors of Blood Kinship

The prevailing nomenclature of the believers' churches testifies to the prominence of the metaphors of blood kinship and notably of brotherhood. We have but to name them: the Brethren of the Common Life, the Unity of the Bohemian Brethren, the Swiss Brethren, the Polish Brethren, the Moravian Brethren, the Church of the Brethren, etc. Brotherhoods or fraternities for devout or religious purposes already existed in late medieval Christendom. Possibly not with the Waldensians and the Unity of the Bohemian Brethren, but surely with the sixteenth century and thereafter the designation "brethren" came to suggest increasingly a relationship based explicitly on the experience of regeneration and hence on the recognition of spiritual brotherhood in rebirth or covenantal adoption as sons of the same heavenly Father. The regenerate basis for the relationship meant that the fraternity of the believers' church was also a sisterhood. A marked characteristic of the Anabaptist conventicle was the prominence of women, a feature also of the pre-Constantinian church. That in Christ there was neither male nor female meant in the formative period of many groups the equality of women and men. Women were prominent among the martyrs. Among Schwenckfeldians, Quakers, and Methodists women also played prominent roles as patronesses and protectresses, which again reminds one of the protecting role of wealthy ladies with their villas in the ancient church, whose names come down to us from the period of the catacombs. In the choirs of Zinzendorf and in the class-meetings of Wesley women were sometimes organized on their own and with their own female leadership.

The major gain for women in the tradition of the believers' church was undoubtedly in the home itself, for the covenantal conception of marriage seemed to equalize the partners in a way that sacramental marriage in the context of a celibate clergy and monasticism had not yet achieved and also in a way quite different from the naturalization of marriage among the classical Protestant reformers with their elimination of marriage from the authentically dominical sacraments and their relegation of wedlock to the order of creation. The covenantal conception of marriage among the radicals preserved in different scriptural form the religious character of marriage as a sacrament, while at the same time it placed much greater stress than in sacramental marriage (as then practiced) on the freedom of the woman alike in betrothal, in marriage, and in the ongoing conjugal life. Although the marital status of the woman was in the first instance a matter of individual freedom and accountability, it would appear that the attitude of Anabaptist or Moravian brethren-husbands toward their wives was also of significance ecclesially in enhancing their respect for spiritual sisters in the conventicle or community.

The importance of regeneration as the basis of brotherhood in the believers' church meant that at some periods and in some regions the believers' church was not only freer from the restrictions of class and nationality than the given churches—Catholic and Protestant—but that participants in it were more responsive to the divine summons to fraternize with persons of whatever race or class. It was partly under the impulse to be evangelical instruments of the fraternization of the human race that the emissaries of the believers' churches have been so often conspicuously identified with missions. Like the missionary friars, they often spoke with more compassion about Jews, Muslims, and pagans than did the representatives of the established church. Some of the more spiritualizing or mystical of the Anabaptists and the Quakers considered it quite probable that the eternal Word and the omnipresent Holy Spirit could in various ways even in the absence of missionaries, bring about regeneration in the hearts of Turks and far-off American Indians. Along with the more intimate and disciplined brotherhood of the gathered Anabaptist conventicle there was also in their view a more embracing spiritual brotherhood. Zinzendorf was expressly concerned with such a brotherhood among peoples of all conditions and colors. He also considered each congregation or commune of the Moravian Brethren "an affiliate (Filial) of the eternal Mother City" until that time when the Commune of Christ would become visible on earth.

5. The Believers' Church and the Metaphor of Comradery

Comrades are, etymologically, roommates. The Roman equivalent was tentfellows within the comradery of men in arms sharing the same shelter (*conturbinium*). If we keep to the etymology, comrades are companions of the barracks; and the relationship of comrades is then not essentially different from that of the companions of the way, in a school, on a job. But soldiers are brought together for a common cause which takes precedence over any individual or personal concern. The church from the beginning has liked to think of itself as a spiritual militia. It organized in antiquity as though modeling itself in polemical parallelism to the Roman Empire. To the ultimate religious claims of Empire it refused to submit, risking martyrdom. The martyrs were the vanguard of the spiritual militia. Comradeship in spiritual arms suggests discipline, readiness for self-sacrifice, a far-flung strategy, all undergirded by an oath (*sacramentum*) of loyalty. A close examination of Judaeo-Christian pacifist groups from the Qumran Essenes to the Jehovah's Witnesses will show that their fellowship is in part that of comrades who have in various ways psychologically interiorized, sociologically transmuted, or eschatologically postponed the martial impulse.

The Hussite and especially the Taborite antecedents of the Unity of the Bohemian Brethren were quite bellicose. The Taborites under General John Ziska fought not only the Catholic crusaders but even the more conservative Utraquist Hussites. The Unity, however, formed in 1467, was programmatically pacifist; but, in sublimating their martial energies, the Brethren spiritualized their warfare in the eschatological context of the Lamb's War. There is something of this transmutation in Hans Hut, once a sympathizer with Thomas Müntzer in the Peasants' War, who became a major Anabaptist evangelist. In his only partial spiritualization of an imminent Armageddon, one is not entirely sure of a wholly benign role of the Turks in protecting the evangelical saints! In the siege of Münster by combined Catholic and Protestant forces, "eschatological" warfare was anticipated under duress and in self-defense.

An apocalyptic vision of warfare was not entirely absent in certain sectors of Quakerism in formation. Although there was not the slightest residue of belligerence in the Moravian Brethren, it is of interest that Zinzendorf provides us with the only instance encountered in my survey of the use of the designation "comrades." He spoke of the communes of the brotherhood as "shelters" (*Her-*

bergen) for the invisible church of Christ in a basic strategy of God "which would make of all the children of God throughout the world *comrades.*"

Although many of the believers' churches were pacifistic, many of them were not. It is quite possible that many in our conference would not include the Scottish Covenanters and the French Camisards, both of the eighteenth century, as representatives of the tradition of the believers' church. It is true that they were not in theory fully congregationalist in polity. It is true also that the eighteenth-century Covenanters or Cameronians (followers of Richard Cameron) very staunchly adhered to the principle of a national, though also a politically free, church. But then so did the Fifth Monarchy Baptists of the Cromwellian period. In any case, in terms of explicit faith and of popular polity and even clandestine conventicular loyalties and fervors, the Covenanters morphologically had much in common with the other groups we have been considering. The Covenanters called for a truly covenanted king, that is, a ruler who would acknowledge the limitations of his own royal power and the kingship of Christ over the church in his realm. The Covenanters would not tolerate any interference of the ruler, of Parliament, of lords and other patrons in the internal affairs of the church, her assembly and her lesser judicatories and convenings. The distinctive action of the eighteenth-century Covenanters was the renewal of the Scottish covenants of the seventeenth century, adapted to new circumstances and in all cases modeled on what they imagined took place in ancient Israel. The swearing or the renewal of the covenants was an act both of a group and of an individual, as with a theological student being readied for ordination. In the most notable of the covenant renewals on the lonely heights of Auchlinsaugh in Lanarkshire in July, 1722, the solemnities among cottars, farmers, a sprinkling of professional men and lesser lairds proceeded thus. The adapted covenants were renewed with a sermon, a pledge, an acknowledgment of national and personal sins, and an engagement to duties, the several stages of the renewal marked by a rising, by upraised hands, and by individual subscription of the bond. Fellow covenanters were in effect comrades determined to restore the sway of Christ the king to Scotland. The covenants in this manner were renewed many times in many places, and by many dissatisfied Presbyterian societies and sectaries, interestingly even by Covenanters (Reformed Presbyterians) in America, in Middle Octarara, Pennsylvania, November, 1743.

6. The Believers' Church and the Metaphor of Fellowship

A fellow is a *socius*, associated with others like himself in a *societas*. The experience of the believers' church, regardless of the terminology used, is that of a fellowship. The *Gemeinde* of Anabaptism was fundamentally a fellowship of those who had separated from the local parish, whether Protestantized or still Catholic. But we hear resonating in the word "fellowship" also the related meanings of fellow classmateship and compatriotism. The Unity of the Brethren was an expression of Czech nationalism as experienced by a certain class in society. And there was a touch of anti-German feeling not only in Hussitism in general but even among the pacifistic Brethren. On the other side, the Hutterite communitarian Anabaptists who streamed into Moravia from a large circle of Germanic lands (from the Tyrol to Hesse) into this Slavic landgraviate felt themselves to be German. Not only did they not have very much contact with surrounding Slavic Bohemians; but also, when a delegation of Polish Brethren with a view to developing their own communitarian settlement at Rakow on the Hutterite model approached the leaders of Hutterite communism, they were rebuffed, technically on theological and ecclesiological grounds, but one detects also a Germanic pride even in these Hutterite exiles. Compatriotism and also classmateship were indeed expressly a factor, when the Hutterite chroniclers include a reference to the bourgeois and even aristocratic elements in the Polish delegations to the Hutterite communes as a reason for suspecting their motive and even their capacity to live as true Christian communists! Yet among the Polish Brethren, there were several lords and former owners of many villages who had conspicuously freed their serfs and exchanged their gentleman's sword for a pilgrim's staff. Nevertheless, it is true, there was no strong move to include converted peasants in the fellowship of Rakow or elsewhere.

The class background of English Congregationalists and of the colonists of Plymouth and Massachusetts Bay is well known, with all the first families interconnected by education in Cambridge, intermarriage, and mutual commercial and planting interests. In New England there was also a class factor in the differentiation between the full communicant members of the church on the one side and on the other the pedobaptized but not "experimental" believers who lived in the parish—the town or subdivision thereof considered ecclesiastically—who supported the minister and the meetinghouse by taxes, and who attended the Sabbath service, but who were unable to profess that saving and lively faith which would qualify them for admittance to communion. The high proportion of "goodmen" and "goodwives," as they appear in the records, in the noncommunicant status in contrast to those entitled "mister" and "mistress" is an indication that something other than the Holy Spirit was helping to draw the lines in the Congregational theocracy. During the Great Awakening many of the converted withdrew from the town parish or society to form a society of their own, as Separate or Strict Congregationalists, some of these to become New Light Baptists. It is generally recognized that in the Separates the class factor was again operative.

Wesley called his groupings, never in his lifetime separated in **England from the Established Church,** "societies." The "sense of Christian fellowship" was especially experienced, said Wesley, and for the first time, when the society was divided into the neighborhood band and the larger class for bearing one another's burdens and caring for each other, "as they had daily a more intimate acquaintance."

What has just been recounted is perhaps more in the nature of describing the class factor in the rise of certain groups than the evidence that fellowship, classmateship, and compatriotism themselves supplied metaphors for the Believers' Church. But it is a major fact of ecclesiastical history, while many of the sixteenth-century and early seventeenth-century groups were disposed to retain the term "parish" and "congregation" (*Gemeinde*) and only unconsciously to restore the sojourner meaning of the scriptural original (*paroikia*: 1 Pet. 1:17), that with the rise of Pietism and its *ecclesiola in ecclesia*, the idea of the gathered church as a society or fellowship gained full ecclesiological status. The term[2] is preserved in the official designation of one denomination surviving from the second half of the seventeenth century, the Society of Friends. Where fellowship has become the regnant metaphor for the gathered church, such terms as "disfellowship," "withholding" and "withdrawing fellowship," and "dismissal" have come to the fore to betoken the moral rupture of fellowship.

7. *The Believers' Church and the Metaphor of Membership*

The verbs most in keeping with the metaphor of the church as a mystical **body with members are as follows:** for adhesion, "to join";

for separation therefrom, "to be cut off/away" or "to be severed" (Mt. 5:30, etc.). To the extent that the body of the church was also thought of in scriptural imagery as an olive tree or a tree of life with branches rather than members, the appropriate verbs would be "to ingraft" and "to cut off" (Rom. 11:22, etc.). Although both the corporal and the arboreal images were fully scriptural, they have generally suggested to free churchmen a rootedness in the orders of creation or a hierarchical structure and an elaborate articulation of organs and functions within the redemptive community not entirely consonant with the spiritual egalitarianism of most of the believers' churches. It is true that the Unity of Brethren managed a kind of apostolic succession in a celibate episcopate, that the neo-apostolic authority of Jakob Hutter was closely imitative of that of Paul, and that John Wesley was on principle as well as by temperament authoritarian in the supervision of the inner life not only of the societies but even of their intimate subdivisions, the bands and classes. It is quite probable also that the fact that, except with the medieval Unity of the Brethren, the Lord's Supper was largely observed in the free churches as a commemoration without any theory of the Real Presence tended to drive the corporal metaphor to the margin of the vocabulary of the believers' churches. It is true that in the communion observed by the South German Anabaptists the imagery of the one loaf occurs, along with the expectation that **the communicants would mutually support each other in the hour of persecution when the wine would become the blood of martyrdom.** It is true further that the doctrine of the celestial flesh of Christ peculiar to the Hofmannite and hence both **Münsterite and Mennonite Anabaptists (and to Schwenckfeld and** Michael Servetus) allowed them to think of the communion as the occasion for the interpenetration of the community of faith with divine substance. But in general the fact is that the believers' churches and kindred groupings we have been considering here all so stressed the accountability of each participant, man and woman, that the image of the church as a mystical body, though not entirely absent (since after all it had high scriptural credentials), has not been characteristic of the believers' churches. One would have to make an exception of Zinzendorf's community, where the imagery abounded of the body of Christ, particularly with reference to his heart and his wounds, and of the symbol of that mystical body, the Lamb slaughtered.

8. The Believers' Church and the Metaphor of Co-Citizenship

We earlier recognized that there are two political images that begin in Scripture and remain interrelated throughout Christian history: (1) the City—at once Jerusalem that is above and the transmutation of eternal Rome and (2) the Kingdom—the Messianic Kingdom foreseen by Israel's prophets, transposed and augmented by the tradition of Christianized Roman imperialism in the conception of the Roman Empire as Holy, the last of the four earthly monarchies before the Fifth Monarchy of Christ in the Millennium. At the time of the Reformation this waning concept was revived under Charles, fifth in succession to Charlemagne. In this era the nearly sovereign city-state had become a political reality again, the imperial city, free or freed of its prince or bishop in temporalities, based on its own elaborate civic constitution with social checks and balances, and annually sanctioned by an oath of allegiance pledged by all male citizens. Despite the potency of the two political metaphors of kingdom and city in the long history of Christianity, there has been little disposition either in the traditions of the given or the gathered churches to speak of believers either as citizens of the heavenly City or as subjects of the Kingdom yet to be. Our phrase "co-citizenship" is, therefore, admittedly an artificial construct to suggest one of the ten avowed or implied metaphors of relationship in the evolution of the church as a community. As for the image of kingdom, it barely appears in our phrase "the *royal* and mutual priesthood of all believers." Yet the conflated political metaphors of kingdom and city are fully as important for the gathered as for the given church, perhaps even more so. The clue to their functioning in the believers' churches is the frequency of the refusal to swear the civic oath or, in the case of groups which did not object to this, the supplementation of the civic oath with the scriptural owning or swearing of a covenant.

The indisposition of the Unity of the Brethren to swear to any kind of oath was largely in keeping with the Dominical mandate (Mt. 5:34, etc.), although this disinclination was one with their partial or complete withdrawal from worldly society. In the case of the Anabaptist refusal to swear an oath, it is quite possible that in addition to the scriptural inhibition there operated also the feeling that believer's baptism was the constitutive act whereby one at hazard of property, profession, and even life became a *Bundesgenosse*, a fellow of the covenant of the good conscience (cf. Luther's translation of 1 Pet. 3:21). As such it was the counterpart of the annual civic oath but, of course, as a testimony of faith it was once for all. In any case the Anabaptist refusal to swear the annual oath is the closest counterpart of the refusal of the pre-Constantinian Christians to offer incense before the imperial statue as a symbolic act of loyalty to the imperial government. For like the early Christians, the Anabaptists felt themselves to be a people whose citizenship was in heaven (Phil. 3:20).

As in the ancient city-state, so in the Anabaptist conventicle the punishment for disloyalty was banishment or exile. The lesser and the greater ban had been observed (and also much abused) within the medieval church, the lesser ban being excommunication, or deprivation of the right to holy communion, and the greater ban involving the civil interdict of a person or region. For Anabaptists who regarded themselves as withdrawn from the world and as nonparticipant in its temporal institutions, the lesser and the greater ban came to the same thing, excommunication having the psychological effect of exile. An erring spouse, for example, was banned by the Anabaptists "bed and board." The discipline of the ban was regarded as the equally important counterpart of believer's baptism in the maintenance of the integrity of the believers' community.

The Hutterite *Gemeinde* was a complete commonwealth with chosen servants of necessity (*Diener der Notdurft*) alongside the servants of the word (*Diener des Wortes*). The Hutterite communitarians built bridges, engaged in collective farming and industry, sent emissaries abroad for new recruits and for parleys with the Moravian magnates, their protectors. The Münsterite Anabaptists were an even more complete commonwealth. The episcopal city's constitution evolved under charismatic leadership from Holland into a theocracy, which at length claimed to be a kingdom of potentially universal sway. Hence the use of an adapted imperial orb as symbol of the onset in Münster of Christ's universal messianic reign among the saints.

The immersionist anti-trinitarian Polish Brethren, scrupulously pacifistic, considered themselves, as individual converts and as a community, called upon to imitate Christ as prophet, priest, and king in a way which involved suffering. He "having suffered for us left us an example" that Christians might die to the world in immersion and rise with him to become "an elect race, kings, and priests." The noblemen among the Polish Brethren tried to carry out their duties at the royal national diet as subjects first of Christ's kingdom, and they always counseled against war and refused, themselves, to use the sword even in self-defense.

Congregationalism, never pacifistic, fulfilled in New England its ideal. While each congregation was independent of every other, ideally the magistrates for the colony as a whole could be drawn only from experiential members of a gathered church, not from the merely baptized supporters of the religious establishment of a town. Moreover, at the beginning only the experiential Christians had the franchise. Because there was thus a real *religious* unity beyond the separate congregation, the phrase "Zion" emerged as a collective term for the unity among not only the congregations spiritually but also temporally among all inhabitants of the colony (later, the province).

When in the course of the Great Awakening the Separates felt that authentic congregationalism had disappeared, Isaac Backus (who passed successively from the Standing Order Congregationalists, with the Strict Congregationalists, to the Baptists) declared: "[T]hose who hold the church to be national cannot build with those who hold it to be congregational." Little more than a century after settlement, some in New England found it appropriate to level against the Congregational churches the same charge that the Congregational puritans had once leveled against the Established Church in England. The depoliticizing of the new believers' church and the separation of it from the church and tax structure of the Standing Order did not mean, however, the disappearance of the political metaphor for the New Light churches. The Separate brethren in their Killingly Convention in Connecticut in 1781, for example, are on record for using the word "subjection," which one might have expected to be used more commonly in all believers' groups. They declared that all who submitted themselves "in a professed Heart *Subjection* to Jesus Christ, as their rightful Lord and Sovereign, to be ruled and governed by his Law prescribed in his Word," were to be accepted as "friends of Christ."

The Covenanters of Scotland were, of course, from the outset very political in their vocabulary. The kingdom they were determined to bring into a covenanted relationship with the God of Israel was the realm of Scotland, but the source of their courageous conviction was their consciousness of their being subjects of Jesus Christ. Even a children's covenant subscribed in Pentland parish in 1683 made clear the sense of Christ's sovereignty taking precedence over the authority of any hereditary king, when it boldly declared of the true Kirk that His foes "have banished her king Christ out of the land, yet

He will arise and avenge His children's blood." Descendants, mayhap, of these children in colonial Pennsylvania were prophetically political in the renewal of the covenants in Middle Octarara when—with reference to the, from their point of view, uncovenanted William III of Orange—they declared in 1743: "We likewise state our testimony against the instalment of William Henry [at the time of Glorious Revolution], because he had neither national nor scriptural qualifications, but exactly contrary thereunto." The ancient church may have been an *imperium in imperio*; the stout Covenanters constituted a covenanted *regnum in regno!*

In Methodism Wesley himself was too much of a Tory to encourage the use of the more political metaphors in describing the church. In defying the lord bishop of Bristol and reluctantly resorting to outdoor preaching, Wesley, however, made the prophetic claim: "The whole world is my parish!" His was also a disciplined parish! The morally erring participants in his societies were warned thrice in the scriptural fashion. If penitent, they were admitted to the penitents' band, pending satisfactory amendment of life and the validation of their love-feast ticket. Though Wesley enjoined obedience to all set in authority, he himself defied it in the cause of an evangelical church; and his self-disciplining followers eventually became skilled in the way of politics.

9. *The Believers' Church and the Metaphor of Elective Confederacy*

The idea of the church as a people in covenant is perhaps the most distinctively Jewish conception, just as the idea of the church as a communion is probably the most distinctively New Testament conception. (The idea of the church as a prospective kingdom draws, of course, equally from both Testaments.) The idea of the covenant is linked with the idea of God's choosing a people of his own and deigning to enter into a special relationship with them. In his mysterious purpose the elect people are allowed to do something pleasing to him, even as omnipotent. In the sophistication of medieval Scholasticism, covenantal theology or federalism came to be grounded in a distinction made between God's absolute potency and his ordered or ordinary power *(potentia absoluta et ordinata/ ordinaria)*. Election was, in a sense, grounded in God's absolute power; for salvation was understood as not depending upon human merit which could never be "condignly" sufficient to merit grace, although conceivably it could be "congruously" sufficient according to the standards set for frail human capacity and proneness to aberration by

God in his ordinary power. The sacraments of the church and also its precepts and counsels were the ordinary means established by God's ordering power to enable the elect to receive his grace at least congruously. Election and a federal theology of pacts (*pacta, foedera*) and promises (*promissiones*) thus already existed in sectors of late medieval Scholasticism when the Reformation of Luther restored the Bible, both in the original languages and in the vernacular, as sole authority. The federal theology of Scholasticism was tremendously vivified and expanded by renewed contact with Old Testament federalism and in the fresh understanding of Christianity itself as a new covenant or testament. This development, among the magisterial reformers, was most marked in Ulrich Zwingli, partly because in the Confederation of the mountain and city cantons of Switzerland there was a political counterpart of the covenant that held together the tribal amphictyony of ancient Israel. The covenant ideal also functioned among the Anabaptists, and then, by way of John Knox, the Swiss ideas reached both England and Scotland. We have already seen how in Scotland covenantalism functioned as an extension of the political metaphor of the kingdom. The covenantal idea is in many ways a richer concept than the kingdom and city metaphors because it says something both about God and about the elect and covenanted believer which activates the individual as well as the group and at the same time satisfactorily correlates God's omnipotent justice with his mercy and forgiving love. Thus a church which understands itself in terms of an elective confederacy is different from a church that thinks of itself wholly in terms of the more purely political metaphors of (messianic) kingdom and (heavenly) city.

The Unity of the Brethren, belonging still to the medieval world, retaining in a Donatist sense all seven sacraments and a celibate clergy, did not make much of the covenantal idea. The Anabaptists, finding the covenant of the remnant in the Old Testament and in the New Testament baptism on confession of sin and as a testimony to faith, readily called themselves *Bundesgenossen*, fellows of the covenant (of a good conscience). Emphasizing man's freedom to work out his salvation in fear and trembling, with his will long ago proleptically liberated by the obedience of the Second Adam, the Anabaptists minimized God's primordial election in the tradition of Augustine as renewed and intensified by Luther and tended to interpret the elective aspect of the elective confederacy of the baptized in terms of the visible chosen remnant with the covenant written on the heart. Among the Hutterites the whole community was an instrument of salvation, likened to Noah's Ark floating on believer's baptism, an elect company in the sense of their adhering to God's commandments as renewed in Christ.

The Polish Brethren, in contrast, partly because of Swiss Reformed and even Italian Reformed elements in their makeup, adhered to the Augustinian doctrine of election. Accordingly, baptismal immersion among them did not acquire the covenantal character of believer's baptism prevalent among the German Anabaptists of all kinds. With the Quakers all sacraments and ordinances were interiorized or disallowed. Hence there was no oath or covenant. But they did speak of themselves as a Peculiar People (cf. 1 Pet. 2:9) and alluded often knowingly and yet somewhat obscurely to their being the mystical seed of Abraham, David, and Christ the King.

With the Congregationalist puritans the covenantal idea, as enriched by Zwingli, Calvin, and Knox, developed along lines somewhat different from what we have already noted among the Scottish Presbyterians and especially the Covenanters of the eighteenth century. In old England there took place within some of the most advanced Puritan Established Church parishes of Congregational convictions a church covenant, by which the "experimental" members of the parish constituted themselves a righteous remnant within the nominally Christian parish of baptized adults and children. In New England the churches were gathered by the owning of the covenant exclusively on the part of experimental believers who could publicly testify to a lively and saving faith. On the supposition that their offspring were presumptively of the covenant (for in their Calvinistic view Christians could not have privileges inferior to those of the covenant under the old dispensation which did include the progeny of all good Israelites), the covenanted communicants of the gathered church were entitled to have their children baptized into the privileges of the local church in covenant. However, it was originally understood that on growing up, these "baptized children of the covenant" would not be permitted to partake of the communion in covenant until they in their turn could publicly testify to the same lively faith experienced by their parents. In an extraordinary way, almost unique in Church history, these Congregationalists were working not only with a traditional pair of terms—the one invisible, holy, catholic church of the elect and the (local) visible church however constituted—but also with a doublet of superimposed churches of their own divising, namely, the local church proper gathered in the meetinghouse for communion and the larger "society," later called "parish," made up of the baptized children and also many adults who could not claim to have experienced a lively faith. Eventually this arrangement was compromised when, to take care of the ever growing number of children of the original birthright baptizands, the latter, who in advanced parenthood could still not profess to have had a saving experience, were allowed nevertheless to have their infants (now of the third generation among the settlers) baptized in hope and by a compromise known as "the Half-Way Covenant." It was in the context of the ebbing ardor and necessary compromises in the ideal of a pure church, for which the Congregational puritans had ventured all in the New World, that the revival of the heart and will in great outpourings of the Spirit became the counterpart in New England and elsewhere of the renewal of the covenants in the Scottish tradition. The revival experience not only qualified one for membership but, as we have noted already, also created the basis for the withdrawal of whole companies of revived believers from the established church-parishes with their "graceless communion" administered by "unconverted ministers" to form the Separate congregations modeled on the original ideal. Separate Congregationalists and the still more consequent Separate Baptists who issued from them readily spoke of themselves as the elect in Zion, thinking of themselves as the righteous remnant in a Puritan Israel that had become worldly. This network of Separates spun out by the Great Awakening were, morphologically, the counterpart of the network of "connection" among Methodist societies, which Wesley continued to think of till his death as primarily the Evangelical *ecclesiolae* within the rationalist, moralistic Established Church of England. Wesley, being Arminian rather than Calvinist in his doctrine of election, was however not disposed, as were the New England Separates, to think of his Methodist Connection in terms of an elective confederacy. He left that to the strict Calvinistic Covenanters of Scotland!

10. The Believers' Church and the Metaphor of Communion

Communion in general is not so much a metaphor as a directly experienced reality of the Christian life, whether in the given or the gathered churches. But communion has something of the character also of the metaphorical by which we have seen the church over the generations attempting to understand and explain itself as a community. In an historical survey of the believers' church in community, the meaning of communion might well be considered the most important of all our topics; and it therefore fittingly comes at the end of our account, although there may be some who would feel that we have already exhausted all the possibilities and that nothing more that

137

is essential need be said. But the fact is that communion and related terms have several religious meanings. The Latin word behind it has given the Germanic word *Gemeinde*, which means variously "parish," "congregation," and "commune" or even "commonwealth," if we think of Hutterite usage. There are basically three *foci* of action and experience in the differentiation of the usages of the word both in English and other languages. There are (1) the sharing in the eucharistic elements, (2) the sharing in gifts of the Holy Spirit, and (3) the sharing in the goods of life. The first is eucharistic communion and by extension the recognition of fellowship with others far and near, departed and yet to be. Eucharistic communion leads over, then, into the second meaning, that of the communion of saints. The latter is based not only on the eucharistic elements but also upon the activity of the Holy Spirit, taking of the things of Christ and drawing believers to one another in him. In many groupings of the believers' churches, especially at their inception, and in the monasteries, convents, and sodalities of the given churches, eucharistic communion and the communion of saints may come to mean also more than even a common purse, namely, a spiritual commonwealth. Although Christian communism, a recurrent phenomenon, represents the fullest expression of our third meaning of communion, we should be prepared to recognize its presence in a variety of less programmatic ways in which Christians have shared each other's burdens in magnanimity and compassion. We should also note that the opposite of communicating with others (in the eucharistic elements) either liturgically or by prayerful intention is to excommunicate. This is usually the consequence of a prior failure to commune in the Holy Spirit and thus to share in the same love and doctrinal illumination vouchsafed by the Spirit, while the intensification of this spiritual communing leads many who no longer take thought as to "mine" and "thine" to communize their goods and services.

Among the Unity of the Brethren the most distinctive characteristic was *jednota* (unity) in the sense of communing with each other in spiritual fellowship and the apostolic communism of the ministers and the "perfect." A readiness to share some goods in common with a common purse was characteristic of all the Anabaptists, although it was only among the Hutterites and the Münsterites that communal sharing led to a communalized system of production and distribution. The Hutterites lived very much as in Israeli *kibbutzim*. The Münsterites carried their communal life, supposedly on an apostolic model, into marriage. As for communion in the

Holy Spirit, it has often gone unnoticed that there were pentecostal outpourings among the Anabaptists comparable to the later revivals. This phenomenon, including glossolalia, is documented notably among the Anabaptists in Appenzell in Switzerland and the circle around Obbe Philips, a group tributary to both the Münsterites and the Mennonites. Belief in the presence of the Holy Spirit in their conventicular interpretation of Scripture was the scriptural sanction for the egalitarian *Sitzerrecht* (see above). The presence of the Holy Spirit with each detached member of the fellowship was also scripturally assured whenever he should be called upon to speak before magistrates. Although the Anabaptists of all kinds were in controversy with several kinds of Spiritualizers on their left, like the Schwenckfeldians and the Franckists, we should not underestimate the extent to which the renewing experience of the outpouring Holy Spirit of the latter days also sustained them. Some Anabaptists, gathering frequently in local and regional synods, looked for some kind of council, which, with the outpouring of pentecostal flames, would be the eschatological counterpart at once of the pentecostal assembly in the upper room and the apostolic council in Jerusalem. The phenomenon of glossolalia is also reported among the Polish Brethren, who had more than one communal settlement like that at Rakow. The freeing of serfs by noble converts to the Brethren and the donning by them of simple clothes were other expressions of the communitarian and egalitarian thrust.

Both the Anabaptists and the Polish Brethren adhered to the view that the soul dies with the body, the latter to be reformed and reanimated in the final miracle of the general resurrection. Hence there was among these groups nothing of what could be called the literal communion of the saints. In contrast, with the Moravian Brethren the full meaning of *jednota* was communion with the departed. Some of their most distinctive services were held at Easter and at other times in the burying grounds. At the elaborate eucharistic liturgies the minister wore a talar or sacramental garment which was understood to be also a gravecloth. The intensely joyful, loud, and protracted singing at worship was conceived by the Moravian Brethren as the principal way of establishing spiritual unity between the living and the departed saints.

The eucharistic communion of the Covenanters took place in a manner already worked out by John Knox with long tables extending consecutively into the nave of the sanctuary or over the heath, with the communicants seated as at a meal, and with a "fencing" of the tables to withhold communion from any who had not sworn the covenant at the appropriate times or who were found otherwise unworthy of the Lord's table.

In Methodism, because of Wesley's enjoining participants in his societies to attend upon the holy communion of the Established parishes or in the dissenting chapels, the quarterly love feast or *agape* gained unusual prominence, modeled indirectly upon what survives thereof in the New Testament but more directly on the usage of the Moravians who observed both love feasts and eucharists.

For all the importance of eucharistic communion in the churches mentioned and also among the early Congregationalists who made such a sharp distinction between, as it were, the society of the baptized and the church of the communicants, it is of some interest that "communion" has never established itself metaphorically as an alternative term for church or denomination, as it has elsewhere, notably among the Episcopalians.

Conclusion

Under the heading of ten scriptural metaphors of togetherness and natural metaphors of community Christianized, we have now sampled the institutions and vocabulary of a limited number of believers' churches and others of kindred constitution or motivation. It has been an exercise in the metaphors of morphology and an attempt to ascertain how ecclesial imagery shapes communities, as well as how the shape of a community of faith produces a special terminology. We have not so much described the constitution of believers' churches as attended to the profusion of terms by which they have variously sought to describe themselves or separate acts and aspects of their togetherness. Although the survey has made no claim to completeness even for the groups selected as illustrations, running up and down a few of the corridors of the believers' churches in the last five hundred years, we have gotten a few glimpses of what the believing community is and was.

It is and was, first of all, not primarily a community of explicit belief. In a way, the term "Believers' Church" puts an unrepresentative stress on belief and implies incorrectly that the given churches are, in contrast, weak in believers. Actually it is the given churches which historically have placed the greatest stress on credal belief. The believers' churches so-called really stress far more than belief, namely: obedience, purity, simplicity, discipleship, covenantal accountability, mutual support, mutual discipline and mutual, though also exclusive, love.

As a consequence of the quest for holiness, the so-called believers' churches are also leavers' churches, communities of come-outers. Those in the tradition of the given or sacramental church with its order and apostolic continuities should see this major characteristic of the believers' church in its formative stage not only negatively, as they do, pillorying it as sectarianism, factionalism, rigorism. For the leavers' church can lay claim in its own way to a venerable tradition which will have to include Abraham leaving Ur of the Chaldees; the children of Israel leaving bondage to Egypt; various remnants within Israel led by the fiery and even vindictive prophet of the still small voice; the disciples of Jesus who were expressly bidden to let kith and kindred go and to leave even the dead to bury the dead; the true or new Israel, as they liked to call themselves, leaving old Israel under the Apostle of the Gentiles; the churches of the magisterial Reformation, repudiating the indulgent penitential amplitude of the basilica of St. Peter's; still later the Congregationalists, who left the Established Church of England; likewise the Separate Baptists who left the Congregational Standing Order in New England; and finally the Freewill Baptists under Benjamin Randall who left the Calvinistic or Regular Baptists in New Hampshire.

The believers' church as the leavers' church is also a free church. It is because of the similarity between the various Calvinistic secession churches in Scotland, Holland, Switzerland, and elsewhere and the believers' churches more narrowly defined that we have presumed to include the Covenanters, the Congregationalists, and the Methodists in the foregoing survey. The freedom of the free churches has often been a combination of sensitivity to the freedom of individual conscience, the resolution not to allow the state or any of its instrumentalities to interfere with the inner life of the community of faith, and a suspicion of non-ecclesial factors in any overdevelopment of the structures above the level of the local congregation. This last characteristic would not have been true of Wesley, but it would characterize the Free Methodists and the Nazarenes and other denominations in the Wesleyan succession of Arminian piety. Regrettably, the complex of sensitivities to both secular and "sacred" interference from without has not immunized the believers' church from those emotions and machinations that can build up in a single congregation of even fully covenanted members overwatchful of each other. Its purity is always precarious, because in each stage in the devel-

141

opment of a believers' community the dynamics of social and temperamental differentiation create new sensitivities as well as "laxism." The conflict between the prophetic and the routinized is often too easily disposed of in terms of the conflict between the rigorists and the laxists, a tension almost as old as Christianity, to the advantage of the rigorists.

Rather, then, than the believers' church, or the gathered church, or the free church, or the pure church, or the rigorist church, it might be best to speak of the pilgrims' church. Pilgrims come from somewhere, they carry something with them, and they seek "the city which hath foundations, whose builder and maker is God." Since this questing mobility is increasingly characteristic in our time of those churches we have called "given," perhaps we can descry converging several bands of pilgrim churches, constituting the New Testament People, God's ongoing Israel in the spirit. Themselves increasingly understanding of and theologically concerned about God's providential guidance of Israel according to the flesh, the New Testament People, given, gathered, and yet to be gathered in, are beholding a new vision of God's purpose for them and new ways in their pilgrimage through contemporary history.

William G. MacDonald

6

A PEOPLE IN COMMUNITY:

Theological Interpretation

In the person and message of William Graham MacDonald the Conference on the Concept of the Believers' Church received an authentic and responsible word from the latest of the major strands in the heritage of believers' churches—the Pentecostal Movement. A native of Virginia, Mr. MacDonald was educated at South-Eastern Bible College, Florida Southern College, and Wheaton College and received the BD and STM degrees from Gordon Divinity School and Concordia Theological Seminary, respectively. An ordained minister in the Assemblies of God, he was instructor in South-Eastern Bible College, Lakeland, Florida, from 1959 to 1962 and assistant professor of theology, Greek and Hebrew in Central Bible College, Springfield, Missouri, from 1962 to 1966. At present he is a candidate for the ThD degree at Southern Baptist Theological Seminary and serves as pastor of the La Grange, Kentucky, Assembly of God. A member of the Evangelical Theological Society and the National Association of Professors of Hebrew, Mr. MacDonald is the author of *Glossolalia in the New Testament.*

Mr. MacDonald's address constituted an exposition both of the post-Pentecostal New Testament church as the Community of the Holy Spirit and of modern Pentecostalism's distinctive understanding of the resurrection "afflation" of the Holy Spirit as different from the Pentecostal "effusion" of the Holy Spirit and the charismatic gifts. In the former he specified ten distinctive marks of the Community of the Spirit, including both formative characteristics and differences from other alternate ecclesiological views. In the latter he sharply distinguished John 20:22 from Acts 2—a distinction analogous to that between Jesus' begetting by the Spirit and Jesus' anointing by the Spirit at the outset of his public ministry—and concluded that baptism in or with the Spirit was used in the New Testament to describe both regeneration and charismatic enduement.

The response to Mr. MacDonald's address was given by Dr. Wayne E. Ward, professor of Christian theology, Southern Baptist Theological Seminary. Dr. Ward commended Mr. MacDonald's "careful analysis of the psychological, sociological, and cultural factors in community," his "rejection of any of these as determinative for true Christian community," and his insistence upon an "ontological" basis for Christian community—"the presence of the Holy Spirit who makes possible the existence of the church." But Dr. Ward strongly rejected Mr. MacDonald's distinction between the "afflation of the Spirit" and the "effusion of the Spirit." "Most modern New Testament scholars believe that the afflation passage in John 20 is a Johannine interpretation of the same event which Luke interprets in Acts 2," he declared. On the contrary, when treating these two passages Mr. MacDonald "begins to marshal biblical texts in such a way as to ignore all questions of sources, dating, authorship, and theological context—not even to mention the stickier problems raised by form and redaction criticism." Furthermore, it "cannot be flatly assumed that all one hundred twenty of the brethren in Acts 1:15 were 'filled with the Holy Spirit and began to speak with other tongues' (2:4), for the latter may refer only to "the eleven apostles and Matthias." Dr. Ward's critique reached its climax in these words:

> I am convinced that in the entire last half of his paper Mr. MacDonald has superimposed upon the Scriptures a preconceived theological system which he has not derived from the Scriptures by sound biblical exegesis. The reason I am so sure that I recognize this in him is because we Baptists also excel in this fine art, and I have had much experience in it myself. We do the greatest honor to the Scriptures and to the divine authority of the written Word when we submit ourselves to the rigorous disciplines of serious biblical exegesis, historical criticism, and spiritual interpretation, even if it shatters our theological systems again and again.

For example, Dr. Ward insisted:

> When Mr. MacDonald says that *glossolalia* are mentioned some eighteen times in Acts and First Corinthians, he is wrong eighteen times. It is never mentioned anywhere, and it is a flagrant example of reading an idea into the biblical text. Such introduction of external theological assumptions into the text itself does violence to the Scriptures.

The MacDonald address and the Ward response brought the Conference on the Concept of the Believers' Church to one of its crucial moments. How are the demands of rigorous biblical studies to be related to the brotherly recognition of the work of God's Spirit in a new expression of the Believers' Church? Dr. John Howard Yoder spoke to the issue:

> I am not sure whether the Anabaptists . . . or the Campbellites sixty years after their origins or the Friends would have come already this far in talking the language of their persecutors. The Pentecostal Movement is in our age the restoration movement protesting against the establishment which all the rest of us represent. It is a test case of our capacity to be the Believers' Church to find a new way of dealing with a new restitution movement as the establishment of other ages did not do.

Moreover, by virtue of the lay-character of the Believers' Church it must be accepted, Dr. Yoder observed,

> that the predominant theology of the Believers' Church must be a layman's theology, so that the critical questions which the scholar must ask [come] after and not before the acceptance of this mode of theologizing.

Dr. Yoder continued:

> We have all said that it is a part of a Believers' Church vision to expect further leading, not to be tied down by creeds or institutions or sacerdotal systems or political systems, but to expect the Word of God to be the source of new vitality through the reality of the Holy Spirit. . . . Here new languages are being found and used in the explicit confidence that everything said is to be tested by the Scriptures and by whether it is the testimony of Christ. And we who have been saying that the Spirit is going to use new methods find ourselves embarrassed by the humbleness of the methods He has chosen to use.

Mr. MacDonald commented on his address:

> I have spoken today in such a way as, I believe, truly represents the millions of people there are now who have gone on in their experience of Christianity, from their beginning in Christ by the new birth . . . by the Spirit into a deeper experience of the Lord, call it what you will. . . . We have in Pentecostal ranks virtually no theologians, and I speak . . . from a perspective that is . . . prejudiced to the simple meaning of Scripture.

The community of faith is a people polarized around the Lord Jesus Christ. No metaphor by itself is sufficient to divulge the nature of this "great mystery . . . Christ and the church" (Eph. 5:32). [1] The intricate and intimate biblical figures of husband/wife (Eph. 5:28-32) and head/body (Eph. 1:22, 23; 5:25) point toward the preeminence of Him in whom our faith stands and through whom we stand. Believers experience "community" not merely within the realm of the human spirit, that is, with one another as religious colleagues, but uniquely in a sense of togetherness with Jesus Christ—a communion which is of Him and through Him and to Him (Rom. 11:26). The mystery, however, lies in the fact that believing people are at once *in* Him "as members of his body" (Eph. 5:30) and, conversely, He is *in* them, making among them His home, His temple (Eph. 1:21, 22).

How do individuals who repent of their sins and believe in the Lord Jesus Christ immediately find themselves to be "A People in Community"? If we search for the answer on the psychological level, we will discover several well-traveled roads, but though they appear to be going in the right direction, they do not lead to the mystery of Christian *koinonia* (1 Cor. 1:9; 10:16; Phil. 2:1; 1 Jn. 1:3, 7).

Misgivings About Community

On the level of human life we recognize the fact that people of common experience tend to cluster about that experience. The survivors of Dachau, though of different nationalities and races, know a kind of "community" in that they share a common history of physical and psychological excruciation. Veterans of Bataan and Corregidor will gather from time to time to reminisce. Yet in the most emotive gatherings of those who have shared the same or similar experiences there remains a degree of emptiness, an upper ceiling of the human spirit, whether the "ingroup" numbers only two or three or up in the multiplied thousands.

What experience is more traumatic and universal than human birth? Yet its failure as an experience to unite all men in a community of brotherhood is well known. When we speak of a mutual experience or similar independent experiences, we recognize a certain unitive power of experience. It brings together people in the present because of their past. But it gives no guarantee of the future and is continually eroded in its unitive function, if experiences of a different nature intervene.

Artists, hobbyists, laborers, fadists, interest groups, and the like have their associations on the basis of some mental, moral, or monetary principle. But their coteries or communities, if we may use the word in this loose sense, ultimately have their roots in an impersonal principle or object, though surely it may have to do with such very personal concerns as civil rights or poverty. The principle may be in the persons concerned, but the persons cannot be in the impersonal principle, as believers are in Christ. This means that, if an individual accepts the pivotal principle, he may belong to the group without necessarily "accepting" as persons every member of the group except in the most general way. In fact, he may come to scorn certain individuals as persons, while maintaining with them only the tenuous tie of one or more mutual interests. Even in those instances where an oath of allegiance is taken to the group and its members as in underworld gangs and certain secret societies, the kind of loyalty engendered is no greater than the strength the human spirit can provide.

Now the visible Church is also amenable to psychological assessment of the nature of its community, inasmuch as the Church is composed of human beings. It has in common the experience of regeneration and therefore can be said to have a certain quality of community on the basis of similar religious experience. The cohesive factor, however, is not so much the psychological side of the experience as it is its divine content. Its true source and nature lie beyond all permutations of the human elements. Too often the Church, like human associations, either looks backward to mutual experiences or forward from the present to humanly conceived goals, without honoring its transcendent Lord in the midst, who is the whole cause and *telos* of its existence. Any church among the churches whose total life can be explained completely by psychological principles, has at that point, if not before, ceased — if it ever was — being part of the Risen Lord's Community. For the Believers' Church is unique and transcendent in that at its center is a "great mystery." It can be accounted for neither by the sum of its human parts nor by a solely psychological appraisal of its men and movements.

Nor can the nature of this community of the faithful be abstracted from the psychological understanding of the fact that there are mysteries in both its doctrines and structure. Common possession of a secret does serve to unite people. The ancient mystery religions and modern secret societies illustrate this fact. But the difference is that the Church preaches her secrets openly and does not conserve them as esoterica. "If our gospel is veiled, it is veiled only to those who are perishing" (2 Cor. 4:3). Leaders in the churches serve as "stewards of the mysteries of God" (1 Cor. 4:1). They serve well when they proclaim "the whole counsel of God" (Acts 20:27). All attempts, therefore, to classify the Church in human categories on the basis of the unifying power of a secret faith fail to find the requisite biblical data to substantiate such a claim. The mystery of the Church does not lie in secret faith formulas, initiation rites, or rules of community; it lies deeper in its ontological structure.

Moorings in Pneumatology

We must ask again the question of the nature of the community of the believing people. So far we have discussed it only in its character as a "great mystery . . . Christ and the church," and noted the mutual indwelling of the two parties. In this pursuit the Virgin Mary's simple and sincere question—"How can this be, since I have no husband?" (Lk. 1:34)—captures the spirit of our question about the union of Christ and His Church. What she sought to know concerning the Incarnation, we seek to comprehend concerning the Church, which is "the fulness of him who fills all in all" (Eph. 1:23). We ask: How can this be, since ". . . all who received him, who believed in his name . . . were born, not of blood nor of the will of the flesh nor of the will of man, but of God" (Jn. 1:12,13)?

The answer to our question of the unity of Christ and the Church, and therefore of the Church's community in Him, has a remarkable correspondence to the revelatory response received by Mary to her question as to how the Son of God could dwell in her womb. The

Incarnation with all its mystery and glory—like that of Christ's presence in the New Humanity in Him—was to come into being by "The Holy Spirit . . . , the power of the Most High" (Lk. 1:35). Similarly sublime words express the spiritual constitution of the community of Christ. The Apostle Paul states unequivocally that believers have their community in the Holy Spirit (Rom. 8:8b, 9):

> and those who are in the flesh cannot please God. But you are not in the flesh, you are in the Spirit, if the Spirit of God really dwells in you. Any one who does not have the Spirit of Christ does not belong to him.

In view of the continuous indwelling of the Holy Spirit in all bona fide believers, we now must speak ontologically of the Church as the Community of the Spirit.

Three theses emerge here which are foundational to further consideration of *he koinonia tou hagiou pneumatos* (2 Cor. 13:14b) as it is experienced in the Community of the Spirit. They are:

(1) A Christian is one who has the Spirit of Christ dwelling in him. [2]

(2) The "fellowship of (or "participation in") the Holy Spirit" (2 Cor. 13:14b) is the essential basis of the corporate community of believers, because in their unity with Christ (Eph. 5:30) they become "members one of another" (Eph. 4:25) in Christ's body (1 Cor. 12:13).

(3) The *newness* of the New Covenant is contained precisely in theses one and two in that God has moved into His new temple so as to dwell in every personal unit (1 Cor. 3:16; 6:19) as well as unitively in the whole structure (Eph. 2:20-22).

Regeneration means "Christ in you," present by His Holy Spirit, cleansing and creating us anew with the breath of His life. By no means is this new creative work of the Holy Spirit to be compared to a general contractor who builds a house, then leaves it to its owners. Just as the Spirit of God hovered over the natural creation during the creative process (Gen. 1:2) and then remained as God immanent "in whom we live and move and have our being" as natural men (Acts 17:28), so in regeneration—the new creation—we must say that the Risen Lord is *received* and *remains* in the human spirit by the Holy Spirit. Regeneration, therefore, should not be given any definition that excludes the continuous presence of the One who works. It is no less than an impartation of the Spirit of God to dwell in man's spirit as his life. The New Testament witness to this fact is abundant: Jn. 20:22; Acts 2:38: Rom. 8:9; 1 Cor. 3:16; 12:13; Gal. 3:2; 4:6; 5:25; 2 Tim. 1:14; 1 Jn. 3:24; 4:13; Jude 19, 20. Paul abbreviated his testimony down to the heart of the matter in these concise words: "For to me to live is Christ"(Phil. 1:21). If we should ask how this is, we hear him reply: "Christ . . . lives in me" (Gal. 2:20). In ontological terms we must say therefore that two spirits are present in one being. The "Thou" is no longer exclusively "there" but "here" *in* me as well. This is the "good news" actualized. This becomes the really new in the New Covenant.

The "Missing Link" in Old Testament Community

It was not this way in the Old Testament period. There was always justification by God's grace by faith in that grace, to be sure. It consisted of "acceptance" by God of a chosen people but without their having the Spirit's inner witness of that acceptance. They had to depend on external signs and God's words of acceptance spoken by the "charismatics." A charismatic was one called to a direct encounter with the Holy Spirit of God. He did not seek out God for his "gifts," but God sought him out and endowed him to minister with the ability that God alone gives.

Israel always had to travel to the appointed place to meet God or, at the very least, to pray in the direction of His sanctuary. It is not so much that God was confined to His temple—for, indeed, this was impossible (Acts 7:48; 17:24)—but God's people as a whole were confined in their experience of Him. Their law which does not rest on faith (Gal. 3:12) could not bring the Spirit (Gal. 3:2). The law "weakened by the flesh" (Rom. 8:3) could not produce therefore the spiritual life which its holy precepts required.

The ordinary Israelite on the basis of the corporate personality principle experienced God in the community of the covenant where he could identify with the charismatic leaders. To the extent that the community as a whole followed and obeyed those in their number upon whom the Holy Spirit came, to that extent the community moved forward in God. It was, by and large, a community experience. The charismatic's anointing was never to be utilized for his own personal advantage. He was given revelations, empowerments, skills, and ministries for the betterment of the chosen community. His *charisma* by the Spirit might take many forms—prophecy, intercession, wisdom, judgment, miracles; yet these were not really given to him so much as to the community through him.

The charismatics themselves were first to recognize the limitations of a community in which all did not share the same Spirit

149

which was upon its leaders. In spite of all the charismatics could do, Israel as a whole behaved as a Community of the Flesh. There was union on the basis of law and ritual experience but not much unity. Moses, weary from having to make every spiritual judgment for the people, had his load lightened by God's sharing with seventy elders the anointing of the Spirit upon him. This elicited from Moses a confession of his illimitable desire for the people of God: "Would that all the Lord's people were prophets, that the Lord would put his spirit upon them" (Num.11:29)! Moses, possibly as no other except Jesus, knew the formidable frustrations of trying to lead un-regenerate men in spiritual victory without the transforming power of the Spirit in their lives. His longing was not foreign to the pur-pose of God for the New Israel of a future day.

Jeremiah prophesied a new kind of covenant to be made in God's own handwriting on the human heart. No individual of the new covenant community would be excluded from a personal knowl-edge of God. He prophesied:

> Behold, the days are coming, says the LORD, when I will make a new covenant with the house of Israel and the house of Judah, not like the covenant which I made with their fathers when I took them by the hand to bring them out of the land of Egypt, my covenant which they broke, though I was their husband, says the LORD. But this is the covenant which I will make with the house of Israel after those days, says the LORD: I will put my law within them, and I will write it upon their hearts; and I will be their God, and they shall be my people. And no longer shall each man teach his neighbor and each his brother, saying, "Know the LORD," for they shall all know me, from the least of them to the greatest, says the LORD (Jer. 31:31-34).

Bone weary with the spiritual frustrations of ministering to unspiritual people, Jeremiah was nevertheless given a vision of a day when all "from the least of them to the greatest" would have the knowledge of the Lord inscribed upon their hearts.

Joel's prophecy gives concrete promise to Moses' and the proph-ets' longings for a spiritual people and translates Jeremiah's "least . . . to the greatest" into, "all flesh . . . sons . . . daughters . . . old men . . . young men . . . menservants and maidservants":

> And it shall come to pass afterward, that I will pour out my spirit on all flesh; your sons and your daughters shall prophesy, your old men shall dream dreams, and your young men shall

see visions. Even upon the menservants and maidservants in those days, I will pour out my spirit (Joel 2:28, 29).

The Mission of Jesus to the Old Testament Community

Let us examine briefly the continuation of this same Old Testament economy during the period of the life of Christ prior to the establishment of "the new covenant" in His blood and the new life in His resurrection. In this period He bears two remarkable resemblances to Moses. First, from another mountain He expatiates on God's holy will for man with such combined simplicity, profundity, and authority that no one could gainsay His "more excellent way." Secondly, like Moses He shared His charismatic gifts with His disciples as Moses did with the elders. Luke tells us in these words:

And he called the twelve together and gave them power [*dunamis*] and authority [*exousia*] over all demons and to cure diseases, and he sent them out to preach the kingdom of God and to heal (Lk. 9:1, 2).

In this donation of spiritual *power*, He who was the Anointed One par excellence, having an immeasurable unction of the Spirit (Jn. 3:34), made His disciples "charismatic" much like the Old Testament prophets, especially those in the tradition of Elijah and Elisha. Further examination of the Twelve's religious experience reveals no doubt about their "salvation." They were justified as were all the Old Testament saints by their faith in the grace of God; they expressed their faith by keeping covenant with God. Had Herod killed them after his murder of John the Baptist, their names were written in heaven and they would have found rest on Abraham's bosom.

But it must be said that they were not yet *regenerated*, although in possession of charismatic gifts of the Holy Spirit. That is, Jesus had given them His power, but not yet Himself, for His time had not yet come. They believed in Him but without *initially* receiving the Spirit when they believed (cf. Acts 19:2). Charismatic though they were, they were still in an external, man-to-man relationship to Christ, strictly dependent on Him for their power, and when He went down in death, they lacked the inner presence of the Spirit to maintain communion with Him whom they one time had confessed to be the Son of God.

Jesus also had spiritual affinities with Jeremiah. Did Jesus not

151

say continually in so many words to the Twelve, "Know the Lord"? Yet at the very last hear His lament as He says to Philip: "Have I been with you so long, and yet you do not know me, Philip" (Jn. 14:9)? Why does Jesus weep over the same Jerusalem that Jeremiah wept over six centuries earlier? His tears are collected in these words: "Would that even today you knew the things that make for peace! . . . You did not know the time of your visitation" (Lk. 19:42, 44). The combined charismatic ministries of John the Baptist, Jesus, and the Twelve had brought a measure of "revival" to Israel—if we understand the Old Testament tradition of that word— but not regeneration! The "revival" had not brought the fulfillment of Jeremiah's prophecy of the new covenant in which all God's people would know Him intimately. Lives were touched and prepared for the kingdom of God, but the real fruition of these charismatic ministries was not seen until after the resurrection of Christ.

The Meaning of the Afflation

It was imperative that the Twelve should know Christ and one another in Him in the fullest sense of unity in community. They had been chosen to become the pillars of the New Israel united with God. In His last discourse with them before He suffered, among the many words He spoke about the coming of the Holy Spirit Jesus said this: "Yet a little while, and the world will see me no more, but you will see me; because I live, you will live also. *In that day you will know that I am in my Father, and you in me, and I in you*" (Jn. 14:19, 20). Here was a promise that meant knowledge of the kind of unity Jesus had known with the Father and experience of a new level of unity with Jesus. Until then they had been in union insofar as community under the old covenant was possible. We remind ourselves that it was at a Passover observance—their last together— that Jesus uttered these words about the new unity that would eventuate between them in the realization of the new covenant. Until then they had experienced Jesus in a man-to-man relationship, as students with their Master, as prophets with the Prophet. Like Old Israel gathered around the tabernacle in the wilderness where Moses spoke for God, so they had gathered about Jesus and pondered His words. As yet they did not know empirically His saying: "I . . . in my Father, and you in me, and I in you." That was intimate *spiritual* truth which the world could not receive (Jn. 14:17), distinctively *Christian* truth, and it could not be known by telling and hearing. It had to await the creative acts of the New Creation in Christ, expressed in those words, "because I live [Act I], you will live also [Act II]" (Jn. 14:19b).

He died. He was buried. Then came "the third day" (1 Cor. 15:4)! On that day He became the firstfruits of a new order of men (1 Cor. 15:20). His creaturely identity is both preserved and transcended in His *soma pneumatikon* (1 Cor 15:44). But He is also in His deity *ho kurios to pneuma* (2 Cor. 3:17). When He appeared to the disciples on His third day, they did not believe for joy (Lk. 24:41; Jn. 16:22; 20:20); they were breathless with amazement in the awe of that stupendous moment! Neither Luke (24:36-49) nor John (20:19-23) records anything they said; Jesus anticipated all their questions. Yes, and more. Only now could He give Himself to His own in a level of unity impossible before. The Community of the Spirit could have its genesis only in the glorification of Jesus Christ (Jn. 7:39). Now He stood in the center like Ezekiel in the valley of bones (Ezek. 37:1-14). In Ezekiel's vision wonderful words of promise were made:

> . . . you shall know that I am the Lord, when I open your graves, and raise you from your graves, O my people. And I will put my Spirit within you, and you shall live, and I will place you in your own land; then you shall know that I, the Lord, have spoken, and I have done it, says the Lord (Ezek. 37: 13, 14).

Here stood One in their midst who could do what neither Ezekiel nor any of the charismatics could do. Now He would give them His Spirit, not as special *charismata* as He had done before, but as His very own *life*. In the hush of that moment so unlike Sinai's shakings and Pentecost's power, "the Author of life" (Acts 3:15) breathed on them saying, *labete pneuma hagion:* "Receive the Holy Spirit" (Jn. 20:22)! Jesus Christ entered their hearts then and there. They were united with Him. The new covenant was sealed in their hearts. The Community of the Spirit had its beginning. The term is applicable for both the relationship—*koinonia* or participation in His Spirit—and the group having that relationship.

This experience was the valley between the twin peaks of Jesus' own charismatic ministry in the Gospels and the Church's in Acts. Or to reverse the topographical figure of the valley, here was the highest peak—the watershed ridge—that separated the old and new covenants. Representative "relationship" in the Old Testament became personal

153

"regeneration" in the New Testament, and the Old Israel, justified in the name of her God, became the New Israel (Gal. 6:16), "justified in the name of the Lord Jesus Christ *and* in the Spirit of our God" (1 Cor. 6:11).

He *breathed* on them! Genesis pictures God as breathing upon the human form of collected elements so as to animate the man He made. Here we have something superior to natural creation. This second divine breathing was upon men already in possession of full humanity. It brought spiritual life by the transmission of Christ's Spirit to them. He breathed on them as a symbolic act of Self-impartation in fulfillment of His prediction: "In that day you will know that I am in my Father [the mystery of Jesus' complete unity with God., and you in me [the mystery of the renewed human spirit's being "in Christ"], and I in you [the mystery of Christ's Spirit in the Church individually and corporately]" (Jn. 14:20). The Risen Lord spoke; He breathed holy Spirit, holy life, Himself, uniting man directly with God's life. Their part was only to receive. When man receives this divine afflation (lit., "breathing on") from the God-man, he becomes a new creation, a Christian—if you please—a *re*generated man. He is still *in God* as His creature (Acts 17:28), but more importantly he is *in God* as a living member of the body of Christ (1 Cor. 12:13), and *God is in him* as his life (Rom. 8:10). He becomes a composite being of body and spirit *plus* Spirit (1 Cor. 6:17), of creation plus afflation—which in itself as *holy* breath is qualitatively an emanation, something which could not be said of the breath natural man received at creation. "Any one who does not have the Spirit of Christ does not belong to him" (Rom. 8:9). This truth is basic, constitutive of the only eternal hope of humanity and consequential for all New Testament theology, especially ecclesiology.

A footnote on Thomas is appropriate here. He missed more than the first Sunday night meeting; he had missed that which was necessary for his faith to be viable (Jn. 20:24-29). In that interval he had the name of Christ as His disciple, but not "the same spirit of faith" (2 Cor. 4:13) the others now had. Significantly, things were different for Thomas from what they had been for Eldad and Medad, two of the seventy appointed elders who were not present at the tent when the elders under Moses were "charismatized" and prophesied. Yet these two received the same gift independently of Moses and they prophesied apart from the sixty-eight. Moses was dispensable for the transmission of *charismata*, but the new covenant sealing is not made apart from Spiritual contact with Jesus Christ.

154

Now Thomas asked for external evidence; he still wanted to know Jesus the way he knew the world; he wanted to know Him the old way He had been known before, the way a man knows another man (2 Cor. 5:16). Thus he assembled with the Community of the Spirit which had told him, "We have seen the Lord." Here was a datum he must check out. Though he was skeptical, he was not cynical. In truth Thomas became the first "quester" for the historical Jesus; his critical faculties were astute; he was honest; he wanted facts. As he sat on the eighth day after the resurrection with that faculty Jesus had trained, he ensconced himself in the quester's chair. His methodology was objective and vastly more empirical than today's source and form critics ever hoped to be. He would not speculate about Old Testament texts and apostolic testimonies; what he wanted was for somebody to produce the *soma tou 'Iesou* (Lk. 24:3) in order that he might make visual and tactile examination.

One of the perennial problems of the Church is that of individuals in *union* with the corporate visible Church who have not the Resurrection faith and therefore do not possess the "unity of the Spirit" (Eph. 4:3). Thomas' eight days are typical of those who would insist on their own epistemological starting point. They are: "scoffers . . . who set up divisions, worldly people, devoid of the Spirit" (Jude 18, 19). Amazingly, we are not told in the records whether Thomas ever touched Jesus when at last he saw Him. But surely Jesus touched Thomas trenchantly! He did not call off Thomas' quest but He did call Thomas to faith's personal encounter (Jn. 20:27b). Evidence grasped in the hands or seen on the screen of the cerebrum is admissible for the eyewitnesses—and Thomas was called to be one of those—but sight is not necessary for all, for faith brings the Spirit with the greater cogency of an internal witness (Jn. 16:13, 14; Rom. 8:16).

The upshot was the termination of Thomas' quest and the commencement of a new understanding of Jesus by a new experience of Him. His exclamation, "My Lord and my God!" was for Thomas not a "new hermeneutic" for the continuation of the old quest, but the conquest of Thomas by the Spirit of Christ. A babe in Christ, Thomas' first words ("My Lord and my God") were those of spiritual worship. Resurrection, lordship, the bestowal of the Spirit and Spiritual worship (Jn. 3:23, 24)—all cohere in the One in whom the Community of the Spirit is polarized. Therefore, really to call Him "LORD" —whether in pure *adulation* as with Thomas, or in personal *obedience* (Rom. 14:8, 17, 18) or in public *oracle* (1 Cor. 12:3)—such can only be done "by the Holy Spirit."

155

Were we to put the cause for the effect, we could call the Community of the Spirit, the Community of the Resurrection. What the disciples totally misunderstood during their years of being taught by Jesus in His external position among them, viz., the *fact* of His death and resurrection and the *meaning* of these events, became the center and substance of their apostolic kerygma. The character of the resurrection is unique. No human saw it. Nobody heard it. It was God's exclusive act. Jesus appeared; He spoke; He breathed on them. It was not a resuscitation, an unchanged restoration of the body of Jesus. Such would have been ineffectual for building that Church Jesus said He would build (Mt. 16:18), for the temple He built in three days had to be the beginning of the Community of the Spirit. Had He returned as He was before, He would not have been able to build after this new order of transmitting Himself and thereafter His gifts.

Neither was His resurrection a metamorphosis into Spirit. Such would have been a renunciation of the Incarnation and a total break in His unity with mankind. But there was a metamorphosis of His body, the *soma psychikon* becoming *soma pneumatikon* (1 Cor. 15:44). Moreover, when "God . . . raised him from the dead and gave him glory" (1 Pet. 1:21), the *pleroma* which was always the possession of the Incarnate Son (Col. 1:19) was shared (Jn. 1:16) with His Church, which mystically became His full body (Eph. 1:23; 4:13), identifiable as such because all the members have His "*one* Spirit" (1 Cor. 6:17; Eph. 2:18; 4:4). The unity of this mystical body, the *pleroma* of Him "who fills all in all" (Eph. 1:23), is secured "in the Spirit" (Rom. 8:9). It is the Community of the Spirit, having been "sealed with the promised Holy Spirit, which is the guarantee of our inheritance until we acquire possession of it" (Eph. 1:13, 14), i.e., "the redemption of our bodies" (Rom. 8:23).

Ministry Gifts

Jesus Christ is Lord in the Church by the Spirit. He is present in it to the degree His Spirit is present. He who was conceived by the Holy Spirit in the formation of His humanity was also three decades later anointed with the Holy Spirit for a full charismatic ministry. His personal experience of the Spirit in His humanity became a model for those who "are Christ's" (1 Cor. 3:23). That is to say, His birth by the Spirit is comparable to our regeneration, and His anointing by the descent of the Holy Spirit is comparable to the filling with the Holy Spirit which the disciples first experienced at Pentecost. He *experienced* the Holy Spirit in His humiliation. He

156

dispenses the Holy Spirit in His glorification. The Scriptures teach three primary stages in His glorification. Corresponding to each of these stages Christ imparts a measure of His Spirit to the Church:

HIS GLORIFICATION	THE CORRESPONDING DONATION	THE RESULT
1. *His Resurrection:*	The afflation of the Spirit	regeneration "participation"
2. *His Ascension and Session as Lord:*	The effusion of the Spirit	saturation *charismata*
3. *His Revelation in the Eschaton:*	The transformation of the mortal body by the Spirit	translation glorification

Peter in his Pentecostal sermon explained that Jesus received "the promise of the Holy Spirit" from the Father and "poured out" the Spirit in the mighty effusion which was seen and heard at Pentecost. **Twice in Luke-Acts we are told the divine purpose in the Pentecost Event for the disciples themselves.** He commanded them to wait in Jerusalem for the *power* of the Holy Spirit (Acts 1:8) with which they would be clothed (Lk. 24:49). Before this in conjunction with the resurrection afflation of the Spirit, Jesus had restored the disciples' authority (*exousia*), recommissioning them as His apostles (Jn. 20:21-23), but the reception of the power (*dunamis*) which would restore and heighten their charismatic ministries was not to be renewed until Jesus entered His glory as Lord of all.

The contrasts between the Resurrection afflation and the Pentecostal effusion (lit., "outpouring") are graphic and instructive. In the former the regenerative breath of Christ was directed to them and received by them (Jn. 20:22), while in the latter the blowing fury of the heavenly wind was heard all about them in the room where they were (Acts 2:2). In the Easter appearances Christ's words burned like a fire in their hearts (Lk. 24:32); in the Pentecost Event the *kavodh Yahweh* (Ex. 13:21) descended to the New Israel, streaming forth in tongues of fire upon their heads (Acts 2:3). In the one instance we hear the Risen Lord speaking Spiritual words (Acts 1:2) *to* the silent Church (Lk. 24:36-48; Jn. 20:19-23); in the other we observe Him as "the Lord, the Spirit" speaking *through* the Church "the mighty works of God" (Acts 2:11) in glossolalia (Acts 2:4-13) and in prophecy (Acts 2:14-40). In the one case believers became "*partakers* of the Holy Spirit" (Heb. 6:4), *drinking* the "living water" of God's Spirit (Jn. 4:10; 7:37; 1 Cor. 12:13); in the other case, they *were filled* with God's Spirit (Acts 2:4). Changing the figure slightly, one may say that the former was the *indwelling* of the Spirit (Jn. 14:17, 18, 23) on a permanent basis (Jn. 14:16); the latter was the *infilling* of the Spirit subject to further replenishments (Acts 2:4; 4:31; 9:17; cf. Eph. 5:18) and further *charismata* (1 Cor. 12:31; 14:1). One was the fulfillment of Hosea's prophecy, "I will be as the dew to Israel" (14:5; cf. Deut. 32:2), the other of Joel's prophecy of rain in abundance (3:23, 24, 28). The John 20:22 Event was a *birth* by the Spirit (Jn. 1:13; 3:3-6), a "washing of regeneration and renewal in the Holy Spirit" (Tit. 3:5); the Acts 2:4 Event is best described as a *baptism* in the Holy Spirit (Mt. 3:11; Acts 1:4, 5; 11:16, 17), since it is the one body, alive in the Spirit-life of His resurrection, upon whom the Spirit is "poured out" (*ekcheo*—Acts 2:17, 33; cf. 10:45) in power and glory.

In the Pentecost experience the rich anointing upon Him whose name is Christ, "The Anointed One," now poured down from heaven over His entire earthly body "all together in one place" (Acts 2:1). They were immersed (*baptizo*) in the Holy Spirit, symbolized visibly by the wind and the fire and realized personally by the glossolalia which evidenced the Spirit's overflowing fullness within. The Spirit of Jesus had filled their environment and filled them too. They were "baptized with the Holy Spirit" (Acts 1:4, 5) by the Spirit's presence without and within. There is a beautiful analogy between the disciples' experience and that of their Lord. As He had been conceived by the Spirit in obscurity and later anointed publicly by the Spirit's coming down upon Him from heaven, so they were born of His Spirit within closed doors and later anointed before the world with the same Spirit from heaven.

We must ask here if it is possible to use the expression "baptized in/with the Holy Spirit" as a synonym for regeneration, rather than limiting it to "Pentecostal" or charismatic connotations as Luke seems to do in Acts 1:4, 5 and 11:16, 17. The problem occurs in Paul's use in First Corinthians 12:13 of *baptizo* juxtaposed with the Spirit so as to indicate the plunging or placing of Jews and Greeks, bond and free, indiscriminately into the body of Christ, where they all "drink of one Spirit." This expression, coupled with his reference to "one baptism" in Ephesians 4:5, reveals his understanding of baptism in the wholistic Hebrew manner of thinking. Therefore, using any part for the whole, he could speak elsewhere of Christian baptism as a rite (1 Cor. 1:14-17), as a mystical relation to Christ's death (Rom. 6:3, 4), or typologically of Moses' baptism in the cloud and the sea (1 Cor. 10:2), or theologically of baptism into Christ (Gal. 3:27) as a realm independent of the law. As Galatians 3:27 demonstrates, Paul is a master of the use of composite figures: "For as many of you as were

baptized into Christ have put on [*enduo*=dress in, wear] Christ."
First Corinthians 12:13 combines the figures of baptism and drinking in
a similar way. Having said all this, we conclude that First Corinthians
12:13a in free application could designate the John 20:22 type of experience which unified the disciples by their mutual reception of the
same Spirit, and First Corinthians 12:13b could well refer to the
drinking of the Spirit in regeneration. But it would be stretching the
figure too far to say that this totality thrust of the verb "baptize" is
comparable to the charismatic understanding of the baptism in the
Holy Spirit in Acts. Jesus told the disciples not to begin to carry out
the Great Commission until they had received this baptism which John
the Baptist had foretold—a baptism which differed in degree, purpose,
and effects from what in the Pauline sense of First Corinthians 12:13
might be called a "baptism" into the one body of Christ. Inspecting
the natural elements that constitute the framework for the spiritual
analogy, we have to recognize that immersion into a body—a solid
structure—is quite different from immersion into water, fire, or
wind in the normal figures.

The protest being made here is against the reasoning that
runs like this. There is only "one baptism"; it is the baptism
(1 Cor. 12:13) of believers by the Spirit into the body of Christ.
Therefore, all the regenerated have been baptized in the
Holy Spirit once and for all, though they be completely lacking in
the power of Pentecost and the *charismata* contemporary at Corinth. This kind of reasoning exists in scores of books written during
the past sixty years. Aside from exegetical considerations, its fallacy
lies in its not reckoning with the fact that the Jerusalem church and
the churches founded by both Peter and Paul possessed not only the
Spirit as life in Christ but also as power for edification and evangelism in a variety of Spiritual *charismata*.

We conclude therefore that the expression "baptized with/in the
Holy Spirit" is an equivocal expression, general enough to apply to
all aspects of the "one baptism" of the Church, but particularly suited
to express immersion into the realm of the *power* and *fullness* of the
Spirit. And here I speak particularly to the Believers' Church as one
in the modern Pentecostal tradition and experience. We contend not
so much for the term as for the experience itself. Call it baptism in
the Holy Spirit (Acts 1:4, 5; 11:10-17), filling with the Holy Spirit
(Acts 2:4; 4:8, 31; 9:17; cf. 13:9), falling of the Holy Spirit upon one in
palpable manifestation (Acts 8:12-18; 10:44-46; 11:15), or an anointing
analogous to Christ's (Acts 10:38), the effect is the same.

In regeneration the inner witness of the Spirit (Jn. 10:27; Rom.

8:16) is expressed outwardly by oral confession of Jesus Christ as Lord (Rom. 10:9, 10; 1 Cor. 12:3), by participation in water baptism (Mt. 28:19, 20; Acts 2:38) and in the Lord's Supper (1 Cor. 11:26). In a similar manner we can speak of the palpable evidence that accompanies a regenerate believer's plunge into the depths of the Spirit. His inner "filling" becomes evident by oral confession of the glory of God (Acts. 2:11; 10:46) in the Spirit-wrought phenomenon of glossolalia, a speaking "to God . . . [of] mysteries in the Spirit" (1 Cor. 14:2). This speaking is understood neither by the speaker himself (1 Cor. 14:14) nor his hearers (1 Cor. 14:2) unless God should choose in special instances, as in the international gathering at Pentecost, to speak through the yielded vessels in the languages known by those who hear, in which case tongues become a "sign . . . for unbelievers" (1 Cor. 14:22). We must hasten to say, however, that glossolalia, having the character of intensely personal communion with God, as valuable as it is for individual edification (1 Cor. 14:4), is not as profitable as prophecy for the edification of the gathered church (1 Cor. 14:4, 5).

Glossolalia, mentioned some eighteen times in Acts and First Corinthians, must not be despised because of its limitations which obtain toward men, but not toward God. *All* the one hundred and twenty spoke in tongues (Acts 2:4), *all* the Gentiles at Cornelius' house (Acts 10:44-46), and presumably all the dozen Ephesians who became the nucleus of that church (Acts 19:6); and the Apostle Paul confessed that he exceeded even the Corinthians in glossolalia in his private life of prayer and praise (1 Cor. 14:18). Remarkably, in the "little Pentecost" at Caesarea among the Gentiles it was glossolalia which was the factor of continuity with the first Pentecost. This led Peter to know that the Gentiles had the same baptism or gift of the Spirit which had first fallen on the Jews, though the theophanies of wind and fire were not repeated.

How do we harmonize glossolalia as an initial indication of the Spirit's *full* control and Paul's classification of glossolalia as the least of the *charismata* (1 Cor. 12:28), a gift not to be exercised by all during the worship of a local church (1 Cor. 12:30)? The principle of community in love must be seen as the decisive element. Paul could say to the Corinthians, "Now I want you all to speak in tongues . . ." (1 Cor. 14:5), because this was their privilege based on their individual experience of the Spirit, but, when the church met together in *koinonia*, it was that the body might be edified as a whole and not merely to indulge individuals in their personalized experience. Thus Paul counseled the desiring of the better gift of prophecy (1 Cor. 14:1, 5), which was a speaking by the Spirit in the language common to the locality, though he did not forbid glossolalia in the common assembly (1 Cor. 14:39) but set limits for the exercise of this gift (1 Cor. 14:27).

Ideally, every member of the Community of the Spirit should be a gift-bearing unit in the mature body of Christ (1 Cor. 1:7). The "gifts of the Spirit," "manifestations of the Spirit," and "varieties of service" or offices are designed to build up the Community of the Spirit (1 Cor. 12:8-10, 28-30; Rom. 12:6-8; Eph. 4:11; 1 Pet. 4:10, 11). The individual gifts are not subject to a precise count. There are overlappings between gifts, as in "gifts of healing" (1 Cor. 12:9) and "working of miracles" (1 Cor. 12:10). The charismatic ministries range all the way from "apostles" and "prophets," as multiplex ministries, to such simple ones as "helpers" (1 Cor. 12:28), exhorters (Rom. 12:8), and "speakers in various kinds of tongues" (1 Cor. 12:28). The gifts and ministries of the Spirit are so fused that it would be difficult to distinguish them except to say that the kind of *charisma* determines the type of office. We conclude, therefore, that the Community of the Spirit is a realization of theocracy according to God's pattern, because Christ is sovereign by the Spirit in the distribution of *charismata* among the members of His body (1 Cor. 12:11).

Included among the ministries are "administrators" (1 Cor. 12:28); this implies a flexibility in church government that is Spirit-directed. Otherwise, there would have been a standardized blueprint of government set forth for all the churches. The first concern of any segment of the Church must always be that the Lordship of Jesus not be obstructed by any system that precludes the freedom of the Spirit to guide in new situations. Perhaps the most impressive factor in this regard in the early Church was the recognition of the Spirit's speaking *within* the Church (Jn. 16:13, 14) so as to direct both individual ministers (Acts 10:19, 20; 13:2; 16:6, 7) and larger groups, e.g., the Council at Jerusalem (Acts 15:28). There, significantly, it is said, "It seemed good to the Holy Spirit and to us . . . ," in reporting the decision of the Church Council to those who were not there. Herein lies an important distinction, "the Holy Spirit and . . . us." Let no one transmute the Christological error of Apollinaris into an ecclesiological one. Neither the human spirit of the individual nor the esprit de corps in the gathered church is ever denied by the presence of the Holy Spirit. Local churches, denominations, and ecumenical endeavors must always discern and differentiate between their corporate psychological entity and the Lord in the midst, under the judgment of His Word and His Spirit. "He who has an ear, let him hear what the

161

Spirit *says* to the churches" (Rev. 2:7, 11, 17, 29; 3:6, 13, 22). The question is not of the Lord's speaking but of His being heard!

A Many-Sided Principle

The basic thrust of this study has been the assertion that the Believers' Church is the Community of the Spirit under the Lordship of Jesus Christ. From this premise the following implications may be drawn:

1. The Community of the Spirit must test the many spirits at large in Christendom. Any spirit that claims to be the Holy Spirit of God must have fidelity and continuity with the crucified and living Lord, Jesus Christ. That is, just as the test of the authenticity of Jesus during His ministry was His conformity to what was previously revealed and known of God, so the test of the genuineness of the Holy Spirit is His conformity to the revelation of God in Christ Jesus. Biblically we observe this in the Spirit's coming in the name of Jesus Christ as "the Spirit of the Son" (Gal. 4:6), "the Spirit of Jesus" (Acts 16:7), "the Spirit of Christ" (Rom. 8:9), "the Spirit of Jesus Christ" (Phil. 1:19), "the Spirit of the Lord" (2 Cor. 3:17).

2. The Community of the Spirit exists wherever there are two or more believers gathered around the Lord Jesus. Historically, geographically, and practically the Church exists as local congregations. Nevertheless, wherever the local believers gather in districts, associations, conferences, synods, conventions, or councils, the basis for their community must still be in the "one Spirit" in recognition of the fact that there is only "one Lord" over all the Church.

3. The Community of the Spirit denies the "super church" concept which is a reversion to the Old Testament state of legal, political, or nominal union. If the Spirit is truly free to lead theocratically, the unachieved goal of the Old Testament, then there will be no need for dependence on an institutional bureaucracy for government.

4. The Community of the Spirit perforates denominational walls. If we acknowledge that others of like precious faith in Jesus Christ have the Spirit of Christ, then not to fellowship them as brethren in Christ is an affront to Christ Himself.

5. The Community of the Spirit preserves individuality while denying both individualism and collectivism. On the one hand individualism does not distinguish self-consciousness and Holy Spirit, and on the other hand collectivism absolutizes the esprit de corps at the expense of both the individual and the Holy Spirit. The fact

that every member has a direct encounter with the Lord by the Spirit secures his individuality.

6. The Community of the Spirit is the foundation for Christian ethics and discipline in the Church. This principle is seen vividly in Paul's shaming of the Corinthians for going before the pagan courts with lawsuits against one another. How is it that Paul can contend that even the "least esteemed" member of the Corinthian church would be competent to judge such matters (1 Cor. 6:1-8)? If he is a Christian, he has the Holy Spirit and therefore can be led of the Spirit in ethical decision. Moreover, possession of the Spirit includes love and mercy and those who are "spiritual" should restore a man overtaken in any trespass in a spirit of gentleness (Gal. 6:1).

7. The Community of the Spirit has but one Teacher. With the Apostle John we regard both truth and falsehood as requiring spiritual identification. There is a "spirit of truth and a spirit of error" (1 Jn. 4:6). Paul, like John, challenged anyone who thought himself to be "a prophet or spiritual" to acknowledge that his teaching was a command of the Lord (1 Cor. 14:37); teaching can be authenticated or disallowed on the basis of its controlling spirit. The Holy Spirit alone is Christ's appointed teacher (Jn. 14:26; 16:13-15). This function He exercises both directly and indirectly. John recognized the direct route by saying, "the anointing which you received from him abides in you, and you have no need that any one should teach you . . . his anointing teaches you about everything . . ." (1 Jn. 2:27). The indirect method is the *charisma* of "teachers" given to the Community of the Spirit (1 Cor. 12:28; Eph. 4:11) to bring the truth before the believers, not teaching down to them as in authoritarianism but being cognizant of *koinonia* in the truth, the "one faith." There must be recognition that only the Holy Spirit can illumine spiritual realities within the soul (1 Cor. 2:12-16) and that all "teachers" must appeal in the verification of their teaching to the same Spirit who resides within those taught (cf. 1 Cor. 7:40).

8. The Community of the Spirit denies sacerdotalism which conceives of unity with Christ in the physical terms of a succession of persons reaching back to Jesus' right-hand man. But we need not try to bring Christ to ourselves (Rom. 10:6-8) by a human ladder. Risen and free He comes to us in His Word by the Spirit.

9. The Community of the Spirit denies sacramentalism which defines unity biochemically in terms of the flesh and not the Spirit. The Risen Christ ate (Lk. 24:41, 42); He was not eaten! But His disciples did receive His Holy Spirit. Our "participation in the blood

of Christ . . . [and] in the body of Christ" (1 Cor. 10:16) in our observance of the Lord's Supper is actualized only through "the *koinonia* of the Holy Spirit" (2 Cor. 13:14). His life can be received in no other way.

10. Finally, the Community of the Spirit denies both spiritualism and universalism because of their failure to concede the particularity of the **Spirit of Jesus. When men confess the Lordship and Resurrection** of Christ and worship Him as a consequence, the Holy Spirit is made visible, so to speak, in them; the Church becomes visible. And to all universalists and optimists who hold that all mankind is in some way the Church we reply, "Any one who does not have the Spirit of Christ does not belong to him" (Rom. 8:9)!

In conclusion I would like to read a statement written eighty-five years ago by an original member and perhaps the most outstanding theologian of the Free Church of Scotland. The words of George Smeaton express well the alternatives before us.

> Another error is the modern notion . . . that believers are not to pray for the Holy Spirit, because He was once for all given on the day of Pentecost. and that the Christian body may not pray for what is already possessed. That rash and presumptuous position, by whomsoever it is held, is discredited by the fact that the apostles who had received the Holy Ghost on the first resurrection day continued with one accord in prayer and supplication for the promise of the Father (Acts 1:14). They prayed for the Spirit though they had received the Spirit. They waited for more of the Spirit that they had in compliance with their Lord's command. [3]

J. Lawrence Burkholder

7

A PEOPLE IN COMMUNITY :

Contemporary Relevance

J. Lawrence Burkholder, Victor S. Thomas Professor of Divinity, Harvard University, brought to the Conference on the Concept of the Believers' Church a rich and diverse background in graduate study, in the Mennonite pastorate, in overseas relief administration, and in teaching both in a liberal arts college and in a university-related divinity school. A native of Pennsylvania, Dr. Burkholder graduated from Goshen College, Gettysburg Theological Seminary, and Princeton Theological Seminary, having received the ThD degree from the last-named institution. During 1944-48 he served in relief administration in the Far East, first as secretary of the Bengal Christian Council Relief Fund in Calcutta, then as associate director of Church World Service located in China, and finally as director of the National Clearing Committee in Shanghai until Chinese Communist troops captured the city. From 1955 to 1960 Dr. Burkholder was professor of Bible and philosophy at Goshen College. A member of the faculty of Harvard Divinity School since 1961, he became chairman of the Department of the Church in 1963.

Dr. Burkholder's sympathetic understanding of and identification with the Believers' Church heritage was coupled with a perceptive and critical awareness of the contemporary religious and human situation. The primary objective of Dr. Burkholder's address was to affirm the urgent necessity of a viable alternative to the present-day hiatus between the heirs of Pietism and the heirs of the Social Gospel and to demonstrate that a renewed Believers' Church, functioning both as a prophetic community which faces society's great issues and as a healing community which binds up man's internal wounds, can become such an alternative. This major objective he sought in the context of the contemporary racial crisis. Dr. Burkholder had himself been in jail in St. Augustine, Florida, by virtue of his sympathetic participation in the Civil Rights Movement. In his diagnosis of the failure of most of America's white churches to confront directly the racial crisis, he alluded to the absence of Negro participants in the Conference on the Concept of the Believers' Church—an absence subsequently explained at least partly as the failure of numerous Negro church leaders to respond to invitations which had been issued to them.

Also of significance for the conference were Dr. Burkholder's distinction between minimal and maximal definitions of the Believers' Church and his prognosis that the Believers' Church is not likely to find many pure embodiments in the present era or achieve any degree of popularity, despite the significance of the Church of the Saviour, Washington, D.C., but may have some of its important characteristics taken up within the churches of "the establishment."

Panel members who discussed Dr. Burkholder's address were Dr. Allen C. Deeter, associate professor of religion, Manchester College, North Manchester, Indiana; Dr. Vernard Eller, associate professor of religion, La Verne College, La Verne, California; Dr. Leland D. Harder, professor of practical theology, Mennonite Biblical Seminary, Elkhart, Indiana; Dr. Walker N. Stockburger, pastor, Trinity Baptist Church, Norfolk, Virginia; and Dr. Nat Tracy, chairman, Division of Religion and Philosophy, Howard Payne College, Brownwood, Texas. Dr. Duke K. McCall, president, Southern Baptist Theological Seminary, served as moderator of the panel.

Dr. Eller called for a "dialectical tension" between Pietism and the Social Gospel rather than a "synthesis" of the two. He pointed then to a linguistic problem: "Pietism" as a term for overwhelming concern for personal salvation is not correct historically, and "Social Gospel" is too closely linked with the old Liberalism of Schleiermacher and Harnack to serve now as a useful term. It is better, said Dr. Eller, to speak of personal and social redemption and possibly also of cosmic redemption. There is need for a new emphasis on eschatology, "the hallmark of the Believers' Church," with a resultant genuine concern for this world. Dr. Harder declared that the Believers' Church needs "the stimulus of a dynamic world" and identified the tension which Dr. Burkholder treated as "one of the most difficult problems" in the history of believers' churches. According to Dr. Deeter, Pietism with its cell group emphasis provides the pattern for church renewal. Yet early Pietism did not stress revivalism, and Clarence Jordan's Koinonia Farm is a modern example of Pietism's social concern. Dr. Tracy stressed the value of cell group or small group procedures, for personal "bankruptcy" draws people together in a "new wholeness." Being must be magnified as well as doing, and a renewed church can then undertake its mission to the world. Dr. Stockburger emphasized that the church must focus attention on the Civil Rights Movement, seeing both its own failures and its opportunities. Yet the church must not be a mere appendage to the Civil Rights Movement. It must not enter the struggle for expediency, but rather out of the motivation of Christian love.

o   o   o

Our approach to the problem of the contemporary relevance of the idea of community depends initially upon the concept of the Believers' Church. The Believers' Church may be interpreted in minimal or maximal terms. It may be reduced to skin and bone by claiming for it only a few essential ideas of church order, or it may be freighted with necessary implications until it takes on the proportions of a total point of view. We may put the options in the form of a question. Do we mean by the Believers' Church a way of conceiving the *practical* life of the church, taking into consideration primarily structural and communal implications, saying as little as possible about the theological content of faith? Or do we mean by the Believers' Church a comprehensive *view of Christianity?*

It seems to me that there are advantages in both ways of thinking, depending upon whether our purposes are *normative* or *constructive*. As a normative concept, it is wise to keep it minimal. For only a few ideas abstracted from the past can be transplanted into the present. It is impossible to recover entire systems. Even though one could argue for an association of ideas as may justify the term, "Believers' Church theology," it is impossible to recover that theology as a package. For example, some of us who belong to the Anabaptist tradition have come to realize that it is impossible to recover the "Anabaptist vision" in its organic unity—there are just too many differences between the outlook of the sixteenth and the twentieth centuries. That is to say, although the Believers' Church in its classical expressions took the form of comprehensive views of Christianity, it would be an anachronistic impossibility to recover them in their totality.

Though we may hesitate to appropriate arbitrarily certain elements of the Believers' Church while discarding others, this is precisely what happens unwittingly anyway in history. History has a way of loosening the Believers' Church from its original theological and cultural moorings and latching it onto other theological and cultural developments. Accordingly, the Believers' Church tradition has been influenced by nearly all of the major developments of Protestantism. Regardless of their original theological orientations, the believers' churches have been fundamentalist and liberal, pietistic and rationalistic, individualistic and socialistic, dispensational and nonhistorical, pacifist and non-pacifistic, segregationist and integrationist. The obvious implication is that as a matter of historical fact the Believers' Church idea is not able to go it alone. It always becomes associated with other ideas in an infinite number of combinations, and for this we can be thankful, even though the possibility of compromise is very real.

If, then, we were to ask, What are the normative ideas of the Believers' Church? we would hold to such *practical* ideas as believer's baptism, covenantal ethics, discipline, congregational decision-making, prophecy, and spiritual discernment and witness. But we would leave unspecified, to a considerable extent at least, many matters relating to the content of faith, the controlling images of thought, the purposes of the church, and attitudes toward the world.

However, if our purpose is to be *constructive* as well as normative, i.e., to formulate a view of the Believers' Church which is relevant to contemporary life, then we must think fairly comprehensively and concretely. We cannot simply test the possibility of this or

167

that essential of church order independently of theological content and cultural bias. We cannot simply say, "Let us baptize believers," regardless of what is believed, or "Let us make decisions," regardless of what is decided, or "Let us discern the truth," regardless of the kind of truth that is considered worthy of discernment. Therefore, we must take up, in conjunction with such normative marks as believer's baptism, discipline, etc., the whole question of the central problems around which the believers may gather. If church people gather together today, it will be for a purpose. What is it?

It seems to me that people will gather together into a Believers' Church for two reasons: (1) to know how to respond as Christians to what is going on in the world, and (2) in order to understand how to cope with problems of personal authenticity and need for wholeness. There is, in other words, an external problem—the problem of the meaning of history, the eschatological problem, the problem of the future, and an internal problem—variously stated as the problem of alienation, estrangement, and guilt. It seems to me that the Believers' Church is the church which may be in a position to meet these issues. In doing so, the Believers' Church would become a *prophetic community* and *a healing community. The challenge to the so-called believers' churches today is to seek to bring these purposes into conceptual and functional unity.*

The tragedy of the church is that it has no way at present by which the problems of the external world and of the individual soul can be seen and worked at together. Churches respond to one or the other but seldom to both. Congregations are split down the middle on whether the church's job is to bring in the Kingdom of God or to save souls. This is a split which also divides theologians between those who would save the city and those who would save the individual, between theologians who are sociologically or existentially oriented. We are all aware that those who would save the city not infrequently despise those who even acknowledge ontological concern. They are criticized as remnants of a tribal culture or of Bible Belt piety. Sometimes they are described as sick people. Pietists, at the same time, deplore social action as secular outrage against established orders which should be left to the lawmakers. This is a split which has its counterpart in the younger, *avant-garde* generation between the "Hippies" and the "Squares." The Hippies seek to heal their brokenness through the psychedelic trance, while the Squares seek radical social change in which the individual is lost in the secular structures. Another way of stating the cleavage is between those who value an "experienced faith" and those for whom religion is no more than to "do justice and love kindness."

But this cannot go on. I believe that *we have reached the theological and cultural moment for a new formulation of the faith which will join two major influences, heretofore considered antithetical.* I refer to Pietism and the Social Gospel. Both Pietism and the Social Gospel have deeply influenced the believers' churches. They go further in describing the inner life and piety of the believers' churches than the idea of the Believers' Church itself. But instead of complementing each other, they have canceled each other out. Instead of completing each other, they have preyed upon one another. *The current question, therefore, is whether what is intended by these interpretations of Christianity can be joined.* They must be brought together if the church is to survive. They must be brought together because the Gospel is incomplete without them and because modern culture poses problems for which the characteristic emphases of Pietism and the Social Gospel are equally relevant. Pietism stands for authentic existence in the face of ontological and moral alienation, and the Social Gospel stands for justice at a time of revolutionary change. If the churches limit their task to one or the other, the Gospel is truncated and the churches lose their point. Salvation is both individual and social. The churches must, therefore, find ways to express this fact both theologically and practically.

If Pietism and the Social Gospel are to be joined, they will both have to be reinterpreted in the process. Fortunately, they offer considerable latitude, since neither is a closed system of theology as such but an approach to Christian life. What is intended by these ways of viewing Christianity is more important than the forms which they have taken. Pietism is concerned primarily with "authentic existence." It has relied upon biblical symbols such as the "new creation," "perfection (completeness)," "forgiveness," "sonship," and "reconciliation." It has emphasized the necessity of right relationships to God and neighbor. Certain existentialist theologians have attempted to find modern psychological equivalents for the language of Pietism. Hence, Tillich speaks of the "New Being," "reunion," "authentic existence," "the new reality," and "ultimate concern." Furthermore, Pietism has upheld the idea of "experienced faith." Religious experience is a necessary accompaniment of faith. The emotions and the will join the mind in affirming the Gospel. Emphasis upon the "heart strangely warmed" is one of the permanent contributions of Pietism, and when the church neglects the emotions, secular expressions are bound to appear.

The Social Gospel will also have to be reinterpreted. It will have to be purged of its superficial view of sin, its tendency to obscure differences between the church and the world, its abhorrence of the cultic, its onesided historicism, its superficial optimism, and its obsession with relevance. But having said this, we must insist that the Social Gospel opens before us the possibility of social salvation and reinstates the hope of the Kingdom of God as God's universal reign. This is the avenue by which the churches join universal history, looking to the time when "God may be everything to everyone." The Social Gospel thus stands for the fact that it is the world which is to be saved and that Salvation history (*Heilsgeschichte*) and World history, man and the "new man" in Christ, the church and the world participate in the same divine purpose.

But you may ask whether it is possible to find a language and a piety which will bring into theological expression all that is meant by "personal" and "social" salvation. At this point, I am emboldened by biblical precedence to suggest that it can be done. We would not insist that all that appears in the Bible represents a single point of view. Nevertheless, one may be encouraged by the way in which various authors of the New Testament hold together different and far-ranging realities. A precedent for the synthesis of such inward and outward concerns as are represented by Pietism and the Social Gospel is found in Romans 8, where Paul links worship with the condition of the universe. Here Christians are depicted as suffering with the universe and this suffering is expressed in the gathered fellowship, literally and audibly by "groans."

> We know that the whole creation has been groaning in travail together until now; and not only the creation, but we ourselves, who have the first fruits of the Spirit, groan inwardly as we wait for adoption as sons, the redemption of our bodies (vv. 22, 23, RSV).

Here is an insight into the "pietism" of early worship by which the local assembly responded intellectually and emotionally to the universal dream of salvation. Thus, the worshiping assembly saw in one sweeping image the correlation of its own destiny and the destiny of the world. The Spirit enabled them to participate in the drama of cosmic salvation. Here the dichotomy of sizes and spheres was overcome. It was not a question of whether the primitive assembly should pay any attention to the totality of existence; the church was caught up in the total process of redemption, although the Christian community and creation were at different stages of redemption. The Christian community literally "groaned" with creation, thus linking religious experience with all that lies outside the church. If the early church could identify religiously with creation, could not the twentieth-century church identify in the same manner with society?

Also, we find in the Pauline corpus a connection between personal salvation and Christ's defeat of cosmic powers. What is more unlikely than a connection between cult and cosmos? Yet Paul placed worship and ritual in a cosmic setting. Nothing lay outside Christian scrutiny, since Christ was Lord of the universe.

Are we able in the twentieth century to construct a theology and a piety which, while making proper distinctions, bring into a single conceptual framework the salvation of the individual and the salvation of the social order? This has not been done by the Free Church tradition to my knowledge. Can we think of a way by which evangelism, social action, pastoral care, prophetic witness, personal morality, and public responsibility participate in the same spirit and express the same redemptive purpose?

Before setting forth something of a practical model of the believers' churches today in which what is best in Pietism and the Social Gospel may be combined, I would like to point to the fact that a paradigm of the Believers' Church may have appeared among us in recent years, in unexpected places. I refer to the early days of the Civil Rights Movement when, under the direction of Martin Luther King, Jr., a number of Negro churches in Montgomery and other places brought together, in a unique way, evangelical piety, prophetic speech, and social action. It strikes me as a unique religious phenomenon that in many Negro churches evangelical theology, language, songs, preaching, and feeling were interlaced with political analysis and social witness. In many religious assemblies on civil rights there was, oddly enough, no such thing as a conscious transition from the religious to the secular, from this world to the next, from the call to Christ and the call to prison. Social protest was grounded in a theology of the cross. It was not an artificial appendix to religious thought but an evangelical religious act. Hymns depicting heaven were used to prepare the spirit for a free society; prayers for eternal salvation and civil rights were said in the same breath. The Bible informed social action as much as personal evangelism.

Not only did the Civil Rights Movement inject into evangelical piety a social dimension, but it also became the occasion for a new form of congregational life. I recall St. Augustine, Florida, when Hosea Williams of Martin Luther King's staff gathered us together in a Methodist church. He preached a sermon on Amos and closed with a moving appeal to the suffering of Christ and His way of nonviolence. Then came the proposal to march. This was followed by discussion, prayer, singing, decision-making, and then action in the streets and jail for over three hundred people. This was for me a paradigm of the Believers' Church, for all of the elements of Free Church life were present—prophecy, discernment, congregational decision-making, singing, prayer, commitment, social action, and suffering.

It occurs to me that one of the tragedies of our time is the fact that the churches, especially the so-called believers' churches, have not been able to see in the Civil Rights Movement the occasion for the revolution of the churches along the Believers' Church pattern. The civil rights issue is a moral issue which is real enough and sufficiently complex to require for its resolution a new and radical view of the structure and life of many churches. Here is an issue in which people are so deeply involved emotionally and morally that its resolution on the local congregational level not infrequently requires a process of discussion, Bible study, spiritual discernment, political awareness, and corporate decision-making along lines of the believers' churches. The civil rights issue constitutes the test case today for many churches of the Believers' Church tradition. If the churches would face the race issue honestly, openly, repentantly, and forthrightly on a local level, they would either be made or broken as believers' churches. As it is, many so-called believers' churches evade this and other moral issues by a thousand deviations and thus perpetuate the "establishment." Shall we call them "established" Free Churches?

But let me cite an exceptional case. About four years ago I spoke to three hundred ministers in Cincinnati on the theme of "The Church as a Discerning Community." I was upholding what is essentially a Free Church ideal. The response of the ministers was one of skepticism. They claimed that I was unrealistic. The churches are simply incapable of discerning the truth, they said. Ordinary people have neither the faith nor the intelligence to know what is really going on and how to respond in a Christian way.

However, I was saved on this particular occasion by a minister who rose and described an event in his congregation which had transformed it, incidentally, into a believers' church. The question was whether this church, just south of Cincinnati, would open its doors to Negroes. The sentiments were high against integration, but the minister laid the groundwork for the resolution of the problem by preaching a series of sermons on the Holy Spirit, citing cases in the Acts of the Apostles. He emphasized the Holy Spirit as a Leader and Teacher of the church in making such moral decisions as inclusion of Gentiles. At the close of the series of sermons, the minister asked the congregation whether they believed the following propositions: that God has a will with reference to moral issues; that He is able to reveal His will to His church, and that the civil rights issue is a moral problem. The (pietist) congregation stood in acceptance of these propositions, with some hesitation regarding the third. Thereupon, the minister proposed that on the following Sunday morning the church should assemble at the regular time to seek the will of God regarding integration, with the understanding that they would remain together in church until God made His will known. The congregation accepted the proposal, and the people spent the following Sunday until midnight (without recess except for potluck lunch and sandwiches for supper) praying, arguing, accusing, forgiving, threatening, rehashing old problems until at about twelve o'clock at night the members, most of whom remained, concluded that God willed that the congregation should be integrated, and a new style of church life was born in the process. The church experienced renewal with a new social dimension added to its life.

By this example, I am not suggesting that theological "frame-up" should be listed among the marks of the Believers' Church! But I am suggesting that a crisis in civilization, such as the civil rights crisis, is the kind of occasion, which, if approached with evangelical presuppositions and social vision, may lead to a new conception of Christianity (combining Pietism and the Social Gospel) and may lead at the same time to the renewal of the church in the form of the Believers' Church.

One may say, parenthetically, that the tragic course of the Civil Rights Movement may be due in part to the fact that the churches at large have been unable to relate evangelical faith to social reform. Hence, some churches have undergone conservative reaction, holding on to individualistic faith, while others have joined the movement with, at bottom, secular attitudes and presuppositions. The pietists have failed to participate in the vision of a free society, and the social gospelers have failed to undergird social vision with genuine religious faith. Hence, the Civil Rights Movement has been taken over by the secularists, the churches having lacked a genius for Christian organization and reform.

Let us now sketch briefly a kind of Believers' Church which may incorporate in its community the intentions of Pietism and of the Social Gospel.

I have in mind a church which is organized first of all as a *prophetic community*. This is a community which may be called a

173

prophetic community because of its emphasis upon the central concern of prophecy, namely, the will of God, and because it is informed by prophetic faith, especially with reference to the revelation of God in history. Furthermore, it may be called a prophetic community, because it is open to the possibility of prophecy today. It is a community of which prophecy is an organizing principle.

Although such an ideal church stands in the tradition of Old Testament prophecy, it takes on such communal dimensions as would make it resemble New Testament prophecy. It also resembles New Testament prophecy, because it assumes that prophecy is the responsibility of the entire community, even though some individuals may be more prominent in this regard than others. We read:

> yea, and on my menservants and my maidservants in those days I will pour out my Spirit; and they shall prophesy (Acts 2:18, RSV).

The question which the prophetic community asks is: "What is God doing in the world today?" This is a way of asking, "What is the will of God?" as His will may be revealed in history.

It is obvious that the prophetic community runs the risk of embarrassment of asking a question which cannot be answered. To ask specifically what God is doing or what God really wills in the present is to become existentially involved in the problem of religious knowledge, in the particular form which it takes in biblical faith. History may not be absurd, as the existentialist philosophers say it is, but it is ambiguous. Hence, the prophetic community, if it is true to its own presuppositions, believes that God does reveal His will in history, but the community is reserved in its claim to be the recipient of that revelation. Nevertheless, it remains open to the possibility that God may speak, and it encourages the members to prophesy as they are called and to participate in a process of testing called "discernment."

Christian prophecy moves on two levels: (1) the attempt to understand the facts, and (2) the attempt to interpret the facts from a Christian point of view. Understanding the facts is a Christian responsibility. All scientific methods which have been developed by the modern world are employed insofar as they may be available to the Christian community. This means that the community is a community of study. The second level is the level of spiritual discernment by which the community exercises its Christian judgment regarding what corresponds to the will of God. It is impossible to say here exactly what goes into Christian judgment; this would require a course in Christian ethics. But most certainly the revelation of God in the historical Jesus is the main clue, together with the wisdom of the church in previous ages and whatever pragmatic factors may seem to apply.

The capacity for Christian judgment based upon the knowledge of redemptive history is one which according to the New Testament grows with Christian commitment and experience. Thus Paul writes in Romans 12:2:

> Be ye transformed by the renewing of your mind, in order that you may attain to the *dokimazein*, the capacity to distinguish what God's will is. [1]

According to Oscar Cullmann, "This 'testing' is the key of all New Testament ethics." [2] But testing is not simply or primarily a personal gift of the Spirit; it is rather the activity of the Spirit in the community. The church is a discerning community—one which is organized to "test" ideas and possibilities governing Christian conduct and the course of world history.

At this point we would draw a distinction between "gnosis" and "discernment." Gnosis frequently appears as private, often esoteric knowledge. Gnosis is, to be sure, a legitimate phenomenon; the possibility of even private revelation is not absolutely excluded in the New Testament. But gnosis is suspect when it does not submit to *dokimazein*, i.e., the critical examination by the community. The New Testament church was severely threatened by men who claimed to know something that the community was incapable of knowing or which lay beyond the judgment of the community. The practical problem behind the letter to the Colossians is precisely that—Christian philosophers with esoteric wisdom seeking to influence the church without their having engaged the church in a process of corporate examination. Regardless of whether the problem at Thessalonica was "gnosticism" or "false prophecy," the resolution recommended by Paul was spiritual discernment:

> Do not quench the Spirit, do not despise prophesying, but test everything (1 Thess. 5:19-21a, RSV).

The mode of *dokimazein* is conversation. One is tempted to say that nothing is more crucial to the prophetic community than the quality of its conversation within the *koinonia*. The community which is organized to "test the Spirit" must be a community in which conversation is both free and required. The prophetic community is one in which each individual is viewed as a channel of the Holy Spirit. Hence, that quality of freedom which elicits speech assumes theological importance. For one's speech could be the Word of God for the occasion. The possibility that God may be speaking makes speech a serious phenomenon in the eyes of the community. An old Anabaptist baptismal formula is the following: "Will you give counsel and receive counsel?" This formula presupposed a communal approach to problems in which every baptized person was expected to participate.

The quality of speech and the quality of *koinonia* go hand in hand. It is a fact of life in the Believers' Church tradition that the condition of the church depends almost entirely upon an atmosphere of honesty and openness. At the same time, it would be less than candid to hide the fact that the structure of the Believers' Church lays almost inhuman demands in this regard upon the community, and it is evident that such practices as conversation and discipline are almost impossible to accommodate at the same time. And yet, the solution to the problem of brokenness is primarily communication with discipline.

In this connection, it may be pointed out that adult baptism is upheld not only because of a Believers' Church view of sin and salvation, but because prophetic discernment presupposes maturity. The question put to the candidate for baptism is not only, "Have you received forgiveness?" but, "Will you participate in the attempt to understand what is the meaning of the age?"

This leads to further comments about where the prophetic community focuses its attention. It attempts to stand in both the Old Testament and the New Testament traditions. In the Old Testament, prophecy is directed primarily to the nation, whereas in the New Testament, prophecy is more concerned with internal problems of the Christian community. To say that the prophetic community must address itself both to the problems of the world community and to the community of believers is not only sound theologically but it is a practical necessity. For it is becoming increasingly impossible to separate personal and social problems, especially under urban conditions.

In this connection, something must be said about the significance of politics. If politics may be defined in the broad sense as that which has to do with the *polis*, [3] then politics will become a major concern of the church. Whether we like it or not, life is becoming increasingly politically determined. Whether we call our culture a cybernetic, technological, or industrial culture, it is increasingly political in character. Business, education, commerce, and communication are coordinated by political power, And, of course, it is obvious that problems of peace and war are so important for the continuation of the human race that the church cannot be disinterested.

The only general rule that can be laid down for the focusing of attention is the necessity of concentrating on important matters. Trivia is the death to the believers' churches. Furthermore, believers' churches must wrestle with crucial current issues. If they do not, they change their character. Although we would not concede that they must move from crisis to crisis in contrast to the established churches which move from grace to grace, we would acknowledge that the believers' churches need the stimulus of a dynamic world in order to exist. Since their reliance upon organizational structures is minimal and their concept of grace is nonsacramental, they need to struggle with the world, while being motivated by an eschatological vision of the future. The world in which we are living—urban, revolutionary, violent, technological—meets the Believers' Church need to be kept on its toes and a bit off balance.

In speaking about the relation of the prophetic community to the political order, one should point out that prophecy as a working concept is felicitous for the Believers' Church. It is felicitous because it implies involvement, even emotional involvement, with the world. Nevertheless, it implies a transcendent loyalty to God which results in sharp selective opposition to particular policies which are deemed immoral. The prophet is not sectarian in the sense in which that word is sometimes used. He is not opposed *en toto* to the world; he is indeed a man of the world. However, he is free to oppose what needs to be opposed and equally free to support what needs to be supported. The prophetic community is a community for which discrimination is a way of life. The function of the prophetic community is to sharpen the powers of discrimination.

One should not conclude the description of the prophetic community without at least raising the question of whether there is any sense in using the term "prophet" today. This is a most problematic issue. We use the word "prophetic" with a wide variety of meanings. Sometimes it means no more than radical criticism, striking social biases, *avant-garde* sympathies, or bearded mumblings. We use the adjective "prophetic" with an abandon with which we do not use the noun "prophet." We have no prophets. At least we have no prophetic office as such. The problem seems to lie in the realm of prophetic inspiration.

I feel that we need not be held up by this difficulty, however. Let us frankly admit that today's prophets will come to their conclusions largely on the basis of historical analyses and scientific understanding rather than direct inspiration. But this use of the reason will proceed from a sensitive spirit and a believing mind. Furthermore, it will represent the spiritual struggles of a believing community. The reluc-

177

tance to say, "Thus saith the Lord," in many cases may actually be an advantage in a secular state.

The Believers' Church today must become a *healing community*. It must seek to heal those who have lost touch with reality and long for authentic existence. The healing community will endeavor to meet the crisis of man as his sense of identity and wholeness is eroded and as traditional identity-bestowing realities are swept from him by a technological society. It will try to create a community in which the plight of the individual may be freely discussed. In that freedom the community will offer manhood by the reinterpreting of traditional symbols and by offering a new set of relationships.

What is needed today is a community which is designed to accomplish under modern circumstances what Pietism has traditionally accomplished, especially through revivals. Many believers' churches have depended upon revivals to supply the basis for their life. Revivals have been the way by which churches have intensified pietistic religion. In the pietist tradition the revival has been the means by which the churches have articulated the message of forgiveness. The revival has been the occasion for the individual to receive his identity as a child of God and as a member of the community. We are not likely to exaggerate the significance of the revival for authentic existence. The revival has been the instrument of Pietism through which converts have seen themselves as people who have been accepted by God and the community. In many villages and rural parts of America, conversion has even carried with it acceptance by the community at large.

But in recent years, the revival, Billy Graham notwithstanding, has been losing its function as a means for the intensification and realization of faith. Hence, many so-called believers' churches are caught in a whirl of unreality. What is needed, therefore, is an alternative to revivalism which will be no less effective in meeting the religious needs of the individual. It must be an alternative which makes it possible for modern man, given his peculiar problems of self-understanding and acceptance, to find God, himself, and his neighbor.

I personally believe that an alternative lies in a new conception of *koinonia*. Such a *koinonia* would address itself in biblical and in modern, psychological terms to the problem of being a human being in a technological society. It would try to understand why people feel and act the way they do, and it would attempt not only to understand the underlying problems of existence, but it would

178

attempt to be a genuine fellowship, which is in itself at least a partial answer to the problem.

I am not suggesting that the Believers' Church is in itself the solution to the problem of modern estrangement. But I believe that an anthropological revolution is occurring, a new concept of man is emerging, to which the theologian must respond with a concept of the "New Man," and to which there must be found no less an ecclesiological counterpart. The typical institutional church, with its center in preaching, may have been acceptable in a less pluralistic age, when communication was possible within a commonly accepted idiom. But today, especially within the city, what is needed is a somewhat less pretentious form of communication in which vastly different views, born of modern specialization, interests, and activities, enter into dialogue. Church life must increasingly take on the quality of a search among a multitude of alternatives and possibilities with the Holy Spirit as the teacher and guide.

I wish that it were possible to set forth at greater length the main lines of the conception of a prophetic and healing community. If there were time, I would discuss decision-making, consensus, discipline, and mission. I would also like to show a possible link between "binding and loosing" and the "New Morality." But we must turn to the question of whether this and other conceptions of the Believers' Church have a ghost of a chance in the contemporary world.

My feelings are ambivalent. It would appear that the Believers' Church in the pure sense will not become a widespread phenomenon in our time. Very few congregations of the American establishment are likely to be transformed into congregations which incorporate all or even most of the marks of the Believers' Church. Among the marks which are most unlikely today are consensus in belief and discipline. Our culture is pluralistic and individualistic, and as a result it is extremely difficult to expect a theological consensus except on vague generalities, and in a day of ethical relativism and behaviorism, our congregations are less and less prone to hold people morally responsible for their actions. Furthermore, the Believers' Church is just too demanding for the masses. For most people today, the Believers' Church implies a level of commitment and sacrifice which exceeds in their minds the benefits of the church. Others feel that the church as an institution, regardless of its form, is no longer in touch with the great centers of power and decision-making in the modern world. The church has been displaced by the university as the source of ideas, and such think tanks as the Rand Corporation are more relevant to

179

the world than the church will ever be. Still others could not care less.

This is not to say that the Believers' Church is technically impossible, or that it should be abandoned as an ideal. Sometimes it is claimed that the Believers' Church is in conflict with urban society. But the city is not ultimately decisive. The existence of the Church of the Saviour in Washington is proof of that fact. The Church of the Saviour defies all those sociological "laws" which are supposed to make genuine community impossible. Its members are scattered. They come from different backgrounds. They represent diverse occupations, races, classes, and temperaments. Yet this church not only exists, but it has risen up to challenge the very foundations of American church life. Thousands of pastors and laymen visit the Church of the Saviour each year, and many churches throughout the nation have been influenced by this disciplined congregation of eighty members. It may be expected that other similar experiments will appear during the present period of ferment, but it is somewhat indicative of the problem that all attempts to duplicate the Church of the Saviour have failed. Radical congregations which attempt to bring into organic unity all or nearly all of the classical marks of the Believers' Church are few and far between.

However, this is just part of the picture. While it is impossible to point to many kosher believers' churches, it is one of the exciting facts of our time that many ideas and practices which have been emphasized by the Believers' Church are being introduced *piecemeal* into the "established" churches. I refer to the renaissance of the laity, study groups, discussions, and missionary outreach. The World Council of Churches' study of the "Missionary Structure of the Congregation" is reminiscent of the Anabaptist search for missionary outreach. I trust that I am not presumptuous in suggesting that almost all that has been discussed under the rubric of "renewal," except liturgical renewal, points in the direction of the Believers' Church.

Just what the end result will be we cannot tell. Rigid ecclesiological systems are breaking down, and we are seeing what would appear to be strange combinations of ideas and practices. Believers' Church ideas and practices are no longer centered in the believers' churches, but they are being dispersed in all kinds of organizations and structures. Oddly enough, the people who are most excited about such ideas are the Roman Catholics. The Catholic Church is undergoing a revolution in which renewal is being greeted with integrity and passion. Renewal among the Catholics is not just a rebellious child of secularization, or a frantic search for the latest gimmick, or an attempt to join the *avant-garde*. Rather, it is the discovery of ways by which faith may express itself. I trust that I am not sanguine when I suggest that one can detect a religious quality about Catholic renewal which is increasingly absent among the Protestants. We must, therefore, wait with thankful hearts and open minds to what emerges from the injection of Believers' Church ideas into structures which were once considered foreign. Will there emerge in history ecclesiological structures which make such distinctions as "church" and "sect" or Believers' Church and the "established church" appear outmoded? Will the Catholic Church find ways by which the strength of its massive institution, with its authoritative structures and ecclesiastical powers, may be combined with Believers' Church practices, thus joining the values of the institution with the *koinonia*? This is another way of asking whether the future of the Believers' Church lies in the local congregation or in the *ecclesiola in ecclesia*.

A PEOPLE UNDER THE WORD

8

A P E O P L E U N D E R T H E W O R D:

Historical Background

The name of Alfred T. DeGroot has frequently been associated both with the history of the Christian Church (Disciples of Christ)—both historiography and history-making—and with the Ecumenical Movement. A native of Virginia, Dr. DeGroot was educated at Lynchburg College, Butler University, and the University of Grenoble (France) and received his PhD degree from the University of Chicago. Now he is professor of church history, Brite Divinity School, Texas Christian University, Fort Worth, Texas, and is one of two "distinguished professors" in that university.

Onetime pastor of Christian churches in Indiana and Michigan, Dr. DeGroot formerly taught at Butler University, Drake University, and Overdale College, England, was dean of Chapman College, and from 1949 to 1956 served as dean of the Graduate School of Arts, Sciences and Professions at Texas Christian. He coauthored with Winfred Ernest Garrison the most comprehensive history of the Disciples movement: *The Disciples of Christ: A History* (1948; 2nd rev. ed., 1958). He is author or coauthor of twenty other books. He has represented the Disciples churches in numerous ecumenical gatherings, including the first assembly of the World Council of Churches, and since 1953 has served as archivist for the World Council's Faith and Order Commission.

The context out of which Dr. DeGroot addressed the Conference on the Concept of the Believers' Church was also more particular, namely, the recent discussions centered around the Consultation on Church Union and particularly the issues faced by the Christian Church (Disciples of Christ)˙if deciding to enter a merged and comprehensive Protestant Church. From an extensive survey of patristic, medieval, Reformation, and contemporary sources Dr. DeGroot concludes that the weight of Christian evidence rests not in favor of "a hierarchical, limited listening community" but in favor of "a believing community, a people under the Word" which is as comprehensive as genuine faith itself. Disavowing the centrality of the issue of ordination, he cautions against "an almost abnormal fascination" with things Greek and Roman.

In his response to Dr. DeGroot's address, Dr. Donald F. Durnbaugh, associate professor of church history, Bethany Theological Seminary, Oak Brook, Illinois, associated himself "both with the approach and the results of Dr. DeGroot" and commended the latter for treatment of "a broad topic from a broad foundation . . . with charity of mind while maintaining clarity of conviction." Dr. Durnbaugh, however, expressed surprise at Dr. DeGroot's "lack of references to the denominational heritages represented at this conference" and observed:

> Surely from the histories of these groups can be gleaned some of the most eloquent affirmations and testimonies on the church as a people of God under the Word to be found anywhere in church history. Possibly the author assumed that these are so well known to this assemblage as to be superfluous. Yet . . . this omission is to be regretted.

Dr. Durnbaugh expressed doubt that member churches within the World Council of Churches must "publicly confess the existence *as churches* of the member bodies" and demurred at the statement that after Vatican I "tradition" in the Roman Catholic Church became "simply whatever the pope now teaches."

Then Dr. Durnbaugh posed six questions for further consideration: (1) "What, in fact, is the appropriate posture, *vis a vis* the Ecumenical Movement, of denominations dedicated to the definition of church as the people under the Word? . . . Is there biblical support for a separated role?" (2) "Does the move of the Roman Catholic teaching toward Scripture and the corresponding move of the World Council of Churches toward tradition have something to say to those in the believers' churches? In what way is Scripture itself tradition, and in what way is it traditioned?" (3) "Is it not true that free churches wrestle with the same problems" of "continuity and institutionalization" which Dr. DeGroot criticizes "in Anglo-Catholicism and Roman Catholicism"? Is it possible, as some have claimed, "that greater abuse of authority is found where there is no established constitutional system of checks and balances in church polity"? (4) "Do not free churches face the same problems" of "acculturation," i.e., "the anomaly of the church baptizing the state or the culture following the 'Constantinian fall,' " as the "writings of Littell, Marty, Berger, and Benton" and the recent research of Gustafson seem to indicate? (5) "How is the church as a people under the Word to judge and respond to" the contemporary "words of the world"? (6) How is the Vincentian canon, quoted with approval by Dr. DeGroot, "to be brought into harmony with the free church emphasis upon the gathered and disciplined church?" "How is the Vincentian definition to be differentiated from a 'spiritualized' concept of the church without visible limit, so opposed in history by free churchmen? . . . In reacting against morphological fundamentalism, has Dr. DeGroot pushed the limits further than the free churches were willing to do?"

º   º   º

The major concern of this paper shall be to look historically at who the *people* are who are under the providence and word of God. Of course, as believers in one God we must affirm that all people are his concern. However, our object is not to pursue the problem of just how the 70 percent of the world's population who are non-Christian fit into that providence. Certainly a great humility must possess us when we consider that the God of history permits a variety of faiths to avoid our company. As we turn apart from the vast majority of humankind at whom the Vatican II fathers peered with mixed feelings as "the people of God," we can the more modestly go about our particular task of identifying and differentiating those who claim to be not only under a very special providence but specifically under the word of God. Across the centuries of Christian history we shall see a varied judgment as to who, within only Christian bounds, are understood to be truly God's people.

In the year of our Lord, 1967, we enjoy a view of *church* vastly different from the strong opinionism that we must review historically. It is the specific accomplishment of the World Council of Churches in this century to bring into effective encounter and fellowship Christian communities that publicly confess the existence *as churches* of the member bodies. In ten years Roman Catholicism has broadened its horizon vastly on this theme. It entered the decade with the long-cherished assumption that it was the one authorized successor to the institution (this conference might say, "if any") begun by the apostles. But the ecclesial character of non-Roman Christian bodies is taken seriously by the decree on ecumenism issuing from Vatican II. Eastern Orthodox churches are described almost as sister churches, and their episcopal celebration of the eucharist is acknowledged as producing the holy assembly of the Lord, his chosen people, his church.

Rome does not acknowledge the sacramental succession of clergy as existing among any of the churches of the West who claim to have it, but, again, it does admit the ecclesial character of these communities. Their baptism and their announcement of the Word is seen as real. Indeed, says Gregory Baum,[1] since the Word is a power unto salvation and the Spirit is free to move as he wills, the institutional perfection of a Church does not guarantee its conformity to the image of Christ. A diocese of the Roman church, for instance though institutionally complete, may yet be made up of members who are transformed into God's People only in an incipient way, while another ecclesiastical community, though lacking many of the elements that make up the Church as institution, may be constituted of men who are, through Word and Spirit, deeply united and sanctified as God's own People. Baum contends that in a complete and balanced ecclesiology the two levels must constantly be taken into account, the Church as institution and the Church as communion with the Lord. In his view, when the Roman church regards herself as the measure of ecclesiastical fidelity, this applies only to the institutional level, i.e., **to the episcopal and papal structure as guarantee of the Gospel**.

187

However, much as this more humble understanding of the character of the church has come to be in recent years on the part of Roman advocates, we must leave it to its proper place in our chronology. The purpose of this conference is to segregate the constitutive aspects of the church as these were perceived in history. How have professing Christians across the centuries delimited and defined the People of God, the *Lumen Gentium*—the Light of All Nations? Apart from the 70 percent, our *Corporis Mystici* consists of those people under the Word. As we make our review, we shall see a checkered understanding of this body. Even Protestant ecclesiology will make the directional error of Vatican I, the unfinished work of which started with structures and government. Free churchmen see the body of Christ to consist of persons in groups who apprehend the nature and call of the gospel. They can take courage that Vatican II quite reversed the direction of its predecessor and began to see the church, in the words of Avery Dulles, "as *a people* [italics mine] to whom God communicates Himself in love."[2]

I

Our concern for a *people* under the Word is reflected in one of the very earliest and most often quoted fathers, Ignatius. Writing to the Smyrnaeans (ch. 8), he says, "Wheresoever the bishop appears, there let the people be, even as wheresoever Christ Jesus is, there is the Catholic Church."[3] This signifies his understanding that the presence of Christ is the essence of the church universal and his judgment that the bishop is the essence of the church local and is its tie to the church universal. When we recall that Ignatius meant by a bishop a local and not a diocesan functionary, quite unrelated to medieval or traditional episcopacy, he becomes a valued witness to the concept of the believers' church. Indeed, we could say he was anti-episcopal, if by that we use the traditional idea, for as George H. Williams says, "Ignatius thinks of himself as instituted by the Spirit of God. There is no thought of his being a successor of an apostle. He is a prophet."[4]

Irenaeus (*c*. 130-*c*. 200) is the first clear delineator of the idea of apostolic succession, but it is important to observe *why* he introduced this novelty. For him the true church was vouchsafed by the true tradition or true apostolic teaching; in our term, the Word. For him episcopal order was related to apostolic teaching; his heavy emphasis was on the latter—the transmission of the truth, the Word. Only later was his emphasis turned upside down. While in the earlier fathers apostolicity lay basically in teaching that accords with the *witness* of the apostles, it came in the course of time to be equated with the episcopal *office* with fidelity in teaching taken for granted. This is as fascinating a development as is what has happened to the Roman Catholic concept of "tradition." Until the vacillating "Pio Nono Secondo" (Pius the Ninth the Second) and his personal declaration of the novel dogma of the Immaculate Conception in 1854 it was the assumed agreement reached by the fathers of the church; but, since that time it is simply whatever the pope now teaches. Pius IX (1846-1878) said, "I am tradition."

Tertullian (*c.* 160- *c.* 220) is like Irenaeus in regard to apostolicity. The apostolic succession really lies in the churches and is demonstrated in their bishops, although apostolic teaching rather than apostolic pedigree of the founder is what really counts. This is seen in the very title of his work, *The Prescription Against Heretics.* [5]

St. Vincent of Lerins (*c.* 434) presented the church with a conception with which it must ever reckon. His succinct Latin definition was, *quod ubique, quod semper, quod ab omnibus creditum est*— i.e., the church is found under such truth as is believed everywhere, always and by everybody.[6] This places a reception of the Word at the center of ecclesial reality.

John of Damascus (*c.* 675-*c.* 749) begins with the same emphasis upon apostolic belief as central to church existence that we have seen in those cited thus far. After describing one hundred and three heresies in his work *On Heresies*, he says, "The Catholic Church has kept itself away from all of these."[7] However, of one group, the Audians, he says that they "form a schism and a faction, but not, however, a heresy. They pursue a well-ordered way of life and profess a faith which is in every respect like that of the Catholic Church."[8] He then describes them as a monastic, puritanical group which had withdrawn from the rest of the church. Thus John's full concept of church stressed the importance, if not the absolute necessity, of fellowship in the mainstream of group agreement.

So thoroughly was the church taken for granted as the paramount fact of medieval life that little time was devoted to reflection upon its nature. Hugo of St. Victor (1097-1141) called the church the body of Christ animated by one spirit and united in a single faith. He asked if it was not "the totality of the faithful—the totality of Christians? "[9] This definition expresses a widespread medieval understanding of the church, which saw it more as the body of Christians than as the body of Christ, for there is little evidence from that period of serious reflection upon the nature of the church in Christological terms. The church was understood more after the manner of an empire to whose powers Christians were subject, rather than as a living organism.[10]

Commenting on the ninth article of the Apostles' Creed, Thomas Aquinas (c. 1225-1274) saw the church as the congregation of the faithful. In his *Summa Contra Gentiles* and his *Summa Theologica*, Thomas deals with the Catholic faith rather than the Catholic Church, defining the Catholic faith as that universally held and opposed to heresy.[11] In this respect Aquinas is like Augustine. But with Boniface VIII and his bull *Unam Sanctam*, 1302, the polemical concept of "one holy, catholic, apostolic" church united in the papacy was declared and has prevailed in Roman thought to modern times.

Beginning in the twelfth century, the Waldenses developed their understanding of the church in the manner in which they presented it to the king of Bohemia in 1508. Their vitalistic concept saw the church as the body of active Christians who embrace and proclaim the evangelical faith. Much the same terminology was employed by Marsilius of Padua (c. 1275-1342). While his major concern was for a political theory which placed the state above the church, he was clear in defining the latter as

> the whole body of the faithful who believe in and invoke the name of Christ, and all the parts of this whole body in any community, even the household.[12]

Quite in opposition to the prevailing hierarchical ideology Marsilius desired that control of the faithful be exercised by a general council of clergy and lay persons elected by the faithful under the direction of their rulers.

As far as the main body of Christendom is concerned, it is with Martin Luther that we see a return to the Word as central to the life of the church. He says,

> Wherever, therefore, you hear or see this Word preached, believed, confessed, and acted on, there do not doubt that there must be a true ecclesia sancta catholica, a Christian, holy people even though it be small in numbers; for God's Word does not go away empty (Isaiah 1v), but must have at least a fourth part, or a piece of the field. If there were no other mark than this one alone, it would still be enough to show that there must be a Christian church there; for God's Word cannot be present without God's people, and God's people cannot be without God's Word.[13]

John Calvin is clear in his proclamation of the church as the elect of God: "all the elect of God are so connected with each other in

190

Christ, that as they depend upon one head, so they grow up together as into one body, compacted together like members of the same body. . . . " [14] But he approximates Luther's evangelical concept, seeing the church in terms of an evangelistic succession extending from the apostles in time and space. [15]

Zwingli's *Sixty-Seven Articles* (1523) saw the church lying in the being of Christ as shared by all those who receive salvation from him. Three of the articles read this way:

VI.   For Christ Jesus is the Leader and Captain, promised and given by God to the whole human race.
VII.   That He might be the eternal salvation and Head of all believers, who are His body, which however is dead and can do nothing without Him.
VIII. From this it follows that all who live in the Head are members and children of God, and this is the Church or communion of the saints, a bride of Christ, *ecclesia catholica.* [16]

Zwingli was clear on his distinction between the visible and invisible church. He said,

We also believe that there is one holy, catholic, that is, universal Church, and that this Church is either visible or invisible. . . . Within the visible Church . . . there are some who are not members of the Church elect and invisible. [17]

That the Anabaptists did not neglect the ecumenical aspect of the church despite their strong emphasis upon its delimitation to believers is apparent in a statement by Menno Simons (*c.* 1496-1561). He said,

Therefore observe that which I write, and let it be unto you a certain rule—namely, where the Spirit, Word, sacraments, and life of Christ are found, there the Nicene article is pertinent, I believe in one holy, Christian church, the communion of saints, etc. [18]

Richard Hooker (1553?-1600) states that the church's confession of Christ must include keeping "that faith" which Christ published unto the world and which the church has received from the apostles as the given belief. [19]

Vatican Council I, 1869-1870, presents us with the most exclusive, even pugnacious, definition of the church. In its *Dogmatic Constitution I on the Church of Christ* the council declared the infallibility of the Roman pontiff in his official magisterium. The opening sentence reads,

But, that the episcopacy itself might be one and undivided, and that the entire multitude of the faithful through priests closely connected with one another might be preserved in the unity of faith and communion, placing the blessed Peter over the other apostles He established in him the perpetual principle and visible foundation of both unities, upon whose strength the eternal temple might be erected, and the sublimity of the Church to be raised to heaven might rise in the firmness of this faith. [20]

Perceptible softening of this brittle delineation without any retreat from its juristic claims (by placing the matter in the realm of mystery) is seen in Pius XII and his encyclical in 1943 entitled *On the Mystical Body of Christ.* He emphasizes that while the juridical principles of the Church are divinely given and contribute to the Church's realizing its divine destiny, it is the Spirit of Christ in the Church that "lifts the Society of Christians far above the natural order" and gives it all "graces," "gifts," and "miraculous powers." [21]

From this changed stance and the fresh winds of Vatican II George Tavard asked in 1963,

Is it at last possible to contemplate the structure of the Church according to other patterns than those of power, of jurisdiction, of authority? Can our episcopate, formed by scholasticism and canon law and accustomed to the exercise of power, see itself in its *ensemble* with eyes which are not the eyes of jurists? [22]

Tavard declared that the ecclesiological issue facing Vatican II was, "Will it be Catholic or simply Latin?" In similar strain and with an echo of Rupertus Meldenius is Lorenz Jaeger, who says,

This catholicity is unity in essentials, liberty in the approved variations in liturgy, theology and canon law, the whole being subject in charity to the Lord and Head of the Church, Jesus Christ, and his visible representative, the pope. [23]

Even more in the direction of a people under the Word is the thought of Hans Küng—but with the safely orthodox reservations. He conceives of the people of God as being in communion in council but also in relation to the papacy. Moreover, the council "is open to the Holy Spirit, who breathes where he will, even outside an official ministry." [24] Küng considers the Lutheran doctrine of the priesthood of all believers to be, first of all, Catholic doctrine and holds that Catholic laymen could directly participate in a general council of the church. But he declares that the central issue in "Catholic-Protestant dialogue" at this point is "the problem of ecclesiastical office and its function." Küng sees Protestants, even via the World Council, unable to constitute an ecumenical council. For him, "the *episkopoi* who represent the individual Churches do not have the powers and authority of their ministry as delegated to them by the people; it is the Holy Ghost who, in succession to the Apostles (Acts 14:22), has placed them as bishops to shepherd the *ekklesia* of God. . . ." Neither is a general council "simply a parliament of the Church."[25] Thus he seems to prefer the pope as the presiding officer of the universal episcopate so as to be its pastoral leader and director much as the bishop is conceived to be in his diocese.

Vatican II's *Dogmatic Constitution on the Church* has a number of generous and inclusive statements about the people of God, but safely concludes:

> They are fully incorporated into the society of the Church who, possessing the Spirit of Christ, accept her entire system and all the means of salvation given to her, and through union with her visible structure are joined to Christ, who rules her through the Supreme Pontiff and the bishops.[26]

However, it is affirmed that the Roman Church is "linked with those who, being baptized, are honored with the name of Christian, though they do not profess the faith in its entirety or do not preserve unity of communion with the successor of Peter."[27] Furthermore, "those who have not yet received the gospel are related in various ways to the People of God"—Jews, Mohammedans, and other non-Christians. Devout persons in these communities are not beyond the reach of salvation.[28]

Eastern Orthodoxy in our day insists no less than does Rome upon the absolute necessity of apostolic succession and of hierarchy to the being of the church.[29] In practice, historic emphasis upon mysticism and devotion gives at least a surface life to fellowship with other Christians. It would be a great service to Christendom if some scholar would write an extensive study of "economy" in the systems of both Eastern and Western Catholicism. Here is a doctrine by which an existential fellowship is declared and supported in relation to those not canonically with the "true" church.[30]

Attracted as this writer is to the value and utility of the Vincentian definition, the cautionary words of Georges Florovsky on the subject are appreciated. He says that "Catholic experience can be expressed even by the few, even by single confessors of faith; and this is quite sufficient." It may happen that in a council the truth will be expressed by a minority.[31]

There is tentative willingness today on the part of the Episcopal signatories to the "Principles of Union" in the Consultation on Church Union by which they would accept from the authorities of non-episcopal communions "a form of commission or recognition," while ministers of non-episcopal churches might "accept a commission through episcopal ordination, as obtaining for them a ministry throughout the whole fellowship."[32] Indeed, since that particular statement of position was written, there has, in quite recent times, been a far greater concession, tentatively, by which no re-ordination would be required in the constituting of the proposed "new church." This willingness is an emergent in the twentieth century and stems from an irenic letter "To All Christian People" issued by the Lambeth Conference of 1920. It said:

> We acknowledge all those who believe in Our Lord Jesus Christ and have been baptized into the name of the Holy Trinity, as sharing with us membership in the universal Church of Christ which is his Body. . . . We believe that God wills fellowship.[33]

This was a perceptible softening of previous interpretations of the Chicago-Lambeth Quadrilateral of 1886, particularly in the light of interpretations which had been made in earlier centuries by John Pearson and other Anglicans.[34]

Pertinent to the vexed problem of orders in COCU is the judgment of one of the editors of the *Journal of Ecumenical Studies.* He says:

> We must confess to a sense of shock upon reading that "essential to such a church . . . is a united ministry, capable of bearing un-doubted and unquestionable authority everywhere." (Proceedings, IV, 30) On such terms no church will ever come into existence. Perhaps we ought not take this astonishing ideal statement so seriously. Surely its authors must have known that no one can make over the clergy of the participating denominations into such an image. Is not a confession of liability to error and dependence upon the Spirit in the church axiomatic to a ministry of mission and renewal? Many Catholics have recently questioned the Pope himself who is supported by the most extended doctrine of au-thority known to Christian history, when he declared that the church entertained no doubts relative to its traditional position on birth control. How can such an "undoubted and unquestioned authority" for the ministry of the new church arise? This phrasing must have been borrowed in a moment of thoughtlessness from the past; it is remote from the reality of a modern church min-istry.[35]

This writer is aware of a certain ambiguity in the current Anglican concepts of just who are the people under the Word. Recognition that non-episcopal Christian bodies are part of one true church is balanced by the reservation that a reunited Catholic church must include the historic episcopate. Arthur Michael Ramsey, present Archbishop of Canterbury, is clear in his stand. He says:

> We are led, therefore, to affirm that the Episcopate is of the *esse* of the universal Church; but we must beware of mis-stating the issue. All who are baptized into Christ are members of His Church, and Baptism is the first mark of churchmanship. Yet the growth of all Christians into the measure of the stature of the fulness of Christ means their growth with all the saints in the unity of the one Body, and of this unity the Episcopate is the expression.[36]

Another who might agree to be called Anglo-Catholic is William Nicholls. Acknowledging that "no one of our separated churches proclaims the integral Gospel," still he contends that "the apostolic succession is one among a number of other elements of Catholicity."[37] But, yielding to another impulse, Nicholls says that it is wrong to make apostolicity the *esse* of the church and unity only its *bene esse*. He argues that, if separated churches are all to some degree of the one church, the burden then is upon those who refuse intercommunion with their brethren in such churches.[38]

It is a pleasure to report that the Free Churchmen who presented to the Archbishop of Canterbury a book entitled *The Catholicity of Protestantism* had done their homework on what is for this writer a favorite volume on systematic—no, let us call it philosophical—theology. I refer to *Robinson Crusoe*. The circumstances of its writing were not, contrary to common belief, a prophetic or clairvoyant faith that someday God would send Walt Disney. The authors of *Catholicity* . . . comment on Ignatius and say:

> It is the presence of the living Christ, recognized, adored and obeyed, which secures the catholicity of the Church. Nothing else is necessary; and if a Christian in whom Christ dwells by faith lives on an island which is otherwise entirely inhabited by devil-worshipping savages, the catholic Church is present in his person, for he represents both his Lord and the people of his Lord. For St. Paul, for St. Ignatius, for the Reformers, and for us, to be "in Christ" is to be in the Church.[39]

More specifically, the authors, quoting the language of the "Declaratory Statement" of the [British] Free Church Federal Council, see the people under the Word to consist of

> "the whole company of the redeemed in heaven and on earth, and we recognize as belonging to this holy fellowship all who are united to God through faith in Christ."[40]

The Free Churchmen criticize "the highly romantic view expressed in *Catholicity* [the Anglo-Catholic report to the Archbishop], of the Church of the early centuries." They think that the Anglo-Catholic authors "have slipped an undefined 'Tradition' into the place of the Word, which is Christ Himself, and treated it as the final authority for the faith and life of the Church." The Free Churchmen argue:

> The notion of the episcopal succession as in itself guaranteeing the "wholeness" of the Gospel can by no device be shown to be derived from Christ Himself. We stand by the view of the episcopate which Irenaeus held, that it has its authority in virtue of its proclamation of the Word; the office is contingent upon the Word; not the Word on the office. He is concerned with the defence and proclamation of the apostolic *kerygma* against "another gospel," that of the false Gnosis of the heretical teachers. Like a modern historian seeking the best and most reliable sources, he appeals to the bishops in the great sees as the most responsible persons who could testify to the pure and unaltered message of the apostles. This testimony is rendered all the more reliable because the historical succession has been brief, well-known and unbroken, in Rome and Smyrna and Ephesus.[41]

The Free Churchmen emphasize their convictions that the one "essential" ministry is that of Christ, which he continues through the church, his body. The Holy Spirit, and not the apostles, is Christ's "plenipotentiary." They point out that the argument in the book, *The Apostolic Ministry*, that the apostles are *sheluchim* and therefore plenipotentiaries has subsequently been shown by reliable scholars to be incorrect.[42] At the vexed point of the ministry, the writers approve the "Declaratory Statement": "The Ministry is an office within the Church—not a sacerdotal order—instituted for the preaching of the Word, the ministration of the Sacraments and the care of souls."[43] They grant that episcopacy "may be seen by all to be the most valuable form of the Ministry for the welfare of the Church; but the efficacy, the reality and the divine origin of other forms are attested by signs manifest to all."[44]

In summary, the concept expressed by the British Free Churchmen is that catholicity is the wholeness of the church in Christ—realized partially as yet, but nonetheless the church's eschatological destiny. It includes all who have been reconciled to God through faith in Christ. Its elements include belief in the Word of God presented in the Bible, faith in God in Christ, the unity of the church, the gospel sacraments, and the office of the ordained ministry. Catholicity centers in Christ present to his church as the visible and spiritual fellowship of all those united with him by faith. It does not center in the historic episcopate and the historic episcopate cannot, on pain of blasphemy, be conceived of as essential to the catholicity of the church.

Daniel T. Jenkins, British Congregationalist, argues that "the nature of catholicity can be determined only in the light of God's Word, Jesus Christ, and that Church Order has significance only in relation to the Gospel." Thus, "the inquiry into the nature of catholicity and thus into the nature of the true Church is the same as the question, 'Is Jesus Christ in the Church?' " Jenkins observes that the Apostle Paul "in the opening chapters of Galatians pours scorn upon those who maintained that a certain kind of connection with the Apostles was necessary before his 'gospel' could be accepted." He sees this passage as "of crucial importance for the Reformed doctrine of catholicity as against that of traditional Catholicism" without deprecating apostolic authority.[45] On apostolicity Jenkins makes this statement:

> We are as ready . . . as traditional Catholicism is, to assert that apostolicity is the essential mark of catholicity, but our position is distinguished from theirs by the fact that we are compelled to insist that it is their *testimony* which constitutes the Apostles as Apostles. . . . It is not their faith or their zeal or their religious genius or any special charismata they possessed, like the gift of the Spirit by the laying on of hands, and certainly not any accident of historical association, but their *testimony* which constitutes them apostles. This is what the argument of Saint Paul in the first two chapters of Galatians already mentioned makes clear. . . . It is hard to believe that the exceptional circumstances of Paul's call are not intended as a reminder to a Church which is always in danger of forgetting it that it is their testimony to a God who retains His Lordship over them and therefore His freedom to work independently of them or even against them which gives their authority to His ministers.[46]

Jacques de Senarclens, a Reformed theologian, argues in 1961 that it is the Holy Spirit who produces the church among us. He said:

What I mean is that we are now at the stage at which we must preach, teach, reflect, and pray for the Holy Spirit that more authentic Christians may arise. Care for the Church as such comes forward. If what we do is successful, we will see then what kind of Church the Spirit will produce among us. On the other hand, if we refuse to take this path and put the cart before the horse, I fear that our ecclesiological discussions will simply lead to new institutionalisms.

It is therefore more important to speak of what creates the Church, than of the Church in and of itself, for the right causes inevitably bring the Church into being, while taken more or less alone, the Church can only deviate from its true nature. [17]

Thomas F. Torrance warns us against starting reunion discussion with the subject of orders, the historic connection of which could issue from the spirit of man and human culture. The Christological and soteriological approach is the necessary basis on which the study of the church in relation to the Holy Spirit can be undertaken. In other words, the *filioque* clause in the historic creed is of decisive importance here. [18]

Markus Barth decries the Presbyterian-Anglican overtures of a few years ago in which "it was considered to swap bishops (or their ordination) against elders and vice versa!" Says Barth:

Renewal of the Church will rather come from a rediscovery of, and obedience to, a more Biblical understanding of ministry and sacrament, than from a high doctrine of the Church. [19]

Karl Barth insists that the identity of the church cannot be equated with the continuity of certain earlier forms, such as "a legal succession . . . of its ministry linking it with the ancient or most modern or most ancient Church." He argues that the mistake of basing apostolicity upon a verifiable so-called apostolic succession in history is that "neither the Holy Spirit nor faith is necessary." [30] Answering the contention that the Holy Spirit in the form of the "particular gift" of "the grace of office legitimately [is] passed from one man to another by means of a fixed rite," Barth asks:

But in that case, who and what is the Holy Spirit? Is He the sovereign God, who as Spirit moves where He will, awakening the hearts of men to the unity of the faith and their lips to attest it?—or is He something quite different? [31]

An important Lutheran view of our subject is the "Declaration of the Ecumenical Committee of the United Evangelical Lutheran

Church of Germany (VELKD) on the Question of Apostolic Succession" in 1957.[52] It sees the whole church by its participation in the Holy Spirit through Baptism being "commissioned and empowered to live out and carry on, in all its fullness, Christ's ministry to the world" and as the apostles blended their ministry with the ministries of the whole church, so must those in special ministries today. The apostolic succession that is of "the essence of the church" is "Christianity's **abiding continuity with her foundation, the apostolic** ministry, and her abiding conformity with the normative witness of the apostles." At the fourth assembly of the Lutheran World Federation in Helsinki, 1963, E. Clifford Nelson said:

> The Church is persons, men and women, called to be the people of God by the Word, sustained as the people of God by the Word, and acting as the people of God by serving the Word. Whether the people of God assemble as local congregations or as synods in specific localities . . . , they are the *ekklesia*, for the one Christ is present whole and undivided in every assembly of believers who are served by and who serve the Word and Sacraments.[53]

He added, "The Church must seek only those historical, earthly, organizational structures which are appropriate to its nature, i.e., the form of a servant. Whatever the form, it stands under the judgment of the Word."[54]

Paul Tillich, a Lutheran, sees the church in ontological terms, but with visible reality. It may always be unfair, even impossible, to characterize his thought in a single quotation, but this one, carefully digested, represents him well:

> The inner-religious profanization of religion, its transformation into a sacred mechanism of hierarchical structure, doctrine, and ritual, is resisted by the participation of church members in the Spiritual Community, which is the dynamic essence of the churches and of which the churches are both the existential representation and the existential distortion. The freedom of the Spirit breaks through mechanizing profanization—as it did in the creative moments of the Reformation.[55]

The modern ecumenical era began with "Edinburgh 1910" (as professionals call it). On our subject that conference dared only to commend comity but in the same breath declare it an insufficient expedient that "must lead to federation and some form of unity in order to present a common front before the enemy."[56] Stockholm,

1925, by the nature of its theme, did not treat ours. Lausanne, 1927, was almost as tentative and vague as the previous meetings. S. Parkes Cadman, a Congregationalist, saw the invisible church as the only universal church. Edinburgh, 1937, sometimes approached, then skirted away from clear delineation of the church and its people. An original and a revised draft on continuity and apostolicity bears this out but will not be given here.[57] On the final day it adopted an "Affirmation of Union in Allegiance to Our Lord Jesus Christ" which emphatically asserted the unity of Christians in the Lord, deeper than their divisions, and the desire to realize the unity willed by Christ for the church.[58] Amsterdam, 1948, dealt specifically with "The Universal Church in God's Design," and this writer as an alternate delegate was in that section. It saw the "deepest difference" in Christendom posed by Protestant and Catholic conceptions. Following normal World Council of Churches procedures it merely "received" the study reports which stated those differences and commended them to the churches for study. Evanston, 1954, spoke more of the church's mission than of its nature. New Delhi, 1961, confronted the subject of the church and its unity, saying,

> We believe that the unity which is both God's will and his gift to his Church is being made visible as all in each place who are baptized into Jesus Christ and confess him as Lord and Saviour are brought by the Holy Spirit into one fully committed fellowship, holding the one apostolic faith, preaching the one Gospel, breaking the one bread, joining in common prayer, and having a corporate life reaching out in witness and service to all who at the same time are united with the whole Christian fellowship in all places and all ages in such wise that ministry and members are accepted by all, and that all can act and speak together as occasion requires for the tasks to which God calls his people.

But it added promptly, "We are not yet of a common mind on the interpretation and the means of achieving the goal we have described."[59] Montreal, 1964, dealt with "The Church in the Purpose of God." However, the very success of the conciliar movement seen in its membership of 212 denominations, all recognized as "churches," means weakness in reaching agreement on complex subjects. The officers at Montreal could only appeal by asking the churches,

> Will you humbly recognize that many of God's gifts to his whole Church cannot be shared by us in our local churches, until we become the one people of God in each place, and are prepared to realize this by new and bold adventures of living faith?[60]

However, a section report did add that

each church or congregation participating in Christ is related to others not by participation in some higher structure but rather by an identity of existence in Christ. In this sense each congregation gathered for the proclamation of the Word and the celebration of the Eucharist is a manifestation of the whole Catholic Church in the very process of becoming what she is in service and witness to the world.[61]

II

Out of the experience of the Christian community across the centuries it is the object of this day's theme in our conference to affirm that the people of God, in the church, are brought into this community by the standards and judgments of the Word more than by any other vehicle of God's disclosure. The Word judges, renews, and re-creates the Church. This Word is held in our hands for our reception and illumination today, being the continuation in time of the original, focal revelation, the Event of Jesus Christ. The Word is Christ, ever awaiting reception by men, who in receiving it become peculiarly and communally his People.

Two problems, closely related, must be confronted here. One was hinted in the introduction to this study. Our very love for the church, the home of the holy community, has caused us to assume that God is limited to a directional scheme in the divine disclosure which is always in the form of God-church-world. We may learn that the divine freedom can challenge the institutional church, on occasions, by choosing to use the world as the teacher of a complacent church, so that one divine thrust may truly be in the direction of God-world-church.

The other "problem" or possibility is indeed the heart of our concern. It is the problem of epistemology, of knowing. What is the best guarantee that a people is in possession of a presumed disclosure? Must some single person or small number among them be seen and accepted as the lenses and filters for the divine light? This consideration is complicated by our recognition that God has used persons, the prophets and Jesus Christ, as the means of great disclosures of his will. The question is, does this revelatory action confine itself to a class, a priesthood, superior to and normally exclusive of the lay community? Or, on the other hand, is the event of Christ a normative and adequate revelation, to which the community of faith relates itself, needing only to establish a means of study and understanding of what is once and for all time given? This latter option is not to deny a life and action of the Holy Spirit; it is, rather, to affirm that the church, the listening community, is the true, appropriate, and more effective means by which the Spirit acts for the guidance of the body of Christ during its earthly sojourn. *The choice is clear: either we believe in a hierarchical, limited listening community, or, we accept a believing community, a people under the Word, as the divinely intended instrument of God's disclosure of his will in every age.*

It is far from original with me to say that any people, any community, requires much time to view, to consider, to evaluate, and to reach conclusions about a problem or group of problems. Gifted individuals favored by circumstances for gathering relevant data may perform the thinking process with comparative rapidity. For a large body of people, such as a nation, or a community spread across nations, to do this requires high levels of communication. They must, first of all, be aware that this process is needed and, indeed, is indispensable. A life of the divine Gospel among men is dependent upon men themselves, men who are conscious of their duty to act as receptors and communicating digestors of truth so far as mankind can know it.

It is this rationale which lies behind the call to this historic first consultation among the voluntary churches. As the conference's Prospectus noted,

> there exists in the heritage of those Christian groups which have insisted upon the baptism of believers, on confession of faith, into visible congregations, an apprehension of the nature of the gospel and of the church which is specific and coherent; which constitutes a theologically valid option and a needed contribution in ecumenical debate. (Prospectus, p. 1.)

The need of laying hold upon the competence of all of God's creation, the whole of humanity consciously committed to discipleship and not just its clergy, in the task of knowing God's will for our day, is emphasized by Hendrik Kraemer. He cautions that "the laity should . . . not be seen primarily as the needy, ignorant and helpless." In many fields the layman is more knowledgeable than the clergy. The very terms "periti" and "lay theologian" tell the clergy more than they may want to acknowledge. What is called for, therefore, is "a *mutual* co-operation of theologians and lay people, in which both are teachers and taught."[62]

The historical background provided in this paper shows that even

202

when the Constantinian events within a century transformed the church from a persecuted community of believers into a persecuting agency ambitious to be empire-wide if not world-wide, perceptive individual leaders never totally lost a view of the believing community as the appropriate vehicle for receipt, perception, and transmission of the divine will, given in Jesus and communicated to and through the disciples. We observed this in Tertullian who saw succession carried by the churches. It was so with St. Vincent, who was concerned for a validating agency, which he perceived in the universal believing community. In similar fashion Aquinas saw the true faith as that which commanded the mind of the vast majority of the Christian community. Luther, of course, was clear in seeing that "God's Word **cannot be present without God's people.**" Hans Küng admits that the Holy Spirit breathes outside of any official ministry and among all believers. Gregory Baum more pointedly delimits the church as hierarchical and visible institution, whereas "God's own People" may be quite another community than that of Rome.

It is from the vantage point of this historic humility that the free and voluntary churches, through this conference, would press upon Christendom the message of their understanding of how, in the divine economy, they have been privileged to regain a valid and true understanding of the whole church as the only effective epistemological instrument for reception of the divine intention for our day and other days. An un-free, state church is denied and rejected, because it cannot but be distorted by the massive influences of an unregenerate society. This is not to say that a community of free churches would be utterly uninfluenced by the pressures of their civil circumstances; it is, rather, to say that there are more opportunities and possibilities for a broad, free body of congregations and persons to hear, consider, and discern the divine intent for the hour and the issue than there are for a ministry or priesthood committed in advance to the pledges it has given to the state for its preferential treatment. We need only remember how readily the state churches have become chaplains to the status quo and have provided chaplaincies for the state at war—even the utter anomaly of "Christian" nation versus "Christian" nation—to see how limited is the un-free church ministry in listening to the voice of the Spirit.

How **easily a concept of ministry-as-office instead of ministry-by-**Word may insinuate itself into the very fabric of the body of Christ is seen in what John A. Mackay refers to as the "fatal comma" which appears in the Revised Standard Version of Ephesians 4:11, 12. That version makes it read that some were entrusted with special gifts (such as prophecy, preaching, and teaching) "for the equipment of the saints, for the work of ministry, for building up the body of Christ." The New English Bible, however, along with Weymouth, Goodspeed, and other translations, omits the comma after "saints." The special gifts were not provided to a select ministry but were "for the equipment *of the saints* for the work of ministry." All saints are a people under the Word.

It was the Free Churchmen who provided a theology by which authority was centered in the whole believing people. Only by this means could there be any such thing as a *consensus fidelium*. Long before the concept of royalty in government, which was a lively reality throughout the nineteenth century, was abandoned, its religious counterpart of a class of priests in sacramental continuity was challenged by the Free Churches. They revived in local congregations genuine encounter as an essential action of religion, which had as its group dynamic "listening to the Spirit." They achieved, as far as humans can achieve, a practical solution of the problem as Miguel de Unamuno delineated it in his great book, *The Agony of Christianity*. He said that

> the agony of Christianity [is] the agony inherent in it and in each one of us. . . . For truth is something collective, social, even civil; that which is true is that upon which we all agree. Christianity is something incommunicable. And that is why it agonizes within each one of us.[63]

It is not necessary for us to present here a full-scale review of the history and "systematic" of the Free Churches. This has been done in a small series of careful expositions, particularly in the past decade. One result has been to remove the myopia by which so able a historian as Preserved Smith could discount them as the "Bolsheviki of the sixteenth century." There is now ground for hope that before long there will be removed the unconscious presumption by which the Bad Boll annual conferences, initiated in 1951, first were termed as between "The *Church* and the *Free Churches*"; or, the equal phariseeism by which a cultured Englishman today can ask quite blandly, "Do you go to church or to chapel?"

What is the Free Church position? It has been misunderstood and hence misrepresented by even so competent a scholar as Joachim Wach in his important book, *Sociology of Religion*. He said it represented persons seeking freedom from the inner controls of personal discipline and the outer demands of political pressure.[64] The truth is the opposite of this; the Free Churches arose from *one fundamental conviction,* that *God is best served by willing and un-coerced devotion.*

There is an almost abnormal fascination today among some church union advocates for the presumed benefits and "religious" qualities of material laying-on-of-hands virtue in ministerial continuity. The **Free Churches see the people under the Word as possessing a more** effective and efficient means of grace in the congregations of con-cerned believers. History has taught them to distrust institutionalism[65] and continuity as such. In the International Conference on the Theological Issues of Vatican II at the University of Notre Dame in March, 1966, the matter of institutionalism was discussed. It is of the essence of the Roman Catholic claim that it is "the" institution of Christianity, authorized by a continuity from Peter. But a truly *historical* look (instead of a purely juristic or even a sentimental stance) at the subject obliges us to see that it was institutionalism itself which put the greatest burdens upon our Lord and the most frequent ob-stacles in the way of the proclamation of the gospel. There is massive biblical witness to the place of institutional *discontinuity* in the life of the church, and hence a place for a ministry of pastors and people that speaks prophetically about the discontinuity in time and space that the Spirit of God ever has employed among his people.

In concluding, though far from completing, our historical back-ground review of the church as the people under the Word, we have the right to take heart from unintending admirers of some Free Church principles. Arthur Michael Ramsey, Archbishop of Canterbury, threatens to sue for disestablishment of the Church of England in order to be free of a Parliament of mixed Churchmen, non-Church-men, and a few of the sons of Abraham.

You may permit me the privilege of voicing a personal concern. In this day of longing for a truly ecumenical church I fear a tendency on the part of some to become fascinated, almost mesmerized, by their rediscovery of the truly great achievements in longevity and in genuine service on the part of ancient portions of the church. As a result, they are tempted to try to reach certain agreements and unions with systems and institutions that are as yet only slightly reformed around the concept of the church as the people of God under his Word. I am reminded of this from some recent reading. One of the masterful works in the history of culture is the set of volumes by Jacob Burckhardt on *The Civilization of the Renaissance in Italy.* In the section on "The Revival of Antiquity" he notes that most of the scholars who rediscovered the ideals of ancient Greece and Rome and thus gave substance to the Renaissance were content with only those two sources. A few saw the values to be gained from Oriental learning, especially Hebrew and Arabic. Almost alone did Pico della Mirandola defend the truth and science of *all ages* against the one-sided worship of classical Greek and Roman antiquity. He wrote:

> "We shall live for ever, not in the schools of word-catchers, but in the circle of the wise, where they talk not of the mother of Andromache or of the sons of Niobe, but of the deeper causes of things human and divine; he who looks closely will see that even the barbarians had intelligence (*mercurium*), not on the tongue, but in the breast." [66]

This more universal view of Christendom may be our need today in our own Ecumenical Renaissance, for the great movement toward unity is nothing less than that. Some will remember with what a vivid sense of new discovery Henry P. Van Dusen returned from a tour of Christian mission areas about a decade ago and wrote almost fervently about his awareness of what he called the "third force" in Christianity—the real evangelicals, Pentecostals, etc., who are making by far the greatest impact in areas that were assumed to be Christian but are far less than that—South America particularly, but not exclusively. This is Mirandola's insight brought down to date. We are in a momentary fascination with things Greek and Roman; they have a particular glitter and a proven genius; but there is a vast area of human reality, of human experience, which is poorly served by literary practitioners with quick evaluations. Truth is what the whole human race can perceive, not just its favored children. The "coming great church" must include faithfully, not just as second class citizens, all of God's children—those who are sometimes termed intellectually "barbarian," if you care to use Mirandola's phrase. This is, indeed, but to return to the unrivaled insight of St. Vincent of Lerins who, some fifteen centuries ago, defined ecumenical Christianity as "that which is believed everywhere, at all times, and by everybody." It is those who have a deep Christian faith not so much on the tongue as in the breast who must be given further hearing in the search for wholeness of faith.

9

A PEOPLE UNDER THE WORD:

Theological Interpretation

Abraham J. Malherbe, associate professor of Bible, Abilene Christian College, Abilene, Texas, was born in Pretoria, Republic of South Africa, is a graduate of the institution in which he now teaches, attended the University of Utrecht, and holds the ThD degree from Harvard University. A specialist in the Greek philosophical and religious background to early Christianity, Dr. Malherbe is presently co-editing an English translation of Gregory of Nyssa's *The Life of Moses* for the "Ancient Christian Writers" series. Formerly minister of the Lexington, Massachusetts, Church of Christ, he was one of the co-founders of the *Restoration Quarterly*.

As a specialist in the New Testament and the early church and as a spokesman from that indigenously American but now international Restorationist expression of the Believers' Church heritage known as the Churches of Christ, Dr. Malherbe in his address raised very important issues. Should each of the denominations within the Believers' Church heritage have stated clearly and precisely their own theology of the Word, so that both common characteristics and essential differences would be identifiable? How should these same communions understand the role of the early church in the formation and functioning of the canon of the New Testament? How is the characteristic tendency of the believers' churches to assume the validity of their knowledge of the historical Jesus to be related to the contemporary critical "new quest of the historical Jesus"? How is the theological diversity within the New Testament made evident by recent developments in biblical theology to be related to the understandings about the normative character of New Testament teaching prevalent among the believers' churches? Have the believers' churches faced adequately the issue of the nature of tradition and the problem of biblical hermeneutics? Do the present-day heirs of the heritage of the Believers' Church themselves actually live in community under the Word of God?

In responding to the address by Dr. Malherbe, Dr. Bruce Shelley, professor of church history, Conservative Baptist Theological Seminary, Denver, Colorado, commended the speaker's emphasis on the Christological and proclamatory nature of the Word and on "the dependence of the church today upon the Word" and then took issue at several basic points. He regarded Dr. Malherbe's stress on the role of the early church in "producing the Word" as giving the church "a greater place in revelation than did either the early church itself or the Reformation." Moreover, Dr. Shelley insisted, Dr. Malherbe had failed to define or clarify his usages of "the Word of God" in reference to Christ, the gospel, and the Bible. That Christ as the Word and Head was "both logically and chronologically prior to the community of faith" and that the "early church possessed from its beginning the Old Testament Scriptures which it regarded as the Word of God" should, according to Dr. Shelley, qualify any insistence on the church as productive of the Word. Dr. Shelley interpreted Dr. Malherbe's call for greater theological clarity as to the significance of the New Testament canon as "asking if we can hold any longer the traditional view of the Bible as the written Word of God, the view so fundamental to the Believers' Church tradition." Dr. Shelley contended that the number of New Testament writings in serious dispute was small and that the majority of the New Testament books were accepted at least informally as having apostolic authority "from the time of their writing."

> The apostles to be sure were members of the earliest church, and in that limited sense the church did produce the written Word, but they never considered the Word of God which they proclaimed a product of the life of the church. It had been delivered to them, they felt, by their Lord and was the fulfillment of Holy Scripture (1 Cor. 15:1-4; Gal. 1:11 f.).

Dr. Shelley held that "the words of the apostles were human words," but more than that they "were the Word of God." Even the second century *regula fidei* can be understood, with "due allowances for changes in wording to counter the Gnostic challenge . . . as that divine truth which the New Testament calls 'the Word of God.' " His final criticism of Dr. Malherbe's presentation pertained to an alleged lack of emphasis upon the ministry of the Holy Spirit in relation to the Word.

o   o   o

According to a worthwhile tradition of the British Parliament, a member of that body "declares his interest" at the beginning of any deliberation that may involve his personal interests. I do well to follow it in the context of this conference. My interest is that of *neo-testamenticus.* I am the only lecturer in this conference who is at present a professional teacher of the New Testament; hence the knowledgeable historical descriptions and erudite interpretations of the Believers' Church have left me with the uneasy suspicion that I may only be related tangentially to the main interests of this conference. But, since martyrdom and suffering are part of the free church tradition, perhaps my submission to you in this address will help to prove that I do after all belong.

It is necessary to make some preliminary remarks about my understanding of the purpose of this conference and of the task of this paper as a hopeful contribution to its realization.

As I understand it, the purpose of this conference is to determine the identity of the "Believers' Church" by focusing attention on

208

those aspects of its life and thought which appear to give it an identity of its own. That there is at least preliminary agreement that the Believers' Church has certain identifiable characteristics is illustrated by the fact that such a conference could be structured along the lines it has been. We do at least share a tentative view of what sets us apart from other believers. That we do have certain common denominators is obvious. But, as we have already learned from the earlier speakers this week, we are not exactly sure what communions should be included in this tradition.

I conceive it my task to contribute to the ascertaining of the identity of the Believers' Church by discussing its relationship to the Word. To discuss a theology of the Word is an exacting task under any circumstances. For the Christian such discussion involves the nature of revelation and the source of faith. To relate the theology of the Word to the doctrine of the church is further complicated, since the nature of that relationship is not always clear. Under the best of circumstances it is not easy to be sure whether a particular view of the church determines its theology of the Word or *vice versa*.

Our immediate task is further complicated by the fact that neither of the two elements with which we are concerned in this paper has been clearly delineated for us. We are concerned to find out more about the identity of the Believers' Church in this conference. Likewise in this paper we are also concerned to explore the theology of the Word that would characterize such a church. From a methodological standpoint one might wish that a theology of the Word had been stated clearly in disciplined theological language for each of the communions represented here. On the basis of these statements one might then proceed to discuss what is generally determinative for or characteristic of a Believers' Church view of the Word. I must confess that I am not aware of such systematic treatments of our present subject. In the absence of such background information on my part our approach must perforce be different.

In any case, I believe that to arrive at a proper view of our identity we must go beyond the merely descriptive task. Mere description may result in our being able to distinguish ourselves as a group with certain identifiable characteristics. If, by using such a descriptive approach, I should succeed in clarifying the view of the Word held by my own communion, or by myself personally, that might possibly be of value as contributing to our identifying one strain in the tradition. It is questionable, however, that such a descriptive effort alone would be capable of reflecting the inner relationship between a particular doctrine of the church and its theology of the Word.

We must also give attention to the theological implications of the basic attitudes we seem to share about the Word. By focusing attention on these as well as on our common view, we shall be able to define our identity more clearly.

What we do seem to share is the view that Jesus Christ is the Word of God and that the Bible, and the New Testament in particular, in some sense at least is related to the Word. I propose that we begin at this point and attempt to work out the implications of this basic statement of faith.

Our discussion will proceed in three stages. An interpretation of the Word will be ventured. Then the nature of the faith that arises in response to the Word will be discussed. Finally, the relationship of the community of faith to the Word will be treated briefly.

The Nature of the Word

The Christian faith looks to Jesus Christ as the origin and ground of its existence. Faith comes into existence as certain things about him are accepted as divine disclosures. The Gospels record that at the beginning of his ministry Jesus called men to be his disciples and that they left all to follow him (e.g., Mt. 4:18-22). The impression conveyed is that it was not in the first instance the content of his teaching that drew men to him. According to the Gospels Jesus called his disciples before he fully engaged in his ministry—thus before he became known for his teaching. The disciples attached themselves to him because there was something about his person that could not be denied.[1] When his teaching did impress his hearers, they recognized that he was more than a teacher. What he said and taught was grounded in who he was (Mk. 1:21-24).

Later, when the church had come into being, the conviction was recorded that, although God had spoken in many and various ways, he had spoken in the fullness of time, in the last days, by his Son (e.g., Gal. 4:4; Heb. 1:2). God had made known to men in all wisdom and insight the mystery of his will in keeping with the purpose he set forth in Christ as the plan for the fullness of time (Eph. 1:9 f.). In the person and life of Jesus God had revealed himself most completely and finally to men. Jesus was the Word of God (Jn. 1:2), bearing the very stamp of the divine nature (Heb. 1:3).

The dramatic character of God's revelation in Christ is reflected in its description as proclamation.[2] The early church remembered Jesus' ministry as one of proclamation. He was remembered as having been sent to proclaim the acceptable day of the Lord, to preach the kingdom of God (Lk. 4:16-22), and to usher it in by his ministry (Mt. 12:28). But his ministry was seen as being at once a statement about his person, and the man and his message were not to be separated. In his life there was a finality—divine history was finding fulfillment. The writings in which the early church introduces us to Jesus themselves exhibit this understanding that God's Word to man was proclamation. Because the Evangelists wished to underscore that God's Word in Christ was one of proclamation, they could not present the real significance of Jesus by means of ordinary biography. They created a new literary form through which to express the meaning of Jesus, viz., the Gospel form. The Gospels have no counterpart elsewhere; they are formed by their content and purpose.[3] They are proclamation and were written to proclaim Christ.

The church which saw God revealing himself in Christ and his proclamation continued that proclamation. What it proclaimed as the Word of God was that God had fulfilled his promises in Christ (Acts 13:44). It did not separate Christ from the message about him. The proclamation of the message was the proclamation of Christ. What it proclaimed was the Word of life himself (1 Jn. 1:1 ff.). To receive that message meant that one received by faith Christ himself (Eph. 4:20 f.; Col. 2:6) as the content of the Word of the Lord (Acts 16:32-34).

Men responded in different ways to the message of Christ. When the response was in keeping with the character of the message, it gave historical concreteness and clarity to the message (cf. Col. 2:6 f.). When the response was inadequate or inappropriate, it provided opportunity for elaboration or for more specific application to human life (cf. Eph. 4:20 f.). Men guided by the divine Spirit applied the Word to life, showing the new value it should have because of Christ. The main characteristic of this application was its Christocentric character. The meaning of Christ for life was detailed. God's revelation had taken place in Jesus, and when man accepted Jesus he became a new creature. His total life received a new orientation. He experienced a veritable metamorphosis (Rom. 12:2). As a new creature he saw everything anew (2 Cor. 5:16 f.). Thus, his moral life was determined by the fact that his body was a member of Christ (1 Cor. 6:15). His relationship with others was given a new value because of his relationship with the Lord (Col. 3:18-25). Even his attitude toward his enemies was to be different because of the teaching of Jesus (Rom. 12:14; cf. Mt. 5:44).

The response to the Word was not individualistic, and the continued application was not made to individuals only. A new humanity

211

was created of believers who had been reformed by Christ. They were united by their life in the Lord and they formed his body, the church of God (Col. 1:18). The meaning of God's purpose in Christ was applied consciously and specifically to this community of faith. Its structure (Eph. 4:7-16), corporate life (Col. 3:12-17), worship (Eph. 5:18-20), indeed, all aspects of its existence were seen to have their goal in the person of Christ.

The New Testament is to be seen as the Word of God in this perspective. It can be described as the Word because it explicates the meaning of Jesus Christ for human life. The New Testament was written by the first generations of Christians as they were led by their experience in Christ and the Holy Spirit to a truer understanding of their own nature and of the nature of the church. The church understood that it was making God's will known. Jesus had promised that the Spirit would lead his followers to all truth (Jn. 14:25 f.), and Christians later affirmed that what they said did indeed reflect the mind of God because it had been revealed to them by God's Spirit (1 Cor. 2:6-13).[4]

This astounding self-consciousness of the church of its own role in the revelation of the Word extended further. There was a sense of finality about what had taken place in Christ. God had spoken finally in the last days in Christ (Heb. 1:2). The church itself came into being in response to the announcement that Christ had ascended and was inaugurating the last days (Acts 2:17). It was the eschatological community, and it shared in the mysteries that God had reserved for it.[5] Because it had possession of the Spirit and was the community of the last days, it knew things even the prophets could not possibly have known (1 Pet. 1:10-12), and it conceived it to be the church's task to make God's will known (Eph. 3:7-10).

The importance of the church in the creation of the New Testament is thus not to be minimized.[6] The church became part of God's revelation by being the response of faith to the Word. It became the historical ground in which the Word was anchored. The form in which the Word was communicated was determined by the conditions and needs of the church's life. But the theological importance of the church vis-a-vis the Word extends even beyond this. The church shared in the process of revelation through its proclamation and its creativity in giving concrete, literary expression to the Word. The apostolic church marked the transition from the life of Jesus to that expression of faith in him that would become normative with the formation of the canon.[7]

The importance of the church is further emphasized by the part it played in the mediation and preservation of the Word. The church continued to apply to itself that growing body of material that it considered to be in agreement with God's disclosures in Christ and with its understanding of its own nature.[5] In this process the church recognized its own limits. The church saw that it did not originate the Word; it only received and transmitted the Word. It did not interpret the Word independently; the interpretation was from God (2 Pet. 1:20 f.). Neither did the church envisage an open-ended development of thought which it could continue to comment on or guide. There was something final about what had been given it. The church was, after all, the eschatological community. It had received all knowledge as it awaited the return of Christ (1 Cor. 1:4-7). The faith had once for all been delivered to the saints (Jude 3, 5). This sense of the finality of revelation and of the church's own limitation contributed to the formation of the canon of the New Testament.

The church had always understood itself to be under the authority of Christ. All authority in heaven and on earth had been given to him. As the church taught what it had learned from him, Jesus was thought to authenticate that teaching (Mt. 28:19 f.). But as the meaning of Christ became expressed in written form, authority was ascribed to these writings also. They were addressed to particular situations with their own problems, yet their particularity did not limit the authority with which they spoke or the demands they made to the churches to which they were first addressed.[9] The writings were concerned to bring the significance of Christ to bear on human life, and such significance, although it was related to particular situations, could not be confined to them. They were soon regarded as having universal application and could be used in churches other than the ones to which they were originally addressed (Col. 4:16).[10] The tendency to see universal applicability in the once particularistic writings contributed further to the formation of the canon.

When the church formed the canon of the New Testament, it was reaching for an authority.[11] Put in another way, when the church gathered the twenty-seven books to constitute the "New Covenant," it invested them with authority for all ages. They had become Scripture. By recognizing the canon, the church affirmed that its creativity in producing Scripture had come to an end. The apostolic church had shared in the revelation of God by virtue of being the historical response to God's disclosure in Christ. The church in its response grounded that revelation in history for all succeeding generations. But just as God's revelation in Christ was a once-for-all event, the church's response to that revelation and its sharing in it had a once-for-all character. It came to an end with the formation of the canon.

The church believed that, although Jesus lived in history and was thus confined historically by time and space, "he is the same yesterday, today and forever" (Heb. 13:8) and that he continues to make demands on men which were articulated during his life in terms real to the conditions under which he lived. In a similar manner the canon of Scripture, although it too came about within a particular historical period, and although it too reflects the experiences of the church during a certain period of its history, has a relevance for all time.

Here again, in forming the canon there is implicit a surprising self-consciousness on the part of the church as to its participation in the formation of the Word. In deciding, perhaps intuitively, what was to be included in the New Testament, the church in fact determined precisely what constituted the once-for-all givenness of the Word for succeeding generations. The performance of such a function could easily be interpreted as the grossest arrogance. The formation of the canon points up the theological and historical importance of the church, just as the writing and transmission of the New Testament do. It is, after all, to the church's witness and interpretation of Christ that we always return.[12] That witness had now been defined in the canon, and the later church would always return to it. But to think that the church considered its share in providing later generations with the Word haughtily or arrogantly is to misunderstand its view of its relationship to the Word.

The paradox of canonization is that in the process the church recognized its own limitations. The formation of the canon was not only a determination of the limit and extent of the Word. It was also a determination of the limit of the church in the process of revelation. By forming the canon the church placed itself under its authority for all time.[13]

An appreciation of the historical character of biblical religion must take at least these factors into consideration. God's revelation did not take place in Christ without involving the church. His act in Christ was seen to be his act and accepted as such by the church. This acceptance and understanding of Christ then became part of the revelation itself, and the church's part in the process of revelation must be taken seriously. This becomes especially obvious when the significance of the canon is related to the church's role in the canonization of the New Testament.

Such a view of the Word is not without its problems. It has in recent years been stressed that we always return to the faith of the early church and that we cannot get back to the historical Jesus.[14] The questioning of even the legitimacy of wanting to find the historical Jesus has at least had the value of stimulating fresh thought on the nature of the Christological and kerygmatic elements in revelation. Even if one takes heart from that element among those engaged in the new quest of the historical Jesus which has a more positive evaluation of the historical Jesus, it can only be done with the realization that there is still a quest going on and that it has its own peculiarities and problems. To affirm the Christological character of the Word does not mean that the statement is intelligible to all hearers. The Believers' Church is more optimistic about the possibility of knowing about the historical Jesus. It sees itself as aligned with the early church in its desire to relate with the historical Jesus. That church proclaimed and delivered the kerygma, but the kerygma was given meaning by the life which lay behind it. The Gospels are proclamation in their nature, but they do not proclaim only the death, burial, and resurrection of Jesus. They also provide information about his life and teaching which were authenticated for the church by his resurrection. The evangelistic and pietistic strains in the Believers' Church have placed great emphasis on the person of Jesus as the focus of God's revelation. The historical nature of the Gospels has seemed so obvious to this tradition that the discussions of the historical Jesus have largely been bypassed. Yet if the Word is to be understood under the Christological aspect, as we have attempted to do in this paper, then attention must be given to the questions raised by the quest of the historical Jesus. The relation between Jesus and the church is of utmost importance to the view presented here.[15]

An awareness of the historical process by which the New Testament came into being also raises questions with respect to the character of the church, of tradition, and of canon. In view of modern research we cannot assume that a church completely united in theological viewpoint created the canon, after which tradition and heresy developed.[16] An effort to understand the historical complexity of the church that produced the New Testament discovers that the church was not a static, homogeneous institution, but it constantly grew and developed as it responded to the Word, while giving it new form.[17] During this process it received and handed on traditions which reflected its diversity.[18] Tradition is not something which only developed after the canon had been formed and which can therefore facilely be dismissed as a later accretion. The phenomenon is already found in the New Testament itself. It is, perhaps, a necessary consequence of the historical nature of the church. It demands our efforts to work out the implications of the fact.[19] Whereas the early church is regarded as theologically very important by some free church communions, the diversity which characterized it and the part it played in the formation of the New Testament are not appreciated in our ranks as they have been elsewhere. We must seek to discover whether and in what manner that developing church and its traditions and diversity can be normative for us. As we do so, we shall not only clarify our own relationship to the Word, but shall also note with interest other communions' views of their relationship to the early church and tradition.

In a similar way we are very conscious today of the process by which the canon came into existence. The development of the canon cannot satisfactorily be ascribed to "the providence of God" without taking that process and its theological implications seriously. Preoccupation with the canon's historical development is increasingly leading to doubt that it has theological significance for us today.[20] On the one hand, we are told that the writings of the New Testament are only part of the body of literature produced by the early church and that it should be used in the same way and with the same limitations with which other early Christian literature is used. Its theological value as a norm for Christian thought and conduct is diminished. The other extreme is found in the statement that, since the church created the canon, it continues to give authority to the canon and interprets and applies the Word with that authority. This view overlooks the truth that the canon is the result of the church's looking for an authority under which to place itself. A determination of the precise theological significance of the canon in light of the critical enterprise is sorely needed, not least of all by the Believers' Church.

The instinct to relate the authority of the canon to the church points, I believe, in the right direction.[21] But the solution is not to place the church over the canon, as has been done in the tradition of Rome, although winds of change can be detected there.[22] Nor is the solution found in the approach of many churches of the Reformation, namely, to place less stress on the significance of the church.[23] The fear of institutions easily leads to a denial of the canon as an important theological datum. The place of the church in the formation of the Word must be recognized, but the limiting character of the canon must equally be stressed.[24] Such an evaluation will lead to a clearer view of the relationship between the Word and the people who live under it. The Believers' Church tradition seems peculiarly suited to make a substantial contribution to the discussion of this problem today. In this tradition there should not be an intimidating fear of institutions on the one hand, nor an excessive dependence on the institution on the other.

One further problem needs to be observed at this point. Even when the canon is taken seriously, the question of how precisely it is to be normative is not settled. Historical study of the New Testament tends to highlight its particularity. We see with increasing clarity what was meant in the original setting or circumstances, but with lessening certainty do we see what it is to mean to us today. Hermeneutics, as we could expect, has taken on renewed significance. The Believers' Church has not given itself to this problem. It has affirmed that Scripture can readily be understood in such a way as to make salvation possible. The evangelistic thrust of our tradition and the lay character of most free church communions tend to emphasize those elements which are regarded as self-evident, and this confidence in the *Allgemeinverständlichkeit* of Scripture determines our approach to the New Testament as a whole. Too frequently what passes for hermeneutics is a method of approach which sees the Bible as a collection of proof texts or propositions which can be systematized according to any principle one might select. Such an approach is oblivious to the character of the New Testament and therefore does it violence.

What has here been described correctly or incorrectly as a Believers' Church view of the Word demands that a hermeneutic be developed which corresponds to this view. As it was the community of faith, led by the Spirit, which produced the New Testament, so it is now the community of believers which seeks to apply the New Testament to itself as it is being guided by the Spirit. The church approaches the interpretation of the Scriptures with an awareness of its own theological importance.[25] As the Word had come into being out of the life of the church, now the Word is again to find its meaning in the life of the church. The church now exercises its creativity, not in producing revelation, but in interpreting it. Yet its interpretation is disciplined by the canonical status of the Word.[26] While the church does justice to the diversity of Scripture and in itself, it does so with a recognition that it must allow the Word to make its demands on the church.

The Nature of the Faith

We now turn to consider briefly the faith which links the people to the Word. The nature of the Christian faith is determined by the nature of the Word. As the Word is Christocentric in character, so also is the faith which comes into existence as a response to that Word. In Paul's statement that "faith comes from what is heard, and what is heard comes by the preaching of Christ" (Rom. 10:17, RSV) he makes the very basic affirmation that faith originates as a response to proclamation. He had earlier belabored the point. "But how are men to call upon him in whom they have not believed? And how are they to believe in him of whom they have never heard? And how are they to hear without a preacher" (Rom. 10:14, RSV)?

The glory of Christ, who is the likeness of God, is made known in the gospel. Preaching takes place so that through it God may give the light of the knowledge of his glory in the face of Christ (2 Cor. 4:4-6). The content of the preaching is Christological and is clearly presented in the New Testament.[27] The burden of the message is that in the ministry, death, and resurrection of Christ the age of fulfillment has dawned, that by virtue of his resurrection Jesus has been exalted to the right hand of the Father, whence he pours out the Spirit and where he intercedes for us when we look to him as Lord.

The preaching has its point in the affirmation that Christ died for us. He died that we might live, and the Word is preached so that we may be saved. It speaks to our condition as sinful men. The consequence is that such a message cannot be preached in a neutral manner. It demands a response from man. He can either accept the person and life of Christ as God's way of reconciling man to himself (2 Cor. 5:17), or he can reject it. If he appropriates God's action in Christ, he does so by faith. The Word that is preached is a word of faith (Rom. 10:8). It demands that man accept Jesus Christ by faith as God's way of disclosing himself. Man's acceptance is in the nature of a response. He does not accomplish this acceptance on the basis of his own resources, nor does he initiate faith. It is a submission to God's will. It is an inner trust and commitment to the Lordship of Christ made as man is moved by the Spirit to confess that Jesus is Lord.

Faith is expressed in confession. Thus, "if you confess with your lips that Jesus is Lord and believe in your heart that God raised him from the dead, you will be saved. For man believes with his heart and so is justified, and he confesses with his lips and so is saved" (Rom. 10:9 f., RSV). The creed is thus in essence the acceptance of the proclamation. It also has Christ as its content. It says something about Christ and man's relationship to him. In the confession of his Lordship man accepts his own sinful nature and sees his

218

salvation as coming from God through Christ. In the proclamation man is confronted by God and in the confession of his faith he places himself under God's demands.

The Believers' Church insists on this understanding of faith as a response to the proclamation of Christ. It has correctly insisted on the soteriological aspects of the proclamation and of faith. Man stands as sinner before God when he hears the preaching, and he is responsible to God for his own response. The church is no intermediary in the sense that it determines the content of the faith or the form of the confession. That is already determined by the content of the Word itself. Neither can the faith of the church stand for the faith of those incapable of responding in faith. Proclamation calls for hearing that will result in a confession of faith. It knows nothing of a vicarious faith.

The Believers' Church's insight into faith as a response of responsible men and women does justice to the basic nature of the Word. It must continue to be stated with clarity and conviction. Yet there are other aspects of faith whose implications we must deal with more fully. There is more to faith than laying hold of salvation when hearing God's demands being made in the Word. The response is, after all, a response of persons who have been formed by the context in which they live. For faith to be the response of such persons, it must be related to their experience and must be expressed in terms of their experience. We observe that this was the case in the New Testament.[28] The proclamation to Jews took place in terms of promise and fulfillment, and the confession of faith was that Jesus was indeed the Christ, the Messiah who had been promised (cf. Acts 13:16-41). To Gentiles, however, who did not operate within the framework of promise and fulfillment, Jesus was presented as the Son of the Creator who had been granted sovereignty over this age and the one to come by virtue of his resurrection and ascension (cf. Eph. 1:19 ff.). [29] Questions are raised for us here which stem from the historical character of the Word. Is there a basic unity under all the diversity in the New Testament?[30] Does the diversity of the forms by which the faith is confessed in the Word provide us with equal freedom to determine the form of the confession for our own day? Is what is ultimately determinative only that the Lordship of Christ be accepted by man in terms meaningful to him personally, regardless of the form which the faith is to take?[31] Or is the significance of the canon such that it places a limit on the form in which the faith is expressed?

When creeds with diverse content and form are thought to have developed only after the closing of the canon, no great problem is

219

posed for the Believers' Church's attitude toward them. But when critical investigation shows that there is a diversity of confessions of faith within the New Testament itself, the problem becomes more real. In our consideration of this problem we need to affirm that diversity within the New Testament does not permit the theological significance of the canon to be dissolved into its historical nature. Yet, we need to determine what the implications of this diversity are for the Believers' Church and its position with respect to ecclesiastical creeds.

Faith is not only subjective in nature. It admits, indeed requires, objective statement beyond the verbal expression of trust in and commitment to Christ. Objective statement of the faith contributes to the clarity and meaning of the response to the Word. But the question arises again as to the degree to which the faith can be described or stated objectively and systematically without lapsing into a creedalism which replaces living proclamation with propositions. Within the Believers' Church the objective, systematic statement of the faith has been accomplished in varying degrees, but this effort has not been endowed with great importance. We do not appear to be troubled so much by the problems that have been posed for systematic theology as a discipline in the period since Troeltsch. Most of us simply lack concern for the enterprise. Perhaps we shall decide that systematic theology is not necessary for a clear apprehension of the Word, perhaps even that it is undesirable. But before we do so, we should investigate whether our understanding of the Word requires or precludes such an endeavor.

Of greater importance to us probably are the questions raised in connection with biblical theology.[32] Need we be concerned with the possibility or need for biblical theology, or should we be satisfied with operating on the level of individual and sometimes diverse biblical doctrines? Is there not an element or principle which underlies these seemingly unrelated doctrines which will allow us to describe the faith as a coherent and meaningful whole? Here again, we must give attention to the demands made by both the historical and the theological aspects of the Word, that is, to both the diversity in the New Testament and its canonicity.

The Community of Faith

Our whole study so far has been concerned with the relationship between the Word and the church, with special emphasis on the nature of the Word and the faith it calls forth. We now turn more specifically to the implications of the Word for the church and the life it is to lead.

The church owes its existence to the Word. It is in response to the proclamation of the Word that man, moved by the Spirit, confesses that Jesus is Lord (1 Cor. 12:3), and it is by the same Spirit that he is baptized into the one body (1 Cor. 12:13). The church is a community created by faith which comes about in response to the Word. The church continues to owe its existence to the activity of God as he calls men to commit themselves to him in faith. It is indeed a company of the committed, a visible group which is the concrete expression of faith.

When the church is viewed in this manner, we escape the tension, found in so much of Protestantism, between Christology and soteriology on the one hand and ecclesiology on the other. The way is prepared for a much higher doctrine of the church. The Christological nature of the Word is extended to the nature of the church. The church does not exist only to make possible the proclamation of the Word. Its relationship with Christ points up another aspect of its existence. Christ, the content of the Word, is responsible for the existence of the church. When men accept the Word, they accept him. He is still the foundation on which the church is built. There can therefore be no uneasy tension between the institution and the faith. The one is the ground for the other.

The high value of the church is reflected in its understanding of itself. We have noticed the church's self-consciousness as it shared in and mediated the Word in its early years. Today the church must still have a high degree of self-awareness. This self-consciousness must not be an arrogance which boastfully points to the superiority of its members; it must rather be the calm conviction that the church has been redeemed by Christ, a remembrance that will keep the church humble. It must not be a pride which makes the church want to exercise authority; it must rather be a self-consciousness that comes from the church's subjection to the Lord. It must not be an assertion of infallibility; it must rather be the sobering knowledge that apostasy begins within the church.

The value of the church does not reside in itself as an independent institution, but in its relationship to Christ. It is not merely another institution or organization. It is an organism of which Christ is the head (Col. 1:18). To say that the church is his body is not only to use metaphorical language (Eph. 4:11 ff.). The relationship between Christ and the church is an ontological one. When one puts Christ on, he is added to the church, and his life is lived in the Lord. The

221

Christological nature of the church does not, however, permit the church to fall into the error of assuming the creative powers of Christ. The early church, which shared in the revelation and mediated it for later generations, had such self-confidence as we are speaking about, but it also appreciated its own limitation. By accepting the canon the church determined to live under its authority.

The Believers' Church has maintained this attitude of respect for the Word. The Word, after all, brings the church into being and it continues to guide the church. Herein lies the church's understanding of its own nature. The Word is normative with respect even to the structure of the church (Eph. 4:11 ff.), and the church must submit itself in this respect also to the Word. In an age in which so great an interest is shown in the church, this insight is invaluable and must not be abandoned. Modern biblical study has illuminated the different phases of the church's structure in the New Testament period. This diversity has led to the paradox that in discussions on Church unity many Protestant leaders deny that the New Testament can be the basis for unity today, while Catholics defend its normative character.[33] The Believers' Church renders vivid witness to its appreciation of the Word by its life as a visible body of believers living under the Word. The church's visible form is represented in the New Testament as being divinely given. The ascended Lord gave as gifts to men the functions or offices which they were to perform (cf. Eph. 4:11 ff.). But the church's relationship to Christ prevents its structure from becoming either an arrangement to be changed or dispensed with at will. It also prevents the other extreme, that it might become a hierarchical organization which can stand between man and God. All believers stand in an immediate relationship with God in Christ, in whom there is no male or female, bond or free. All stand as equals before God. The structure is given so that all may serve God and each other in mutual subjection. When the body functions in this manner, it is built up as it grows into Christ who is its head.

The church's whole endeavor as an ordered society is occupied with and determined by the Word. It is the church which holds forth the Word of life. The church understands that it is God's plan that through it his manifold wisdom should be made known. The church enjoys this privilege because God realized his eternal purpose in Jesus Christ its Lord (Eph. 3:10-12). In its proclamation the church invites men to lay hold of the promises of God recorded in his Word. In its worship it shares in the great acts of God proclaimed in his Word through its commemoration of them. In its expectation the church lives in hope for the glory promised by the Word.

Faith finds further objective expression in the life that believers live under the Word. When followers of Christ show entire and true fidelity, they adorn the doctrine of God (Tit. 2:10). This life is not determined by the context in which they live or by the situations to which they address themselves. Its content is determined by the Word itself. Having been born anew of the living and abiding Word of God which was preached to them, they live a new life because they have **tasted the kindness of the Lord (1 Pet. 1:22-2:3). Christ is now** their motivation and their standard.

The church knows that it is a redeemed community, because it has been washed and sanctified and justified (1 Cor. 6:11). Even a way of life which may have been worthy of praise before baptism now loses its secular character as the Spirit sanctifies it. This special quality of life can be lived only within the church, where the Spirit dwells. The church is concerned to bring to fulfillment that life under the Word. The church does not judge the world by the Word under which it has placed itself. Judgment of outsiders is left to God (1 Cor. 5:12 f.). The church judges only itself by God's standards. Although the church still lives in the world, it is not of the world. It does not allow the world to break into its life to secularize it and estrange it from the Word. Its life is so dominated by the Word that it becomes a witness to outsiders.

Conclusion

In conclusion, we may summarize by saying that the Believers' Church sees the Word as being basically the proclamation of Christ which demands a response from man. The stress on the relationship between the church and Christ results in an ecclesiology whose implications must still be drawn. In particular, the relationship between the church and the historical Jesus and the church's creativity with respect to the writing and the canonization of the New Testament on the one hand and its interpretation on the other must receive further attention. Such investigation will contribute to a clearer understanding of what it means to be a people under the Word. We may find demands being made upon us which will require the utmost courage of us. As the church originally measured itself by the proclaimed Word, it must now live under the written Word in an age in which the world threatens to break into it. Its survival as the body of Christ depends on its ability to live under the Word in a manner appropriate to the nature of the Word itself.[34]

10
A PEOPLE UNDER THE WORD:
Contemporary Relevance

Dale Moody is widely known and respected as a theologian who takes seriously the exposition and authority of the Holy Scriptures. His interest in Christian unity has led him into wide and fraternal contacts with Christians of the various traditions. These two concerns are reflected in his address to the Conference on the Concept of the Believers' Church.

A native of Texas and a graduate of Baylor University, Southern Baptist Theological Seminary (ThD), and the University of Oxford (D Phil), Dr. Moody has studied in Union Theological Seminary, New York, and the Universities of Zürich, Basel, and Heidelberg. He is a member of the Faith and Order Commission of the World Council of Churches and is the author of *Christ and the Church* (1963), *The Hope of Glory* (1964), *Baptism: Foundation for Christian Unity* (1967), and *The Spirit of the Living God* (1968). A teacher on the faculty of Southern Baptist Theological Seminary since 1945, he is Joseph Emerson Brown Professor of Christian Theology. Formerly the pastor of Baptist churches in Texas, Indiana, and Kentucky, Dr. Moody continues to be in great demand as a Bible teacher and preacher in numerous churches.

Dr. Moody contends that neither the Holy Spirit mediated through religious experience, the church as historic institution, nor the Bible as the written Word of God can be the ultimate seat of authority in Christianity, for only Jesus Christ can rightly have that role. Applying this Christocentric understanding of authority, he investigates briefly the present state of scholarly discussion in the various major Christian traditions or communions concerning the nature and structure of the church, the ministry of the church, baptism, and the Lord's Supper.

Members of the panel that reacted to Dr. Moody's address included Dr. Clifton J. Allen, editorial secretary, Sunday School Board of the Southern Baptist Convention, Nashville, Tennessee; Dr. Ross T. Bender, dean, Goshen College Biblical Seminary, Goshen, Indiana; Dr. Wilmer A. Cooper, dean, Earlham School of Religion, Richmond, Indiana; Rev. Mr. Riley M. Mathias, director, Christian Education Department, General Association of General Baptists, Poplar Bluff, Missouri; and Dr. Roy Bowen Ward, assistant professor of religion, Miami University, Oxford, Ohio. Moderator of the panel was Dr. Wayne E.

Ward, professor of Christian theology, Southern Baptist Theological Seminary.

Dr. Allen expressed agreement with Dr. Moody's address but stated that he had expected more emphasis on the relevance of the Bible for the formulation and interpretation of the concept of the Believers' Church. He then posed a series of questions dealing with the internal implementation and the sharing with the wider Christian community of the concept of the Believers' Church. Dr. Bender expressed disappointment as to the address's lack of more specific treatment of the problem of ministry and of the role of theological education in the heritage of believers' churches. Dr. Cooper stated his opinion that various speakers in the conference had taken considerable liberty with the subjects assigned and that the addresses had tended to be "personal denominational position papers rather than scholarly objective presentations of the subjects." He called for more emphasis on the work of the Holy Spirit in the life of Christians and more stress on the laity. Mr. Mathias spoke of the danger of putting the Bible in a position that lessened the work of the Spirit, of the fact of great differences between the cultural situation today and that at the incipiency of believers' churches, and of the dangers in mere unification of church structures. Dr. R. B. Ward commended Dr. Moody's Christocentric understanding of authority and his approach to biblical criticism. He called for clearer recognition of the complexity of the issue of the biblical canon and identified "the battle of the Bible" as the "crucial question" for the Believers' Church.

o   o   o

Authority is a suspect word in current theology. Much of this is due to its association with authoritarianism and claims of infallibility, but it does not seem that authority can be escaped in any field of knowledge. In the smallest matter we accept authority on sufficient evidence, and religious faith is no exception. It is not a question of whether there is authority but of which authority is supreme.

In an effort to bring this into focus for present discussions of Christian differences and to make some proposal toward the unity of the faith, a twofold approach will be made. First of all, an analysis of authority as represented by conflicting Christian traditions will be made; then there will be the application of these conclusions to some problems that prolong schism in the body of Christ. In all that is said there is the basic assumption that it is the will of God for "the unity of the Spirit" to be manifest in "the unity of the faith" (Eph. 4:3, 13).

An Analysis of Authority

In *the search for authority* in Christian faith three major positions have developed. The first is the authority of the *Spirit*. One can never get to the roots of Christian origins until this new power of the Spirit is noted. In what is generally regarded the first document of the New Testament, an early Christian hymn exhorts (1 Thess. 5:17-21):

> Without ceasing, pray!
> In all things, give thanks!
> The Spirit, do not quench it!
> Prophecy, do not despise it!
> All things, prove them!
> The good, hold to it!

Before New Testament churches were institutionalized and the New Testament writings were canonized, this was the major perspective. Of course they had the Old Testament,' but without the authority of the Spirit the first Christians would have remained Jews or proselytes.

The first effort to write "the story of salvation" in Christ and his church, the Acts of the Apostles, has been rightly called the Acts of the Holy Spirit. Even the Gospel of Luke, the former treatise that precedes Acts, is a Gospel of the Spirit. Luke-Acts represents the Pentecost tradition. The promises of the Old Testament begin to be fulfilled in the death and resurrection of Jesus, and the witness to this is the gift of the Spirit. "Being therefore exalted at the right hand of God, and having received from the Father the promise of the Holy Spirit, he has poured out this which you see and hear" (Acts 2:33; cf. 5:32).'

This is even more pronounced in the Paraclete tradition of the Fourth Gospel. The longest hymn preserved in the New Testament is the great hymn on the Paraclete as the Spirit of truth (Jn. 14:15-17, 25 f.; 16:7-15).

> When the Spirit of truth comes,
> he will guide you into all the truth;
> for he will not speak on his own authority,
> but whatever he hears he will speak (16:13a).

This is sufficient to illustrate the importance of the authority of the Spirit, but it should not be assumed that the disciples of New Testament times accepted all claims to spiritual guidance. First John 4:1-6 is enough to dispel this notion.

The generations that followed saw a decline in this type of authority. The clergy, the canon, and the creed became more and more central, but the upsurges of Montanism and mysticism indicate how hard it was to quench the Spirit. The authority of the Spirit has survived to find its clearest expression in the Quaker movement. According to Robert Barclay, an educated friend of George Fox, even the Scriptures must be esteemed as "a secondary rule, subordinate to the Spirit, from which they have all their excellency and certainty."[2]

The second *search for authority* made the *church* supreme. The authority of the historical Jesus was transferred to the church as a historical institution. The Acts of the Apostles indicated that the things Jesus "*began* to do and teach" in the days of his flesh were continued in the church after the disciples were baptized by the Holy Spirit (Acts 1:1). The authority of the church came from this continuous action of Christ through his disciples.

Since the twelve apostles were the link between the historical Jesus and the church, the authority of the church took the form of apostolic authority. The apostles were the spokesmen for the church in the early days of the Jerusalem church. The Fourth Gospel, with all its emphasis on the Spirit of truth, made much of the reception of the Spirit by the disciples on the first day of the resurrection. Jesus said: "Peace be with you. As the Father has sent me, even so I send you" (20:21). Then: "Receive the Holy Spirit. If you forgive the sins of any, they are forgiven; if you retain the sins of any, they are retained" (20:23).

Apostolic authority in Matthew's Gospel was focused more sharply on Peter. Debate still rages on whether the *petra* of Matthew 16:18 has reference to Peter, Peter's faith, or Christ. Oscar Cullmann's detailed study of Peter concludes that it has reference to Peter.[3] Even a Protestant as conservative as William Sanford LaSor, of Fuller Theological Seminary, accepts this conclusion.[4] A good argument can still be made for the *petra* being Christ, as in First Corinthians 10:4 and First Peter 2:7, but this is not the major point of debate.

The crucial matter for many Protestants is not apostolic authority, even the apostolic authority of Peter in the primitive church. Apostolic succession, which includes the claim of the Papacy that the keys of Peter were transmitted to the long succession of the Roman Bishops, is to be distinguished from apostolic authority. Could there be *any* successors to the apostles as eyewitnesses of the historical revelation? This question was sharpened by the claims of primacy and infallibility in the developing church.

The claim of Rome to speak with the authority of the Spirit goes back to the end of the first century. Clement of Rome, writing about A.D. 95, warns Corinth: "But if any disobey the words spoken by him through us, let them know that they will involve themselves in transgression and no small danger" (ch. 59). They are later called to obedience to what was "written through the Holy Spirit" (ch. 63), but there is no doubt that the authority of Rome is supported by the claim that both Peter and Paul died the martyr's death there (ch. 5). This authority is a dominant tradition in the first five centuries.[5]

Papal primacy is not yet a claim of papal infallibility. Many

Protestants would be able to accept Rome as *a* primatial see, even as *the* most honored see of Christendom, if it were not for the claims of Pius IX in A.D. 1870. The claim brushes aside even the consent of the Church, for the "definitions of the Roman Pontiff of themselves—and not by virtue of the consent of the Church—are irreformable." This has now a century later made problems for progressive Roman Catholics as well as for Protestants. It is now common knowledge that Charles Davis made his decision to leave the Roman Catholic Church while in turmoil over this problem. Papal infallibility is more of a problem for Christian unity than the Marian dogmas. The Marian dogmas of 1854 and 1950 are hardly problems for Eastern Orthodoxy as they are for Protestants, but papal infallibility the Orthodox are not likely to accept.

Vatican II has put the authority of the whole Church of God in a new perspective. For nearly a thousand years East and West have disputed their rival claims. For nearly five hundred years Protestants have protested what they believed were abuses and errors of Rome. The last generation has raised the questions of life and death. Must a solution be found for this family feud in the household of God? Some are terrified at the very thought that these bleeding wounds should be healed. These defensive attitudes are to be found in all camps. Some Roman Catholics have built-in resistance against all Protestants, and some Protestants would fall flat if Roman resistance should cease.

A third *search for authority* exalted the *Scriptures* above all claims of personal inspiration and all ecclesiastical pronouncements, conciliar or papal. At the very beginning of the church there was no serious doubt about the authority of the Old Testament. It is not only Mark and Matthew that assume this in their Gospels, but the more Gentile Gospels of Luke and John are firm on this (Lk. 16:31; 24:44-49; Jn. 5:39).

The question of the New Testament canon was a central issue in the struggle against Gnosticism in the second century, but this was over by the fourth. Athanasius spoke of the authority of the twenty-seven books of the New Testament in his Paschal letter of 367, and this was quickly confirmed by Jerome in the East and the Synod of Carthage in the West in 397.

The *canon* of the Old Testament did not become a problem until the Reformation. Marcion had rejected the whole Old Testament in the second century, but this was soon considered heresy. Luther segregated the Apocrypha in his German Bible, but the Geneva Bible eliminated the Apocrypha altogether. F. D. E. Schleiermacher suggested the relegation of the whole Old Testament to an appendix, but the Old Testament with the Apocrypha has returned in the Revised Standard Version, though the Apocrypha has been published in a separate volume.

The problem of the Old Testament canon is hardly an issue for critical scholarship in both Roman Catholic and Protestant thought. Both *The Jerusalem Bible*,^⁶ the fruit of Roman Catholic labor, and *The Oxford Annotated Bible*^⁷ with its representative Protestant perspective may be purchased with the Apocrypha, and the notes are surprisingly the same. When the joint Catholic-Protestant Bible is published, the Bible may become the broadest base of all for brotherly relations.

The problem that remains for conservative Protestantism is the acceptance of critical scholarship. If one assumes that critical scholarship has won the day, he will be surprised about the reception given *The New Scofield Reference Bible*^⁸ that goes forth with the blessing of Billy Graham. We are told that Moses wrote the whole Pentateuch about 1450-1410 B.C. It is even suggested that Moses could have written the account of his own death in advance! On the very page where the "first" and "second" covenants are set forth in Hebrews 8 there is a note on the eight covenants (p. 1317). One can hardly expect critical study from those unable to count!

This illustrates how difficult it is to use the Scriptures as supreme authority when there is so much difference between the critical and the conservative approaches to the contents. It is all but impossible for one using the *New Scofield Reference Bible* to come to any broad agreement with those who agree with the basic conclusions of the *Oxford Annotated Bible*. Both may agree on the formal statement that the Scriptures are supreme on all matters of faith and even order, but their applications of this statement will have different results. The battle of the Bible is still a crucial question for conservative Protestantism.

Even where there is general agreement on the canon and composition of the Bible, the conflict with ecclesiastical tradition remains. The Scriptures belong to tradition too, but this is *apostolic tradition*. The real conflict is between this *apostolic tradition* canonized in the New Testament and later *ecclesiastical tradition* that either distorts biblical faith by majoring on minors or deviates altogether from New Testament teaching.

In Roman Catholic theology the Marian doctrine of perpetual virginity and the dogmas of immaculate conception (1854) and bodily assumption (1950) are examples. Conservative Protestants are too prone to assume that Luther or Calvin or Wesley can only be reinterpreted but never rejected. Too many think they can only be misunderstood, but they are never mistaken. Evangelical Protestants do much the same with Fundamentalism. My own denomination has a large group of people who will break fellowship over the five points of Landmarkism, none of which is in Scripture; then they will set themselves against the very words of the Bible.

All three searches for the *seat of authority* point to Christ, and each is incomplete without him at the center. The Spirit enables one to confess Jesus as Lord (1 Cor. 12:3), but the Spirit himself is not the authority for faith. He bears witness to Christ, not himself (Jn. 15: 26). For "he will not speak on his own authority, but whatever he hears he will speak" (16:13). He who puts the authority of the Spirit above the authority of Christ has reversed directions.

The role of the church is to be the body of Christ and to bear witness to the Head who is Christ. All who are in Christ are in the body of Christ, and no denomination or any other group of members has the right to say they alone constitute the body of Christ. The body is to manifest the manifold wisdom of God, not to magnify her own authority and rights in the world (Eph. 3:10).

The sole *seat of authority* belongs to Christ, and to this the Scriptures bear witness. Scripture is indeed inspired by the Spirit, but the Scriptures point to Christ. Jesus himself, speaking of the Old Testament, said (Jn. 5:39 f.):

> You search the scriptures,
>> because you think that in them you have eternal life;
> and it is they that bear witness to me;
>> yet you refuse to come to me that you may have life.

As then, so now, he who puts the Scriptures in the place of Christ misses the life found in Christ.

Spirit, Church, Scripture—these three—are all subordinate to him who said (Mt. 28:18-20, RSV revised to accord with the short form of Eusebius):

> All authority in heaven and on earth
>> has been given to me.
> Go therefore and make disciples of all nations
>> in my name [short form],
> teaching them to observe all
>> that I have commanded you;
> and lo, I am with you always,
>> to the close of the age.

Yet we will not be able to discern his authority, unless the Scriptures are put above subjective claims of the present and objective traditions of the past.

Application of Authority

Many of the barriers that hinder Christian unity are in the area of ecclesiology. There are other problems, but four in the field of ecclesiology are here singled out for consideration. They are the Church, the ministry, baptism, and the Lord's Supper.

Studies on the church in the twentieth century have developed in two major stages. Until the last few years the discussion has been on the *nature* of the church, and a large amount of agreement has resulted. *The Realm of Redemption* by J. Robert Nelson, first published in 1951,[9] has compiled much of the results reached. By 1953 J. E. Lesslie Newbigin, in his little classic, *The Household of God* (1954),[10] was able to bring the Protestant, Catholic, and Pentecostal views of the church into a synthesis that many would accept. To speak of the church now as the people of God, the body of Christ, and the fellowship of the Spirit is to express views that only the obstinate obscurantist cares to dispute.

Ecumenical dialogue has produced an interesting shift of emphases. Protestants, once shy of the body of Christ metaphor as a Roman Catholic characteristic, have come to put most stress on this very point. Roman Catholics, on the other hand, in their new openness toward their "separated brethren," tend more and more to think of the church as the people of God. All this is to be welcomed, especially when both Protestants and Catholics take note of that "third force" in the Church that may be called the Pentecostal concern with the Holy Spirit.

The problem of the present has turned toward that which a renowned Roman Catholic, Hans Küng, has called *The Structures of the Church*.[11] This raises again the debate on whether the structures are to be congregational, presbyterial, or episcopal. An application of the Scriptures to this question does not yield three different structures but three different stages.

If one begins with the first church, the church of Jerusalem, a good argument for congregationalism may be made if one does not go beyond the Upper Room! Congregationalism has talked as if the Church never got beyond one hundred and twenty souls in one room. This hardly lasted when there were three thousand, five thousand, then a great multitude in the *one* church of Jerusalem. Obviously they met in many rooms in many houses of worship, but they never thought of but one church. The very term "churches of Jerusalem" would have sounded strange. One could speak of "the churches of Judea" (Gal. 1:22) but not of "the churches of Jerusalem."

It soon becomes clear that the one church in Jerusalem had many meeting places, many elders, and one general overseer in James (Acts 11:30; 12:17). This *presbyterial* structure was reproduced by Barnabas and Saul in the new churches which they established (Acts 14:23). The Hellenistic Jewish letters which we call James (5:14), First Peter (5:1-4), and Hebrews (13:7, 17, 24) have much the same structure. This does not mean that one congregation had many elders, but that the one church of several congregations had many elders or leaders or rulers.

All churches seemed to start as house churches or Christian synagogues, but they soon developed into a presbyterial structure with one church to a city with many elders to look after the many meetings. Before the end of the New Testament an episcopal structure has been added to the congregational and presbyterial, added not supplanted. James was a bishop in Jerusalem in all but name. It is beyond question that Timothy was more than just one of the many elders in Ephesus (1 Tim. 4:14; 5:17-22).

It is when the bishop of one church claims authority over the bishop of another church that development goes beyond the New Testament. However, there was a certain primacy of Jerusalem and James as Acts 15 indicates. The primacy of Rome is a later claim growing out of circumstances, but the long years of growth and mission into all the world raises serious doubts even in Roman Catholic minds as to how much primacy should be retained today. All this is to focus the question of structure. There is no dogmatic solution claimed.

The ministry of the church follows logically from this survey of the nature and structure of the church. The charismatic ministry of all members of Christ's one mystical body parallels the nature of the church as the place of an official ministry parallels the structure of the church.

It is often said that Paul's view of ministry was charismatic. This is certainly dominant in his letters, especially in First Corinthians and Ephesians, but there is more. The charismatic hymn in First Thessalonians 5:17-21, already quoted, appears in a context of conflict between the official and the charismatic functions in the church. This was indeed a church of "brethren" (5:12, 14), as was the Jerusalem church (Acts 12:17), but it was not without official leaders, *proistamenoi* (rulers) they were called. The rulers of the synagogue were *presbuteroi* (elders), so the kindred word *proistamenoi*, "those who labor among you and are over you in the Lord" (5:12), is used in the church of Thessalonica.

The most developed stage of an official ministry in the Pauline tradition is not found until the Pastoral Epistles. The question of authorship is not the crucial question as long as these writings are accepted as canonical and are at least in the Pauline tradition. There is the *episcope* (office of bishop) and one *episcopos* (bishop) for the first time. Up until this point bishops and presbyters (elders) are apparently synonyms. It may be so here, but Timothy is certainly a presiding elder who sees that the elders get paid, rebuked for their sins, and ordained by the laying on of hands (1 Tim. 5:17-22). There are also deacons and even an order of widows who take a pledge (1 Tim. 3:8-13; 5:9-16).

No plea is here being made for an official ministry that reproduces all the details of the first century, but it is difficult to understand those who zealously proclaim the New Testament as the *only* rule of faith and order and who adapt so readily to secular substitutes such as associations and executive secretaries, the first coming from the seventeenth century and the second from the nineteenth. The claim that the New Testament order is valid only in the local congregation is untenable. The so-called Free Church tradition assumes all too easily that the congregationalism of the sixteenth century and afterward recovered *all* the order in the New Testament. This is difficult to defend on the grounds of the New Testament. Too often we in America confuse New England with the New Testament. We must be reminded constantly that the great *kairos* is in the first century, not in the sixteenth, seventeenth, or any other.

The present situation becomes acute at this point. Many are rediscovering the New Testament theology of the laity, the ministry of the whole people of God in the world. Roman Catholics have experienced a striking renewal in this regard, and in this we personally rejoice. Friends of mine who are Roman Catholic laymen have rejoiced in this new recognition that the clergy is not the whole church. At times I have even cautioned them not to overdo the work of the laity!

Caution grows out of evidence that an unhealthy anticlericalism has taken hold of many Protestant groups. This has resulted in a bad image for the clergy and serious hesitation of youth to respond to even deep conviction that God calls them to a clerical vocation. Much of this may be due to the conduct and quality of the clergy, but this should be corrected. It will not be well when those with the finest character and keenest minds no longer accept the *kleros* of the *laos* of God. The sheep will surely stray from the fold. All members are ministers, but every group develops some type of leadership. Even among brethren there are always "big brothers" or "weighty friends."

This gets around to the rather vague theology of ordination that dominates many so-called brethren or believers' groups. In panic from any signs of a special priestly class and the untenable claims of apostolic succession, both of which are here rejected, ordination to an official task in the church has become questionable, even suspect. The book, *Ordination and Christian Unity* by E. P. Y. Simpson,[12] has surveyed the situation from a point of view held by some Baptists, but his solution is far from satisfactory. Here, however, the renewed discussion may begin.

Baptism, which was intended to be a sign of unity, has often become the cause of division. If the authority of Scriptures is accepted as standard, some progress toward unity can be made. If subjective judgment and ecclesiastical tradition are put above Scripture, divisions will continue. There is more agreement today on the meaning and mode of baptism in apostolic times than there has been since primitive times. It may help to summarize both, but again discord may be created. I hope not.

If evidence from the New Testament is gathered together, a group of major and a group of minor meanings of baptism may be classified. The major meanings are purification, identification, and incorporation. The term purification is used in both its ceremonial and moral meanings. Baptism arose as a ceremony to remove the ceremonial uncleanness of Gentile proselytes coming over to Judaism. In Qumran Jews baptized themselves daily to wash away uncleanness. These are called Daily Baptists!

Ceremonial purification became moral with the repentance baptism of John the Baptist. His baptism was "a baptism of repentance for the forgiveness of sins" (Mk. 1:4). In the preaching of Peter in Acts 2:38 and in the baptism of Paul in Acts 22:16 this meaning is continued, but this is not the distinctive teaching in Acts.

The distinctive teaching in Acts is identification with Jesus Christ. The term identification is used to describe baptism "in the **name of Jesus Christ**" (2:38; 10:48) or "**in the name of the Lord Jesus**" (8:16; 19:5). Baptism was a sign that those baptized belonged to the one in whose name they were baptized. This is indicated most clearly in Paul's preaching (1 Cor. 1:13-15), but this is not Paul's distinctive view.

Paul's distinctive view is incorporation into Christ or into the body of Christ. "For as many of you as were baptized into Christ have put on Christ" (Gal. 3:27). "For by one Spirit we were all baptized into one body" (1 Cor. 12:13). Radical distinctions between water baptism and Spirit baptism were not made by Paul, as in rationalistic dualism later, but of course Spirit baptism was primary. Water baptism without Spirit baptism would be mere ceremony with no dynamic. The profoundest baptismal theology in the New Testament is the great hymn in Romans 6:1-11. There those baptized are said to be grafted (sumphutoi) into Christ (6:5).

Minor meanings of baptism found in the New Testament are indicated by the words regeneration, illumination, and salvation. Another baptismal hymn, found in Titus 3:4-7, speaks of "the washing of regeneration" (3:5), and this is generally thought to have reference to baptism. The washing does not automatically effect regeneration, but it is a sign of regeneration when rightly received. It is rightly received by faith.

Baptism as illumination was the understanding of Justin Martyr in the second century (Apol. 61, 65), and this may be the idea behind the term in Hebrews (6:4; 10:32). Baptism was a sign that one had passed out of darkness into the light of the Lord.

Baptism as a sign of salvation appears as a comment in the midst of the baptismal hymn in First Peter 3:18-22. "Baptism, which corresponds to this [Noah's flood], now saves you, not as a removal of dirt from the body but as an appeal to God for a clear conscience by the resurrection of Jesus Christ" (3:21). This is one of the clearest distinctions between outward sign and inward reality, between ceremony and conscience.

The modes of baptism have been studied carefully in recent years, and there are some general agreements here too. Self-immersion was the mode in both orthodox baptism of proselytes and the more sectarian baptism of Qumran. John's baptism was no doubt by immersion, but there is no evidence as to how it was performed. Single immersion was continued in Acts, but the baptism of the Ethiopian eunuch was administered by a deacon, Philip (8:38). Trine immersion was administered from the second century, and this is the mode in the East until this day.

Trine immersion continued in the West, but the practice of clinical baptism as a secondary form by trine pouring became equal to immersion at the Council of Ravenna in 1311. After that, many variations developed in the West, and it is only in recent times that efforts have been made to reform theology and practice on a large scale. If there is to be a unity in "one baptism," this problem must be reexamined in the light Scripture gives on tradition. I have tried to make a beginning in my book, *Baptism: Foundation for Christian Unity.*[13]

Much has been said about "the believing church," and this indeed needs definition. A beginning may be made with "believer's baptism." All traditions that practice baptism profess to believe in believer's baptism. Roman Catholics, building on Augustine's doctrine of infant guilt and practicing infant baptism, locate faith in the Church, not in the infant or the parents.

Luther retained both the belief in infant guilt and the practice of infant baptism, but this was greatly modified by his doctrine of justification by faith. Out of this came the distinctive Lutheran doctrine of infant faith, a view that still appears in Lutheran writings.

Reformed theology has a theology of the covenant child that presumes that all children born of a Christian household are regenerated. Infant regeneration fills the place in Calvinism that infant faith does in Lutheranism.

Anglican theology has moved away from the Augustinian theology; so the Baptismal Reform Movement and others have promoted the view of primitive wholeness that calls for a service of dedication and blessing for Christian children coming before instruction and a conscious confession of faith.

Believers' churches can learn much from this theology and practice, and they can add much vitality to it. A unity of the two traditions will give strength to both. Groups that baptize preadolescent children are pushed into paedobaptism by the lack of a theology and practice that clarifies the status of the Christian child.

The Lord's Supper was also intended to be a sign of unity, but it too has become a scandal and has led to schism. It has caused some to discard all sacramental practice along with the rejection of all clergy, but this is not the way to restore New Testament faith and practice. A reverent restudy of the whole problem is the right way. The state of the question may be of some help.

The sources of the Lord's Supper reach back to the meals Jesus had with his disciples during the days of his flesh and the Last Supper at the last Passover he had with them. One may generalize by saying that Love Feast plus Last Supper equals Lord's Supper. This is the picture that appears in First Corinthians 11:17-34, although there is only a communion with the loaf and the cup in First Corinthians 10:16 f.

The significance of the Lord's Supper is indicated by the words used. In reference to the present it is a thanksgiving (a eucharist) and a communion in reference to both God and man. As a covenant and as a remembrance it is a link with the past event of the death and resurrection of our Lord. It also points to the future as it is linked with the kingdom of God and the coming of Christ in glory.[14]

The service of the Lord's Supper has ranged all the way from the simple order described in First Corinthians 11 to the elaborate mass of Roman Catholics. The one cup and one loaf have been modified by most traditions, and the restoration of the basic forms requires much reform. Any approach that is rigid is likely to shatter the service even more. Radical innovations are not likely to be helpful either. Here is an area in which patience and understanding are at a premium, and the teachings of the Scripture will need to be put above all denominational traditions.

All four of the areas sketched have potential for both unity and schism, but the purpose of this survey has been to give a setting by which divisions can be healed. This healing will require many contacts and much discussion among all who are eager to maintain "the unity of the Spirit in the bonds of peace." Brethren groups and believers' churches have suffered much from isolation from one another and lack of contact with other Christians. Historical circumstances help to understand why this is the case, but the time has come for more contact between separated brethren, even our brethren who today may seem far away.

Until recently those who are "near" have generally required that those "far away" agree fully in doctrine and practice before there is intercommunion. On such grounds interdenominational conferences will need to wait a long while before the visible symbol of our unity in Christ becomes evident. It may be that less rigidity at this point would help not only the so-called believers' churches but all churches to draw near to that unity for which we all so fervently pray.

A PEOPLE IN THE WORLD

11

A P E O P L E   I N   T H E   W O R L D :

Historical Background

"The dean of American church historians" is the term which Dr. George Huntston Williams of Harvard has applied to Dr. Kenneth Scott Latourette of Yale. Known throughout the world for his seven-volume *A History of the Expansion of Christianity,* Dr. Latourette led the way in achieving a universal, rather than merely a Europacentric, perspective in the writing of the history of Christianity. Sterling Professor of Missions and Oriental History, Emeritus, Yale University, he was the author of more than fifty volumes, including *The Development of China, The Development of Japan, The Chinese: Their History and Culture* (two volumes), *A History of Christianity,* and *Christianity in a Revolutionary Age* (five volumes). Dr. Latourette, a native of Oregon, received three degrees from Yale University and then served as traveling secretary for the Student Volunteer Movement for Foreign Missions and as a faculty member of the College of Yale in China. After teaching in Reed College and in Denison University, he joined the Yale University faculty in 1921. Dr. Latourette lectured in numerous universities and theological seminaries.

Onetime president of the American Baptist Convention and a member of the drafting committee for the Constitution of the World Council of Churches at Utrecht in 1938, Dr. Latourette identified himself personally and sympathetically with the heritage of Believers' Churches while at the same time being critical of the heritage and its fruitage. After explaining the close alliance between church and state in the West during the pre-modern centuries and after noting the role of believers' churches in the attainment of the separation of church and state in the United States, Dr. Latourette pointed out that the leading American evangelists of the nineteenth century had not been members of "believers' churches" and that the alleviation of certain of the social evils of the eighteenth and nineteenth centuries had been largely stimulated by Evangelicals who were not identified with believers' churches. More significant, he asserted, had been the missionary outreach of certain believers' churches during the nineteenth and twentieth centuries. Dr. Latourette presented to conference participants the challenging and provocative question, "What is the distinctive function of believers' churches in the Church Universal?"

In replying to Dr. Latourette's address, Dr. Pope A. Duncan, president of South Georgia State College, Douglas, Georgia, called for more "recognition of the very profound psychological, sociological, and cultural factors which played such a major role in shaping the relationship of church and state in western Europe during Roman and Medieval times" so as to avoid the dangers of being "too hard on the state and too easy on the Church" and of judging "people of another age . . . by modern norms." He surmised that the absence of a resident Anglican episcopate in colonial Virginia may have significantly strengthened the Anglican laity and demurred as to Dr. Latourette's statement that "from contact with the Mennonites, the English Baptists arose." He asked whether it is true that believers' churches "are still recruiting mainly from the lower economic levels of the population" and, if so, how this should be evaluated in the light of Roman Catholic strength among the masses. As to the secularization of colleges established by believers' churches, Dr. Duncan asked whether this might mean the colleges "are therefore freer to be significant institutions of higher education and less denominational propaganda agencies."

Concurring with Dr. Latourette, Dr. Duncan suggested that those within believers' churches "are often apt to claim too much" for their movements "in the achievement of goals as they relate to such matters as religious liberty, evangelism, missions, social action, and moral living." Moreover, he concurred that "in believers' churches a large proportion of the members have less than wholehearted commitment and . . . in official churches great hosts of members have experienced the new birth." The believers' churches, affirmed Dr. Duncan, need to be more involved ecumenically, if for no other reason than to discover whether there is "any longer any real distinction between believers' churches and others" and thus whether the Believers' Church heritage still has "a unique contribution." He concluded:

> Perhaps we are now to justify our existence largely in terms of acting as the symbol of the freedom of the Spirit—continually to remind ourselves and others that authoritarianism and institutionalism are median means at best—that God's winds blow whither they will. This being true, we can make a significant contribution to the ecumenical dialogue— especially as we constantly remind others that the institutionalization of the Ecumenical Movement and the development of authority figures in it must always be so tentative as to permit the freedom of the Spirit to operate at every stage.

o   o   o

The planning committee for the Conference on the Concept of the Believers' Church has asked me to speak on the historical background. By the committee's decision the conference has been limited to the centuries which began with the Reformation. Properly, the committee suggested that this paper deal with such topics as religious liberty, church and state, Christian vocation, church and world, mission and witness, and service.

As all historians know, at the beginning of the Reformation church and state had long been closely interrelated, and because of that association, religious liberty was greatly restricted. That situation arose from the fashion in which Christianity had spread. Until

Constantine's espousal of the faith, Christians and the church had been persecuted, and sometimes, notably on the eve of Constantine's adoption of the Christian name, by the persecution furthered by Diocletian. Most of Constantine's successors favored the church. Eventually some of them proscribed the pagan cults. However, the conversion of the population of the Roman Empire was not due primarily to imperial favor, but chiefly to the initiative of earnest Christians. This is seen, for example, in the work of Martin of Tours.

The combination of the support of the state with the labors of missionaries had been earlier seen in the creation of the two first states to bear the Christian name—Edessa and Armenia.

That same combination of cooperation between missionary effort and government action persisted in the conversion of Europe outside the Roman Empire. Thus in the Netherlands, Germany and in their early efforts in Scandinavia missionaries were supported by the Carolingians. Boniface, the great English missionary in Germany, was aided by them. Charlemagne's program among the Saxons was in that tradition. In Norway the efforts of Olaf Tryggvason and Olaf Heraldsson, kings who furthered conversion through force, were assisted by missionaries from England who carried on the work of instruction of the neophytes. The conversion of the Magyars by Stephen was aided by German and Slavic missionaries. The winning of peoples on the eastern shores of the Baltic, notably the Esths and the Letts, was partly through the Knights of the Sword and the Teutonic Knights and partly by German missionaries. The conversion of the Bulgars was chiefly through their king, Boris, with the assistance of missionaries from Constantinople.

As a result of the adherence to the faith of the peoples of Western and Central Europe, of which we have mentioned only a few, church and state were closely associated. Struggles between the two were chronic, chiefly in the efforts of the state to make the ecclesiastical structure subordinate and of the ecclesiastical authorities to render all society really Christian, to achieve independence of the political magnates, and to bring them to conformity to Christian standards. However, except for the Jews and for the Moslems in the Iberian Peninsula and for a time in Sicily, all Western and Central Europeans became members of the Catholic Church. From time to time movements to deepen the Christian life arose, some through monastic orders and some by those whom the official church branded as heretics and sought to enlist the secular arm in stamping out. Among the latter were the

Cathari, the Waldensians, and the Lollards and the Hussites. They were significant, but few if any stood for the full separation of church and state or religious freedom or even religious toleration. Religion was regarded as a territorial affair and church and state as ideally one.

We must hasten to note that in this close association of church and state Christianity was not unique. It was in accord with the widely accepted belief that religion is an integral feature of culture and that to preserve itself and to prevent chaos the state must support a particular religion. That conviction was responsible for the persecution of Christianity by the Roman imperial structure. Similarly, for centuries the Persian rulers supported Zoroastrianism; the Chinese state was built on Confucianism and from time to time attempted to eradicate or at least to curb Buddhism, Islam, and Christianity as politically and culturally a menace. From its beginning, Islam and the state have been closely intertwined. To a slightly less degree Buddhism has enjoyed the support of the state in Ceylon, Burma, and Siam (Thailand).

In the Reformation and much of the post-Reformation centuries the situation was not basically changed. The principle of *cuius regio eius religio*, while adopted in a Germany badly fragmented politically and religiously, in effect was applied elsewhere. Thus in Denmark, Norway, Sweden, and Finland the state supported Lutheranism. For the sake of political unity the Bourbons first sought to limit Protestantism and then to crush it. The majority in Scotland became Presbyterian, and the monarchs in England and Wales and to a certain extent in Ireland endeavored to enforce conformity to the Anglican establishment.

Most of the attempts at the renewal of life in the post-Reformation period sought to operate through the state churches. A few examples may be given. The Oratory and the Theatines did it in Italy. Ximenes de Cisneros sparked the reform in the Catholic Church in Spain, and a little later the Basque, Ignatius Loyola, founded the Society of Jesus, which enlisted much of the new life in the Catholic Church. New movements of several kinds brought new vigor in the Catholic Church in France. In the Netherlands, Germany, Denmark, and Norway the Pietists remained within the state churches. Even the Moravians led by Zinzendorf endeavored to retain a place in the state church in Bavaria. In England the Puritans endeavored to transform the Church of England.

In the colonies established by Western Europeans in the sixteenth and seventeenth centuries the effort was made to continue the relation between church and state typical of the mother countries. In this Spain and Portugal succeeded in Latin America, and the French in Canada. In the Thirteen Colonies which in their independence became the basis of the United States similar attempts were seen, with the exception of Rhode Island and Pennsylvania, but with less success than in the Spanish, Portuguese, and French colonies. In Massachusetts and Connecticut, Congregationalism had close ties with the state. In New York, Maryland, and the four colonies south of the Potomac, the Church of England was established. But in them it suffered from the lack of a resident episcopate. Throughout the eighteenth century until independence the Society for the Propagation of the Gospel in Foreign Parts (Anglican, founded in 1701) made valiant efforts to remedy the situation. But in 1776, so far as can be determined, only about five out of a hundred of the population were members of churches. The overwhelming majority were Protestant in their European background, but religiously a vacuum existed which, as we shall see, was progressively filled, chiefly by believers' churches. As a result, the overwhelming majority of the membership of believers' churches in the entire world is now in the United States.

As is well known, most believers' churches as they are today had their beginnings during the Reformation, chiefly as Anabaptists. They had varied origins and were multiform. They were persecuted by the state churches, both Protestant and Catholic. As a result, all but the Mennonites were eliminated. From contact with the Mennonites the English Baptists arose, but until the nineteenth century they were a small and badly divided minority. In the sixteenth, seventeenth, and eighteenth centuries other believers' churches arose. Prominent among them, although still a small minority, were the Friends.

The rapid growth of believers' churches was in the nineteenth and twentieth centuries. It was part of a widespread awakening in Protestantism. Not all of that awakening was in believers' churches. Indeed, much of the initiative and most of the outstanding leadership was not from them. In England they were chiefly Anglican. That was true of the Wesleys. They never left the Church of England, and their followers were in societies which only gradually severed their ties with that church and became separate denominations. In the Church of England were Evangelicals, some but not all of them quite independent of the Wesleys. In the Thirteen Colonies the Great Awakening of the eighteenth century had as its outstanding leaders Theodore Frelinghuysen, Jonathan Edwards, and George Whitefield, none of them members of believers' churches.

In the course of the nineteenth and twentieth centuries the majority of the population of the United States became members of churches. A large minority are either Roman Catholic or Orthodox. Of the Protestants not quite half are connected with churches which represent communions that in Europe had state ties—chief among them Lutheran, Anglican, Presbyterian, and Reformed. The majority of the Protestants are in believers' churches. We need to remind ourselves, however, that the large majority of the outstanding professional evangelists through whom the Protestant gains were achieved were not in believers' churches. Lyman Beecher, Charles G. Finney, and Dwight L. Moody were Congregationalists, and Billy Sunday was a Presbyterian. Only the latest of that notable succession, Billy Graham, is a member of a believers' church. Of the thousands of evangelists less prominent in the public eye, a substantial proportion, possibly a majority, have been in believers' churches, but hundreds of thousands have not been in them. For example, many have been Methodists, the denominational family which, next to the Baptists, is the largest of the Protestant bodies.

We remember, and rightly, that the separation of church and state made substantial progress earlier in the United States than in any other country and that prominent in achieving the separation were the Baptists and the Friends. Before independence they had brought it about in Rhode Island and Pennsylvania. We must note, however, that the separation is not complete and that other factors than believers' churches have had a major share in that achievement. To be sure, the Federal Constitution forbids the Congress of the national government from making any "law respecting an establishment of religion or prohibiting the free exercise thereof," and it expressly declares that "no religious test shall ever be required as a qualification for any office or public trust under the United States." Yet not until 1831-1833 did the last remnants of establishment disappear in individual states. That was in Massachusetts. Moreover, several state constitutions require belief in God for holding office or serving on a jury. A few make acceptance of the Old and New Testaments a condition for holding office. Legislation has been enacted to protect the observance of Sunday. National days of thanksgiving have been proclaimed by the Presidents and some governors of states. The armed forces and the houses of Congress have chaplains.

Several reasons for the separation of church and state in the

246

United States have been given. Among them are the multiplicity of denominations and the influence of the Enlightenment.

The trend toward the separation of church and state, largely pioneered in the United States, has continued in other parts of the world, both in what is usually thought of as "Christendom" and in lands where other religions are in the majority. The sources have been numerous. Significantly the Declaration of Human Rights by the United Nations had its origin in the initiative of Protestant bodies, but not exclusively in believers' churches.

Obviously, closely related to the connection between church and state has been the individual's relation to the call of God. If by the fact of being born in a state where all are automatically members of the official church one is regarded as a Christian, baptism and confirmation can be purely formal. Fortunately, in thousands having that formal connection, by the pleading of the Holy Spirit and the individual's voluntary response, the new birth takes place which in principle is characteristic of the members of the believers' churches, with the accompanying belief that God has a purpose for every life which each Christian must seek to find and commit himself to fulfill. As a matter of experience and observation, for a large proportion of the members of believers' churches the connection is through parents or friends and entails no conscious wholehearted commitment. Here is a chronic problem of believers' churches.

Similarly a recurring temptation to believers' churches is disobedience to the apostolic command: "be not conformed to this world," and ignoring the question: "What do ye more than others?" We must be sobered by the risen Christ's message to the Seven Churches. They were all "younger churches" which were supposedly believers' churches, whose original members had supposedly come out of darkness into light. Yet in only one (Rev. 2:8-11) can the Spirit find no fault, and the church in Laodicea to which Paul wrote at least one letter — a letter which we do not have — and who we know once to have had enough conviction to write to at least one fellow member of the Christian fellowship (Col. 4:16, 17), had become lukewarm and had conformed to a prosperous environment (Rev. 3:14-22).

It is sobering to recall that the movements to eliminate some of the crying social evils of the eighteenth and nineteenth centuries were chiefly not from members of believers' churches but from Evangelicals in the Church of England and from Congregationalists and Presbyterians who were the products of the Great Awakening and of other revivals. Thus Wilberforce, an Anglican who had had a warm Evangelical conversion, led in the fight to abolish the African slave trade, and the Seventh Earl of Shaftesbury, an Anglican, from his boyhood an earnest Evangelical, led in Parliament the fight for legislation to curb some of the intolerable exploitation of labor in the early stages of the Industrial Revolution. Samuel Hopkins, a faithful disciple of Jonathan Edwards, having as a guiding principle "universal disinterested benevolence," from his pulpit in Newport, Rhode Island, a city which thrived on the slave trade, fearlessly denounced slavery, and some of Finney's converts spearheaded the movement to abolish Negro slavery in the United States. The peace movement of the first half of the nineteenth century had most of its leaders from Congregationalists. The outstanding leader of the W.C.T.U. was Frances Willard, a Methodist. The Anti-Saloon League, a nondenominational organization, had its origin and early leadership in Oberlin, a strong Congregational center.

Yet we must hasten to add that Friends, notably Woolman, were pioneers in fighting slavery. Latterly the American Friends Service Committee has been foremost in relieving the suffering arising from the wars of the present century. While most of the spokesmen for the Social Gospel were Congregationalists and Methodists, the leading theologian of the movement was Walter Rauschenbusch, a Baptist.

In the amazing nineteenth- and twentieth-century effort to spread the Gospel throughout the world, believers' churches have been prominent. We think at once of William Carey who in founding the (English) Baptist Missionary Society in 1792 led the way in a new era in Protestant missions. We are aware of the striking record of the Seventh-Day Adventists in global missions and of the expanding program of the Southern Baptists. We are impressed with the increasing prominence of the Pentecostals in Latin America. Here is a movement, increasingly indigenous, which is multiplying, notably in Brazil, Chile, and Colombia. Yet most of the spread of Protestantism in Asia, Africa, Latin America, and the islands of the Pacific has not been by believers' churches. It has been chiefly by Evangelicals in other than believers' churches.

A striking feature of believers' churches is that they have been and are still recruited mainly from the lower economic levels of the population. That has been true in the United States, the British Isles, the Continent of Europe, Asia, and Latin America. For this we ought not to apologize. We do well to recall that as the climax of his credentials to the messengers from the questioning John the

Baptist, Jesus said that "the poor have the Gospel preached to them" (Lk. 7:18-23). Believers' churches have been relatively less prominent in higher education and scholarship than have other Protestant churches. From believers' churches have come some notable scholars. Believers' churches have given birth to a few outstanding universities. On the frontiers of settlement in the United States and Canada through heroic and sacrificial effort they shared in founding colleges. Yet the colleges and universities created by them have succumbed more rapidly to the secularizing trends which have been marked in most institutions of higher learning founded by Protestants. Why this should be true is not clear. But it poses thought-provoking problems to believers' churches.

With this comment I venture to close this paper. It is thought-provoking but it is not pessimistic. In it lies a basic question: What is the distinctive function of believers' churches in the Church Universal?

12

A P E O P L E   I N   T H E   W O R L D :

Theological Interpretation

The Conference on the Concept of the Believers' Church, if not born as his idea, matured from infancy in the mind and heart of Dr. John Howard Yoder and reached one of its climactic moments with the delivery of his address. A native of Ohio, he attended the College of Wooster before graduating from Goshen College and subsequently attended the University of Akron. Dr. Yoder is associate professor of theology in the Associated Mennonite Biblical Seminaries of Elkhart and Goshen, Indiana, is associate director of the Institute of Mennonite Studies at Elkhart, and serves as consultant to the Mennonite Board of Missions and Charities. He represented the Mennonite Central Committee in Europe from 1949 to 1957, first directing relief activities in France and later participating in ecumenical conversations on questions of war and the peace witness of the church. He was awarded the ThD degree by the University of Basel in 1962 after completion of a dissertation dealing with the conversations between the earliest Anabaptists and the Swiss Reformers between 1523 and 1538. Dr. Yoder has written several booklets on Christian pacifism, ecumenism, and missionary methods. He serves as convenor of the continuation committee of the Conference on the Concept of the Believers' Church.

In his address, the oral presentation of which had to be condensed, Dr. Yoder closely and carefully differentiated the Believers' Church understanding of the life and mission of the church from what he called the "theocratic" (cf. Puritan) and the "spiritualist" (cf. Pietist) understandings and contended that "the distinctness of the church of believers is prerequisite to the meaningfulness of the gospel message." Then he reinterpreted Menno Simons' four marks of the church on mission—holy living, brotherly love, witness, and suffering—in the context of contemporary thinking about mission and delineated how such a Believers' Church could better meet contemporary needs in evangelism, as to the meaning of history, and in congregational life than the "theocratic" and the "spiritualist" patterns.

The response to Dr. Yoder's address was presented by Dr. C. Emanuel Carlson, executive director of the Baptist Joint Committee on Public Affairs, Washington, D.C., and formerly dean of and professor of sociology in Bethel College, St. Paul, Minnesota, an institution of the Baptist General Conference of America. Dr. Carlson commended Dr. Yoder for his "clarity of thought and scope of information" but criticized his use of typology. Dr. Carlson asserted:

Dr. Yoder indicates his awareness that the three types are arbitrary formulations in his own mind for the purposes of analysis and communication. He sets them up as a heuristic device, but on them he later builds his "polemical approach" as though they contain some essence of reality. This gives us difficulty.

Dr. Carlson's own contention constituted a thrust toward more contemporaneity.

There is a sense in which the only world in which God's people live is the world that is contemporary. If the experiences of the past are to help us, they must contribute to our competence for Christian living. What then are the practical requirements for a viable concept of the "Believers' Church," seen as the people of God in their mission in the modern world?

Dr. Carlson called for three basic "characteristics" in such a contemporary believers' church.

First, there is need for "a screen," or "some insights that will help us in *direction and selectivity*" as we respond to the many formulations of our Christian past, the "enormous diversity of custom, traditions, and social conventions," and the challenge of "a scientific, technological, urban society." The social sciences must be employed, he argued, so as "to gain precision of mission." This does not mean the sanctioning of acculturation. Rather it means being better able to know when to conform and when to be nonconformist. It means being better able to decide how church and government ought to be related.

Secondly, there is a need for "creative equipment" by which God's people may be "operative servants of God" and "creators of the future." Dr. Carlson asked:

How much help can the sixteenth century give us in this matter? We all have in our histories what may be called *formative* periods, whether it be sixteenth, seventeenth, eighteenth, or nineteenth century. Are we really justified in asking "history" to answer our questions of *function* and *structure* for the twenty-first century? *Can we be a "formative generation"?* Is that required of a "Believers' Church"?

Dr. Carlson posed other questions regarding the service ministries of contemporary churches. Thirdly, the Believers' Church concept of today should

open the nature and meaning of the Christian's spiritual life to all those who seek to live and serve Christ. It should be so formulated that it leads us to a constant renewal of worship, of prayer, of meditation, of attitudes, and all the graces of the Spirit.

Trends in the renewal of liturgy and toward an "equipping" ministry were commended.

Dr. Carlson concluded:

In short, we must respond to the call to be as creative as the sixteenth century was. And in the face of these needs we are pressed back to the same Word, the same Lord, and the same Spirit as those courageous people of other centuries. But the answers must be ours.

The Yoder address and the Carlson response left unanswered at least two related questions. One is whether all the conference participants, embracing as they did the various historical expressions of the Believers' Church heritage, could accept the Believers' Church type set forth by Dr. Yoder in contradistinction to the "theocratic" and "spiritualist" types as being consonant with and expressive of their own heritages. To put it into negative terms, was the type too strictly Anabaptist-Mennonite to serve comprehensively? Or positively, is this type the trunk line of the Believers' Church? The second question is how these same conference participants would see the needed contemporary "type" of the Believers' Church—whether without theocratic and spiritualist elements, whether an open-ended admixture of the historic types, or otherwise.

o   o   o

I must begin with a plea for indulgence in favor of those of us who were assigned to prepare our papers well before the conference but who now come to present them after three full days of our work together. If either the Holy Spirit or the spirit of man has been at work the past three days, then by definition the progress of these meetings must have gone beyond the point which could have been foreseen when our writing needed to be completed. It is therefore impossible for such a paper as this nearing the end of the study to be fully apropos. It is not possible ahead of time to prepare for such an eventuality by greater depth of research or complexity of treatment. I shall therefore request the liberty of a sweeping resort to typology and oversimplification for the sake of discussion.

We may situate the problem before us by taking stock of the rehabilitation which Anabaptism, as one specimen of the Believers' Church, has undergone at the hands of the writers of history in the last half century. Beginning with Troeltsch, the opinion has become increasingly widespread that the Anabaptists were, without knowing it, and prematurely, "the wave of the future." What they called for by way of separation of church and state and voluntary expression in matters of religion has now been widely accepted.[1] They have proved their point. Just as the magisterial Reformation was the particular form of Protestantism which dominated northern Europe from 1555 to the age of Enlightenment, so sectarian Protestantism is the official form of North American religion, so much so that even the Lutheran and Anglican denominations must be structured and supported as voluntary associations.

We could take this to mean that, since their point has been made, their followers and descendants should lay this issue aside and go on to more important matters. Why keep on belaboring an issue everyone has already accepted?

Such a way of arguing from the cultural acceptance of certain free church positions might be appropriate for some matters of detail, such as the rejection of religious persecution and the Crusade. But as the point of departure for a fundamental understanding of the mission of the Believers' Church, such an approach would be wrong in more ways than one.

First of all, such an assessment of the tapering off of the uniqueness of the Believers' Church is questionable in method. It fixes upon a negative, corrective, formal difference between the sixteenth-century believers' church and the magisterial tradition. For the Anabaptists and all who have followed in their train, the rejection of the church-state tie has, however, not been an issue debated in its own right, but a reflection of or a deduction from their concept of the nature of Christian discipleship and community. Instead of finding the uniqueness of the Believers' Church defined at that central point from which it was possible, *even* in the sixteenth century, to *derive* the concept of religious liberty, such an approach as we have suggested fixes on the derivative concept itself.

Secondly, this approach is wrong in the incongruity of the measures it uses. To say that the Anabaptist position on church and state has "triumphed" is to say that it has become the dominant social form of a given society. Its prescriptions with regard to the withdrawal of the state from matters of religion have been translated into legal form in some countries. The course of the mainstream of history reflects the acceptance of the sectarians' complaint. But all of these ways of stating the "success" or the "progress" of the free church social critique presuppose precisely what the Anabaptists and their spiritual relatives denied, namely, that the course of history and the structures of society are the most significant measures of whether men are doing the will of God. As far as these first free churchmen were concerned, the rightness of their position had no necessary connection to whether it would succeed, in one generation or in twenty,[2] in being adopted by a whole society.

One conclusion which nevertheless does follow from the widespread acceptance· in our society of some elements of the free church critique is that, since our society thinks it has accepted that critique, we cannot restate it without encountering a misunderstanding. "What more do you want?'' the interlocutor asks. "You have your separation from the state and your liberty of conscience. Did we not agree about all the other essentials?''

If thus we are to seek to unfold from its own heart the vision of the community of believers, we cannot do so simply, without encountering distortion and misunderstanding; for all the terms which we shall need to use have been preempted and all the issues have been crystallized. Whatever we say must be distinguished from what some-one else has already said, using the same words, but meaning something else. If then we are to break through to a renewed focusing of the real issues, we must run the risk of speaking with types and caricatures, recognizing the dangers of distortion, trusting that the point to which our conversation has come will enable this simplified approach to be used without profound injustice.

The Classical Options

Let us take for a moment the terrain of the sixteenth-century Swiss and South German Reformation as the source of our typology. The same demonstration could be derived elsewhere as well; it seems that the same possibilities spring forth in every age.

In the development of the Reformation under the shadow of Huldrych Zwingli, to the theological left and the geographical southwest of the Lutheran Reformation, three different streams of spiritual vitality may be usefully distinguished.[3] Despite the presence of borderline figures, the types are very clearly distinguishable. They are not three different positions along one clear continuum, with one of them mediating between the other two; each goes off in another direction. They can best be described with a triangular image.

At one corner of the triangle, claiming to carry to its logical conclusion the Reformation principle of the restoration of original Christianity, is Anabaptism, as best exemplified in Michael Sattler and Pilgram Marpeck. Anabaptism is now long recognized as a major landmark, though not the first nor the last, in the history of the concept of the Believers' Church. Their appeal, over against Zwingli himself, was to the same text which he himself had in January, 1523, used with such great effect against Johannes Faber: "Any plant that is not of my heavenly Father's planting will be rooted up"(Mt. 15:13).[1]

At another corner of the triangle, claiming to carry to its

logical extreme the dismantling of externals and the search for the true inwardness of *faith alone*, we find the so-called "Spiritualizers," best represented by Caspar Schwenckfeld. Their appeal was to the kind of argument Zwingli had employed in his tract of 1522, "Clarity and Certainty of the Word of God,"[5] namely, true inwardness and a religious certainty neither supported nor diluted by outward marks.

In the third corner we find those who carry to its ultimate implementation the logic of theocratic humanism which Zwingli had borrowed from Erasmus, whereby the word of God, as spoken by the "prophet" to the whole society, brings about the renewing of that society according to the will of God. This is the path which Zwingli himself took beginning ·in 1523, in which he was followed· by the Reformed churches along that crescent from Calvin's Geneva through Heidelberg and the Netherlands to Edinburgh.

Each of these parties saw itself standing in a one-dimensional polarity with regard to the other two. From the perspective of Zwingli and Calvin, the Spiritualizers and the Anabaptists were alike in their wrongheaded divisiveness and their undermining of Christian government. They shared the error of Martin Luther in his rejection of the theocratic vision and his relegation of government to a realm outside the gospel.

From the perspective of Caspar Schwenckfeld, the Anabaptists and the magisterial Reformation alike were too concerned for outward forms. Both of them had, like Luther, failed to carry to its consistent conclusion the logic of their withdrawal from the Roman Church with all her ceremonies.

From the perspective of Pilgram Marpeck, the Spiritualizers and Zwingli were very similar. Both of them denied the ultimate importance of proper church order. Schwenckfeld, because only spiritual reality matters, made no issue of outwardly challenging the established forms of Christendom and therefore suffered no severe persecution as did the Anabaptists. Zwingli, with almost the same arguments, could conclude that, since the true church is invisible, therefore the church which we organize cannot be the true church anyway; thus nothing stands in the way of our organizing it as we please, or more precisely, as good public order demands. Since faith is invisible, it was equally appropriate for Zwingli to baptize all infants and for Schwenckfeld to attach no importance at all to baptism. Since the Lord's Supper is a simple external ceremony, it is equally possible to teach (Zwingli) that its meaning is that of "signifying" a message distinct from the symbol itself,

255

or (Schwenckfeld) to abandon it. Thus both Schwenckfeld and Zwingli, in the name of a deeper spirituality, withstood the Anabaptists' call to bring into being a visible congregation of committed believers.

As normal as it was for each of these three parties to see the other two merging in their rejection of its own favorite concern, we do well following the guidance of Ernst Troeltsch (as reiterated pointedly by Franklin H. Littell in a landmark article [6]) to see the triangular character of this division. It is important to determine this in a bygone context because we in our day suffer the same temptation to see our problems in polarities rather than triangles.

With careful discernment we would probably find the same pattern recurring in every critical period of renewal, whether it be the Bohemian Brethren between Utraquists and the solitary Peter Chelcicky, or Alexander Mack between the radical and the churchly Pietists, or George Fox between Cromwell and the Ranters. In drawing from this patterned history a consistent descriptive typology, let us settle arbitrarily on a terminology whose use may accompany us in our contemporary and systematic argument. Within the Reformation to the left of Luther, as within free churchdom ever since then, let us recognize and label these three distinct types of stance, each with its own coherence.

Let us characterize as theocratic that vision of the renewal of the church which hopes to reform society at large in the same blow.[7] Whether the church and state as administrative agencies be merged, as with Bullinger or Erastus, or be quite distinct as with Calvin and the Scots, is a matter quite subordinate to the common Christian take-over of all society for the greater glory of God which is common to both polities.

For the theocrat, the locus of historical meaning is the movement of the whole society. Better that the young and the dissenters do the will of God grudgingly than not at all. Since there is power in every society, it will best be exercised by the Christian, be his calling farmer or statesman, banker or industrialist. The preacher or prophet must not seek to govern the state or the economy—that would be to relapse into clericalism, but it shall be governed by men who in their Christian calling do what God demands as the preacher has interpreted it to them.

Second, let us label as spiritualist the reaction, in the footsteps of Schwenckfeld, which moves the locus of meaning from society to the spirit.[8] Spiritualism does not indeed withdraw from all forms. **It remains in the frame of the theocratic society to** which it reacts. Like Schwenckfeld, by giving no specific social form to its dissent, it leaves the established church in place. Like **Spener preaching to princely households or Francke building schools,** it contributes readily to the social structures whose spiritual inadequacy it at the same time points up. But all of this outward form, it insists, is vanity, unless the deep inward reality can be found.

Our third type, the *Believers' Church*, stands not merely between the other two but over against both of them. With spiritualism it castigates the coldness and the formalism of official **theocratic** churchdom, but it corrects that formalism not by seeking to have no forms at all, nor by taking refuge in para-churchly forms, but rather by developing those forms which are according to Scripture and which are expressive of the character of the disciples' fellowship.

With **the theocratic vision, it rejects the individualism and the** elite self-consciousness of the spiritualist. But the social form which it proposes as an alternative to individualism is not the undifferentiated **baptized mass of the reformed** *corpus christianum,* **but** the covenanted fellowship enjoyed with others who have pledged themselves to following the same Lord.

We said at the outset that we would attempt to catalyze our conversation by bringing into the arena a blunt typology. Now we may say more precisely that we bring a triangular typology into what had seemed like a bipolar debate. We shall claim that the church is called to move beyond the oscillation between the **theocratic and the spiritualist patterns, not to a compromise between** the two or to a synthesis claiming like Hegel to "assume" them both, but to what is genuinely a third option.

The Message Is the Medium

Few assumptions have been more widely shared in Protestant thought than the identification of the messages of Paul and Luther with the promise of a new hope for the individual in his subjectivity. Luther in his rejection of the cultural religion of the Middle Ages, following Paul in his rejection of cultural Pharisaism, raised as his banner the *pro me* of the forgiven sinner. That God is gracious *to me* is the good news that Zinzendorf, Wesley, Kierkegaard, and today both Rudolf Bultmann and Billy Graham (in their very different ways) have derived from Luther, and have labored to keep unclouded by any effort to derive from it (or to base it upon) a social program or any other work of man. To safeguard the pure gratuitousness of grace, any binding correlation with man's works must be studiously kept in second place.

This assumption—to put it crudely, that Paul was a Lutheran—is now being dismantled under the impact of the exegetical theology of this century. Not only does biblical theology in general discover a fuller meaning to the dimension of *peoplehood* in all the working of God throughout the Bible story; not only does one find in Jesus' proclamation of the coming of the Kingdom in the Gospel accounts a dimension of genuine social creativity and in the calling of the twelve the nucleus of a new community. Today such scholars as Markus Barth and Hans-Werner Bartsch are finding as well even in the writings of Paul, yea even in *Galatians* and *Romans*, a hitherto unnoticed dimension of community extending even into the meaning of such words as *justification*.[9]

Since Protestantism from Luther to Bultmann has so broadly assumed such a correlation between "Gospel" and subjective awareness of guilt and forgiveness, one cannot emphasize too strongly how significant is this exegetical breakthrough. The work of God is the calling of a people, whether in the Old Covenant or the New. The church is then not simply the *bearer* of the message of reconciliation, in the way a newspaper or a telephone company can bear any message with which it is entrusted. Nor is the church simply the *result* of a message, as an alumni association is the product of a school or the crowd in the theater is the product of the reputation of the film. That men are called together to a new social wholeness is itself the work of God which gives meaning to history, from which both personal conversion (whereby individuals are called into this meaning) and missionary instrumentalities are derived.

The centrality of the church in God's purposes is stated in a figurative way in the first vision of the *Apocalypse*, where the question of the meaning of history is represented to the seer in the form of a sealed scroll. When it is announced that the Lamb that was slain is worthy to open the seals and unroll the meaning of history, the "*new song*" in which all the heavenly creatures join proclaims that the meaning of the sacrifice of the Lamb was that he has "purchased" "for God" a priestly kingdom out of "every tribe and tongue and people and nation" (5:9 f.).

Almost the same language is used in the sermonic context of *First Peter* 2, where the phrase "priestly kingdom" finds its counterpart, "royal priesthood," in addition to three other parallel collective

258

nouns describing the church as a people claimed by God for His own. Here "having received mercy" and "being a people," after having been "not a people," are synonymous.

The same statement is made more systematically in *Ephesians*. Here the Apostle claims to have been given understanding of a mystery hidden not only through the ages but also to the other apostles, which has been revealed first of all in his ministry and then in his understanding of that ministry. The creation of one new humanity by breaking down the wall between the two kinds of people of whom the world is made, Jews and Gentiles, is not simply the result of reconciliation of individuals with God, nor is it an ad hoc organization established to support the propagation of the knowledge of individual reconciliation. This creation of the one new humanity is itself the purpose which God had in all ages, is itself the "mystery," the gospel now to be proclaimed.

In every direction we might follow in exposition, *the distinctness of the church of believers is prerequisite to the meaningfulness of the gospel message*. If what is called "the church" is the religious establishment of a total society, then the announcement that God has created human community is redundant, for the religiously sanctioned community is identical with the given order. The identification of the church with a given society denies the miracle of the new humanity in two ways; on the one hand by blessing the existing social unity and structure which is a part of the fallen order rather than a new miracle, and on the other hand by closing its fellowship to those of the outside or the enemy class or tribe or people or nation. If any concept of meaningful mission is to remain in this context, it must be transmuted to the realm of subjectivity, calling a few individuals to a depth of "authenticity" which separates them from their brethren.

Pragmatically it is self-evident that there can be no procedure of proclamation without a community, distinct from the rest of society, to do the proclaiming. Pragmatically it is just as clear that there can be no evangelistic call addressed to a person inviting him to enter into a new kind of fellowship and learning if there is not such a body of persons, again distinct from the totality of society, to whom he can come and with and from whom he can learn. But this congruence between **the free visible existence of the Believers' Church and the possibility** of valid missionary proclamation is not a merely pragmatic or instrumental one, but is founded deeply in the nature of the gospel itself. If it is not the case that there are in a given place men of various characters and origins who have been brought together in Jesus Christ, then there is not in that place the new humanity and in that place the gospel is not true. If, on the other hand, this miracle of new creation has occurred, then all the verbalizations and interpretations whereby this brotherhood communicates to the world around it are simply explications of the fact of its presence.

Tools for the Study of the Church: The Notae Missionis

The classical instrument for the interpretation of the mission and nature of the Church is the concept of the "marks" which are the absolute minimum standards which enable one to recognize the existence of a particular church. "The church is wherever the Word of God is properly preached and the sacraments properly administered." From this definition of classical Protestantism we may appropriately begin our analysis.

The shortcoming of this statement is not simply its petitionary character. Obviously, the entire meaning of these two criteria is utterly dependent upon what "properly" is taken to mean. Conceivably one could pour all of any theology into these two phrases. This observation does not demonstrate that they are either right or wrong, but only that they were not coined with the intent that they serve usefully as principles of discrimination in ecumenical conversation. They were not really meant as "marks" in the sense that they could be used objectively by some third party to determine whether in any case of conflict a given entity calling itself "church" really is one.

But a more fundamental flaw in this statement of criteria is that the point of relevance in their application is not the church but its superstructure. The place you go to ascertain whether the word of God is properly preached in a given church is the preacher, or conceivably the doctrinal statement by which that ecclesiastical body is governed. The place you go to see whether the sacraments are being properly administered is again the officiant. The concentration of your attention might be upon his way of proceeding or it might focus upon his understanding of the meaning of the sacrament. But in either case it does not focus upon the congregation.

Now certainly it is taken for granted that there will be a congregation present. As a matter of fact since all of the Reformation statements were produced by state churches, we can be sure that the total community is assumed to be present under pain of punishment by the state. Yet the presence of the community is not part of the definition. How many persons are present, in what attitude they are listening, what they understand, how they respond to what they have heard, to what they commit themselves, how they relate to one another, and with what orientation they return to the week's activities is not part of the definition of the church. We thus have criteria which apply to recognizing the legitimacy of a magisterial superstructure, but not to identifying a Christian community.

The churches of the Reformed tradition were attempting to remedy this gap when they added a third criterion, namely, "proper discipline." This is again a petitionary definition which could be expanded to include much more, but in the Reformation setting it applied primarily to the synod pattern of government, the fourfold ministry, and some kind of moral control over the behavior of members. It is clearly just as petitionary as the other two.

It is thus highly significant when today pioneering thinking about the nature and the mission of the church begins with statements of her task which look quite different from the classical Reformation marks. In his book, *The Pressure of Our Common Calling*,[10] Willem A. Visser 't Hooft identifies three functions of the church: witness (martyria), service (diakonia), and communion or fellowship (koinonia). To some extent these labels could be interpreted as overlapping with the older ones. "Fellowship" might include proper use of the sacrament of the Lord's Supper; "witness" would have something to do with proper preaching of the word. Yet each of these functions is clearly more than that. It is characteristic of all three that they reach out into two dimensions quite different from the earlier description.

First of all, the three functions of witness, fellowship, and service all have to do with the Christian church *as a community* of people. They ask about the relationships and the behavior of the Christian community. It would not be possible to measure whether these requirements have been met by looking only at the functioning of the preacher or at the doctrinal stance of the church hierarchy. They test, or describe, the *congregation*.

Secondly, these descriptions of the function of the church are characterized by the relationship in which the church stands *to the world*. Ministry and witness demand the world beyond for the function to be meaningful. Even "fellowship" implies a relation, in a sense a negative one, in that by definition one's "fellow" is not every other human being but one with whom one has entered into a particular relationship which does not include all others. These marks test, or describe, a *mission*.

Similar in substance, although different in detail, is the proposal of Stephen Neill in his book, *The Unfinished Task*.[11] Bishop Neill suggests that to the traditional Reformation marks there should be added three more: "fire on earth" (missionary vitality), suffering, and the mobility of the pilgrim. Again these are descriptions of the total Christian fellowship in the midst of the world, and not of a leadership body.

What these two senior statesmen of the modern ecumenical movement are saying was said in the sixteenth century by Menno Simons. To the two standard Lutheran marks (which he of course would have defined quite differently in detail from Luther), Menno added four more: holy living, brotherly love, unreserved testimony, and suffering.[12]

We could attempt to exposit the arguments in favor of including these added dimensions in a normative description of the church. But since the testimony of Visser 't Hooft and Neill demonstrates abundantly the currency of this kind of thinking, an expository argument should not be necessary here. We shall therefore limit our concern to two other comments by way of exposition of their continuing contemporary relevance.

First, by way of introduction, let us note the interrelation of the two dimensions which we have observed to be common to these new marks. They have to do with the congregation rather than solely the preacher; and they see the church in relationship to the world rather than looking at her "by definition" or "as such." How do these two dimensions relate to one another?

It would be possible to add either one of these dimensions to the standard Lutheran criteria. Martin Luther himself, for instance, thought seriously of the possibility of the creation of a committed Christian community, to which he testified in the oft-quoted preface to his "German mass" of 1526. It would have been desirable, he said, that in addition to a continuing use of the Latin liturgy and to the introduction of the high Lutheran liturgy there might have been in the third place new corporate expressions in visible congregations. Pietism later sought to fill this gap by creating circles of believers. Yet without the dimension of outward mission, this type of gathering around common pious experiences is immediately threatened with stagnation and becomes little more than communal introspection.

On the other hand, it is also possible to add to magisterial Protestantism the element of propagation. Some early visions of missionary responsibility, especially as sometimes linked to the early commercial colonial corporations of Britain and the Netherlands, could assume it to be quite adequate to think of the missionary task as adequately discharged by the propagation of right preaching and right sacramental practice in other parts of the globe; but in the absence of the creation of a genuine indigenous community this turns out to be pure paternalism and makes the elements of sacramentalism and clericalism all the more distasteful by the alien form in which they are exported into another society.

Thus peoplehood and mission, fellowship and witness, are not two desiderata, each capable of existing or of being missed independently of one another; each is the condition of the genuineness of the other.

Secondly, and at greater length, after having accepted on the word of Visser 't Hooft, Neill, and Menno that the marks of mission and of community are indispensable, we must interpret how and why **it is the stance of the Believers' Church, rather than of the** spiritualist or theocratic traditions, which most adequately meets these criteria. Menno's outline will be as good as any other scaffold.

Nota 1. Holy Living

For it is God's will that by doing right you should put to silence the ignorance of foolish men (1 Pet. 2:15, RSV).

The late Harold S. Bender, dean of the ingroup historians of Anabaptism, gathered into one article[13] the testimonies to the striking quality of life which even according to the testimony of their adversaries was typical of the sixteenth-century Anabaptists. Certainly the same testimony could be duplicated from the history of the other believers' churches. **This is not to suggest that the Believers' Church** tradition is alone in its ethical concern. As a matter of fact the epithets, "puritan" and "pietist," currently used to identify those other traditions,[14] have had their greatest (and their most pejorative) currency as descriptive of particular ethical styles. Pietism designates for many a regimen of abstinences from personal gratification, and Puritanism a pattern of social control, both of them predominantly expressed in negative form. In none of these three traditions is there lurking any of that acquiescence in the lower level of the masses' moral performance of which Lutheranism and Anglicanism are accused, nor any of the antinomianism of the enthusiasts. Yet the ethical **concern in the three settings** is not of the same nature.

With regard to the substance of ethics, spiritualism and theocracy are more alike than different, for the concentration on personal authenticity and on social control is not contradictory but complementary. The man who is truly regenerated and who therefore is humble and unselfish will certainly make the best statesman. Or to say it the other way around: he who governs men most needs the illumination and the counsel and admonition of the gospel. So the typical context of moral decision is that of the ruler; how shall all society be managed? What are the evils and how may they be eliminated? What is the will of God and how may we assure its being done? What shape should our society have? The samples of decision-making dealt with in the ethics text are those persons in "responsible positions": in government, in business leadership.[15] The paradigms are not drawn, as so often in the New Testament ethic, from the underside of social relationships: the wife, the child, the slave, the subject. And what the father or the ruler or the banker is to do is not derived from either the words or the example of Jesus, but from what any honest and reasonable person in that same position would do. The imperatives are defined by the situation (or, as an old system said it, "the station"), and not by the positive word of the covenant God. Thus from John Calvin to Harvey Cox those who have seen the total social order as the locus of the doing of the will of God have differed only in their language from those others, from Philip Spener to Norman Vincent Peale and Howard Pew, who place their trust in the personal integrity of those in high places.[16]

The alternative to all of this is the biblical demand that holiness is the separateness of a called *people*, and the *distinctiveness* of their social existence. The need is not, as some current popularizers would suggest, for most Christians to get out of the church and into the world. They have been in the world all the time. The trouble is that they have been *of* the world too. The need is for what they do in the world to be different because they are Christian; to be a reflection not merely of their restored self-confidence nor of their power to set the course of society but of the social novelty of the covenant of grace. Instead of doing, each in his own station or office, whatever any reasonable person would do in the same place according to the order of creation, the need is for what he does there to be judged and renewed by the difference which it makes that Christ, and not mammon or mars, is his Lord.

So much for the interior concerns of ethics: the Believers' Church is a presupposition of biblical ethics. But now how is that community which is marked by holy living peculiarly the missionary community?

First of all, in that the moral nonconformity of the Christians is an indispensable dimension of their visibility. If the church is visible in that these people keep their promises, love their enemies, enjoy their neighbors, and tell the truth, as others do not, this may communicate to the world something of the reconciling, i.e., the community-creating, love of God. If on the other hand those who call Christ "Lord, Lord" do whatever the situation calls for just as do their neighbors, then what is communicated about their "religion" will probably be that they have preachers and Sunday gatherings and prescribed ceremonies. The visibility of the witness, and thereby the concept of what it means to hear and accept it, is then misplaced.

Secondly, ethics is mission in the sense currently, and properly, being pointed to by the advocates of the "new worldliness." Civil rights advocacy or responsible concern for peace in Vietnam or for food in Mississippi or India can in given circumstances be not only prerequisite for the credibility of preaching but actually themselves the necessary proclamatory action. Likewise when the more ordinary social structures are asked to determine the "shape of the mission," it is only meaningful for Christians in a business or a factory to gather as a "missionary task force" if there is some available definition of what difference their faith makes in their behavior there.[17]

Nota 2. Brotherly Love

Now the company of those who believed were of one heart and soul (Acts 4:32a, RSV).

Menno's second mark of the true church is "brotherly love." With Visser 't Hooft's *koinonia*, this moves the locus of definition from the administration of the sacrament to the meaning of the sacrament. As we suggested before, the loving brotherhood was part of the vision of Martin Luther. But, contrary to the changes which he felt he was fully authorized to make in the external forms of the magisterial church, Luther felt it improper to seek actively to form at his own initiative a group with this quality of relationships, without the prior presence of the people required to form it, for fear of its becoming a clique.

As Luther thus recognized, this is the point where voluntaryism makes all the difference. You can make people come to church, but you cannot make them love one another. The criterion of unfeigned love is therefore the index of the voluntary character of the fellowship.

Menno has the reputation, which at least some of his colleagues and successors did something to earn for their movement, of practicing discipline with an unloving and unbending rigor. Yet significantly, the ban or "discipline" is not, as with Calvin, part of the definition of the church. Brotherly love is. Here we have a pointer to the structural difference between church discipline, even when it extends to the point of excommunication, within the voluntary church tradition, and the very different meaning which such discipline could have in a state church system like those of Geneva, the Netherlands, Scotland, and New England. It is the concern to "win the brother" (Mt. 18:15) which stands behind the discipline of the Believers' Church, not a desire to inflict suffering, or teach a lesson, or protect the reputation or the standards of the church.[18]

It is by no means far-fetched to suggest that this very quality of aggressive concern for the brother is a dimension of mission most regrettably lacking in modern Christendom. In the framework of puritan theocracy, with the coercive character of its social sanctions, the effect of "love" in later years was appropriately to soften the pressures and punishments. But when the congregation's "binding and loosing" is the implementation of the commonly covenanted commitment to a manner of life dictated by grace, then to leave the brother alone in his sin is not love at all but irresponsibility. Like the child who misbehaves because it is a sure way to get parental attention, my brother's sin may testify more to his solitude than to either his carnality or his freedom.

Now that in the secular city the given solidarities of the clan and the village cannot be counted on to provide willy-nilly a place for every man to belong, one may well rejoice in the new freedom which urban anonymity gives him to choose his own associates; but then the question of salvation is posed all the more acutely. Can I find that loving community, for the sake of the finding of which it was good to be freed? If not, then in the words with which Jesus described just this fate, "the last state of that man is worse than the first" (Mt. 12:45c).

Nota 3. Witness

> . . . for truly in this city there were
> gathered together against thy holy servant Jesus,
> whom thou didst anoint, both Herod and Pontius
> Pilate, with the Gentiles and the peoples of
> Israel, to do whatever thy hand and thy plan
> had predestined to take place. And now, Lord,
> look upon their threats, and grant to thy
> servants to speak thy word with all boldness . . .
> (Acts 4:27-29, RSV).

The third of the distinctive marks of the church according to Menno is "that the name, will, word, and ordinance of Christ are constantly confessed in the face of all cruelty, tyranny, tumult, fire, sword, and violence of the world, and sustained unto the end." Just as Menno had previously sharpened the definition of the "right use of the sacraments" by insisting that they are not to be administered undiscriminatingly to the impenitent, so here the accent in the definition of witness as a mark of the church is not simply on the holding forth of a message but on the readiness to do so in the face of hostility from the world. Thus the initial and the derived meanings of the word, *martyria*, are linked. This is, as we have noted, one of the points where the marks of the mission as stated by Visser 't Hooft and Neill would strikingly coincide with those of Menno.

As has been increasingly demonstrated by historical studies, beginning in 1952 with one chapter of *The Anabaptist View of the Church* by Franklin H. Littell[19] and building up to the massive Heidelberg dissertation[20] of **Wolfgang Schäufele dealing with the missionary consciousness and activity of the Anabaptists** (1966), the concept of a missionary witness is structurally incompatible with the sociological and political posture of the established church, since all of the subjects in a given country are already within that church, and in any other *regio* everyone by the same token is the responsibility of some other *religio*. By the same token, only the Believers' Church is structurally committed to and dependent upon a witness addressed to those who are not its members—dependent, that is, both for its own survival and for the accomplishment of its task.

It is noteworthy that in Menno's interpretation of this faithful witness the accent does not fall upon the subjective response of the hearers. Whether many will hear and be converted, or any, does not enter into the discussion of this mark. Thus the debate which has been raging for two centuries about whether the subjective conversion of individuals is the core of the definition of missionary witness is not the central issue. What is central is that the witness be proclaimed without compromise in the face of opposition.

We find in this statement the clear reflection of a particular polemical theme of the sixteenth century. Beginning in the early 1520's, a debate was simmering in both Lutheran and Zwinglian quarters about the concept of *Schonung*, the indulgence or caution or forbearance with which the reformer takes account of the limited understanding of his faithful. In order not to shock the flock with too radical a reformation message, the true preacher of the Word, although convinced that the judgment of Scripture must reject radically much of the inherited Catholic system of piety, will be careful to criticize and dismantle only one point at a time and to move only as fast as his constituency can follow.

This is another point at which the theocratic and the spiritualist streams could agree. Zwingli and Luther argued in favor of *Schonung* in order to bring all of society along; for the greatest danger would be to jeopardize the religious unity of the Christian people. Schwenckfeld, on the other hand, was equally committed to *Schonung*, leaving untouched the traditional ceremonies, because it is not worth the trouble to change them and because the very act of centering one's attention on changing them attributes to external forms more attention than they merit. For Zwingli, then, the concept of "witness" is limited to the issue of the authority of the preacher and his wisdom in properly establishing the dosage of novelty which his listeners can tolerate at any one time. For Schwenckfeld "witness" is an expression of concern for the conversion and the inward vitality and authenticity of the life of the individual.

In both cases "forbearance" had the effect of guaranteeing that the impact of the witness on the social order would not be revolutionary nor lead to suffering. Thus the whole problem of the strategy of "reformation" versus "restitution" was encapsuled in the issue of "forbearance," and in that in turn was enclosed the difference between witness and pedagogy as keynotes of the definition of mission. Is the faithfulness with which the Church has discharged her mission to be measured by how well she "brings along" the crowds or the authorities? Or the children of the faithful? Or by the unbending conformity of her testimony to the character and person of Him to whom it points?

Thus the issue does not become central which past debate on evangelism has stumbled over. By concern for "who says what to whom" a hopeless polarity has been set up in the interpretation of "lay witness." For the spiritualist it means buttonholing people about their souls; to the theocrat it means speaking to relevant issues from a Christian perspective. For Menno it is both, but neither is the unique focus; for the crucial issue is not that there must be one particular idea content, but that the witness must avoid his testimony's being diluted or distorted by what men want to hear.

As we shall see later in the more polemical section of this study, exactly the same debate is still with us. On the one hand there are those for whom the focus of concern in the faithful witness of the church is the subjective authenticity of the conversion with which the listener manifestly responds. The locus of the meaning of the act of witness is therefore in the listener. Then we shall of course expect him in turn to be a witness and also, secondarily, to change society around him by his faithfulness in his calling. On the other hand there are those for whom the witness of the church centers on a strategy of directed social change. Witness is needed in order that this change shall be called forth. Wisdom is needed that it may be guided at the pace which is set by the institutional possibilities of the agencies which the church can get to listen: change is itself the objective.

Free church theologians have been trying to choose between these options, and they thereby fall short of the originality of their own heritage. Menno would have addressed to both the criticism that the "witness" was being diluted by opposition: on one hand by withdrawing from a direct challenge to the orders of society and on the other by setting goals in terms of what the authorities can reasonably be asked to do.

Nota 4. The Cross

A servant is not greater than his master. If they persecuted me, they will persecute you (Jn. 15:20 b,c, RSV).

Fourthly, according to Menno and Stephen Neill, the true missionary congregation is marked by suffering. This suffering, like that of the faithful servant in First Peter (2:18 ff.; 3:14-18; 4:1, 12-16), is not the result of misbehavior but of conformity with the path of Christ. It is not the resigned acceptance of limitations or injustice in an imperfect world, but the meaningful assuming of the cost of nonconformed obedience.

It is no accident that the word "martyr" has the double meaning of testimony and innocent suffering. The suffering of the church is not a passing tight spot after which there can be hope of return to normalcy; it is according to both Scripture and experience the continuing destiny of any faithful Christian community.

Here again our threefold typology will be of assistance in clarification. For medieval mysticism, for Thomas Müntzer, and for Zinzendorf the "cross" is an inward experience in which the self struggles with doubt or with pride until it is brought to that brokenness and surrender which permits the mystical vision. The concepts of cross and surrender (Gelassenheit) then have basically an inward meaning.

For the theocratic world and for the usage of pastoral care across the ages, to have "a cross to bear" means to live with an incurable illness or a difficult mother-in-law or poverty; in other words, a kind of suffering, built into one's own social situation, for which one may or may not be partially to blame, but which is mostly the simple result of where one finds oneself, not of a particular moral commitment. If in this context there is such a concept as "surrender," it must be simply the acceptance of one's being who he is and where he is as "where God has placed you."

For the Believers' Church on the other hand, as for the young Zwingli from whom the Anabaptists learned it, "the cross" is to be understood much more narrowly as that kind of suffering which comes upon one because of his loyalty to Jesus and his noncomformity to the world. "Surrender" has certainly an inward dimension; but its confirmation will be found in one's joyfully doing, in the world, regardless of cost, the will of God. The New Testament scholar, Ethelbert Stauffer, who in his New Testament studies has given special attention to the concept of discipleship and to the conflict between Christ and Caesar, has also written an interpretation of the meaning of suffering in Anabaptism,[21] in which the demonstration is clear that suffering is not simply the regrettably unavoidable cost of holding to those positions which merit salvation, but is rather a participation in the victory of Christ over the powers of this age. The same could be said, for instance, of Quakerism, whose concept of the Christian mission was summed up in the phrase, "The War of the Lamb."[22]

Now it is possible for anyone to agree with the early free churches (and with Stephen Neill) that readiness to suffer is part of the faithfulness of the church and that suffering may often be characteristic of the experience of the faithful church. But this leaves two questions still open. First of all, is there not considerable danger of seeking suffering or glorifying it for its own sake? Here the distinction already made over against spiritualistic and theocratic concepts of the cross is helpful. Mysticism and monasticism can glorify suffering for its own sake because it is thought of as a tool in the discipline of the soul. The theocratic vision on the other hand, can consider it as a not necessary, because incalculable, dimension of Christian faithfulness, arising as Providence permits out of the order of things. If, however, one sees the cross of the Christian, as the language of the New Testament indicates, as the reflection of and participation in the character of the saving work of Christ, then one does not seek it, but when it comes neither does one consider it simply as a matter of having been providentially chosen for a hard time.

But in our context the perhaps more difficult question is what this mark of suffering has to do with faithfulness in mission. The simple answer would be to ask what suffering had to do with the mission of Jesus, but such a cryptic response is not enough. Since the free church definition was developed over against the religious establishment, the place to look for this answer is not on the foreign mission field (for there every church is a free church in the first generations), but in the conflicts of the Reformation. The free churches arose out of attempts at reformation in various times and places where other leaders of that reformation process wanted not to stay with the status quo but to move slowly and strategically. The process of reformation, never complete (*ecclesia semper reformanda*), was conceived as a gradual curriculum, in which the authorized teacher would move his total flock progressively from apostasy or paganism into true evangelical faith. For ⁺his reason, he argued, one must not say everything at once; one must₍ ⁾t be too radical; one must respect the conscience of the weak. Since t..c time when the argument from the tender conscience of the weak brother was used by Zwingli in favor of maintaining the usage of the mass after he had condemned it as theologically wrong, the same debate has been repeated many times at the birth of every free church movement. The "cross" which the gradualist reformer is unwilling to bear is therefore not necessarily outright persecution, death, or exile, but simply the tension and rejection, on the part of the mass of the population or the established authorities, which would need to be faced by someone committed first of all to restructuring the church according to the will of God. Thus willingness to bear the cross means simply the readiness to let the form of the Church's obedience to Christ be dictated by Christ rather than by how much the population or the authorities are ready to accept. When stated in this way it is then clear that the readiness of the church to face suffering thus understood is precisely the only way in which it is possible to communicate to that society and to its authorities that it is Christ who is Lord and not they. The preacher who tailors his message to what the people will understand is not simply making a practical mistake of "not moving fast enough"; he is failing by the very structure of his approach to communicate one particular thing, namely, that his loyalty to Christ is the sole absolute.

Mission Compromised

For the label "Believers' Church" to be meaningful, it must be assumed that there is some other kind of church, or more precisely some other concept of the church, not structured upon faith in the same way, with which it stands in tension. To know honestly what it means to affirm that the community of believers is the form of the mission, we therefore must face as well, in loving polemics, the real possibilities of unfaithfulness and the serious claims of other options. How could it happen that the Church could become Christendom? Wherein lies the essence of that apostasy whereby what calls itself church, continuing to do great deeds avowedly in the name of the Lord, defeats his purposes instead?

The Roman and Eastern forms of Catholicism, when they speak of one another as "apostate," date that fall from grace with their breach of hierarchical communion. When Magisterial Protestantism sought a date for the Fall of the Church, it was found somewhere after the fifth century, so that the ancient creeds could all be retained. Anabaptism found the root still deeper, at the point of that fusion of church and society of which Constantine was the architect, Eusebius the priest, Augustine the apologete, and the Crusades and Inquisition the culmination. If the reconciliation of all races and peoples is the mission, then the sacralization of one people or, even worse, of one bearer of sovereignty, or the identification of the Kingdom with the movement of one society, is its denial. But now this thesis demands application to the current scene.

Compromise 1. Evangelism

For one major portion of our study we have not the liberty of choosing our own topic. Current debate on the mission of the church in the world has been radically and publicly polarized again in the last year around contradictory definitions of the meaning of evangelism.

Perhaps the word "contradictory" is too strong for some. There are many for whom the two polar positions seem extreme and who would seek somehow to mediate between them. But the debaters on both sides are right at least in principle; there is no papering over the difference between two ultimately incompatible points of orientation.

On the one hand, symbolized internationally by the July, 1966, World Conference on Church and Society in Geneva, and in the United States by those parallel concerns for which "the secular city" and "get where the action is" are the slogans, we have the contemporary form of the theocratic program. It finds the locus of meaningfulness in the course of the history of a society or of the world at large and calls upon the church to discern God as the agent of that movement and upon Christians to join him in bringing it about. Now with regard to ethics, the particular standards of moral evaluation for such issues as work and leisure or sexuality will in this context have a quite different outline from what used to be called "puritan." But our

272

typology here is dealing with the question of the locus of the meaning of history, and on this structural level it can hardly be doubted that the vision of the "secular city," which David Little has perceptively called "the social gospel revisited," is today's edition of the Genevan theocratic vision.

On the other hand, in that position, represented internationally by the October, 1966, World Congress on Evangelism in Berlin, and locally by the presence of Billy Graham at the National Council of Churches General Assembly in December, there is the continuing vitality of that stream of churchmanship which sees the locus of all meaning in the stance of the soul. What should matter ultimately to a person is the destiny of his own soul; in his concern for the welfare of others, the good he seeks for them is of the same kind.

Now it does not solve this problem at all to temper one of the extreme positions by adding a few elements of the other. It is possible for instance to add to spiritualism a recognition of the serious social concern which will be expressed by the converted person, while still holding a conception of the saving experience which is completely individualistic. Or on the other hand it is possible to recognize that only a personally convinced and committed person will be effective as an agent of social change and that every significant social cause is carried by a few firmly committed, "converted" individuals whose devotion and effectiveness can only be explained as unique divine gifts, while still holding that what ultimately matters in God's purpose is the building of better society. But such mitigation of the extremes does not change their opposition.

It is already no easy task simply to describe the current polarization of the meanings old and new of evangelism and revolution, to say nothing of attempting to lead this discussion to a wholesome conclusion. But if instead of seeking to mediate or to assign percentages to these two components of the Christian missionary responsibility, we were to bring to bear our tripartite typology, we might be partly freed from the dilemma. For if it is the predominant purpose of God neither to direct all of world history coercively toward a predetermined end, nor to make individuals whole each by himself, but to constitute a new covenant people responding freely to his call, then the strong and weak points of the earlier debate fall into a new configuration. The error of spiritualism is not adequately tempered by insisting that saved individuals will get together sometimes or that saved individuals will be socially effective. But neither is it to be corrected by replacing personal change and commitment with the remodeling of the total society. The complement to personal decision is the "new humanity" of covenant community. Preoccupation with making world history come out right or making the secular city be the city of God is not adequately tempered by saying that even the best technopolis would still be imperfect or that there will still need to be voluntary associations within the coming great society. But neither must concern for the social dimension of the kingdom be replaced by a mere call to a new attitude.

The political novelty which God brings into the world is a community of those who serve instead of ruling, who suffer instead of inflicting suffering, whose fellowship crosses social lines instead of reinforcing them. This new Christian community in which the walls are broken down not by human idealism or democratic legalism but by the work of Christ is not only a vehicle of the gospel or fruit of the gospel; it is the good news. It is not merely the agent of mission or the constituency of a mission agency. This is the mission.

Compromise 2. History

It was predictive of this major contemporary debate when in 1961 the Study Commission on the Missionary Task of the Church of the World Council of Churches identified as one of the continuing questions far from being resolved the issue of the relationship between the work of the church and the course of secular history:

> What is the relation between the Course of the Gospel and what is going on in the world? What is God's redemptive purpose in and for world history?

The Commission's response to this question was modest and moderate. While solidly affirmative about Christian social responsibility and the partly biblical origins of radical social criticism, the statement maintained a distinction in kind between the Church and the wider history, between her faithfulness and her social efficacy, and between her hope and secular messianisms. But this study did not become a landmark, and in the broader stream of "Church and Society" talks the same modesty has not always been evident. So the debate goes on.

This same question comes to the surface in contemporary ecumenic debate on a number of levels, all the way from the attitude to take toward particular power structures within a given local society to the interpretation of the whole course of world history as this reflects the impact of "Christianization" and "secularization." But whatever the breadth of the view, the structure of the thought is the same.

In opposition to what it identifies as "pietism," the currently prevalent mode of thought prominent in World Council circles identifies the structures of secular society as the locus of the meaning of mission. On the broadest level this means interpreting the process of secularization itself as an outworking of the desacralization which is the **impact of the biblical witness.**[23] **It is itself the ultimate goal of the** witness of the church. In the local context, as has been developed in considerable length in the extended series of studies on the Missionary Structure of the Congregation, the emphasis has constantly been laid upon turning one's attention away from the church and what goes on within in order to discern instead what it is that God, independently of the church if need be, has been doing in the world, namely, in the structures of society and their evolution, so that, having discerned this working, the church can welcome it and join it. Between the two extremes of philosophy of history and techniques of social change, the most typical and journalistically attractive discussion deals with "revolution" as the not clearly defined label for the profound and rapid social change which all agree is needed in most of Asia, Africa, and Latin America if men are to be able to live together in dignity. Since it is needed, this revolution must be approved of by the church, however it comes; it must be discerned as both inevitable and the will of God.

A careful encounter with this new mood in Christian social ethics under the heading of mission would go far beyond the scope of the present study. Our concern is only to point out that, in spite of its undeniable originality in detail, such a position is in its structure but another form of the theocratic conception of the mission of the church. It is very aware of the differences, since the old Puritanism labeled as "Christian" the society whose structures it supported, and now these societies are accepted as "secular." Yet the powers at work and the forces upon which one relies, the evils one identifies and the images one nurtures of how men should live together have the same shape. The old theocracy could baptize the world. Now that the world will **no longer be baptized, the church nonetheless claims it in spite** of itself as the "latent" church and proclaims its salvation whether it will or no. In earlier centuries the rulers did at least sometimes what they were told to do by preachers, especially within the Zwinglian tradition. Today churchmen claim to discern a revelation of what God is doing in what the powers of this world are doing anyway for their own reasons. The world has "come of age," but we still baptize it as our baby.

Certainly **the testing of this new Constantinianism is not furthered** by the spiritualistic alternative, which is all that most critics seem able to propose. The spiritualistic critic argues (rightly as far as that goes) that no juggling of the structures of society can do away with the effects of human sinfulness, so that the promises of a new secular optimism are deceptive, in addition to being less than the New Testament gospel, because they bypass the element of personal guilt and reconciliation. But as we saw before, this critique does not have an alternative social ethic of its own. Then in effect those who criticize the "gospel of the secular revolution" presuppose in its place that they shall continue to give their blessing to the present anti- or pre-revolutionary order, which is sanctified for them by virtue of the fact that some at least of the persons who hold office within it are Christians doing their duty in a secular vocation.

Thus in spite of the vast difference in focus and language, the theocratic and spiritualist social ethics are structurally the same. One sanctifies the present or recent order and the other the future order, but both make that total order the framework of social ethics. One sanctifies the coming order because it is what matters the most under the Lordship of Christ; the other leaves things as much as possible as they are because this is not what matters the most spiritually, but the logical outcome is the same. Both derive the substance of their ethics from the "vocation," i.e., from the naturally discernible structures and values built into the social order, present or evolving.

It would be possible to argue on either side of the thesis that, if Christians are to be in servitude to the principalities and powers, it at least is better that it be the powers of the future than those of the past. But from the context of the covenant community the argument should rather be that such servitude, whether past or future, is part of what we have been freed from by the work of Christ and the gift of his Spirit.

The context of the covenant community represents a radical alternative to both the theocratic and the spiritualist views of historical movement, first of all, because the community is a *discerning* community. The promise of the presence of the Holy Spirit is clearly correlated in the New Testament with the need for the church prophetically to discern right and wrong in the events of the age. Not all visible events are God at work, not all "action" is divine, not every spirit is of Christ (1 Cor. 12:3; 1 Jn. 4:1). We cannot "go where the action is" until we know *which* action should be blessed and joined and which should be denounced. Precisely because a community of faith is distinct from the wider society not only in membership but also in decision-making structures and values, it can be the agent of responsible moral discernment.

The church is qualified to be such an agent of discernment, secondly, because she is committed not simply to doing "good," whatever that may be and wherever it may be found, but because she has in her allegiance to Jesus Christ *criteria* of good and evil which are significantly different from those which prevail in even the most respectable segments of the larger society. However much it makes sense to modern Western thought, the ethic of vocation which tells each Christian simply to do what is "called for" by the inherent and unambiguous standards of his "office" finds no support in the New Testament. After a long stretch of time when, under the impact of Albert Schweitzer, the study of New Testament ethical thought was paralyzed by the idea that the irrationally radical ethic of Jesus was conditioned upon his mistaken expectation of the end of history, more careful study is now beginning to rediscover a consistent pattern of ethical thought in the several strands of the New Testament literature. This is not an "interim ethic" in the sense that its logic depends upon the expectation of an early end of the world. It is derived not from any such calculations but simply from Christology.

The difference between this New Testament ethic and that of our age is most clearly demonstrated by what Jesus says about serving and ruling. " 'The kings of the Gentiles exercise lordship over them; and those in authority over them are called benefactors. But not so with you . . . ' " (Lk. 22:25, RSV; cf. Mt. 20:25). In modern parlance, "public service" has become the standard euphemism for the exercise of power, thus fulfilling in the name of the "Christian calling" what Jesus ironically said about pagan rulers, namely, that they glorify the exercise of power over men as being "benefaction." Now Jesus and the New Testament writers following him do not reject rulership because the world is coming to an early end, nor because it is ethically impure (when measured, as Reinhold Niebuhr would measure it, by the standards of absolute selflessness), nor because the people who exercise it are always evil brutes. They do not say that the world can get along without such powers; but neither do they suggest that Christians in all those positions could do a much better job. They simply say that it was the mission of the Son of Man to serve and not to rule and that his disciples will follow him in the same path. If there is to be any solid critique of the contemporary wave of enthusiasm for religiously glorified revolution, it must not be in the name of religiously glorified conservatism nor of

277

social unconcern or withdrawal, but rather an expression of an ethic of social involvement as servants derived from the man Jesus, whose Messianity and Lordship we affirm and of whom we confess (whether the "action" to this effect be visible or not) that his way of servanthood shall triumph.

Thus what is questionable about the "gospel of revolution" as currently being propagated by the popularizers is not that it is too revolutionary but rather that it is just a new edition of the same old pattern of seeking in the name of God to make history come out right instead of seeking in the train of Christ only to be servant.

Compromise 3. The Congregation

It is characteristic of policy statements within the study processes of the World Council of Churches that the centrality of the local congregation is always affirmed. In one classical statement, the paper on "A Responsible Society" with which the veteran ecumenical statesman J. H. Oldham launched a slogan which was to find a wide echo, the development began with such an affirmation:

> The church is concerned with the primary task of re-creating a true social life in two ways. In the first place, its greatest contribution to the renewal of society is through the fulfillment of its primary functions of preaching the Word and through its life as a worshipping community.[24]

It was only after this statement of priorities that the development then moved on in a very significant sequence to the work ethic of the individual, then to the morality of decisions in small groups, and lastly to the discussion of the form of the political order.

As a series of further study conferences and programs circled the globe between Amsterdam and Evanston, applying the concept of responsible society especially to the strategy of the churches in areas of rapid social change, every conference and every document continued to reaffirm this preamble (Bangkok 1949, Lucknow 1952, Evanston 1954, India 1960). But as far as the actual subject matter of study was concerned, the sequence very rapidly became the reverse. The discussion turned first on a picture of what the total social order should be, then on the decision-making of power groups and leadership groups within a society, only thirdly on individual ethical responsibility in the vocation, and then the place of congregational life was left for last.

At New Delhi, 1961, the concern for the congregation was refocused, partly because of the emphasis laid by the Faith and Order Commission on the thesis that the unity we seek is not so much an organizational change on the national or world level but rather the possibility for "all in each place" to be united in fellowship and in mission. There then began the series of studies on the "Missionary Structure of the Congregation" which is beginning in these months to be brought to some concluding statements. The course of this study may be summarized roughly as follows:

A. One begins with the starting assumption that the parish structure, which has obtained in European Christianity and its cultural extensions where colonization has planted "Christian culture," was appropriate and at least in principle adequate as an expression of the responsibility of the church to and for and in a stable society prior to the Industrial Revolution.

B. The changes which have taken place in social organizations and communication through the revolutionary cultural developments and movements of peoples in the last century and one-half make it clear that the residential parish is no longer the cultural home or *oikos* of the living of modern man. If then the Christian congregation is to discharge the responsibility which hitherto has taken the shape of the residential parish, it must learn to adapt itself to the new shape of the life of modern man. This, a consensus of the writers in this stream of study processes would seem to be saying, calls for the breaking up of the traditional concept of "congregational life" along two different lines.

C. The first line of bifurcation is the definition of that shape which society provides to the church and to which the church shall adapt herself.

(1) There is, first of all, the actual matrix of the basic life experiences which replace the residential neighborhood with a group of people gathering around a particular function. For the children and their teachers this is the school; for the wage earners it is the factory or the office; for the housewives it is the shopping center; for students, the university. These are therefore the *oikoi* in which new task forces should gather, each taking, for that segment of society, a kind of "parish" defined functionally rather than spatially, the same

279

type of function which the church in the old days tried to take for the neighborhood. These will be groups much smaller and less rigidly organized than the traditional congregations.

(2) But it will also be necessary to move to groups much larger than the ordinary congregation. Modern man with his media of communication and transportation feels "at home" in a total urban area. The "world" with which he is familiar is that which is within a traveling distance of a few hours from his home and in which, if he has lived there a few years, he can feel that he knows his way around and recognizes the major landmarks and the leading personages. There will, therefore, have to be some kind of organization on this level, that of the metropolitan complex or the "human zone." As Hans J. Margull summarizes it, "Man's life formerly lived in his small parish is now being lived in a large and specific region, and it came to us to affirm that nothing less than such a region ought to be seen as a parish."[25] In a somewhat comparable way, Stephen C. Rose in his vision of *The Grass Roots Church*[26] suggests a regional pattern which might bring forth congregations many times as large as the present ones.

D. The other line of bifurcation distinguishes not size or scale but functions. While the terminology varies and the lines are variously drawn between them, the distinction is usually in some way drawn between those functions which have traditionally defined the inner life of the church and those which express her mission. One may speak of the "instituted means of grace" as continuing to be administered by the traditional residential parish and then of the "prudential means of grace" as the forms of missionary creativity.[27] Or the distinction may run between education and ministry or between "chaplaincy" and "abandonment." Wherever Christians gather, the meeting may be spoken of as in some sense a congregation, but out of respect for the momentum of history or for some genuine function served by the historic structures, these two patterns shall be retained side by side, and the gatherings which seek to discern and to implement God's will for a given social need shall be distinct from those which affirm his saving work in the past in the language of Scripture and liturgy and proclamation.

Our purpose here cannot be to carry on a substantial conversation with this stream of study and popular writing. It must suffice to indicate at which points this line of thought makes assumptions which cannot be taken for granted from the perspective of the Believers' Church tradition, so that it comes to conclusions which are less than convincing.

The first of these assumptions is the one which underwent no examination in this study process, namely, that *until* the Industrial Revolution the parish pattern was quite proper, whereby a given area was assumed to be the responsibility of one given pastor by virtue of the baptism of all members of that community, whereby moral tutelage was exercised by the church organization with the backing of government, and whereby the pastor was named to that place by the church hierarchy. All of these aspects of the historic parish pattern, of which the geographical limitation of areas of responsibilities is simply the mechanical outworking, have been challenged for centuries by the Believers' Church tradition. In fact the first formal reproach addressed to the Anabaptists in 1525 by Huldrych Zwingli was that they interfered with the standard geographically limited parish authorities by migrating and itinerating without governmental authorization. Fox and Wesley were subject to the same reproach. So the believers' church has been since its origins a group of people who have not been brought together by geographical contiguity, but rather who were drawn together, often from considerable distances, even before the Industrial Revolution, by a common commitment. For this heritage, where the church is thought of as the people gathering from many quarters rather than as the agency ministering to an area, the greater flexibility of modern urban society facilitates rather than undermines the expression of its unity. You *can* do it in the city. It is becoming increasingly more difficult for any particular segment of population to feel itself a parish, i.e., the self-evident field of ministry of a given church office or officer; but it is becoming from generation to generation easier for those who want to gather on a voluntary basis with others of common commitment to do so.

Since from this perspective the parish pattern was questionable in the first place, it can hardly be the most constructive way of meeting the modern world to accept and then update the parish assumptions. What was really wrong with the parish was the most wrong not when it became obsolete but when it worked the best, namely, when there was no challenging of the proprietary claim which the local parson had over the allegiance and the beliefs of the people of his village by virtue of his having been named by the local lord.

The "missionary structure" study process has in one way repeated the pattern of the "responsible society" studies. The movement of study topics has been decidedly away from serious attention to what Margull calls "the normal local congregation." Of course, without having discussed together what is considered "normal" and by whom, we cannot know how serious such an omission was. But both those who like and those who question the actual substance of the rapidly expanding treatment of social and political ethics in the name of "mission" recognize that there are issues having to do with the functioning of existing congregations which have not been seriously dealt with. The conviction of the Believers' Church tradition would need to raise serious question about the segregation of three different strands of church life which results from this development. On the one hand there is the picture of the mass of membership in the mammoth congregations of the "human zone," most of whom are not expected to take any active part in the life of the visible community beyond attending the services of liturgy and receiving the sacraments, because their "mission" is in their daily life. On the other hand there are the task force groups gathered around specific missionary interests, but segregated by these interests along lines of occupation, class, capability, and interest. Then thirdly, somewhere between these two types of groups and serving to relate them to one another, but subject to neither, there would be the professional staff responsible for institutional continuity, the use of facilities, specialized services like counseling and education which could be provided only by "the church." This staff would be organized on the level of the mammoth congregation or the "human zone."

It is the conviction of the Believers' Church tradition that all of these necessary functions need to be more integrally related to one another than such a trichotomy would dictate. The face-to-face encounter of the small group wrestling with a given task is vitiated if separated from the liturgical celebration and proclamation of the miracle of reconciliation. The service of the "magisterial" leadership of the congregation is vitiated if it is carried on independently of the government of a visible body in which those special ministries find their legitimacy and their only effective control. The massive celebrations of proclamation and liturgy are vitiated if most of those who attend are not at some other point called to account for a deep personal participation in the disciplined exchange of fraternal concern. Since the "missionary structure study" was not established to be a conversation with the Believers' Church tradition, this comment is not a final evaluation but rather a statement of continuing agenda. The alternative we would suggest would not be to depreciate any of these severally defined and designated functions, but to recognize as most important not that they be seen as separate functions but rather the means of their coordination. Or to put the matter in terms of the slogan, instead of the "missionary structure of the congregation" we would have asked to see more about the congregational structure of the mission.

Envoy

If space permitted, we should argue further the link between the liberty of the Believers' Church, as it used to need to be affirmed over against the *Volkskirche*, and ecumenical concern today as it is in turn dictated by and strengthened by mission, constituting itself a dimension of mission. How evangelism, mission, and unity are interlaced cannot be adequately rehearsed here. Nor need it be repeated that only a church free from the promise to sanctify a given society can conceive its mission as universal. We could argue further that the congregationalism of the Believers' Church provides an alternative definition of "the unity we seek," more real than the spiritualist "spiritual unity" of like-minded believers and yet more realistic than the theocratic vision of a nationwide merger of polity structures. We could demonstrate from history how much of the original momentum of the modern Ecumenical Movement came from the way the "mainstream" church structures were bypassed by voluntaryistic groupings like the Evangelical Alliance and the Student Volunteer Movement. But we have already come to the point where the parallelism in the structure of the argument from one issue to the next has begun to confirm the inner coherence of the Believers' Church stance, and further exposition would have diminishing returns.

Let us then simply conclude by reiterating with reference to mission the thesis stated in the conference prospectus. That in the Believers' Church heritage there exists "an apprehension of the nature of . . . the church which is specific" we have sought to demonstrate by contrasting it with those views which locate mission in the heart or in the total course of history. That this apprehension, beyond being specific, is also "coherent, a theologically valid option and a needed contribution in ecumenical debate" we have sought to display by observing how uniformly relevant it is to issues currently being debated less satisfactorily in the terms dictated by other traditions. Should the conference body deem the demonstration unconvincing, I would remain certain that the flaw has been in the argument and not in the thesis.

13

A P E O P L E I N T H E W O R L D:

Contemporary Relevance

Louis P. Meyer brought to the Conference on the Concept of the Believers' Church a twofold contribution: the insights and skills of one who is daily confronted with the challenge to the churches of changing, urban America, and a denominational heritage which has combined a nineteenth-century restorationist origin with a consistent concern for Christian unity. A native of Texas and a graduate of Anderson College, Anderson, Indiana, and of Oberlin School of Theology, Oberlin, Ohio, Mr. Meyer served as pastor of Church of God congregations in Indiana, North Carolina, and Ohio. Since 1957 he has been the secretary of the Department of Evangelism, Board of Church Extension and Home Missions of the Church of God, Anderson, Indiana. As the representative of that board, Mr. Meyer has actively participated in many interdenominational organizations. He now serves on both the Commission on Evangelism and the Commission on Urban Church Life of the National Council of Churches. Since 1962 he has been a member of the Board of Directors of the Urban Training Center for Christian Mission in Chicago, a national interdenominational cooperative experiment in which twenty denominations are seeking to find creative ways whereby the churches may serve more adequately human needs in urban America, and since 1966 he has served as vice-president of that board. In addition to his secretaryship, Mr. Meyer has been visiting instructor in pastoral work in the School of Theology of Anderson College.

Mr. Meyer confronted those concerned with the heritage of the Believers' Church—a heritage described and interpreted in detail during the conference by historians and theologians—with the challenge of contemporary America. How are God's servant people on mission, renewed and united, to minister to mobile, increasingly urbanized Americans whose nation faces complex international responsibilities? Can the churches which profess to be churches of committed and disciplined believers bring a sense of meaning and purpose to those threatened by an impersonal society, recognize the legitimate strivings for freedom on the part of today's youth, and give an effective witness in behalf of world peace? If so, these churches must find a true balance between personal salvation and social redemption, must equip the whole *laos* of God for witness and servanthood, must strike "a balanced rhythm" between gathering and scattering, and must flexibly and creatively adopt, as did their spiritual forebears, new patterns and forms of ministry.

Members of the panel which discussed Mr. Meyer's address included Dr. T. Eugene Coffin, executive secretary for evangelism and church extension, Friends United Meeting, Richmond, Indiana; Rev. W. Barry Garrett, director of information services, Baptist Joint Committee on Public Affairs, Washington, D.C.; and Dr. Joseph R. Shultz, dean of Ashland Theological Seminary, Ashland, Ohio. Moderator of the panel was Dr. Kenneth L. Chafin, Billy Graham associate professor of evangelism, Southern Baptist Theological Seminary.

Dr. Coffin responded to Mr. Meyer's address by urging that the concept of the Believers' Church stands or falls with its application to the local congregation. It is relatively easy to talk historically and theologically of the Believers' Church, said he, but in becoming contemporary we become "more foggy and confused." Dr. Coffin commended the stress on youth, called for more emphasis on the testimony to peace, and warned against too much fighting among Christian groups and against the church's becoming a victim of the "success syndrome" so as to be a stumbling block to Asian, African, and European Christian brethren. Indeed Christians should not undertake God's work in the way in which the unbelieving world does its work. Mr. Garrett identified as the central question how the believers' churches can flexibly and effectively extend their ministry in today's world. Particularly did he stress the need to work out the relationship to the developing public policy of the United States which is increasing the scope of government services in education, health, welfare, family planning, civil rights, poverty, censorship, urban renewal, etc. Should the churches seek government aid for the promotion of religious activities? What should be the public policy in regard to the use of public funds by and for church-related institutions? How should religion and education be related, and what should be the role of the churches in public education? In the absence of direct subsidies to churches what should be the tax policy? Can we practice religious liberty and the separation of church and state and at the same time adequately meet human need? In the light of the New Testament can a nation be a "Christian nation"? Dr. Shultz, endorsing Mr. Meyer's emphases, noted that the collapse of old traditions may be good and not all bad, for we may now have come to the disestablishment of the established believers' churches. He too stressed the problem of the institutional "success" of the churches, the challenge of urbanization, and the need for openness to freedom, tension, struggle, dialogue, disestablishment, voluntaryism, and newness.

o   o   o

All week we have been concerned with the Believers' Church—the strengths, weaknesses, and relevance of this movement in history. Now we come to the relationship and relevance of the Believers' Church to the contemporary world. We have had some excellent historical and theological perspectives given to us regarding the Believers' Church—heritage and past. Now we must come to the inevitable question which we all must ask, "What is the relevance, meaning, and place of this in today's world?" Or, to phrase the question in another form, "What does Christian obedience demand of us who belong to this Believers' Church tradition?"

The Church in Biblical Perspective

Let us now make a brief review of what it seems that we have been hearing this week. The Believers' Church understanding of the biblical message is that the Church is the direct result of God's action and initiative. It is God's act and plan. (This is one reason for our church movement's insistence on the name "Church of God.") It is sustained and guided by God's power—the Holy Spirit. By its very nature, the Church is God's instrument, brought into being by the Creator to serve His will and purpose. It is the *whole* people of God (both laity and clergy), those who have consciously responded to His call—the fellowship of faith, the household of God, the spiritual body of Christ, and the new community. The church is God's *pilgrim people, servants of Christ* at God's disposal for whatever mission *He* chooses. By her very nature, then, the Church is a missionary and an evangelistic instrument. She exists for others. She was created to serve man on the basis of his need in the name of Christ. She is to be the tangible or visible incarnation of God's love through Christ.

We have also said that the Believers' Church movement has stressed that the Bible teaches that *every member* is called and equipped with the necessary gifts for service unto God. Both laity and clergy are to join in God's creative process of redemption. This mission is impossible unless every member of the body takes his assignment and service gift seriously.

As I understand it, the *arena for God's mission* and the church's obedience *is the world.* The primary object of God's mission is the world of uncommitted men. The church is under assignment to be *God's task force team* in the world; the focus is not on itself—organization or structure, but on God's mission and its assigned task in that mission. It is a task force whose responsibility includes helping each person realize his highest fulfillment in life through Christ. The gathered body is to be the new community which is the training ground and enlistment center for new converts. The members of the task force are to live and conduct themselves in their private and corporate life together in such a manner that they bear witness to the world (to be a sign) of what God intends for all mankind.

It is *through faith* that the *church anticipates* the *meaning of human existence.* This gives her hope for the future. This faith and this hope are her "headstart," or distance from the world. In this way the church does not address the world from above, or as her opponent, **but rather from ahead. She declares that the Lordship** of Christ is over all the earth but not yet completely accepted by man. His Lordship is dynamic and gives courage to expect great things from God's power through the Holy Spirit.

If we are to be responsible believers, we must take seriously the mission field God has assigned to us—the contemporary world. We must take seriously its shape and its needs.

The Current Situation

All of us are aware of the unprecedented rate of change today. In our lifetime we have seen transportation change from the Model T Ford to the space capsule. We have seen our communication system change from the crank telephone to Telstar Satellite. We have observed how the agriculture of the nation has changed from over half the population producing food and fiber to only four percent doing so today. As has often been pointed out, change is not new in the history of man, but the *rate of change* in our day is new. Because so much change has been crammed and compacted into the last forty years, someone has said, "1927 was a thousand years ago!"

1. *Urbanization*

Perhaps the most far-reaching change in the shape of our world is the change from the rural (agrarian) to the urban (industrial-technological). Our nation and the world are becoming urbanized. This does not refer only to the population or size of a community. "Urbanization" is thought of today by some as a *process,* an *attitude,* a *view of life,* a view of how man and groups view life. It is a heterogenic view rather than a homogeneous view. This view is largely fed and shaped by mass communication (radio-television-news-magazines) and by our educational system. This is resulting in a *massive change* in the way men live together, a change that brings *diversity* and *disintegration of tradition.* The urbanization process is drastically affecting man's value system. (Cf. the "new morality," abortion laws, etc.) A person under the pressures of metropolitan life finds his traditional wisdom inadequate (cf. Appalachian whites moving to uptown Chicago). Because of this, our day is called "the *age* of *collapse* of *traditional wisdom.*"

The *process of urbanization* is rapidly accelerating. According to

287

the United States Census Bureau, *ninety percent* of the net growth in population is being absorbed in the metropolitan areas of our nation (7,200 per day). This population growth and mobility rate (twenty percent move annually; 11,200 people move daily) is too *rapid* for our institutional life. Government, education, the judicial system, and our vast voluntary systems of society, including the church, are all caught in the swift currents of change. In an effort to cope with these changes, society is becoming more and more *power-structured.* The individual is dwarfed in this technological, automated, computerized age. Individual solutions to problems are almost nonexistent. Individual man is caught in the system! Many are saying that the solution lies in interdependence and cooperative living.

Metropolitan life today is greatly fragmented. We have the inner-city, the central city, and the many suburbs. We have one metropolitan area spilling into the next (megalopolis). The complexity and multiplicity of governing bodies makes such daily needs as adequate transportation, communication, education, and sanitation very complicated. *In an age of great fluidity, we find ourselves hampered by sluggish institutionalism* (cf. reapportionment: legislative, judicial, religious). While the institutional life of our nation struggles desperately to come up with solutions to the problems of today, the new year arrives to make these solutions obsolete and leaves a new and more complex set of problems demanding immediate attention.

2. *The Religious Scene*

The church does not escape the impact of rapid social change. All religious groups are in ferment. All are deeply affected. There is deep religious restlessness. Religious "institutionalism" is finding survival more difficult every year. There is a crisis in the local church. There has been an alarming exodus by the clergy from the traditional residential pastorate. I foresee in the immediate future a real crisis here.

All churches today are interested in *renewal,* as evidenced by Vatican II, the 1966 Evangelism Conference in Berlin, the current round of "Church in Society Conferences," and Roman Catholic-Protestant dialogues. There is a new openness among denominations. This very conference attests this. Some denominations are merging (cf. the Methodist and Evangelical United Brethren voted yesterday). Other similar denominational groups are talking merger (cf. the Consultation on Church Union). In all church circles, there is a rebirth of interest in the laity. For example, the University of Notre Dame just this year, for the first time in history, placed a majority of lay-men on its controlling board. There is some evidence that the Roman Catholics are more serious about the priesthood of all believers than the Protestants. Add to this the rebirth and renewal of non-Christian religions in our world.

3. *The International Scene*

To prolong our brief view of the contemporary world, let us take a squint at the political world—the world of nations. On the inter-national front, the United States finds herself the strongest nation in history—with more wealth, affluence, and military power than any other nation. She is having difficulty shouldering her world leader-ship with seasoned maturity. The problems are many and over-whelming—new nations, East-West cold war, the struggle between the "have not nations" and the "affluent nations." Facing such com-plex problems and with such awesome destructive power at her dis-posal, the urge to "rattle the rocket," when new conflict arises, rather than diplomatically provide the leadership the world needs, is an ever-present temptation. With such power at her disposal, there is mounting evidence that the United States is on her way to becoming a world police force with troops from Europe to Korea and from Japan to Vietnam. What appropriate word and deed do those who belong to the Believers' Church movement have for our nation in such an hour as this?

Now let us turn to some areas of relevance for the Believers' Church tradition in these changing times. A crucial question is, "How do we accept the future and change?" A thing to be feared and resisted? Or accepted as part of God's continuing action and presence?

Contemporary Relevance

Historically the Believers' Church tradition has been remem-bered or depicted more for its separation from the world than its creative involvement in the world. Sometimes the principle of separation has been given overtones of cultural primitivism, with refusal to use buttons, automobiles, and with the use of peculiar dress and peculiar speech. Basically, however, what is stressed is a discontinuity between the Christian ethic and style, and that of the self-affirming *spirit of the times.*[1]

1. *Religious Liberty and Voluntaryism*

Since its earliest beginnings, our nation has acknowledged complementary roles for the church and the state. Today the issue of prayer in public schools has focused the nation's attention again upon this historic position. The experience and history of the Believers' Church movement should serve the followers of this stream of Christianity quite ably in helping others to see the validity of maintaining *separation*. The attitude of the government toward religion ought to be encouraged—that of benevolent neutrality.

Ours is a day of *religious and cultural pluralism*. Here the tradition of the Believers' Church on voluntaryism and religion is very apropos.

In our mass society, *"individuality"* tends to get lost in the ghettos, the bureaucracies, and the digits of the computer. The Believers' Church tradition, which places most of its weight upon the worth of the individual as an instrument of God, needs to reinterpret individuality as to its relevance and real meaning in metropolitan life.

2. *The Generation Gap*

Unquestionably a phenomenon of our day is the *youth culture*. The *"generation gap"* is familiar to all. No church concerned with relevance can overlook this development. Forty-seven percent of the United States population is under twenty-five years of age! In the 1970's these will make up over half of our population.

Young people are struggling to discover their selfhood. Many of their radical views ought not sound *too new or come as a surprise to those of the Radical Reformation tradition*. These youth are deeply concerned and preoccupied with *"individualism"* and *"freedom."* We have been reminded here this week that these are cornerstone concepts for the Believers' Church tradition. What sympathetic understanding and help do we have for these youth? Where is the "port of entry" into their minds with these same concepts from the church's viewpoint? Are we open and flexible enough to explore dialogue and experimentation with them?

3. *Peace*

In the view of many of us, no more important issue faces the United States and the world today than that of peace. The Believers' Church movement has been deeply concerned about this issue down through the years. However, in light of the Vietnam conflict and other confrontations, many Christians under the banner "to fight Communism," even those who claim to be of the Believers' Church tradition, are finding it difficult to separate their Christian convictions from the contemporary culture. What William Klassen said to Mennonites is applicable to all believers' churches, namely, that we have so identified with Western Powers, we no longer have a balanced view of being above and yet related to both sides.[2] Certainly the issue of war and peace needs to be placed higher on the priority list of every church in America. Perhaps the followers of the Believers' Church movement need to launch a new offensive in this direction.

4. *Personal Salvation and Social Redemption*

Two very distinct poles of thinking regarding the church's mission exist in Christendom today. In fact, every denomination has people from both poles of thought! One focuses on the "individual." The other focuses on "society." According to one view, the church's primary task in the world is that of "individual salvation." The other pole tends to deal exclusively with social redemption or the renewal of society. Articles in recent religious journals give the impression that one must choose either one or the other view.[3]

Those who hold rigidly to the view of "personal salvation only" tend to ignore the world and its needs. Christian commitment is interpreted in so personal a way that religion is "privatized" and interpreted as being for local consumption only. Such an interpretation does not help the convert to adjust redemptively to the modern world. Withdrawal and escape are too often the result of following this view.

Those at the other extreme of the spectrum tend to treat the mission of the church exclusively as social redemption. History shows that with this perspective only there is the tendency for mission to degrade to mere activism or at best humanism. Through constant involvement in the world but without personal commitment to Christ and His work, one tends to forget on whose mission he is.

From the biblical perspective it is true that personal commitment is required, but so is involvement in the world. Social concern is implied in the great commandment, "You must love the Lord your God with all your heart, with all your soul, and with all your mind, *and* you must love your neighbor as yourself" (Mt. 22:37-39). In the Church of God we have been strong on the first half, but weak on the latter. This horizontal dimension is a vitally necessary one, especially in a mass culture.

The *Gospel* must be related to the *totality of life*; otherwise, private experience will replace public responsibility. Overstress upon individual conversion can become a pietistic diversion of energies and resources. It gives the impression that the preaching of an individualistic gospel will produce a reconciliation of society. The pages of history do not support this hypothesis.

We have said that the Believers' Church is composed of persons who have consciously responded to—made a volitional decision concerning—God's call. They are a committed people. This could be the means of renewal in the church today, if this decision is made in light of both individual commitment *and* social responsibility.

A changed people is a *responsible* people. At times the Believers' Church movement has tended to withdraw from society and its complex needs, but *inherent* in the *basic concept* of the *Believers' Church* is the fact of involvement. A responsible people feel responsible for the world where God has placed them. There is an urge to "get the message out." There is a response to the aching needs of the world. (Cf. American Friends Service Committee, Mennonite World Relief, CROP, Heifer, Inc., etc.)

The secular, skeptical urban man of today sees the church as just another institution out to better itself. The verbal Word—proclaimed or read—will not be effective enough to reach him. The church which dwells only here, as its method of evangelism, is basically talking to itself. The spoken Word alone will not change the secularist view or belief. Deed must be locked inseparably with Word. Evangelism cannot be effective and true to the New Testament teaching without these two in balance. The prophetic Word and the servant deed must go hand in hand. Christ came among us as His first sermon text (Lk. 4:18) said, "to preach the good news" (there's the Word), and "to set at liberty those who are oppressed" (there's the deed). We should recall also the Final Judgment scene (Mt. 25:31-46). Could the Believers' Church movement help bring this balance between these two present conflicting emphases in Christendom?

5. *Laity in the World*

Today the layman is coming into his own. The clergy domination of the church is slowly giving way. Now full attention ought to be given to the position of the layman as the missionary church in the world. According to Scripture every Christian is inescapably involved in mission. Every Christian is called. Every believer has a ministry.

In the world the laity is the very spearhead of the Christian mission. The Church has talked loudly and produced many books, but this is still a largely unexplored field as far as "world" evangelism and mission are concerned.

The metaphors Christ used when He spoke of the church as "salt" and "light" have real meaning when applied to the laity of the church. The adherents to the Believers' Church tradition could make an invaluable contribution to today's ecumenical world if they would develop ways of training the laity for their daily life in the world. It is one thing to proclaim a doctrine and recall a history. Quite another thing it is to implement it. While there are signs of breakthrough at this point, even most of the "new" places of training are still dominated by the clergy (cf. *M.U.S.T.* in New York and U.T.C. of Chicago).

6. *The Whole Congregation*

In the depersonalized urban world the individual Christian has a difficult time in achieving God's intended purpose for himself and for his family. The structures of power are many and seemingly impervious as far as the individual is concerned. In this setting it seems to me that the Believers' Church emphasis upon personal response to God's call and association together in a congregation may have some clues for meeting the needs of man in urban society. More work and experimentation is needed in the field of the *corporate witness* of the congregation. While it is true the individual is to witness in his day-to-day contacts, it is also true that the local church or congregation has a corporate witness to make.

For example, the corporate life of the congregation ought to bear witness to the *unity* of the members in Christ (Gal. 3:27, 28). There are terrifying disruptions and brokenness in human life today. The church is called to witness to the world of a unity that can come from commitment to Christ.

The congregation's *dependence upon the Holy Spirit* (Eph. 1:11-14) could be a strong witness to a world so insecure. People living by joy, hope, and confidence rather than by fear and hate is certainly a note that is needed today.

In the fragmented urban life of today the church of the future could become far more relevant. Her witness and servanthood could be greatly improved if she had a *wholistic approach*, both in her program and her concept of the total community or metropolitan area. There is an open door for the church to develop and plan in this manner, both denominationally and ecumenically. For example, let us suppose that a denomination has four congregations in the inner-city, twelve in the central city, and eighteen in the suburbs. It is rare indeed if these thirty-four congregations ever meet and *plan together* on a metropolitan and ecumenical basis. Perhaps the church can begin ecumenically approaching her task in the metropolitan area in this manner and thus help others toward a wholistic approach to meeting man's needs in our cities. But too often most of our churches are adding to the metropolitan divisiveness rather than contributing to its solution.

Also it seems to me that, if in our urban culture the Believers' Church is to be relevant for meeting the needs of man through the the local congregation, far more effort must be put into interpreting the work and mission of the church in terms of *servanthood*. The style of life of the Christian for the latter half of the twentieth century must be that of a servant. This is how the mission is to be carried out. In this role the church is truly unique and different from any other institution. To find an institution willing to give herself freely, lovingly, and without strings attached is indeed "good news" to modern man so harassed by the divisive and destructive and de-humanizing elements of society.

7. Servanthood

The church is to become available among men. The members of the body of Christ in the world today must subordinate their plan of life to that of others; they must be among those of need. The church is assigned her place among people who need to be served. If the church tries to go about her work outside the sphere of service, she withers and chokes on self-concern.

The Christian servant is also the Christian witness. A congregation committed to Christ and dedicated to servant-love inevitably becomes a witnessing community. When the Christian and his congregation identify with the pain and suffering of others who have no claim on them, the non-Christian world takes note.

In community witness and service there are times when the church will bear witness in different ways. On occasion, dynamic action in society is called for (against unfair housing practices, corrupt government, etc.); at times, simply the presence of a worshiping community witnesses to men of God. Again there are times when a word must be spoken, when the Name must be named. The congregation which simply talks and preaches about the Gospel without a daily life of love and service has no convincing power. The church's healing and serving ministry in the struggle for justice and human fulfillment always points to the reality of Christ.

8. *A Balanced Rhythm*

How is the congregation so deeply involved in the wounds and problems of the world to keep her balance and biblical perspective? I feel this is possible only as she learns how to develop the *balanced rhythm* of gathering and scattering, coming and going. She must learn the delicate balance between involvement and reflection.

She gathers regularly as a fellowship for refreshing, reviving, clarifying, training, seasoning, and maturing. The gathered help prepare each other for his part in God's mission in the world. But at all times it must be kept in mind that the gathering is not an end in itself. This has been a fatal error of many churches of the past. There must be a scattering, an involvement in the world. There must be a church without walls—God's servant people sent out to witness to what God has done and is doing, to call attention to His continuing acts in the affairs of men today, and to bid every man to claim his inheritance in Christ.

Unless this rhythm is properly established and kept in balance, congregational life becomes stale and boring. If she gathers only or places major emphasis here, her mission sooner or later becomes that of self-preservation. If the emphasis is exclusively that of scattering, she loses sight of her uniqueness and her God-assigned mission. The church, according to God's plan, gathers for nurture and discipline and then scatters for service, reconciliation, and redemption.

9. *A New Day and New Forms*

There have been times in the history of the Believers' Church when its adherents did not fear breaking with tradition.

> From the initial stages of the Anabaptist movement there was no hesitancy to cut away the unholy accretions of the ages. . . . Reformation was out of the question. The Anabaptists saw their task as building anew on the original foundation.[4]

A basic question that confronts all churches today is, *"How can we effectively extend the ministries of the church in today's world?"* To make the effective contribution God intends for His Church, some radical changes will doubtless be necessary. Institutionalism is in many areas of our lives. In many respects it is both rigid and binding. Many churches are so bound by tradition and institutionalism that they cannot be effective in the twentieth century. There are indications that in America the religious market is "topping out." Much of the blame for this is laid on religious institutionalism.

Most of the church's efforts for generations have been in the residential communities of our nation. Today man has many gathering points, many marketplaces in addition to the residential. He has a gathering place at his work. He has a gathering place where he trades (supermarket and shopping center). He gathers for recreation—his leisure community. He gathers also in industrial, manufacturing, and professional communities. Can the church learn how to relate and listen to him in these places? Can she discover the art of *redemptive listening* in our space age?

There are indications that in her past the Believers' Church was flexible enough to deal with change.

The Free Churches began with a radical break from the parish and regional territorial pattern of state-church Catholicism and Protestantism. Their view of church history was "primitivist," with the period of the New Testament and early church enjoying normative significance; a "fall of the church" at the time of the establishment of Constantine; a restitution of the true church dating from their own movement. For them, "apostolicity" meant "true to the apostles," not mere continuity.[5]

Furthermore, in early American history, according to Littell, the Free Church leaders held out for separation of church and state. This was a *new form* of church life for that day. They felt that voluntary service and commitment were superior to any churchmanship enforced by law. The success of this new form—religion separate from state—was achieved in the nineteenth century because the leaders of the various religious bodies developed new methods (mass evangelism) which won people back to the churches on a voluntary basis. The Roman Catholics did this through the new method (for that day) of the parochial school system.

These are but two examples wherein the followers of the Believers' Church movement were willing to differ radically with those about them, if they felt this was in keeping with the teachings of Scripture. In our day of pluralism, secularism, and urbanism, can the Believers' Church be flexible and ingenious enough to develop some new plans, methods, and ministries? This is a day when the Free Churches' tradition and heritage should serve them well.

Every month innovations are introduced in our society. Every month new doors of opportunity open to the church that is willing to take some risks. Over two hundred "new cities" are now in various stages of being planned. Last year General Electric Corporation passed a resolution to set aside $800 million to develop a new city somewhere in the United States. In the metropolitan areas it has been demonstrated that the traditional, residentially oriented church program is ineffective. In light of this I would hope that the followers of the Believers' Church movement would seek to encourage new ministries organized around the places where people work, play, and shop, and would give leisure hours to the peace movement, civil rights movement, or to whatever mission Christian obedience calls them. This may mean some present institutions of the church must die, but could we refuse, if this brings new life?

Notes

Chapter 1. The Concept of the Believers' Church

1. Williston Walker, *A History of the Congregational Churches in the United States* (New York: Christian Literature Co., 1894), p. 307.

2. John Winthrop, *The History of New England from 1630 to 1649*, ed. James Savage (Boston: Little, Brown and Company, 1853), I, 355.

3. John Norton, *The Answer to the Whole Set of Questions of the Celebrated Mr. William Apollonius, Pastor of the Church of Middleburg*, trans. Douglas Horton (Cambridge, Mass.: Belknap Press of Harvard University Press, 1958), p. 88.

4. x, 3; *The Cambridge Platform of Church Discipline, Adopted in 1648, and the Confession of Faith, Adopted in 1680* (Boston: Perkins & Whipple, 1850), p. 64.

5. Walter M. Abbott, ed., *The Documents of Vatican II* (New York: Guild Press/ American Press/Association Press, 1966). pp. 672-696; cf. my "Response," pp. 697-700.

6. John Owen, *The True Nature of a Gospel Church and Its Government (1689)*, abr. and ed. John Huxtable (London: James Clarke & Co., Ltd., 1947), pp. 44 f.

7. John Robinson, *A Justification of Separation from the Church of England* (n.p.p.: n.p., 1610), p. 221.

8. Rufus M. Jones, *Studies in Mystical Religion* (London: Macmillan Co., 1923).

9. Robert Friedmann, "Conception of the Anabaptists," *Church History*, IX (December, 1940), 341-365.

10. Cf. the brilliant typological discussion distinguishing the established churches from the restitutionists in George H. Williams, *The Radical Reformation* (Philadelphia: Westminster Press, 1962), introduction.

11. Quoted and discussed in John Howard Yoder, *Täufertum und Reformation in der Schweiz: I. Die Gespräche zwischen Täufern und Reformatoren, 1523-1538* (Karlsruhe: H. Schneider Verlag, 1962), p. 20. Distributed in North America by Herald Press, Scottdale, Pa.

12. Michael Novak, "The Free Churches and the Roman Church; the Conception of the Church in Anabaptism and in Roman Catholicism: Past and Present," *Journal of Ecumenical Studies*, II (Fall, 1965), 426-447.

13. Karl Holl, "Luther und die Schwärmer," *Gesammelte Aufsätze zur Kirchengeschichte* (6th ed.; Tübingen: J. C. B. Mohr, 1932), I, 420 ff.

14. Cf. Franklin H. Littell, "A Common Language," *Journal of Ecumenical Studies*, III (Spring, 1966), 362-365.

15. "Cambridge Platform of Church Discipline," iii, 5, in *op. cit.*, p. 53.

16. Cf. Franklin H. Littell, *The Origins of Sectarian Protestantism* (London, New York: Macmillan Co., 1964), p. 36. For the essentials of Joachimitism, all scholars are profoundly indebted to Ernst Benz, *Ecclesia Spiritualis: Kirchenidee und Geschichtstheologie der franziskanischen Reformation* (Stuttgart: W. Kohlhammer Verlag, 1934).

17. Cf. Franklin H. Littell, "The Radical Reformation," in Stephen Charles Neill and Hans-Ruedi Weber, eds., *The Layman in Christian History* (London: SCM Press Ltd., 1963), pp. 261-275.

18. Cf. Franklin H. Littell, "Sectarian Protestantism and the Pursuit of Wisdom: Must Technological Objectives Prevail?" in Donald A. Erickson, ed., *Public Controls for Nonpublic Schools* (Chicago: University of Chicago Press, 1969).

19. Cf. Franklin H. Littell, "The Work of the Holy Spirit in Group Decisions," *Mennonite Quarterly Review*, XXXIV (April, 1960), 75-96.

20. Cf. Franklin H. Littell, "New Light on Butzer's Significance," in *Reformation Studies: Essays in Honor of Roland H. Bainton*, ed. Franklin H. Littell (Richmond, Va.: John Knox Press, 1962), pp. 145-167.

21. John H. Miller, ed., *Vatican II: An Interfaith Appraisal* (Notre Dame, Ind., London: University of Notre Dame Press, 1966), pp. 273 f., 326 f.

Chapter 2. A Believing People: Historical Background

1. See H. H. Rowley, *The Unity of the Bible* (New York: Meridian Books, 1957), p. 1, fn. 2.

2. *Ibid.*, pp. 1-8.

3. It is interesting to observe that Mennonites, Baptists, and Disciples sometimes claim the same ancestors. See Thieleman J. van Braght; *The Bloody Theater or Martyrs Mirror of the Defenseless Christians Who Baptized Only upon Confession of Faith, and Who Suffered and Died for the Testimony of Jesus, Their Saviour, from the Time of Christ to the Year A.D. 1660*, trans. Joseph F. Sohm (5th English ed.; Scottdale, Pa.: Mennonite Publishing House, 1950), for an early Mennonite work that assumes historical connection between Mennonites and earlier "heretical" parties. Hereafter cited as *Mirror*. A more recent Mennonite work which takes a modified position along similar lines is Delbert L. Gratz, *Bernese Anabaptists*, "Studies in Anabaptist and Mennonite History," no. 8 (Scottdale, Pa.: Herald Press, 1953). Baptist works which attempt to establish some sort of historical connection abound. The most popular of these is James Milton Carroll, *The Trail of Blood* (Lexington, Ky.: Ashland Avenue Baptist Church, 1931). This pamphlet is based upon earlier works by Orchard, Crosby, Ray, and others. A more sophisticated work that attempts to establish a spiritual connection between the medieval evangelicals and modern Baptists is Albert Henry Newman, *A History of Anti-Pedobaptism from the Rise of Pedobaptism to A.D. 1609* (Philadelphia: American Baptist Publication Society, 1897). Alfred T. DeGroot in his *The Restoration Principle* (St. Louis: Bethany Press, 1960) traces the principle of restoration of the church on an apostolic pattern through the centuries. This is a well-documented and balanced volume from the pen of an able church historian of the Disciples of Christ.

4. 1 Peter 2:10 (RSV).

5. Section 4, Walter M. Abbott, ed., *The Documents of Vatican II* (New York: America Press, 1966), p. 666.

6. Hans Denck, a sixteenth-century Anabaptist and outstanding Hebraist, became one of the first Anabaptists to take the gospel to the Jews. This interest in the Jews and attempt to help them became a characteristic of the Mennonites and of the early American and English Baptists.

7. *Sociology and Psychology of Communism*, trans. Jane Degras and Richard Rees (Boston: Beacon Press, 1960), p. 291.

8. Matthew Spinka, *John Hus' Concept of the Church* (Princeton, N.J.: Princeton University Press, 1966), p. 396. This is the most extensive modern treatment in English of Huss's ecclesiology. Matthew Spinka is a recognized authority on Huss and the movements which claim him as their founder. Cf. Matthew Spinka, ed., *Advocates of Reform: From Wyclif to Erasmus* (Philadelphia: Westminster Press, 1953) for a biographical sketch of Huss and his treatise, "On Simony," pp. 187-278.

9. See Ernesto Tron, *Historia de las Colonias Valdenses Sudamericanas* (Montevideo: Libreria Pastor Miguel Morel, 1958).

10. *De veritate sacrae Scripturae* (London, 1905-1907), introd. 25, quoted by Spinka, *Advocates of Reform*, p. 26.

11. A. G. Dickens, *The English Reformation* (New York: Shocken Press, 1964), pp. 30 f.

12. *Ibid.*, pp. 33-35.

13. Kenneth A. Strand, *German Bibles Before Luther* (Grand Rapids: William B. Eerdmans Publishing Company, 1966), p. 15.

14. See E. G. Schwiebert, *Luther and His Times* (St. Louis: Concordia Publishing House, 1950), pp. 278-283.

15. Quoted in *ibid.*, p. 286.

16. Cited by Roland H. Bainton, *Studies on the Reformation* (Boston: Beacon Press, 1963), p. 107.

17. *Ibid.*, pp. 4, 5.

18. John J. Kiwiet, *Pilgram Marbeck: Ein Führer in der Täuferbewegung der Reformationszeit* (Kassel: J. G. Oncken Verlag, 1957), pp. 16 f. Marpeck's dissatisfaction with the moral ineptitude of the Lutheran movement made him favorably inclined toward the Anabaptists, who insisted that the Christian life involved all of life and demanded ethical and moral behavior commensurate with the profession of faith.

19. See William A. Mueller, *Church and State in Luther and Calvin* (Nashville: Broadman Press, 1954). This work contains an excellent discussion of the subject based on the sources.

20. See W. R. Estep, *The Anabaptist Story* (Nashville: Broadman Press, 1963), pp. 4, 5, fn. 3, for a summary of the more important works and discoveries prior to 1962. Since 1962 the following are the more important works: Rollin Stely Armour, *Anabaptist Baptism: A Representative Study* (Scottdale, Pa.: Herald Press, 1966); Torsten Bergsten, *Balthasar Hubmaier: Seine Stellung zu Reformation und Täufertum, 1521-1528* (Kassel: J. G. Oncken Verlag, 1961); Hans Joachim Hillerbrand, *A Bibliography of Anabaptism, 1520-1603* (Elkhart, Ind.: Institute of Mennonite Studies, 1962), distributed in North America by Herald Press, Scottdale, Pa.; Irvin Buckwalter Horst, *Anabaptism and the English Reformation to 1558* (Nieuwkoop: B. De Graaf, 1966); John S. Oyer, *Lutheran Reformers Against Anabaptists: Luther, Melanchthon and Menius and the Anabaptists of Central Germany* (The Hague: Martinus Nijhoff, 1964); Leonard Verduin, *The Reformers and Their Stepchildren* (Grand Rapids: Wm. B. Eerdmans Publishing Company, 1964); Gunnar Westin and Torsten Bergsten, eds., *Balthasar Hubmaier: Schriften*, "Quellen zur Geschichte der Täufer," vol. 9 (Gütersloh: Gerd Mohn Verlagshaus, 1962), distributed in North America by Herald Press, Scottdale, Pa.; George Huntston Williams, *The Radical Reformation* (Philadelphia: Westminster Press, 1962).

21. George Huntston Williams and Angel M. Mergal, eds., *Spiritual and Anabaptist Writers*, "The Library of Christian Classics," vol. 25 (Philadelphia: Westminster Press, 1957), p. 22.

22. Fritz Blanke, *Brüder in Christo: Die Geschichte der ältesten Täufergemeinde (Zollikon, 1525)* (Zurich: Zwingli-Verlag 1955), pp. 42 ff. Published in English, trans. by Joseph Nordenhaug as *Brothers in Christ* (Scottdale, Pa.: Herald Press, 1961).

23. Jean Rilliet, *Zwingli: Third Man of the Reformation*, trans. Harold Knight (Philadelphia: Westminster Press, 1964), p. 58.

24. See the account of the second disputation of Zürich in *Huldreich Zwinglis Werke*, ed. Melchior Schuler and Joh. Schulthess (Zürich: Friedrich Schulthess, 1828), I, 459-540. See John Howard Yoder, "The Turning Point in the Zwinglian Reformation," *Mennonite Quarterly Review*, XXXII (April, 1958), 128-140, for a thorough discussion of the disagreement between Grebel and Zwingli on issues of the October disputation.

25. Quoted by Harold S. Bender, *Conrad Grebel, c. 1498-1526: The Founder of the Swiss Brethren Sometimes Called Anabaptists* (Goshen, Ind.: Mennonite Historical Society, 1950), p. 98.

26. *Huldreich Zwinglis Werke*, I, 529, and Yoder, *op. cit.*, p. 128.

27. A. J. F. Zieglschmid, ed., *Die älteste Chronik der Hutterischen Brüder* (Ithaca, N.Y.: Carl Schurz Memorial Foundation, 1943), p. 47. The full account is also given in Zieglschmid, ed., *Das Klein-Geschichtsbüch der Hutterischen Brüder*, (Philadelphia: Carl Schurz Memorial Foundation, 1947). Josef Beck, in his edition of *Die Geschichts-Bücher der Wiedertäufer in Oesterreich-Ungarn . . . in der Zeit von 1526 bis 1785* (Wien: Carl Gerald's Sohn, 1883), pp. 19, 20, gives the same account. English translations of this first baptism are given by John Christian Wenger, *Glimpses of Mennonite History and Doctrine* (Scottdale, Pa.: Herald Press, 1947), pp. 24 f.; Bender, *op. cit.*, p. 137; and Williams and Mergal, eds., *op. cit.*, pp. 41-46.

28. *Mirror*, p. 567.

29. Quoted in Robert Friedmann, "Claus Felbinger's Confession of 1560," *Mennonite Quarterly Review*, XXIX (April, 1955), 151.

30. See Bender, *op. cit.*, pp. 138 ff.

31. See Ekkehard Krajewski's definitive biography on Felix Manz, *Leben und Sterben des Zürcher Täuferführers Felix Manz: über die Anfänge der Täuferbewegung und des Freikirchentums in der Reformationszeit* (Kassel: J. G. Oncken Verlag, 1957).

32. See John Allen Moore, *Der starke Jörg: die Geschichte Jörg Blaurocks, des Täuferführers und Missionars* (Kassel: J. G. Oncken Verlag, 1957).

33. Williams and Mergal, eds., *op. cit.*, pp. 297-390.

34. See J. A. Oosterbaan, "The Theology of Menno Simons," *Mennonite Quarterly Review*, XXXV (July, 1961), 187-196, 237, for a perceptive summary of Menno's theology.

35. Horst, *op. cit.*, p. 61.

36. Champlin Burrage, *The Early English Dissenters in the Light of Recent Research* (Cambridge: University Press, 1912), I, 237.

37. The Historical Commission of the Southern Baptist Convention is in the process of securing photostatic copies of this entire body of materials from the Mennonite Archives in Amsterdam.

38. J. De Hoop Scheffer, *History of the Free Churchmen*, ed. William Elliot Griffis (Ithaca, N.Y.: Andrus & Church, 1922), p. 8. See also Lonnie D. Kliever, "General Baptist Origins: The Question of Anabaptist Influence," *Mennonite Quarterly Review*, XXXVI (October, 1962), 291-321, for an opposing position to that of De Hoop Scheffer.

39. Walter H. Burgess, *John Smith the Se-Baptist, Thomas Helwys, and the First Baptist Church in England* (London: James Clarke & Co., 1911), pp. 181-185.

40. W. L. Lumpkin, *Baptist Confessions of Faith* (Philadelphia: Judson Press, 1959), p. 119.

41. *Ibid.*

42. *Ibid.*, p. 120.

43. *Ibid.*

44. *Ibid.*

45. *Ibid.*, pp. 120 f.

46. *Ibid.*, pp. 122 f.

47. From *A Short Declaration of the Mistery of Iniquity* (London: Grayes Inne, 1612), reproduced from the copy presented by Helwys to King James I, now in the Bodleian Library (London: Kingsgate Press, 1935), p. xxv.

48. *Ibid.*, pp. xxiii xxiv.

49. Lumpkin, *op. cit.*, p. 140.

50. *Ibid.*, p. 115.

51. Isaac Backus was one of the early Baptist ministers who was reared a Congregationalist and became a Separatist under the influence of the Great Awakening. See T. B. Maston, *Isaac Backus: Pioneer of Religious Liberty* (Rochester, N.Y.: American Baptist Historical Society, 1962).

52. William L. Lumpkin, *Baptist Foundations in the South: Tracing through the*

Separates the Influence of the Great Awakening, 1754-1787 (Nashville: Broadman Press, 1961). In this work Lumpkin traces the Separate Baptists from their rise in New England to the area of their greatest success in the South.

53. See John L. Nickalls, ed., *The Journal of George Fox* (Cambridge: University Press, 1952), pp. 25 f.

54. William Tallack, *George Fox, the Friends, and the Early Baptists* (London: S. W. Partridge & Co., 1868), pp. 65-88. See also William C. Braithwaite, *The Beginnings of Quakerism*, 2nd ed. rev. by Henry J. Cadbury (Cambridge: University Press, 1955).

55. *Op. cit.*, p. 26.

56. See Braithwaite, *op. cit.*, which is the standard history of the movement. An excellent brief sympathetic survey is: Henry van Etten, *George Fox and the Quakers*, trans. and rev. E. Kelvin Osborn (London: Longmans, 1959).

57. **Philip Jacob Spener, *Pia Desideria*, trans. and ed. Theodore G. Tappert** (Philadelphia: Fortress Press, 1966), p. 23.

58. *Ibid.*, p. 29.

59. *Ibid.*, p. 16.

60. Donald F. Durnbaugh, *European Origins of the Brethren; A Source Book on the Beginnings of the Church of the Brethren in the Early Eighteenth Century* (Elgin, Ill.: Brethren Press, 1958), pp. 120-124.

61. **See Timothy L. Smith, *Called unto Holiness; The Story of the Nazarenes: The Formative Years*** (Kansas City, Mo.: Nazarene Publishing House, 1962), for a detailed account of numerous "Holiness" and "Pentecostal" groups related to the Nazarenes. Additional information on the more Baptistic Assemblies of God may be gleaned from C. C. Burnett *et al*, *In the Last Days: An Early History of the Assemblies of God* (Springfield, Mo.: Assemblies of God, 1962).

62. Winfred Ernest Garrison, *Alexander Campbell's Theology* (St. Louis: Christian Publishing Company, 1920?), p. 113.

63. The most important debate, due both to the stature of his opponent and to the maturity of Campbell's own views, was that with N. L. Rice. See *A Debate Between Rev. A. Campbell and Rev. N. L. Rice on the Action, Subject, Design and Administration of Christian Baptism; also, on the Character of Spiritual Influence in Conversion and Sanctification, and on the Expediency and Tendency of Ecclesiastic Creeds as Terms of Union and Communion: held in Lexington, Ky., from the Fifteenth of November to the Second of December, 1843, a Period of Eighteen Days*, reported by Marcus T. C. Gould and H. Euclid Drapier (Lexington, Ky.: A. T. Skillman & Son, 1844); and Alexander Campbell, *Christian Baptism* (Nashville: Gospel Advocate Company, 1951).

Chapter 3. A Believing People: Theological Interpretation

1. Sections I-III of the following were also delivered, in slightly altered form, as part of an address given to the 1967 annual meeting of the Catholic Theological Society of America. This address, entitled "Original Sin in Ecumenical Perspective," was published in the *Proceedings of the Catholic Theological Society of America*, xxii (1967), 33-50. By permission of its editor Daniel V. Flynn, the sections common to both addresses appear here.

2. This insight has become axiomatic nowadays. The developing self, with its individuality and distinguishing idiosyncracies, is at the same time social in its make-up. The writings of George H. Mead continue to be representative of this widely shared viewpoint. Consult especially *Mind, Self and Society from the Standpoint of a Social Behaviorist*, ed. Charles W. Morris (Chicago: University of Chicago Press, 1934).

3. For a phenomenological description of the way an awareness of "limitation" erupts in human experience see Gordon D. Kaufman, "On the Meaning of 'God': Transcendence Without Mythology," *Harvard Theological Review*, LIX (April, 1966), 105-132. Where our discussion goes beyond Kaufman is in more explicit reference to the way not only personal relationships and volitional strivings but especially future expectations provide an experiential base for the notion of God as ultimate Limit.

4. I am indebted to H. Richard Niebuhr who first disposed me to view revelation as an event that illuminates and shapes subsequent events. One finds this position articulated in *The Meaning of Revelation* (New York: Macmillan, 1941). I have since come to think and speak of revelation as an historical *a priori*.

5. **Harvey G. Cox, *The Secular City: Secularization and Urbanization in Theological Perspective*** (New York: Macmillan, 1965), has something of this doublesidedness in view when he distinguishes between an "open secularity" and a "closed secularism." Even though the heroism of the "secular city" does judge ecclesiastical narrowness in whatever form, the demonic potentialities of a secularist orientation should never be overlooked.

6. We share with Schleiermacher a strong emphasis upon the communal context of faith. He viewed Christianity as a monotheistic, ethically sensitive religion, whose consciousness of God is specifically anchored in the experience of redemption through Jesus Christ. This is developed in *The Christian Faith*, ed. H. R. Mackintosh and J. S. Stewart (**Edinburgh: T. & T. Clark, 1928**). The Christian Church takes shape around that particular point where the consciousness of God—as the One who relates to all of life—takes sensible form in the man from Nazareth. We are locating the church in human culture as those institutionalized patterns of thought and behavior which revolve around man's anticipations of the future, especially as concretized in the man on the cross.

7. Romans 8:38, 39.

8. Ephesians 1:9, 10.

9. For a fuller discussion of the theme of original sin see the article mentioned above: "Original Sin in Ecumenical Perspective."

Chapter 4. A Believing People: Contemporary Relevance

1. "Society of Friends," *Mennonite Encyclopedia* (Scottdale, Pa.: Mennonite Publishing House, 1959), IV, 561.

2. Harold S. Bender and C. H. Smith, *Mennonites and Their Heritage* (Scottdale, Pa.: Herald Press, 1964), pp. 42-45.

3. "Membership in the Body of Christ as Interpreted by Classical Pietism," *Brethren Life and Thought,* IX (Autumn, 1964), 30 f.

4. *Catholic Quakerism* (Gloucester, England: privately published, 1966), p. 8.

5. George Fox, *Gospel Truth Demonstrated* (London: T. Sowle, 1706), p. 782; **or** *Works* (Philadelphia: M. T. C. Gould, 1831), VI, 85.

6. Fox, *op. cit.*, pp. 115, 172, 223 f., 436, 450, 463; Fox, *A Catechisme for Children* (London: Gyles Calvart, 1657), p. 61; Fox, *Newes Coming up out of the North Sounding Towards the South* (London: Gyles Calvart, 1654), pp. 19 f., 43.

7. Fox, "A Sermon . . . Preached at a General Meeting Held at Wheeler St. in London, on the First of the Fourth Month 1680," in *A Sermon . . . by Thomas Story . . . 1737; Together with Corresponding Extracts from . . . Elias Hicks . . . with an Appendix Containing an Original Sermon of George Fox* (Philadelphia: S. Potter, 1825), p. 64.

8. Benson, *op. cit.*, p. 19.

9. Isaac Penington, *Works*, 1761 edition, I, 556, quoted in Benson, *op. cit.*, p. 20.

10. Benson, *op. cit.*, p. 35.

11. *Ibid.*, p. 38.

12. *Ibid.*, pp. 24-27.

13. John L. Nickalls, ed., *The Journal of George Fox* (Cambridge: University Press, 1952), p. 27.

14. (Richmond, Ind.: Friends United Meeting, 1966), p. 14.

15. Benson, *op. cit.*, p. 36.

16. *Ibid.*, p. 23.

17. *Ibid.*, pp. 23 f.

18. Cooper, *op. cit.*, p. 10.

19. Tertullian, *De idololatria*, ch. 19 quoted in Roland H. Bainton, *Christian Attitudes Toward War and Peace* (Nashville: Abingdon Press, 1960), p. 73.

20. Robert Barclay, *Apology for the True Christian Divinity* (stereotype ed.; Philadelphia: Friends Book Store, 1908), proposition 15, section 15, answer to objection 6, p. 537.

21. Nickalls, ed., *op. cit.*, p. 357.

22. Hugh Barbour, *The Quakers in Puritan England* (New Haven: Yale University Press, 1964), pp. 1 f., 40, 183, 208.

Chapter 5. A People in Community: Historical Background

1. Just as the *chaburah* or dining fellowship of the friends of God and strict observance of his Law was the mark of the separatist or pietist within the context of old Israel at the time of Jesus Christ, so the monastic conventicle with its vow and severer dietary and other regulations was the mark of the separatist and pietist temperament expressing itself within the context of the medieval catholic *corpus christianum*. In any case, believer's baptism is not the sole or indispensable criterion for the existence of an authentic believers' church.

2. In New England, in consequence of the unitarian-trinitarian schism in the Standing Order of Massachusetts, "society" came commonly to be used polemically for the more inclusive liberal townspeople over against the sometimes diminutive church of experimental believers qualifying for communicant membership and generally conservative in theology. In the famous court decision in the Dedham Case in 1820, the liberal (unitarian) parish or society were deemed the owners of the town meetinghouse, since they supported it financially, rather than the "church" of communicant members.

Chapter 6. A People in Community: Theological Interpretation

1. Biblical quotations in this address follow the Revised Standard Version.

2. We are using the term "Spirit of Christ" just as Paul used it in Rom. 8:9, i.e., synonymously with the (Holy) "Spirit" and the "Spirit of God."

3. *The Doctrine of the Holy Spirit* (London: Banner of Truth Trust, 1882, 1961), p. 47.

Chapter 7. A People in Community: Contemporary Relevance

1. Translation by Oscar Cullmann, *Christ and Time: The Primitive Christian Conception of Time and History*, trans. Floyd V. Filson (London: SCM Press Ltd., 1951), p. 228.

2. *Ibid.*

3. Cf. Paul L. Lehmann, *Ethics in a Christian Context* (London: SCM Press Ltd., 1963), pp. 81-86.

Chapter 8. A People Under the Word: Historical Background

1. See "A Note on Ecumenism at Vatican II," *The Ecumenist*, III (November-December, 1964), 1-3.

2. Walter M. Abbott, ed., *The Documents of Vatican II* (New York: America Press, 1966), p. 12. Hereafter cited as *Documents*.

3. *The Epistles of St. Ignatius, Bishop of Antioch*, trans. J. H. Srawley (London: Society for Promoting Christian Knowledge, 1900), II, 41.

4. "The Ministry of the Ante-Nicene Church" in H. Richard Niebuhr and Daniel D. Williams, eds., *The Ministry in Historical Perspectives* (New York: Harper & Brothers, 1956), p. 30. See also the apt use of this ideology as given in *The Catholicity of Protestantism*, cited below in footnote 39.

5. *On Prescription Against Heretics*, chs. 20, 21, 32, 36; trans. Peter Holmes, *The*

Ante-Nicene Fathers (Buffalo: Christian Literature Publishing Co., 1887), III, 252, 258, 260.

6. *A Commonitory*, ch. 2; trans. C. A. Heurtley, *A Select Library of Nicene and Post-Nicene Fathers*, 2nd series, vol. 11 (Grand Rapids: Wm. B. Eerdmans Publishing Company, 1955), p. 132.

7. Concl. parag.; *Saint John of Damascus: Writings*, trans. Frederic H. Chase, Jr., "The Fathers of the Church," vol. 37 (New York: Fathers of the Church, Inc., 1958), pp. 161-163.

8. Parag. 70, *ibid.*, p. 128.

9. Quoted by David Schley Schaff, *John Huss: His Life, Teachings and Death, After Five Hundred Years* (New York: C. Scribner's Sons, 1915), p. 306.

10. I am indebted for the substance of this paragraph to O. D. Johnson, "The Concept of Catholicity and Its Place in the Thought and Life of the Christian Churches (Disciples of Christ)," ThM Thesis, Brite Divinity School, Texas Christian University, January, 1967.

11. Cf. Thomas Aquinas, *On the Truth of the Catholic Faith; Summa Contra Gentiles*, I, 2, trans. Anton C. Pegis (Garden City, N.Y.: Hanover House, 1955), p. 62; Thomas Aquinas, *Summa Theologica*, II-II, q. 1, arts. 8, 9, trans. Fathers of the English Dominican Province (London: Burns Oates & Washbourne Ltd., 1920), VII, 19-28.

12. *Defensor Pacis*, discourse two, II, 3, trans. Alan Gewirth, *Marsilius of Padua, the Defender of Peace* (New York: Columbia University Press, 1956), II, 103.

13. "On the Councils and the Churches," III, 1, *Works of Martin Luther* (Philadelphia: A. J. Holman Co., 1931), V, 271.

14. *A Compend of the Institutes of the Christian Religion by John Calvin*, ed. Hugh Thompson Kerr, Jr. (Philadelphia: Presbyterian Board of Christian Education, 1939), p. 152, excerpting *Institutes*, IV, 1, 2.

15. "The Adultero-German Interim," ch. 10, in *Tracts and Treatises in Defense of the Reformed Faith*, trans. Henry Beveridge, "Calvin's Tracts and Treatises," vol. 3 (Grand Rapids: Wm. B. Eerdmans Publishing Company, 1958), pp. 204 f.

16. Philip Schaff, *The Creeds of Christendom* (Grand Rapids: Baker Book House, 1967), III, 198.

17. *Zwingli and Bullinger*, trans. G. W. Bromiley, "The Library of Christian Classics," vol. 24 (London: SCM Press Ltd., 1953), pp. 265 f.

18. Menno Simons, "Reply to Gellius Faber," *The Complete Writings of Menno Simons*, trans. Leonard Verduin and ed. John Christian Wenger (Scottdale, Pa.: Herald Press, 1956), p. 754.

19. *The Works of Mr. Richard Hooker* (New York: D. Appleton & Co., 1890), I, 220, col. 2.

20. Henry Denzinger, *The Sources of Catholic Dogma*, trans. Roy J. Deferrari (St. Louis: B. Herder Book Co., 1957), parag. 1821, pp. 451 f.

21. Pius XII, *The Mystical Body of Christ*, trans. G. D. Smith (London: Catholic Truth Society, 1944), parag. 61, p. 38.

22. Quoted in Michael Novak, *The Open Church, Vatican II, Act II* (New York: Macmillan, 1964), p. 118.

23. Lorenz Jaeger, *The Ecumenical Council, the Church and Christendom*, trans. A. V. Littledale (London: Geoffrey Chapman Ltd., 1961), p. 128.

24. Hans Küng, *The Council in Action*, trans. Cecily Hastings (New York: Sheed and Ward, 1963), p. 56.

25. *Ibid.*, pp. 57-62.

26. Section 14, *Documents*, p. 33.

27. Section 15, *Documents*, pp. 33 f.

28. Section 16, *Documents*, pp. 34 f.

29. G. V. Florovsky, "*Sobornost*: The Catholicity of the Church," in E. L. Mascall, ed., *The Church of God: An Anglo-Russian Symposium* (London: Society for Promoting Christian Knowledge, 1934), p. 62.

30. Cf. Georges Florovsky, "The Orthodox Churches and the Ecumenical Movement

Prior to 1910," in Ruth Rouse and Stephen Charles Neill, eds., *A History of the Ecumenical Movement, 1517-1948* (Philadelphia: Westminster Press, 1954), pp. 169-215.

31. Florovsky, "*Sobornost:* The Catholicity of the Church," pp. 70 f.

32. *Documents of the Christian Church*, ed. Henry Bettenson, "The World's Classics" (London: Oxford University Press, 1943), p. 444.

33. *Ibid.*, p. 441.

34. *Anglicanism,* comps. Paul Elmer More and Frank Leslie Cross (New York: Macmillan Company, 1957), pp. 23-39.

35. Elwyn A. Smith, "Turning Point for the Consultation on Church Union," *Journal of Ecumenical Studies,* IV (Spring, 1967), 294.

36. Arthur Michael Ramsey, *The Gospel and the Catholic Church* (2nd ed.; London: Longmans, Green and Co., 1956), pp. 84 f.

37. William Nicholls, *Ecumenism and Catholicity* (London: SCM Press Ltd., 1952), pp. 96, 104.

38. *Ibid.*, pp. 90, 128-130.

39. R. Newton Flew and Rupert E. Davies, eds., *The Catholicity of Protestantism* (London: Lutterworth Press, 1950), pp. 21 f.

40. *Ibid.*, p. 33.

41. *Ibid.*, pp. 25 f.

42. *Ibid.*, pp. 104 f.

43. *Ibid.*, p. 35.

44. *Ibid.*, p. 107.

45. Daniel T. Jenkins, *The Nature of Catholicity* (London: Faber and Faber Ltd., 1942), pp. 13, 20, 23.

46. *Ibid.*, pp. 24-26.

47. *Bulletin of the Department of Theology of the World Presbyterian Alliance, The World Alliance of Reformed Churches,* II (Summer, 1961), 2-4.

48. *Ibid.*, pp. 4-8.

49. *Ibid.*, p. 14.

50. Karl Barth, *The Doctrine of Reconciliation,* "Church Dogmatics," Vol. IV, Part 1, trans. G. W. Bromiley (Edinburgh: T. & T. Clark, 1956), pp. 704, 715.

51. *Ibid.*, p. 716.

52. *Lutheran World,* IV (March, 1958), 419-424.

53. *Proceedings of the Fourth Assembly of the Lutheran World Federation, Helsinki, July 30-August 11, 1963* (Berlin, Hamburg: Lutherisches Verlagshaus, 1965), p. 283.

54. *Ibid.*, p. 281.

55. Paul Tillich, *Systematic Theology* (Chicago: University of Chicago Press, 1963), III, 259.

56. *World Missionary Conference, 1910: Report of Commission VIII, Cooperation and the Promotion of Unity* (New York: Fleming H. Revell Co., n.d.), VIII, 19 f.

57. See *The Second World Conference on Faith and Order*, ed. Leonard Hodgson (New York: Macmillan Co., 1938), pp. 315, 318, 347, 235.

58. *Ibid.*, pp. 275 f.

59. *The New Delhi Report: The Third Assembly of the World Council of Churches* (New York: Association Press, 1961), pp. 116 f.

60. *The Fourth World Conference on Faith and Order, Montreal 1963*, ed. P. C. Rodger and Lukas Vischer (New York: Association Press, 1964), pp. 39 f.

61. *Ibid.*, p. 46.

62. Hendrik Kraemer, *A Theology of the Laity* (London: Lutterworth Press, 1958), pp. 114 f.

63. Trans. Pierre Loving (New York: Payson & Clarke Ltd., 1928), p. 19.

64. (Chicago: University of Chicago Press, 1944), p. 148.

65. It is the central issue of institutionalism which has caused great ecclesiastical commotion in England recently. Charles Davis was a priest and England's leading Roman Catholic theologian who served among the *periti* at Vatican II. In a renuncia-

tion of the Roman Church late in 1966 which may be as important as John Henry Newman's acceptance of Rome a century ago, he defended his action by saying, "I do not think that the claim the Church makes as an institution rests upon any adequate Biblical and historical basis. I don't believe that the Church is absolute, and I don't believe any more in papal infallibility." *Time*, LXXXVIII (December 30, 1966), p. 42.

66. (New York: Harper & Brothers, 1958), I, 210.

Chapter 9. A People under the Word: Theological Interpretation

1. See Ferdinand Hahn, "Die Nachfolge Jesu in vorösterlicher Zeit," in Ferdinand Hahn, August Strobel, and Eduard Schweizer, *Die Anfänge der Kirche im Neuen Testament* (Göttingen: Vandenhoeck und Ruprecht, 1967), pp. 9 ff.

2. See Hermann Diem, *Dogmatics*, trans. Harold Knight (Philadelphia: Westminster Press, 1959), pp. 141-147; G. Clarke Chapman, Jr., "The Proclamation-History: Hermann Diem and the Historical-Theological Problem," *Interpretation*, XVIII (July, 1964), 329-345.

3. Cf. E. Hennecke and W. Schneemelcher, *New Testament Apocrypha*, trans. and ed. R. McL. Wilson (Philadelphia: Westminster Press, 1963), I, 71-80.

4. For the theological significance of inspiration beyond its relevance to the New Testament alone, see D. M. Stanley, "The Concept of Biblical Inspiration," *Proceedings of the Twelfth Annual Convention of the Catholic Theological Society of America*, vol. 13 (1959), pp. 65-89.

5. Cf. Ernst Käsemann, "Ministry and Community in the New Testament," in his *Essays on New Testament Themes*, "Studies in Biblical Theology," No. 41 (London: SCM Press Ltd., 1964), pp. 63 ff.

6. For a clear presentation of the process, see C. F. D. Moule, *The Birth of the New Testament*, "Harper's New Testament Commentaries," Companion vol. 1 (New York: Harper and Row, 1962).

7. The Apostles' unrepeatable function was their grounding of the Christian message in history. For the view that they represented canonicity from the very beginning of the church, see K. Holl, "Der Kirchenbegriff des Paulus in seinem Verhältnis zu dem der Urgemeinde," *Gesammelte Aufsätze zur Kirchengeschichte* (Tübingen: J. C. B. Mohr, 1928), II, 44-67.

8. Cf. Moule, *op. cit.*, pp. 51 ff.

9. See, for example, Wolfgang Schrage, *Die konkreten Einzelgebote in der paulinischen Paränese: Ein Beitrag zur neutestamentlichen Ethik* (Gütersloh: Gerd Mohn, 1961), pp. 117 ff., who discusses the general validity of Pauline ethical instruction.

10. Adolf Harnack, *Die Briefsammlung des Apostels Paulus und die anderen vorkonstantinischen christlichen Briefsammlungen* (Leipzig: J. C. Hinrichs, 1926), pp. 7 ff., believes that the general value of Paul's letters was immediately recognized by the churches and that this led to their collection in a corpus. On the early church's concern with the problem of particularity and universal validity, see N. A. Dahl, "The Particularity of the Pauline Epistles as a Problem in the Ancient Church," in *Neotestamentica et Patristica, Eine Freundesgabe, Herrn Professor Dr. Oscar Cullmann zu seinem 60. Geburtstag überreicht*, ed. W. C. van Unnik (Leiden: E. J. Brill, 1962), pp. 261-271; Krister Stendahl, "The Apocalypse of John and the Epistles of Paul in the Muratorian Fragment," in *Current Issues in New Testament Interpretation: Essays in Honor of Otto A. Piper*, ed. William Klassen and Graydon F. Snyder (New York: Harper and Brothers, 1962), pp. 239-245.

11. Moule, *op. cit.*, pp. 178 ff.; Harnack, *The Origin of the New Testament and the Most Important Consequences of the New Creation*, trans. J. R. Wilkinson, "Crown Theological Library," vol. 45 (London: Williams and Norgate, Ltd., 1925).

12 Cf. Helmut H. Koester, "One Jesus and Four Primitive Gospels," *Harvard Theological Review*, LXI (April, 1968), 203-247.

13. See Oscar Cullmann, "The Tradition," *The Early Church*, trans. and ed. A. J. B. Higgins and S. Godman (London: SCM Press Ltd., 1956), pp. 55-99.

14. See James M. Robinson, "Kerygma and History in the New Testament," in *The Bible in Modern Scholarship: Papers Read at the 100th Meeting of the Society of Biblical Literature, December 28-30, 1964*, ed. J. Philip Hyatt (Nashville: Abingdon Press, 1965), pp. 114 ff., for a judicious assessment of the present state of the discussion.

15. *Ibid.*, pp. 118 ff.

16. The revival of interest in Walter Bauer, *Rechtgläubigkeit und Ketzerei im ältesten Christentum* (Tübingen: J. C. B. Mohr, 1934; 2nd ed., 1963), is indicative of the seriousness with which the diversity of the early church is being investigated. See also Arnold Ehrhardt, "Christianity Before the Apostles' Creed," *Harvard Theological Review*, LV (April, 1962), 94; Koester, "Gnomai Diaphoroi: ｊThe Origin and Nature of Diversification in the History of Early Christianity," *Harvard Theological Review*, LVIII (July, 1965), 279-318.

17. See R. M. Grant, " 'Development' in Early Christian Doctrine: Review Article," *Journal of Religion*, XXXIX (April, 1959), 120-128; John Knox, *The Early Church and the Coming Great Church* (Nashville: Abingdon Press, 1955), p. 129; Reginald H. Fuller, *The New Testament in Current Study* (New York: Charles Scribner's Sons, 1962), pp. 137 f. These Anglican scholars see the development of Christianity in the second century as the natural unfolding of what is already implicit in the apostolic preaching. Consequently, the discovery of *Frühkatholizismus* in the New Testament causes them no theological embarrassment (see notes 21, 23, 25).

18. C. F. D. Moule, "The Influence of Circumstances on the Use of Eschatological Terms," *Journal of Theological Studies* XV (April, 1964), 1-15, ascribes the diversity to the different circumstances to which the message was addressed rather than to a straight-line development. Käsemann, "Ministry and Community in the New Testament," p. 89, claims that what makes the process questionable theologically is that the development "is associated with, and founded on, not need and historical necessity but a theoretical principle of tradition and legitimate succession; so that, in effect, the Spirit is made to appear as the organ and the rationale of a theory."

19. For the problem of tradition in the New Testament, see Klaus Wegenast, *Das Verständnis der Tradition bei Paulus und in den Deuteropaulinen*, "Wissenschaftliche Monographien zum Alten und Neuen Testament," vol. 8 (Neukirchen: Neukirchener Verlag, 1962), and Birger Gerhardsson, *Memory and Manuscript: Oral Tradition and Written Transmission in Rabbinic Judaism and Early Christianity*, trans. Eric J. Sharpe, "Acta Seminarii Neotestamentici Upsaliensis," vol. 22 (Uppsala: Almqvist & Wiksells, 1961). For the theological implications of such material in relation to the problem of heresy in the early church, see Koester, "Häretiker im Urchristentum als theologisches Problem," in *Zeit und Geschichte: Dankesgabe an Rudolf Bultmann zum 80. Geburtstag*, ed. Erich Dinkler (Tübingen: J. C. B. Mohr, 1964), pp. 61-76.

20. This is a Protestant legacy from F. C. Baur, who dissolved theology in history. For a recent sympathetic treatment of Baur, see Peter C. Hodgson, *The Formation of Historical Theology: A Study of Ferdinand Christian Baur* (New York: Harper and Row, 1966).

21. It occasions no surprise to note that those scholars who detect a nascent catholicism in the New Testament and value it low theologically have a corresponding view of canon (cf. fn. 23).

22. See, for example, D. M. Stanley, "Reflections on the Church in the New Testament," *Catholic Biblical Quarterly*, XXV (July, 1963), 387-400.

23. The current discussion of *Frühkatholizismus* in the New Testament, represented, for example, by the writings of Ernst Käsemann, clearly expresses the relatively low estate in which the church is held.

24. Cf. W. G. Kümmel, "Notwendigkeit und Grenze des neutestamentlichen Kanons," *Zeitschrift für Theologie und Kirche*, XLVII (December, 1950), 277-313.

25. Hans Küng, *The Council in Action; Theological Reflections on the Second Vatican Council,* trans. Cecily Hastings (New York: Sheed and Ward, 1963), pp. 159-195, insists that the whole canon be taken seriously but claims that only the Catholic Church can do justice to the catholicism in the New Testament.

26. See Diem, *op. cit.,* p. 236.

27. Cf., for example, C. H. Dodd, *The Apostolic Preaching and Its Developments* (New York: Harper and Brothers, 1936).

28. E.g., Oscar Cullmann, *The Earliest Christian Confessions,* trans. J. K. S. Reid (London: Lutterworth Press, 1949); Vernon H. Neufeld, *The Earliest Christian Confessions,* "New Testament Tools and Studies," vol. 5 (Leiden: E. J. Brill, 1963).

29. Eduard Schweizer, "Two New Testament Creeds Compared," in Klassen and Snyder, eds., *op. cit.,* pp. 166 ff.

30. Cf. Willi Marxsen, *Der "Frühkatholizismus" im Neuen Testament* (Neukirchen: Verlag des Erziehungsverein, 1958), who sees the variety of the confessions in the New Testament as being united by the proclamation of Christ.

31. Cf. E. Schweizer, "Variety and Unity in the New Testament Proclamation of Jesus as the Son of God," *Australian Biblical Review,* XV (December, 1967), 1-15.

32. For discussions of the problem, see Stendahl, "Biblical Theology: Contemporary," *The Interpreter's Dictionary of the Bible,* ed. George Arthur Buttrick *et al* (New York: Abingdon Press, 1962), I, 418-432; Stendahl, "Method in the Study of Biblical Theology," in Hyatt, ed., *op. cit.,* pp. 196-209; Leander E. Keck, "Problems of New Testament Theology," *Novum Testamentum,* VII (June, 1964), 217-241; Herbert Braun, "Die Problematik einer Theologie des Neuen Testaments," *Gesammelte Studien zum Neuen Testament und seiner Umwelt* (Tübingen: J. C. B. Mohr, 1962), pp. 325-341.

33. E.g., Käsemann, "Unity and Diversity in New Testament Ecclesiology," *Novum Testamentum,* VI (November, 1963), 290-297; Käsemann, "The Canon of the New Testament and the Unity of the Church," *Essays on New Testament Themes,* pp. 95-107; Raymond E. Brown, S.S., "The Unity and Diversity in New Testament Ecclesiology," *Novum Testamentum,* VI (November, 1963), 298-308.

34. An abridgment of this address was published in *Mission,* I (September, 1967), 80-84.

Chapter 10. A People Under the Word: Contemporary Relevance

1. This and subsequent biblical quotations, unless otherwise indicated, are taken from the *Revised Standard Version.*

2. *An Apology for the True Christian Divinity; Being an Explanation and Vindication of the Principles and Doctrines of the People Called Quakers* [1678] (Philadelphia: Friends Book Store, 1908), proposition 3.

3. *Peter: Disciple, Apostle, Martyr,* trans. Floyd V. Filson (2nd ed.; Philadelphia: Westminster Press, 1962).

4. *Great Personalities of the New Testament: Their Lives and Times* (Westwood, N.J.: Fleming H. Revell Company, 1961), p. 87.

5. E. Giles, ed., *Documents Illustrating Papal Authority,* A.D. *96-454* (London: S.P.C.K., 1952), pp. 1-3.

6. General editor, Alexander Jones (London: Darton, Longman, & Todd, 1966).

7. Ed. Herbert G. May and Bruce M. Metzger (New York: Oxford University Press, 1962).

8. Ed. C. I. Scofield; chm., editorial committee of new edition, E. Schuyler English (London: Oxford University Press, 1967).

9. (London: Epworth Press).

10. (London: SCM Press Ltd.).

11. Trans. Salvator Attanasio (New York: Thomas Nelson and Sons, 1964).

12. (Philadelphia: Judson Press, 1967).

13. (Philadelphia: Westminster Press, 1967).

14. See my chapter in Duke K. McCall, ed., *What Is the Church?* (Nashville: Broadman Press, 1958), pp. 79-96.

1. This estimate is distilled in Roland H. Bainton's characterization: "an amazingly clear-cut and heroic anticipation of what with us has come to be axiomatic." "The Anabaptist Contribution to History," in Guy F. Hershberger, ed., *The Recovery of the Anabaptist Vision: A Sixtieth Anniversary Tribute to Harold S. Bender* (Scottdale, Pa.: Herald Press, 1957), p. 318.

2. What Bainton has said very pointedly about the Anabaptists would be as true of any other believers' church group; namely, that the positions they took were not so calculated as to contribute effectively to social progress or democratization, even if such developments may have been the long-range implication of their witness. "Let it now be said that the worth of their endeavor is not to be judged in the light of their contribution to history. They took their stand in the light of eternity regardless of what might or might not happen in history. They did not fall into the error of those who treat the way of the cross as if it were a weapon; . . . the cross is not a strategy. It is a witness before God, no matter whether there may or may not be any historical consequences" (*Ibid.*, p. 325).

3. This classification is sliced along a different axis from that proposed by George H. Williams in his introduction to *Spiritual and Anabaptist Writers*, "The Library of Christian Classics," vol. 25 (Philadelphia: Westminster Press, 1957), pp. 28-35. Williams identifies three kinds of Anabaptists and three kinds of Spiritualists, with the magisterial Reformation not included on the chart. To relate this typology to that of Williams, it could be said that we are here dealing with a transversal section of his repertory: evangelical spiritualism, evangelical Anabaptism, and evangelical magisterialism.

4. The form which this concern for restoration took in the sixteenth century was *sola scriptura*; the differences of degree all the way from Anglicanism through Lutheranism and Zwinglianism to Anabaptism were differences as to how much authority Scripture was to have over against Christian tradition. Yet we should take care not to misinterpret the appeal to Scripture through the categories of a later Protestant scholasticism. Anabaptists coupled their appeal to Scripture with an accent on the "Inner Word," analogous to the later Quaker concept of "Christ's coming to teach His people today." Thus the issue is the authority of Christ versus the authority of men, not the Christ of Scripture versus the present Christ.

5. See text in *Zwingli and Bullinger*, trans. and ed. G. W. Bromiley, "The Library of Christian Classics," vol. 24 (Philadelphia: Westminster Press, 1953), pp. 59-95.

6. Franklin H. Littell, "Church and Sect (With Special Reference to Germany)," *The Ecumenical Review*, VI (April, 1954), 262-276.

7. If one were free to use labels without regard for the emotional coloring of words, this type should have been called "puritan," and it would not be unfair to history so to label it. Since, however, in our culture this label has strong value-laden overtones, positive for some and negative for others, I have chosen another label. Nonetheless a few scattered references to Puritanism as an historical phenomenon representing this stance have had to be retained.

8. Here the historically fitting name would be "Pietist," but this is an even more feeling-laden term. Much of what has been historically labeled "Pietist" has been at the same time very much in the Believers' Church format, especially the Brethren and Methodist origins. Much of what is currently condemned as "pietist" by one stream of ecumenical thinkers is not congruent with historical Pietism at all.

9. Hans-Werner Bartsch, "Die historische Situation des Römerbriefes," *Communio Viatorum*, VIII (Winter, 1965), 199-208; Markus Barth, "Jews and Gentiles: The Social Character of Justification in Paul," *Journal of Ecumenical Studies*, V (Spring, 1968), 241-267. The conclusions of these men are all the more striking in that they arise out of the critical-exegetical expertise of the Continental university style of theology with no hidden apologetic-sectarian agenda. Barth's earlier *Acquittal by Resurrection* (New York: Holt, Rinehart and Winston, 1964), also "mixes" faith and sociology in a way which creatively disgruntles the purists.

10. (London: SCM Press Ltd., 1959), esp. p. 28.

11. (London: Edinburgh House Press, Lutterworth Press, 1957), pp. 19 f.

12. "Reply to Gellius Faber," *The Complete Writings of Menno Simons, c. 1496-1561,* trans. Leonard Verduin and ed. John Christian Wenger (Scottdale, Pa.: Herald Press, 1956), pp. 739-744.

13. " 'Walking in the Resurrection': The Anabaptist Doctrine of Regeneration and Discipleship," *Mennonite Quarterly Review,* XXXV (April, 1961), 96-110.

14. Cf. footnotes 7 and 8.

15. When testing ethical generalizations for their applicability, the standard paradigmatic question (regarding war, for instance) is not "What should a Vietnamese peasant do?" nor "What should a teenage Christian draftee do?" but rather "What should Dean Rusk do?"

16. We cannot here go into detail in the analysis of the logical structure of the ethics of the vocation, to demonstrate how the coincidence of spiritualist and theocratic ethics is explained by the natural law character of their ethical standards. It must suffice to suggest that there is a very logical connection between the absence of a visible committed community in sociology and the impossibility in epistemology of deriving an acceptable ethic from the positive moral teaching of the Bible.

17. From the Believers' Church perspective one is at a loss to understand the juxtaposition of two emphases which constantly recur in the "mainstream" traditions:

    (a) When speaking on the general topic of social involvement and Christian vocation, our magisterial brethren argue the importance of "taking responsibility for" the course of events in politics, the economy, the university, etc. Often one has the impression that "taking responsibility" means "taking charge" and that it is being understood within the framework of Christendom's assumptions. Over against the spiritualist's unconcern for the mundane, this concern for the course of events is valid, though it is theocratic in its unspoken trust that control over how things turn out is always desirable or usually possible.

    (b) When, however, one turns to the narrower theme of the ethical standards which should guide the Christian in this realm of vocational responsibility for society, the same thinkers will argue strongly against a specifically Christian ethic. They reject pacifism, for instance, while admitting that is the position of Jesus and the apostles, because one's social ethics must be drawn from the order of nature. They reject the ideals of poverty and chastity, any kind of withdrawal, any kind of non-generalizable ethic, fearing monasticism, legalism, and the like.

Now it is possible to see, if Christian ethics were different from non-Christian ethics, why Christians would have a duty to bring their contribution to bear on society; for in that case they would be doing something which no one else can. If, however, one argues at the same time that there is no difference in substance between the standards which Christians apply and those which intelligent honorable non-Christians can perceive and attain, it is not self-evident that much remains of the case for involvement.

18. An outline for study of the discerning and forgiving functions of the community is offered by *Concern,* "A Pamphlet Series for Questions of Christian Renewal," no. 14 (Scottdale, Pa., 1967).

19. (n.d.p.: American Society of Church History), ch. 5.

20. *Das missionarische Bewusstsein und Wirken der Täufer,* "Beiträge zur Geschichte und Lehre der Reformierten Kirche," vol. 21 (Neukirchen: Verlag des Erziehungsvereins, 1966).

21. "The Anabaptist Theology of Martyrdom," *Mennonite Quarterly Review,* XIX (July, 1945), 179-214.

22. Hugh Barbour, in his definitive *The Quakers in Puritan England* (New Haven: Yale University Press, 1964), identifies the phrase "War of the Lamb" as the standard early Quaker characterization of their place in the movement of history. See his fourteen

citations in the index, p. 267. Cf. the contribution of T. Canby Jones to this symposium.

23. The theses of Arend Th. van Leeuwen to this effect have been given wide currency, partly through ecumenical agencies. The publication of the Study Division of the World Council of Churches, *Study Encounter,* treated the theme in its second issue (1965), and van Leeuwen was the featured speaker at the First Assembly of the Division of Overseas Ministries of the National Council of Churches in October, 1965.

24. *The Church and the Disorder of Society,* vol. 3, "Man's Disorder and God's Design" (New York: Harper and Brothers, 1948), p. 127.

25. *Concept,* "Papers from the Department on Studies in Evangelism of the World Council of Churches," Fascicle XII (December, 1966), 11.

26. (New York: Holt, Rinehart and Winston, 1966), esp. chs. 5, 6.

27. This distinction made by John Wesley, *Works,* VIII, 322-324, is reinterpreted by Colin W. Williams, *Where in the World? Changing Forms of the Church's Witness* (London: Epworth Press, 1965), pp. 61-64.

Chapter 13. A People in the World: Contemporary Relevance

1. Franklin H. Littell, "The Importance of Anabaptist Studies" (Paper with limited circulation, 1966), p. 5.

2. "The Nature of the Church," in *The Lordship of Christ: Proceedings of the Seventh Mennonite World Conference, Kitchener, Ontario, Canada, August 1-7, 1962,* ed. Cornelius J. Dyck (Elkhart, Ind.: Mennonite World Conference, n.d.), p. 647.

3. For an important historical study related to this issue, see Timothy L. Smith, *Revivalism and Social Reform in Mid-Nineteenth-Century America* (New York: Abingdon Press, 1957).

4. William R. Estep, *The Anabaptist Story* (Nashville: Broadman Press, 1963), p. 178.

5. Littell, "The Historical Free Church Traditions Defined," *Brethren Life and Thought,* IX (Autumn, 1964), 83.

Report of the Findings Committee

First Preface: On the Nature of the Findings Possible in a Meeting Such as This

We have noted during our meetings a profusion of varied lists of the distinctive "marks" of the Believers' Church identity. This does not refute the thesis that there is such an identity; it rather points to the character of that identity.

The believers' churches have no creeds but many confessions. The question of the faithfulness of a given confession to Scripture, and to its own time and place, must be asked within that diversity and not in abstraction from it.

This diversity of expression has numerous causes:

(1) local authority in polity;
(2) the lay character of the Believers' Church theology;
(3) necessary adaptations to the issues of different times and places, in the outworking of the expectation that under the Holy Spirit "new light will break forth from the Word of God" as needed.

Our apprehension of this common identity has been hampered by a lack of agreed terminology which results from the way in which, in the past, in contradiction to our expressed views of spiritual unity, we have ignored or talked past one another.

Nevertheless we do discern, within the mode of discernment which is fitting here, a commonality of stance which underlies the profusion of formulations. This consensus is ascertained not as the fruit of our conversational process here, but as already given to us through our several, largely separate, histories.

(To this report we append a "Summary of Believers' Church Affirmations" formed by the summation of the numerous statements made by our speakers. Most of the positions here named would be held to by all the groups represented here; many of them would not be representative of the other major Christian traditions.)

We thus confirm the truth of the traditional affirmation, which we had already made without updating our expression of it, that the gift of unity is prior to our discovery and articulation of it. This meeting has contributed to the renewed discovery of this commonality and has given us some intimations of the call to articulate it in our age. If we acknowledge the gift, we must as well accept the challenge to manifest it in future brotherly relationships.

(1) The order and content of the following draft follow the June, 1967, program outline. This outline might be found somewhat questionable in its sequence when judged from a biblical point of view. Since the concept "Believers' Church" differs from other understandings of the church most strikingly with reference to the place of individual commitment, the first day was given to the discussion of the meaning of individual belief. Yet from biblical perspective there might have been some other point at which it would have been more appropriate to begin.

Then, there are significant gaps in the program's treatment of material. There is little reference to ethics or to social witness. The issues of civil rights and race were brought in only by J. Lawrence Burkholder, and then as an example to illustrate another issue. The conference participants never felt free to discuss directly the attitude of the Believers' Church toward militarism or Vietnam.

Another gap was that there was little direct Scripture study. Still another was the telescoping of the last day's program, so that the theme for the fourth day, "A people in the world," received proportionately less study time, even though the missionary dimension of the church's life was frequently alluded to at other points during the conference.

The following draft accepts these limits as fixed by the program itself and speaks only to the topics which come within this scope.

(2) The statement of each issue in the following draft concludes with the recognition of problems and dangers with which "we are left." This "continuing agenda" should not be interpreted as an indication of doubt as to the affirmations from which the questions flow. Nor is it meant specifically as support for the argument that there needs to be an organization to carry on more common study of these themes. The recognition of these problems and dangers is intended rather as an indication of sobriety about the very limited extent to which the Believers' Church position can be thought of as having been adequately defined and implemented.

(3) The unity to which we here testify is not the result of the discussion process at Louisville. It is rather a unity which was "taken on faith" by the Planning Committee and which the Findings Committee believes has been confirmed, although often it was not the subject of full and direct discussion. Strictly speaking, then, what follows is not the *findings* from the conference but rather an understanding of the character of the concept of the Believers' Church as illuminated by the conference.

I. We have found ourselves in agreement that the most visible manifestation of the Grace of God is His calling together a believing people.

   A. The congregation is therefore constituted by the divine call to which men and women respond freely in faith.

The shorthand label "Believers' Church" therefore points first of all not to the doctrinal content of beliefs held, nor to the subjective believingness of the believer, but more to the constructive character of the commitment in defining the visible community.

We therefore reject any pattern of establishment or any church practice (of which pedobaptism is only the most explicit example) whereby Christian allegiance is affirmed, imposed, or taken for granted without the individual's consent or request.

We are left with uncertainty as to how the reality of regeneration subjectively experienced relates to psychological and social causalities.

We are left with the problem of understanding the child, his possible religious experiences, and his relationship to the believing community, in such a way as to respect the integrity both of his person and of the congregation's discipline.

We are left as well with the problem of understanding our relation to those pedobaptist traditions which by virture of thorough nurture, meaningful confirmation, and faithful discipline may affirm that they also are constituted of freely committed believers.

B. The believer in Jesus Christ manifests a new quality of life which many of us have preferred to call discipleship.

Discipleship is brought about by the regenerating and sanctifying work of the Holy Spirit, who enables and sustains a life otherwise impossible. Its model is the perfect humanity of Jesus Christ, especially in His servanthood and His cross. It is sustained by the mutual discipline of the congregation, which supplies discernment, admonition, moral solidarity, and forgiveness.

We therefore reject any pattern of indiscriminate membership not conditioned upon commitment to discipleship, whatever be the age of the person admitted to membership, or any pattern which does not provide to the new members the needed resources for growth in maturity and obedience.

We are left with the danger of locating Christian perfection in the believer rather than in Christ and His Spirit.

We are left as well with the danger of imposing our vision of obedience upon the unconvinced, or of defining it legalistically without reference to changes in the ethical context.

C. Every believer participates in the full ministry of Christ. Every believer is a priest; every believer is a prophet or preacher.

Every believer participates in that servanthood which Jesus revealed as the mode of His rule. Every believer is endowed with a gift, the exercise of which is essential to the welfare of the body.

We reject the concept of ministry as a unique sacramental, professional, or governing caste, and the concept of "laity" as usually defined negatively from that perspective.

We are left with the question whether the subordination of teaching, like other ministries, to the life of the congregation might increase the church's susceptibility to ideological conformity to the world or to alien forms of church life.

We are left as well with the question whether believers' churches, as time passes, can give to new charismatic leaders the same hearing and support which their founders once received.

II. We have found ourselves in agreement that the particular local togetherness of the congregation is the primordial form of the church.

A. The congregation is called to a prophetic life whereby in the exercise of personal gifts, study both of Scripture and of contemporary reality, and Spirit-led group process the will of God is discerned in a given time and place.

We reject:

(1) administrative processes or patterns of congregational life which either deny the right, or avoid the responsibility and challenge, to exercise this discernment;
(2) habits of thought which are slow to believe that God's will may thus be known to the church;
(3) that laxity in discipline which permits membership to be divorced from participation in this common obedience.

We are left with uncertainty about the readiness of men in our day, whether in "believers' churches" or elsewhere, to accept the challenge of such openness and mutual responsibility.

B. The congregation is called to a sanctifying, healing life whereby in praise, confession, forgiveness, and reaffirmation of covenant men grow in liveliness and in the authenticity of their communion with God. The instrument of this healing is not so much a professional service or an intellectual illumination of

317

the meaning of selfhood, as it is the actual experience of redemptive personal relationship in admonition and acceptance and mutual caring. The structural separateness of the voluntary community is the indispensable form; these loving relationships are the substance.

We reject the routinization of patterns of worship which hamper the believer's freedom to share and to receive.

We are left with the dangers of prescribing or routinizing particular new patterns of worship or of personal experience.

C. The congregation is called out of the wider society for a communal existence within and for, yet distinct from, the structures and values of the rest of the world. This distinctness from the world is the presupposition of a missionary and servant ministry to the world. At times it demands costly opposition to the powers of the world.

We reject any view of the world which fails to reckon with its fallenness and any view of the church which simply identifies her membership, or her goals, with the world in its rebelliousness.

We are left with the danger of misunderstanding separation from the world in terms of geographic or social distance or of a merely ethical or cultural nonconformity, and with the further danger of precipitately applying the concept of separation from the world to other Christians from whom we differ.

We are left as well with the task of interpreting ecclesiologically the significance of the *corpus christianum*, that acculturated Christianity or Christianized culture which is both the progeny and the parentage of the restoration churches. Some would hold that the case for the Believers' Church, or for movements of restoration, is refuted by these churches' arising from, or degenerating into, forms of "Christendom."

D. The centrality of the congregation dictates a specific Believers' Church style of ecumenical relations. This is not the spiritualized concept of a purely invisible unity. Nor need it be denied that councils, boards, conventions, associations, and synods may have any ecclesiological significance. The import which congregationalism has for these other agencies means rather that their authority is that of the "congregational" character, procedures, and unity of conviction which is given them as they meet. They cannot authoritatively bind other, local congregations which meet more frequently, whose members know one another better, and whose responsibilities are for the total life of their members.

We reject that vision of the ecumenical task which seeks to relate the "faith" or the "order" or the administrative structures of entire "denominations" or "communions" and which makes decisions by instructed delegates, proportional representation, and majority votes, and other processes which are not congregational in character.

We reject as well the assumption that the visible unity we seek would take the form of one agency (board, convention, association, council, or "Church") seeking or claiming to gather, represent, or lead all Christians.

We are left with the dangers of anarchy, competitiveness, and isolationism which threaten when the rejection of "high" or magisterial visions of unity is not coupled with an equally statesmanlike vision and an equally passionate commitment to a freer, more fluid, more missionary, and more costly manifestation of the unity of Christ's body.

III. We have found ourselves in agreement that the Word of God creates, judges, and restores the church.

A. It belongs to the particular, historical character of Christian faith that its foundation and therefore its norm is fixed in the events to which the Apostles testify. The church exists where these events are reported and their meaning interpreted by believing witnesses to believing hearers. The recognition of the New Testament canon fixes the normative authority of the apostolic witness.

We reject the concept of continuing traditional development as a norm independent of Scripture. We reject as well any historical interpretation which would fail to read the Old Testament as interpreted by the New or the New as testifying to Jesus Christ.

We reject as well any narrowing of the listening community by the claims of hierarchical authorities or expert interpreters.

We are left with the danger of so oversimplifying the doctrine of the perspicuity of Scripture as to bypass the necessary historical and contextual requirements of correct interpretation.

We are left as well with reticence and difficulty in recognizing and evaluating those changes in teaching, emphasis, and interpretation which arise within our own history.

B. Since the life of churches is—like the gospel events—historical, particular, and contingent, the church may be disobedient. If the church persists in disobedience and hears and follows alien spirits, she may become apostate. In this event, the Holy Spirit calls men to the restoration of faithful belief and practice according to the New Testament norm.

We reject any concept of the indefectibility of the church which would by definition make apostasy impossible and restoration unnecessary.

We are left with the temptation to exaggerate the possibility or desirability of imitating in particular details the cultural forms of New Testament church life.

We are also left with the recurrent temptation to justify separation when every effort has not been made to bring about acceptance of the truth by the larger body, or to justify as "restoration" what is simply schism.

C. Jesus promised His disciples that by the Holy Spirit He would continue to lead them into all truth, to instruct them in the meaning of what they had already heard, and to renew that meaning in new situations. This continued instruction and guidance are limited by but not limited to the verbal content of canonical Scripture.

We reject any concept of the closing of the canon which would limit valid Christian witness to the repetition of words of Scripture.

We also reject any concept of "New Light" which would not be subject to the "testing of the spirits" by the norm of the New Testament witness to the Incarnation and Lordship of Christ.

We are left with semantic uncertainty as to whether this continued guidance and instruction beyond the apostolic age should be called "revelation."

IV. We have found ourselves agreed that the mission of the church in the world is to work out her being as a covenant community in the midst of the world.

A. The visible community is the organ of missionary proclamation. Integration into its fellowship and style of life is the goal of the evangelistic call to individuals.

We reject the concept of evangelism which is limited solely to moving individuals, in their self-concern, toward a sense of forgiveness, self-acceptance, and assurance.

We are left with the danger that the congregation might understand its proclamation as recruitment of support for its institutional program.

B. The visible community is the organ of witness to the surrounding society. As discerning community it is led by the Holy Spirit to develop criteria of moral judgment in social issues. As forgiven community she brings to bear the qualities of compassion and love. As paradigmatic community the church is the pilot agency in the building of new patterns of social relations. The democratization of the power structures of society and the development of welfare concerns are pioneered and preached by the covenanted community.

We reject the idea that the churches' primary role in social changes is to call upon the larger social order to accept some immediately available change in power structures or to call for the maintenance of the social status quo.

We reject as well the idea that it is not the concern of the church to speak to issues of public morality as these arise in social, economical, political life.

We are left with the unmet need for the church to think about her social witness in forms which run ahead of rather than behind the world's own efforts to solve its structural problems.

John Howard Yoder, Goshen, Indiana, Chairman
William L. Lumpkin, Norfolk, Virginia, Vice Chairman
John J. Kiwiet, Oak Brook, Illinois, Secretary
Paul D. Brewer, Jefferson City, Tennessee
Donald J. Burke, Edmonton, Alberta, Canada
Donald F. Durnbaugh, Oak Brook, Illinois
Dean Freiday, Elberon, New Jersey
Charles Garrison, Lexington, Kentucky
Glenn O. Hilburn, Waco, Texas
Harold L. Phillips, Anderson, Indiana
Maynard Shelly, Newton, Kansas
David Stewart, Austin, Texas

August 10, 1967

Summary of Believers' Church Affirmations

(1) LORDSHIP OF CHRIST

The will of God is central in history.
God's will is best discerned from the life and teachings of Christ.
It is possible to ascertain Jesus Christ from the Scriptures.
Jesus Christ is head of the church; it does not belong to its members.
The events of the cross and the resurrection shape the church.

(2) AUTHORITY OF THE WORD

The Word is authoritative for the church.
The church believes in a living Word.
Additional light can break through the written word.
Inspiration can never be contrary to the written word.
The church helped form the canon of the New Testament and put itself under its authority.

(3) RESTITUTION (RESTORATION) OF THE CHURCH

The church may become apostate (is not indefectible).
The apostolic church is the model of the church, even though it cannot be fully recaptured or imitated.
Radical discontinuity can also be faithfulness.
The church is visible.

(4) SEPARATION FROM THE WORLD

The church consists of a pilgrim people.
The church's prior allegiance is to the coming kingdom.
The church's methods are not of the world (Lamb's War).
The church recognizes the demonic capabilities of the world as well as its potential.

(5) LIVING FOR THE WORLD

The church exists not for itself but as the suffering servant.
By separation from the world's standards the church is free to serve the world.
The church listens for God's voice in the world.
The church lives to proclaim and witness to the good news.
The church lives not from grace to grace but from crisis to crisis.
The church is open to new forms of witness and proclamation.

(6) COVENANT OF BELIEVERS

The church consists of the voluntary membership of those confessing Jesus Christ as Lord.

The covenant is a personal relationship and mutual commitment between God and His people.

The church tests the spirits and is receptive to the action of the Spirit.

Uncoerced faith is a mark of true religion.

God has His purpose for every believer.

(7) FELLOWSHIP OF THE SAINTS

The church is composed of regenerate membership.

The church maintains an ethical as well as doctrinal emphasis.

God gives the grace to permit obedience to His commands.

The church is called to be a peacemaker.

Each member is at once priest, prophet, and preacher.

The church is not hierarchical, sacramental, or sacerdotal in its essence.

The church is composed of those who will suffer for Jesus Christ and His faith.

(8) RELATION TO OTHER CHRISTIANS

The Believers' Church is mindful of the Christian matrix from which it came.

It sees unity as the fellowship of restored congregations.

It understands that the Spirit of God can break through denominational boundaries.

It feels called to provide its voice in the ecumenical conversations.

Donald F. Durnbaugh

July 7, 1967

A Resolution of Consensus and Commitment

A Resolution of Consensus and Commitment by the Participants of the Conference on the Concept of the Believers' Church, Southern Baptist Theological Seminary, Louisville, Kentucky, June 30, 1967.

Being assembled in conference on the concept of the Believers' Church and understanding ourselves as heirs of various Free Church traditions, we profess to have discovered in history and in our present fellowship a common scripturally based heritage, which is relevant for contemporary life and which is developing in churches of other traditions.

By study and comparison we have noted that this heritage includes the following acknowledgments: the Lordship of Christ, the authority of the Word, church membership regenerated by the Spirit, the covenant of believers, a need for a perpetual restitution of the church, the necessity for separation from the world and proclamation and service to the world, and a special conception of Christian unity.

We, therefore, commit ourselves this day to study together our common heritage, to remember one another in prayer, to promote a wider awareness of our common stance, and to seek to multiply contacts with one another in days to come.

Roster of Conference Committees

Interdenominational Planning Committee

Dr. Owen H. Alderfer
Dr. Donald F. Durnbaugh
Dr. James Leo Garrett, Jr., Chairman,
    1966-67
Dr. E. Glenn Hinson, Chairman, 1965-66
Dr. T. Canby Jones
Rev. William G. MacDonald
Dr. James D. Mosteller
Dr. Gene W. Newberry
Dr. W. Morgan Patterson
Dr. Richard M. Pope
Dr. Joseph R. Shultz
Dr. John W. V. Smith
Dr. John Howard Yoder, Secretary

Southern Baptist Theological Seminary Committee

Miss Mary Jean Aiken
Rev. T. R. (Bob) Allen
Dr. Leo T. Crismon
Dr. Paul M. Debusman
Dr. James Leo Garrett, Jr., Chairman,
    1966-67
Dr. W. Bryant Hicks
Dr. E. Glenn Hinson, Chairman,
    1965-66
Mrs. Theda Howell
Rev. Paul G. Kirkland
Dr. Hugh T. McElrath
Rev. Chester A. Molpus
Dr. W. Morgan Patterson, Vice Chairman,
    1966-67
Mr. W. M. Pattillo, Jr.
Dr. C. Penrose St. Amant
Dr. Wayne E. Ward

Findings Committee

The members are listed at the end of the Report of the Findings Committee.

Committee for Continuing Conversations

Dr. Owen H. Alderfer, Ashland Theological Seminary, Ashland, Ohio 44805

Dr. Donald F. Durnbaugh, Bethany Theological Seminary, Oak Brook, Illinois 60523

Dr. Everett Ferguson, Abilene Christian College, Abilene, Texas 79601

Mr. Dean Freiday, 2 Garfield Terrace, Elberon, New Jersey 07741

Dr. James Leo Garrett, Jr., Southern Baptist Theological Seminary, 2825 Lexington Road, Louisville, Kentucky 40206

Dr. T. Canby Jones, Wilmington College, Wilmington, Ohio 45177

Rev. William G. MacDonald, Anchorage Apt. No. 7, 7832 Highway 51, North, Millington, Tennessee 38053

Dr. James D. Mosteller, New Orleans Baptist Theological Seminary, 3939 Gentilly Blvd., New Orleans, Louisiana 70126

Dr. Gene W. Newberry, School of Theology, Anderson College, Anderson, Indiana 46012

Dr. W. Morgan Patterson, Southern Baptist Theological Seminary, 2825 Lexington Road, Louisville, Kentucky 40206

Dr. Richard M. Pope, Lexington Theological Seminary, 631 So. Limestone St., Lexington, Kentucky 40508

Dr. Joseph R. Shultz, Ashland Theological Seminary, Ashland, Ohio 44805

Dr. John Howard Yoder, Institute of Mennonite Studies, 3003 Benham Avenue, Elkhart, Indiana 46514 (Chairman)

Bibliography

I. The Believers' Church°

Armour, Rollin Stely. *Anabaptist   Baptism: A Representative Study.* "Studies in Anabaptist and Mennonite History," no. 11. Scottdale, Pa.: Herald Press, 1966.

Bainton, Roland H. *Christian Attitudes Toward War and Peace.* New York: Abingdon Press, 1960.

——. *Studies on the Reformation.* Series Two. Boston: Beacon Press, 1963.

Banowsky, William Slater. *The Mirror of a Movement: Churches of Christ as Seen Through the Abilene Christian College Lectureship.* Dallas: Christian Publication Company, 1965.

Barnes, William Wright. *The Southern Baptist Convention, 1845-1953.* Nashville: Broadman Press, 1954.

Beasley-Murray, George Raymond. *Baptism in the New Testament.* London: Macmillan; New York: St. Martin's Press, 1962.

Bender, Harold S. *These Are My People.* Scottdale, Pa: Herald Press, 1962.

Benson, Lewis. *Catholic Quakerism.* Gloucester, England: The Author, 1966.

Blakemore, William B. *The Discovery of the Church: A History of Disciple Ecclesiology.* Nashville: Reed, 1966.

Blanke, Fritz. *Brothers in Christ.* Trans. Joseph Nordenhaug. Scottdale, Pa.: Herald Press, 1961.

Boyd, Malcolm. *Underground Church.* New York: Sheed and Ward, 1968.

Brack, Peter de B. *The Political and Social Doctrines of the Unity of Czech Brethren in the Fifteenth and Early Sixteenth Centuries.* The Hague: Mouton, 1957.

Brinton, Howard. *Friends for 300 Years: The History and Beliefs of Friends Since George Fox Started the Quaker Movement.* New York: Harper and Brothers, 1952.

Brumback, Carl. *Suddenly . . . from Heaven: A History of the Assemblies of God.* Springfield, Mo.: Gospel Publishing House, 1961.

°This bibliography is introductory and select, consisting only of books and pamphlets related to the believers' churches, contains none of the writings of the early leaders of these movements, and is confined to English language publications.

Campbell, Will D. *Race and the Renewal of the Church*. Philadelphia: Westminster Press, 1962.

Carrillo de Albornoz, A. F. *The Basis of Religious Liberty*. New York: Association Press, 1963.

Climenhaga, A. W. *History of the Brethren in Christ Church*. Nappanee, Ind.: E. V. Publishing House, 1942.

Conn, Charles W. *Like a Mighty Army, Moves the Church of God, 1886-1955*. Cleveland, Tenn.: Church of God Publishing House, 1955.

Davies, Horton. *The English Free Churches*. London: Oxford University Press, 1952.

DeGroot, Alfred T. *The Restoration Principle*. St. Louis: Bethany Press, 1960.

Douglas, James. *The Non-Violent Cross. A Theology of Revolution and Peace*. New York: Macmillan Company, 1968.

Driver, Christopher. *A Future for the Free Churches?* London: SCM Press, 1962.

Durnbaugh, Donald F. *The Believers' Church: The History and Character of Radical Protestantism*. New York: Macmillan Company, 1968.

——. (comp. and trans.) *European Origins of the Brethren: A Source Book on the Beginnings of the Church of the Brethren in the Early Eighteenth Century*. . . . Elgin, Ill.: Brethren Press, 1958.

Dyck, Cornelius J. (ed.) *A Legacy of Faith. The Heritage of Menno Simons*. Newton, Kan.: Faith and Life Press, 1962.

Eastwood, Cyril. *The Priesthood of All Believers: An Examination of the Doctrine from the Reformation to the Present Day*. Minneapolis: Augsburg Publishing House, 1962.

Edge, Findley B. *A Quest for Vitality in Religion*. Nashville: Broadman Press, 1963.

Estep, William R., Jr. *The Anabaptist Story*. Nashville: Broadman Press, 1963.

——. *Baptists and Christian Unity*. Nashville: Broadman Press, 1966.

Etten, Henry van. *George Fox and the Quakers*. Trans. and rev. E. Kelvin Osborn. New York: Harper Torchbooks; London: Longmans, 1959.

Friedmann, Robert. *Hutterite Studies: Essays by Robert Friedmann Collected and Published in Honor of His Seventieth Anniversary*. Ed. Harold S. Bender. Goshen, Ind.: Mennonite Historical Society, 1961.

——. *Mennonite Piety Through the Centuries*. Goshen, Ind.: Mennonite Historical Society, 1949.

Garrett, James Leo, Jr. *Baptist Church Discipline*. Nashville: Broadman Press, 1962.

——. *Baptists and Roman Catholicism*. Nashville: Broadman Press, 1965.

Garrison, Winfred Ernest, and DeGroot, Alfred T. *The Disciples of Christ: A History*. St. Louis: Christian Board of Publication, 1948. Rev. ed. Bethany Press, 1958.

Gee, Donald. *Spiritual Gifts in the Work of the Ministry Today*.

Springfield, Mo.: Gospel Publishing House, 1963.

Gilkey, Langdon. *How the Church Can Minister to the World Without Losing Itself.* New York: Harper and Row, 1964.

Gilmore, Alec (ed.) *Baptism and Christian Unity.* London: Lutterworth Press, 1960.

——. (ed.) *Christian Baptism: A Fresh Attempt to Understand the Rite in Terms of Scripture, History and Theology.* London: Lutterworth Press, 1959.

——. (ed.) *The Pattern of the Church.* London: Lutterworth Press, 1963.

Harrison, Paul M. *Authority and Power in the Free Church Tradition; A Social Case Study of the American Baptist Convention.* Princeton, N.J.: Princeton University Press, 1959.

Haselden, Kyle. *Mandate for White Christians.* Richmond, Va.: John Knox Press, 1966.

Heering, G. J. *The Fall of Christianity.* New York: Fellowship Publications, 1943.

Hershberger, Guy F. (ed.) *The Recovery of the Anabaptist Vision: A Sixtieth Anniversary Tribute to Harold S. Bender.* Scottdale, Pa.: Herald Press, 1957.

——. *War, Peace, and Nonresistance.* Scottdale, Pa.: Herald Press, 1944.

Hill, Samuel S., Jr. *Southern Churches in Crisis.* New York: Holt, Rinehart and Winston, 1967.

Hillerbrand, Hans J. *A Fellowship of Discontent.* New York: Harper and Row, 1967.

Hudson, Winthrop S. (ed.) *Baptist Concepts of the Church.* Philadelphia: Judson Press, 1959.

Ironside, H. A. *A Historical Sketch of the Brethren Movement.* Grand Rapids: Zondervan, 1942.

Jenkins, Daniel. *Tradition, Freedom, and the Spirit.* Philadelphia: Westminster Press, 1951.

Kelsey, George D. *Racism and the Christian Understanding of Man.* New York: Scribner, 1965.

Klassen, Peter J. *The Economics of Anabaptism, 1525-1560.* The Hague: Mouton & Co., 1964.

Kraemer, Hendrik. *A Theology of the Laity.* Philadelphia: Westminster Press, 1958.

Lasserre, Jean. *War and the Gospel.* Scottdale, Pa.: Herald Press, 1962.

Lindley, D. Ray. *Apostle of Freedom.* St. Louis: Bethany Press, 1957.

Littell, Franklin Hamlin. *The Free Church.* Boston: Starr King Press, 1957.

——. *The Origins of Sectarian Protestantism: A Study of the Anabaptist View of the Church.* New York: Macmillan Company, 1964.

Lumpkin, William L. *Baptist Confessions of Faith.* Philadelphia: Judson Press, 1959.

McCall, Duke K. (ed.) *What Is the Church?* Nashville: Broadman Press, 1958.

MacDonald, William G. *Glossolalia in the New Testament.* Springfield, Mo.: Gospel Publishing House, 1964.

McGavran, Donald A. *The Bridges of God: A Study in the Strategy of Missions.* New York: Friendship Press, 1955.

Macgregor, George Hogarth Carnaby. *The New Testament Basis of Pacifism and the Relevance of an Impossible Ideal.* Nyack, N.Y.: Fellowship Publications, 1960.

Moody, Dale. *The Spirit of the Living God.* Philadelphia: Westminster Press, 1968.

Murch, James DeForest. *Christians Only: A History of the Restoration Movement.* Cincinnati: Standard Publications, 1962.

Neill, Stephen C., and Weber, Hans-Ruedi. *The Layman in Christian History.* Philadelphia: Westminster Press, 1963.

Nichol, John Thomas. *Pentecostalism.* New York, Evanston: Harper and Row, 1966.

O'Connor, Elizabeth. *Call to Commitment.* New York, Evanston: Harper and Row, 1963.

Payne, Ernest A. *The Anabaptists of the Sixteenth Century and Their Influence in the Modern World.* London: Carey Kingsgate Press, 1949.

——. *The Fellowship of Believers.* London: Carey Kingsgate Press, 1952.

——. *The Free Church Tradition in the Life of England.* London: SCM Press, 1944.

Reid, John Kelman Sutherland. *The Authority of Scripture: A Study of the Reformation and Post-Reformation Understanding of the Bible.* London: Methuen, 1957.

Roark, Warren C. (comp.) *The Church.* Anderson, Ind.: Warner Press, 1946.

Rose, Stephen C. *The Grass Roots Church.* New York: Holt, Rinehart and Winston, 1966.

Shelley, Bruce Leon. *By What Authority? The Standards of Truth in the Early Church.* Grand Rapids: W. B. Eerdmans Publishing Company, 1965.

Southard, Samuel. *Pastoral Evangelism.* Nashville: Broadman Press, 1962.

Stokes, Anson Phelps, and Pfeffer, Leo. *Church and State in the United States.* Rev. one-vol. ed. New York, Evanston: Harper and Row, 1964.

Tavard, Georges Henri. *Holy Writ or Holy Church: The Crisis of the Protestant Reformation.* London: Burns and Oates, 1959.

Torbet, Robert G. *Ecumenism: Free Church Dilemma.* Philadelphia: Judson Press, 1968.

——. *A History of the Baptists.* Rev. ed. Valley Forge, Pa.: Judson Press, 1963.

Trueblood, D. Elton. *The Company of the Committed.* New York, Evanston: Harper and Row, 1961.

——. *The Incendiary Fellowship.* New York, Evanston: Harper and Row, 1967.

Verduin, Leonard. *The Reformers and Their Stepchildren.* Grand Rapids: William B. Eerdmans Publishing Company, 1964.

Walton, Robert C. *The Gathered Community.* London: Carey Kingsgate Press, 1952.

Watkins, Keith. *The Breaking of Bread: An Approach to Worship for the Christian Churches (Disciples of Christ.)* St. Louis: Bethany Press, 1966.

Webber, George W. *The Congregation in Mission; Emerging Structures for the Church in Urban Society.* New York: Abingdon Press, 1964.

Weber, Hans-Ruedi. *Salty Christians.* New York: Seabury Press, 1963.

Wenger, John C. *God's Word Written.* Scottdale, Pa.: Herald Press, 1966.

Westin, Gunnar. *The Free Church Through the Ages.* Trans. Virgil A. Olson. Nashville: Broadman Press, 1958.

Williams, George Huntston. *The Radical Reformation.* Philadelphia: Westminster Press, 1962.

———. *Wilderness and Paradise in Christian Thought.* New York: Harper and Brothers, 1962.

Williams, George Huntston and Mergal, Angel M. (eds.) *Spiritual and Anabaptist Writers.* "The Library of Christian Classics," vol. 25. Philadelphia: Westminster Press, 1957.

Wilson, Bryan R. (ed.). *Patterns of Sectarianism: Organisation and Ideology in Social and Religious Movements.* London: Heinemann Educational Books Ltd., 1967.

Yoder, Gideon G. *The Nurture and Evangelism of Children.* Scottdale, Pa.: Herald Press, 1959.

Yoder John Howard. *The Christian Witness to the State.* Newton, Kan.: Faith and Life Press, 1964.

———. *The Ecumenical Movement and the Faithful Church.* Scottdale, Pa.: Mennonite Publishing House, 1958.

II. The Conference on the Concept of the Believers' Church

Dodds, Robert C. Ecumenical Problems: "The Radical Protestant," *The Iliff Review,* XXV (Spring, 1968), 39-47.

Durnbaugh, Donald F. "Exploring the Relevancy of the Believers' Church," *Messenger,* CXVI (August 31, 1967), 14 f.

"Free Church Ecumenism," *Christianity Today,* XI (September 1, 1967), 1157 f.

Garrett, W. Barry. "'Believer's Church' Meeting Finds Common Stand," *The Baptist Record,* LXXXVIII (July 13, 1967), 1 f.

Jones, T. Canby. "Concept of the Believers' Church," *Quaker Outreach* no. 40 (August-September, 1967), 2.

Knight, George W. "Believers' Church: A Study in Contrasts," *The Maryland Baptist,* L (July 13, 1967), 3.

[Knight, George W.] "Kentuckians Attend Believers' Church Sessions," *Western Recorder*, CXLI (July 31, 1967), 9.

Knight, George W. "Lessons from the Believers' Church Conference: The Church Under Tension," *Home Missions*, XXXIX (February, 1968), 24f.

Littell, Franklin Hamlin. "The Importance of Anabaptist Studies," *Archiv für Reformationsgeschichte*, LVIII, Heft 1 (1967), 15-28, esp. 17.

Meade, Dave. "U.S. Churches Undergo Triple Reformation," *Chicago Daily News* (September 9, 1967), 25.

[Newton, Jim.] "Authority of Scriptures Urged as Ecumenical Basis," *Capital Baptist*, XIII (July 13, 1967), 8.

[Phillips, Harold L.] "The Concept of the Believers' Church," *Vital Christianity*, LXXXVII (September 10, 1967), 24.

Shelly, Maynard. "Deliberation on the 'Believers Church,' " *The Christian Century*, LXXXIV (August 23, 1967), 1077-1080.

——————————————. "The Case for a Separated Church," *Baptist Herald*, XLV (November 15, 1967), 10, 11, 18, 23; *Baptist Standard*, LXXIX (October 25, 1967), 12 f.; *Canadian Mennonite*, XV (October 24, 1967), 5; *Christian Leader*, XXX (December 5, 1967), 4 f.; *Church Advocate*, CXXXII (February, 1968), 9-11; *General Baptist Messenger*, LXXXII (November 30, 1967), 4 f.; *Gospel Herald*, LX (October 31, 1967), 984, 997 f.; under title, "Making a Case for Separation," *The Mennonite*, LXXXII (October 24, 1967), 640-642; *The Schwenckfeldian*, LXV (July, 1968), 10 f., 13; under title, "Ecumenical Dialogue," *Vital Christianity*, LXXXVII (December 3, 1967), 3 f., 12.

——————————————. "An Experience with New Light," *Baptist Herald*, XLV (October 15, 1967), 10 f.; under title, "When Old Radicals Meet the New Radicals," *Baptist Program* (December, 1967), 11, 13; *Baptist Standard*, LXXIX (October 18, 1967), 12 f.; *Canadian Mennonite*, XV (October 17, 1967), 4; *Christ for the Nations*, XX (February, 1968), 7 f.; *Christian Leader*, XXX (November 21, 1967), 4 f.; *Church Advocate*, CXXXII (January, 1968), 7 f., 11; *General Baptist Messenger*, LXXXII (November 23, 1967), 4 f.; *Gospel Herald*, LX (October 24, 1967), 960 f.; under title, "New Light Comes from Radical Churches," *The Mennonite*, LXXXII (October 17, 1967), 624 f.; under title, "An Experience with New Life," *Mennonite Brethren Herald*, VI (October 20, 1967), 7 f.; *The Schwenckfeldian*, LXV (April, 1968), 6 f.

——————————————. "The Marks of a Missionary Congregation," *Baptist Herald*, XLV (November 1, 1967), 11 f.; *Baptist Standard*, LXXIX (October 11, 1967), 12 f.; *Canadian Mennonite*, XV (October 10. 1967), 5; *Christian Leader*, XXX (November 7, 1967), 4 f.; *Church Advocate*, CXXXII (December, 1967), 9 f., 21; *General Baptist Messenger*, LXXXII (November 9, 1967), 4 f.; *Gospel Herald*, LX (October 10, 1967), 910 f.; under title, "Mission Marks the Congregation," *The Mennonite*, LXXXII (October 10, 1967), 608 f.; *Mennonite Brethren Herald*, VI (October 13, 1967), 7 f.;

The Schwenckfeldian, LXV (January, 1968), 6 f.; *Vital Christianity*, LXXXVII (November 19, 1967), 3 f., 8.

——————————————. "Models for a New Church," *Baptist Herald*, XLV (November 1, 1967), 13 f., 22; under title, "Tomorrow's Church," *Baptist Program* (January, 1968), 13-16; *Baptist Standard*, LXXIX (November 1, 1967), 12 f.; *Canadian Mennonite*, XV (October 31, 1967), 5; *Church Advocate*, CXXXII (March, 1968), 15-17; *General Baptist Messenger*, LXXXII (December 14, 1967), 4 f.; *Gospel Herald*, LX (November 7, 1967), 1012-1014; under title, "Finding New Models for Church Life," *The Mennonite*, LXXXII (October 31, 1967), 657 f.; *The Schwenckfeldian*, LXV (October, 1968), 12 f.

——————————————. "The Undying Fire of the Reformation," *Baptist Herald*, XLV (October 15, 1967), 6 f., 23; under title, "What Is a Believers' Church?" *Baptist Program* (November, 1967), 11, 13; *Baptist Standard*, LXXIX (October 4, 1967), 12 f.; *Canadian Mennonite*, XV (October 3, 1967), 1; *The Christian*, CV (October 29, 1967), 8-10; *Christian Leader*, XXX (October 24, 1967), 4 f., 21; *Church Advocate*, CXXXII (November, 1967), 8-10; *Covenant Companion*, LVI (October 20, 1967), 6 f., 26; *Evangelical Visitor*, LXXI (January 15, 1968), 5, 12; *General Baptist Messenger*, LXXXII (October 26, 1967), 4 f.; *Gospel Herald*, LX (October 3, 1967), 892-894; under title, "Reformation Fire Still Burns," *The Mennonite*, LXXXII (October 3, 1967), 594-596; *Mennonite Brethren Herald*, VI (October 6, 1967), 6 f., 10; *Pentecostal Evangel*, no. 2787 (October 8, 1967), 26 f.; *The Schwenckfeldian*, LXIV (October, 1967), 10 f.; *The United Brethren*, LXXXII (October 25, 1967), 3 f., 18; *Vital Christianity*, LXXXVII (October 22, 1967), 5 f., 11.

[Slaght, Lawrence Townsend.] "Conference on the Concept of the Believers' Church," *The Watchman-Examiner*, LV (August 10, 1967), 483-489.

Stewart, David. "Report on Believers' Church Conference," *Mission*, I (September, 1967), 34.

Indexes

INDEX OF SCRIPTURE REFERENCES

INDEX OF NAMES OF PERSONS

337

340

341

THE EDITOR

Since 1959 James Leo Garrett, Jr., has been professor of Christian theology at Southern Baptist Theological Seminary, Louisville, Kentucky. He served as chairman of the two committees that gave guidance to the Conference on the Concept of the Believers' Church. A graduate of Baylor University (AB), Southwestern Baptist Theological Seminary (BD, ThD), Princeton Theolgoical Seminary (ThM), and Harvard University (PhD), Dr. Garrett has studied at the Catholic University of America and the University of Oxford and formerly taught theology at Southwestern Baptist Theological Seminary. He is a member of the American Society of Church History and American Academy of Religion. He has served in Baptist pastorates in Texas and as lecturer in various seminaries and universities and on other occasions in North and South America and Europe.

Dr. Garrett is a member of the Walnut Street Baptist Church, Louisville, Kentucky. He is married to Myrta Ann Latimer and has three sons.

He has written *Baptist Church Discipline* and *Baptists and Roman Catholicism* and co-edited *The Teacher's Yoke: Studies in Memory of Henry Trantham.* A specialist in the history of Christian doctrine. Dr. Garrett now serves as the first chairman of the newly constituted Study Commission on Cooperative Christianity of the Baptist World Alliance.